History and Status
of
American Physical Education
and Educational Sport

Earle F. Zeigler
Ph.D., LL.D., D.Sc., FAAKPE
The University of Western Ontario, Emeritus
(formerly of the University of Illinois, U-C
and The University of Michigan)

TRAFFORD

2005

Note for Librarians: A cataloguing record for this book is available from Library and Archives Canada at www.collectionscanada.ca/amicus/index-e.html
ISBN 1-4120-5897-x

Printed in Victoria, BC, Canada. Printed on paper with minimum 30% recycled fibre. Trafford's print shop runs on "green energy" from solar, wind and other environmentally-friendly power sources.

TRAFFORD

Offices in Canada, USA, Ireland and UK

This book was published on-demand in cooperation with Trafford Publishing. On-demand publishing is a unique process and service of making a book available for retail sale to the public taking advantage of on-demand manufacturing and Internet marketing. On-demand publishing includes promotions, retail sales, manufacturing, order fulfilment, accounting and collecting royalties on behalf of the author.

Book sales for North America and international:
Trafford Publishing, 6E–2333 Government St.,
Victoria, BC v8t 4p4 CANADA
phone 250 383 6864 (toll-free 1 888 232 4444)
fax 250 383 6804; email to orders@trafford.com
Book sales in Europe:
Trafford Publishing (uk) Ltd., Enterprise House, Wistaston Road Business Centre,
Wistaston Road, Crewe, Cheshire cw2 7rp United Kingdom
phone 01270 251 396 (local rate 0845 230 9601)
facsimile 01270 254 983; orders.uk@trafford.com
Order online at:
trafford.com/05-0798

10 9 8 7 6 5 4 3 2

DEDICATION

To the late Fred E. Leonard, A.M., M.D.
Oberlin College, Ohio

and

To the late Bruce L. Bennett, M.A., Ph.D.
The Ohio State University, Columbus

*"Two fine gentlemen who dedicated their lives
to physical education and educational sport!"*

Contents
(Conceptual Index)

Preface

The publication of another book on the history of physical education and sport in the United States requires justification. This seems necessary because there have been five books with a similar title dating back to 1941. These five publications are:

(1) Norma Schwendener's *A History of Physical Education in the United States* (NY: A.S. Barnes, 1941),

(2) Arthur Weston's *The Making of American Physical Education* (NY: Appleton-Century-Crofts, 1968,

(3) Earle Zeigler's edited and co-authored *A History of Physical Education & Sport in the United States & Canada: Selected Topics* (Champaign, IL: Stipes, 1975,

(4) Paula D. Welch and Harold A. Lerch's *History of American physical education and sport* (Springfield, IL: Charles C. Thomas, 1981), and

(5) Richard Swanson and Betty Spear's *History of sport and physical education in the United States* (New York; McGraw-Hill, 1995, 4th Ed.).

I argue here, however, that there is indeed a definite need for *this* book right now whether used by professionals in the field as a general reader or by a university professor as a textbook for his class. Physical education, including what is here called *educational* sport, is a field that early in the 20th century is facing one more crossroad in its torturous historical development. Thus, the assertion that there is a need can be justified because this is the first such book that takes what might be termed an *"analytic"* or *"vertical"* approach to the history of American physical education and educational sport. All of these other fine histories approach the subject in a chronological, more traditional manner (in a "horizontal" way). Also, some are now either out of print, difficult to locate, or somewhat out of date.

(In passing, however, I should mention also a book that was difficult to locate, but which most effectively traces aspects of American history about health, fitness, and sport in three separate time periods from 1830 to 1940. I refer to Harvey Green's *Fit for America: Health, Fitness, Sport, and American Society* (Baltimore, MD: The Johns Hopkins University Press, 1986). Although rarely, if ever, referred to, Green's profusely illustrated history is a gold mine for professionals in "what came before" in the fields of American health education, physical education, recreation, and sport.)

Having stated that there is a "definite need" for this analytic approach to the field's history, I understand, of course, that some people really enjoy reading history, while others can take it or leave it. A very few can't stand it in any form-- not even in a highly adventurous novel. But this latter group is decidedly in the minority. Most people seem to respect history, and more so if they were personally involved in the making of it. Perhaps it's a case of revering--and not speaking evil-- of the dead. Whatever the reason, just about everybody pays lip service to history and believes that it belongs in the educational curriculum at various points along the way. This is true all the way up the line--in fact, even to the required historical review of related literature in a Ph.D. thesis!

Interestingly, based on my assertions in the previous paragraph, a visitor to America viewing the educational system for the first time might be apt to think that history, in one form or another, is the most important subject in the curriculum. Based on the overall time spent on it, this might seem to be true. The child has it forced upon him throughout his early school years; some facets of it are thrust upon him or her in during the middle-school experience; and world history and American history are typically included in the high school years. Even at the university level, there is no escape without a variety of course experiences involving a greater or lesser amount of history typically related to the area covered by the specific course involved.

The student specializing in physical education and educational sport is fair game for the history ploy at a slightly later stage of development. There may have been a standard history course included, as required or elective, during the general-education course experience that all universities claim as a necessary part of the university curriculum. Then, in the professional physical education curriculum, a separate history course has been a tradition. However, such a course has often been combined with the history of health education and/or recreation as well. Now, with the advent of the "*discipline* of kinesiology curriculum," along with the opportunity for a second relationship with the professional education unit on campus for teacher certification, the place of the former "history of p.e." course has been challenged. Further, we now find the term "history and philosophy of" or "social foundations of" emerging in course titles as a decreased time allotment in provided to the "second-class" social-science and humanities aspects of the professional curriculum. I heartily deplore this trend. As has been said before, "If you don't know where you've been, and why you went there, how can you know where you're going?"

With such an array of courses covering the history of "this and that" to a greater or lesser extent, yet with varying teaching methodologies, one might expect the new graduate student in physical education/kinesiology to have a reasonably good understanding of history. Such understanding should be both general and specific--i.e., general in regard to the world, somewhat more specific about the United States, even more specific about general professional education, and very specific about specialized professional education related to physical education and educational sport. A type of "historical competence" should be the end result of such experiences.

Would that such were the case! As a matter of fact, the average graduate registering for a course in the history of physical education and sport--*if he/she even does so!*--seems to possess but a hazy concept of the sweep of the human's history on Earth. In addition to the lack of information about the chronology of events, the student is completely inadequate if questioned about what might be designated as the persistent or perennial problems that humans have faced down through the centuries. General or specific questions about educational history, even in the Western world, cannot typically be answered either. After making these observations, this somewhat disheartened professor hardly dared to inquire about historical knowledge and perspective relative to the history of sport and physical activity.

Just how matters got this way is difficult to explain. Criticizing students' earlier teachers--or their parents!--will not solve the problem. Jokingly, I might say that the blame should be placed on parents in the final analysis for bringing such stupid offspring into the world. I don't wish to be either pessimistic or foolishly idealistic about the status-quo. I can only recommend a *melioristic* approach--i.e., to take the situation as you find it and work to make it better. Thus I am pleased to state that, beginning in the mid-1960s, the situation began to improve because of improved historical research leading to the development of the discipline of sport history. *However, for a variety of reasons, the same cannot be said for the history of physical education--i.e., the teaching of physical activity skills in exercise, sport, physical recreation, and dance to children and young people primarily. but also to people of all ages and all conditions from "womb to tomb"! That concept seems to have been "lost in the shuffle."*

Basically, therefore, this analytic history of American physical education and educational sport is an attempt to rectify the prevailing situation--i.e., to provide one up-to-date, insightful textbook on the subject for aspiring teachers of physical activity education and coaches of educational/recreational sport. However, I add quickly that this is not a book that would help the reader become a star on a "Jeopardy-like" television show about physical education history. I do hope that by looking at our history analytically that it will clarify for the prospective teacher/coach how and why the present disintegrating situation came about. I sought to do this by offering the a sequence of narratives, studies, essays, and analyses, both chronological and critical, that will lead him or her to comprehend what has happened in this aspect of people's live from America's early days to the present. I want the reader, as an embryonic professional, to grasp the historical thread or timeline depicting people's greater or lesser involvement in purposeful or purposeless physical activity since America was first settled.

Interestingly, after approximately two hundred years, during which time people were involved in subsistence physical activity and indigenous physical recreation and games, some nineteenth-century European leaders in organized physical activity brought their varying ideas about physical training and gymnastics to the "New World." Those directing the effort after the American Civil War adopted the name "physical education" for a new national association in the 1980s. What then gradually developed on this soil has been termed an unique "American system" of physical education. Over the decades of the 20th century, this "American program" has included to greater or lesser extent, at the several levels of education, elements of health education, physical education, physical recreation, sport, and dance.

On March 25, 2004 in Reston, VA, the National Association for Sport and Physical Education (NASPE) released a revised, second edition of *Moving into the Future: National Standards for Physical Education*. These national standards were proclaimed to be "an essential tool for developing, implementing, and evaluating K-12 school physical education programs." They sought to "identify that students should know and be able to do as a result of a quality physical education program. The six national content standards in the news release are as follows:

1. Demonstrates competency in motor skills and movement patterns needed to perform a variety of physical activities.
2. Demonstrates understanding of movement concepts, principles, strategies, and tactics as they apply to the learning and performance of physical activities.
3. Participates regularly in physical activity.
4. Achieves and maintains a health-enhancing level of physical

fitness.

5. Exhibits responsible personal and social behavior that respects self and others in physical activity settings.
6. Values physical activity for health, enjoyment, challenge, self-expressions and/or social interaction.

This is an outstanding set of standards that NASPE has released for the guidance of professionals in American physical education and educational sport.

Nevertheless, after 60+ years in the profession, and also after reading such an excellent, updated statement of "standards for physical education," I find myself hard pressed not to be pessimistic about the future of the field. How can this be so? To give an answer to this question, I decided to offer you my assessment of the present situation. I did this by "looking into the future" and then offering some recommendations to a struggling profession. Instead of listing them at this point (in the Preface), I decided to include them in Chapter X, the final chapter in this book.

Now it is time to explain how--and why, also!-- I organized what I have called an *analytic* history of American physical education and educational sport. First, in the **Preamble**, I have included a brief "excursion" into philosophy of history. This is in an effort to place the profession in broad historical perspective. Then, in **Chapter I**, because the reader needs a review of the historical milieu in which my subject took place, I decided to trace the social and education foundations of the United States from the Colonial Period to the present day. Next, in **Chapter II**, I prepared an historical precis of the history of physical education and sport in America. This chronological (so-called horizontal or longitudinal) treatment of physical education's history was followed in **Chapter III** by what I have termed "An *Analytic* Approach to the History of Physical Education and (Educational) Sport." In this unique approach to history that was recommended to me almost 60 years ago by my doctoral adviser at Yale, the eminent John S. Brubacher, the history of a subject (in this case physical education) is viewed horizontally as a series of persistent problems that humans have face since their original involvement with the "problem." These may be categorized as (1) *social forces* and (2) as what I have termed as) *professional concerns*. Values (and accompanying norms), for example, is one of the social forces discussed. Similarly, the curriculum in physical education is one of the professional concerns considered.

In **Chapter IV**, a brief history of *undergraduate* professional preparation for physical education is presented. Here I trace this important topic (another professional concern!) for a period of 100 years, from its inception in 1861 to 1961 when a national conference on the subject was held. After this I offer in **Chapter V** a similar historical treatment, this time a history of graduate study in physical education from its beginning in 1891 to approximately 1975.

Following this, in **Chapter VI**, the reader will find a comprehensive analysis of the entire 20th century in what I have titled "American Physical Education in the 20th Century: An Analytic Review." In this analysis I looked at the developing professional curriculum in great detail. I concluded with what I believe to be the best curriculum model for professional development of a physical activity educator at the present.

In an effort to become more specific about the field's history during the fourth quarter of the 20th century, I decided to present in **Chapter VII** the results of a comparative study between the United States and Canada as to their respective approaches to professional preparation in the field.

Teachers and coaches in physical education and educational sport are all managers or administrators, but to varying degrees. Accordingly, I felt it important in **Chapter VIII** to include a brief history of the field's inadequate involvement with management theory and practice as an aspect of its professional curriculum.

In **Chapter IX** the history of what may be called "sport and physical education philosophy" is traced from its informal origin in the late 1800s to the end of the 20th century. After analyzing the history of this subject, the author concluded that professional preparation in this aspect of the field's body of knowledge became inadequate from the standpoint of the professional practitioner beginning in the late 1960s. Recommendations for the 21st century are made

In **Chapter X**, I introduced the subject of ecology as an unique social force, a persistent problem that was called to my attention in 1970 by a graduate student. (Back then it was typically called "conservation of natural resources.") I now understand that the impact of this subject, or social force, is absolutely crucial to the future of all humankind.

In addition to the comparative study between the United States and Canada explained in Chapter VII, I decided to broaden the reader's perspective "geographically" also in **Chapter XI.** I did this by describing the results of a study I carried out in the mid-1990s as to the status of physical education worldwide. To this I appended a listing of some 13 "principal principles" that I have "unearthed" by steady informal analysis over the past 50+ years. These are principles that physical education can lay claim to as a result of the scientific efforts of scholars and scientists in our field and related disciplines over the last half of the 20th century.

Finally, in **Chapter XII**, I closed out this analytical history of physical education and educational sport by daring to take a look at the future and what it might hold for the profession. The eminent historian, Allan Nevins, argued that history's rays should shine in three directions: "backward," at "our feet," and in the direction of "the future." So, after having looked at the past in a variety of ways, I made a brief review of some of the "future forecasting" carried out by scholars in other fields. Then I made some recommendations as to what our profession "should avoid." in the years immediately ahead. The chapter, and the book, is concluded by a listing of 20 recommendations regarding what we need to do if the profession is to reach its potential in society.

A few words about the two-pronged dedication of this volume seems appropriate. Professor Leonard dedicated his early *A Guide to the History of Physical Education* "to the memory of Dr. Edward Mussey Hartwell who first in America blazed the trail which I have tried to follow." Be that as it well may be, I felt that this book should be dedicated to Dr. Fred E. Leonard for his valuable pioneering effort. Secondly, I decided to dedicate this physical education history also to the late Dr. Bruce L. Bennett of The Ohio State University, Columbus. Bruce was a good friend, a fine colleague, a "solid physical educator, a true sportsman, and an outstanding historian of physical education.

Our profession and (now) discipline most assuredly needs to know "where it has been, how it got there, and where it should be going from here." By such continuous, careful assessment, the guideposts for the future should be somewhat more readily apparent. We need all of the help we can get--and then some!--in the years immediately ahead. Writing from both an American and Canadian perspective (as a dual citizen), it is not difficult to see that the future of the United States is being challenged as perhaps never before in its relatively short history. A careful study and understanding of the history of American physical education and educational sport is a prerequisite to a full understanding of the overall situation.

Earle F. Zeigler
Richmond, BC, Canada

PREAMBLE

A professional in physical education and educational sport must start from the beginning to comprehend the place of this specialized field in world society. For this reason a brief excursion into the philosophy of history is introduced at this point in an effort to place the profession in broad historical perspective. (A philosophy of history can be defined as a systematic body of general conceptions about the sum total of past happenings in the world.)

PERSPECTIVE

Living our lives from day to day we sometimes forget that the planet Earth originated more than 4 billion years ago (or earlier!). Early man and woman, we are told, had their beginnings some one million years ago and have used crude tools for something less than half that time.

Three hundred thousand years have elapsed since the mutation of sub-man into man. We now know that many tribes roamed and settled at various points in prehistoric Europe during a warming trend at the time of the Wurm Glaciation of the late Pleistocene Epoch from 35,000 to 25,000 years before the present. Nevertheless, the beginnings of the first true civilizations as we know them are actually less than 10,000 years ago. (See, for example, *Cooke et al.*, 1981.) The great religions are the product of the past 2,500 years. As types of political state go, democracy, is the youngest of infants, its official origins dating back only several centuries to the late 18th century. Is it any wonder that perfection appears to be a long way off?

Even arguing that improvement in different areas took place during the second half of the 20th century presents us with a two-sided coin. On the one hand, a great variety of significant changes occurred, and they are undoubtedly having a significant, positive effect on many parts of the world. In the so-called advanced nations, developments such as the use of electrical and nuclear energy, the increase in specialized weaponry, mechanization of the farm, technological advancement in production, the "exploding" cities, the extended life expectancy, and a higher standard of living for the "favored few" can be substantiated. However, these developments are offset to a degree by the knowledge that the underdeveloped nations are experiencing a rising nationalism that is proving to be troublesome along with an increasing birth rate and accompanying rapid growth of population, poverty, and enormous debts to the more prosperous nations.

Nevertheless, Commager in 1961 argued that the forces of good had gone steadfastly ahead despite the presence of much evil and inequality in the world. He was pleased that civilization had actually survived the wars of the 20th century to that point. He also expressed satisfaction that the United Nations had been created, had survived, and had grown in power and influence. Further, in addition to the end of Western colonialism, the more prosperous nations were accepting considerable responsibility for the welfare of unfortunate countries. Still further, he was encouraged by the vast progress in the natural sciences, the development of electronics, and the formidable advances in medical science. Still further, along with the rapid growth of Big Government--a boon or a "disaster" depending upon one's political philosophy-an unprecedented educational revolution was occurring. Finally, it was considered truly noteworthy that there was increasing recognition of both intellectual and material equality among peoples, a development that conceivably could eventually destroy most of the artificial inequalities of color, race, and class that exist in the world.

There is no doubt but that truly significant social change occurred in the 20th century. The most advanced nations, after moving from the pre-industrial stage to the industrial stage, are now progressing (technologically at least) to what is being called the post-industrial stage of the 21st century. This has been considered as progress by some, but it appears to be causing a great deal of job dislocation. Since the time when Commager was so optimistic about the future, another spectre--in addition to the ever-present threat of nuclear attack because of such destructive devices as nuclear warheads--has appeared that is casting strong shadows of gloom among many about the future. The stark fact is, however, that a large majority of people on Earth are conducting their lives in a manner that indicates clearly that they still don't appreciate the gravity of the human's precarious plight on Earth.

What is alluded to here is the stark necessity for the continuing development of *ecology* as a discipline. Ecology may be defined as the field of study that treats the relationships and interactions of people and other living organisms with each other and with the natural (or physical) environment in which they reside. For a variety of reasons, humans can no longer proceed on the assumption that their responsibility is to "multiply and replenish the earth" with little thought to the future. Now there are more than 6 billion (six *thousand* million) people on earth, and the various nations are struggling to develop an economy to cope with the almost unbelievable demands surfacing daily.

When we take a hard look at the economic situation, therefore, it has become apparent that certain extremely difficult choices may well have to be made during the next few decades. In 1972 Murray explained that most of the world's countries were striving to create a continuous-growth economic system, but ecologists were warning us increasingly that many countries may be forced to shift to no-growth economic models. The ecological argument is simply this: the quality of the planet is moving rapidly to the point where it will soon become precarious for life as we have known (or envisioned) it to continue. We are surrounding ourselves--each one of us in the advanced nations to the extent that we can afford it--with an ever-larger shell of consumer technology. In the process the earth is steadily being polluted to an ever more dangerous and life-threatening point. In fact, North America "leads" the world in this respect. If the ecological model postulated has any significant validity, then it and the prevailing economic model being followed are on a collision course that will result in disaster (38-39, 64-65, 70, 72)

In summary, we have reached the point where the world's problems must be solved for its very survival. This can be explained as follows: Humans have achieved a level of mastery over Earth's flora and fauna, but the exponential increase in the number of people alive is placing intolerable pressure on the world's resources. However, we haven't truly answered the hard questions about the extent to which nature's self-renewing cycles have been disturbed. The answers that we are starting to get--as we continue to ask the right questions--will be extremely difficult to accept. They are indicating that future "hardship" will be required to rectify Earth's plight. Unfortunately, we are finding that these obvious "answers" are not being accepted wholeheartedly and followed immediately by positive steps on the part of the majority of citizens. They are seemingly largely unaware and therefore somewhat recalcitrant about being asked to alleviate the destructive conditions with remedies that could conceivably renew Earth for its ongoing task.

Thus, people are now being faced with a number of threatening, stressful "ifs." Accordingly, two types of global problems are present: those that are mostly *understandable* and those that are mostly *uncertain*. Those who are attempting to forecast the future are now referring to (a) the *possible* future, (b) the *probable* future, and (c) the *preferable* future (Melnick, 1984, p. 4).

QUESTIONS

All of these difficult questions raised have a relationship to philosophy of history that will become even more apparent throughout this chapter. As we ponder this topic, we begin to realize that there are a number of unanswered questions. As presumably enlightened human beings, and as dedicated professional teachers and coaches, we have an obligation to come up with satisfactory answers to these basic questions relating to survival and progress. Attempting to put this discussion about the historical development of humankind in further perspective, we might ask the question, What is history? Is everything historic? Are we referring to the actual order of events as seen by an interpreter (the historian)? A student of history might ask whether the philosophy of history seems to approve or challenge one type of political state over another? If this were true, this would imply that there is just one way of looking at history or that there is simply one correct philosophy. If there are many philosophies of history, can we even argue that one is paramount?

Approaching this issue from another angle, we might question the validity and reliability of historical research. Is it possible to construct a valid philosophy of history that is fact and not at least part fiction? Is it possible for historians to record facts scientifically? It has been said that good history has depth as well as surface, the assumption being that "depth" is equated with scientific endeavor. However, "history is never above the melee," wrote Nevins in 1962 (p. 23) Yet, Woody (1949), for example, had deprecated the fact that those who have written about education and its history--or even about general history--have slighted "physical culture" perhaps through bias:

Despite the fact that lip service has been paid increasingly to the dictum "a sound mind in a sound body," ever since western Europe began to revive the educational concepts of the Greco-Roman world, there is still a lack of balance between physical and mental culture, both in school programs and among those who write of education. This is evident in many quarters, even where a certain universality of outlook ought to reign. Turn where one will, it is impossible to find physical culture adequately presented in books dealing with the general history of education. Written in keeping with a dominant rationalism, these books have been concerned chiefly with intellectual movements and institutions for mental improvement (vii).

Written history appears to have begun with the ancient Greeks. It was written also, but perhaps not quite as well, by the Romans. In these early histories, we are often faced with a dilemma: can a disinterested observer write history as effectively as someone who has lived through the passing events. Of course, this introduces a further disturbing problem that is difficult to answer. What constitutes acceptable history? Is a simple, factual, chronological listing of events satisfactory? Some would argue that history must show the connection between a series of events. Further, should it have a broader scope and seek to place any such events in societal perspective over a fairly long period of time?

And then we find some histories of the world with strong religious overtones that would have us believe unequivocally that God's purpose is gradually coming to pass. Whether one accepts one or more of these accounts, we are all still faced with the question of possible moral evolution. We know that history has often been destructive as well as cumulative. The question arises whether the history of humankind shows strong (or even probable) trends toward *emergence*. It may be wishful thinking, but we can't help but hope that people will soon evolve a formula that will help all people of the world live together in relative peace and harmony.

NEED FOR, AND POSSIBILITY OF, HISTORICAL RESEARCH

Looking at the actual conduct of historical research, there is no argument but that historians need to uncover as many primary sources as possible to write the best history. If only one mind passes between the historian and the material about which he is writing, there is a much greater chance of an accurate report. The possibility of a forged document, for example, or of a firsthand observer's inaccurate report only increases the difficul of writing fine history.

Because it may be so difficult also to locate an objective observer, some historians have felt it necessary to retrace the steps of the incidents that the historian hopes to describe later. Witness the historian of the 20th century who felt it advisable to hire an elephant to prove that it had been possible for Hannibal to cross the Alps by this means of transportation. One further step seems required: that the historian employ the highest type of reflective thinking before completing his work.

Experimental (group method) researchers, and even those who undertake what is called descriptive research, may repeat and check on their earlier observations. Unfortunately (for the historian at least) history does not repeat itself exactly. Because historians cannot themselves "see" what has happened, their attitudes will undoubtedly influence their work. They must make some assumptions as to the rationality of the universe. Presumably this would be necessary if a rational human hoped to make sense out of the world in which she or he lives.

Thus we might agree that complete objectivity of history is an impossibility. It must be pointed out, however, that ever-improving scientific techniques of investigation are becoming available to the historian. Nevertheless, it seems as though we may always need people with penetrating insight who will have flashes of intuitive genius while writing and interpreting the history of humankind. Such individuals would undoubtedly be employing a degree of speculative philosophy as part of their approach to the problem of historical interpretation. In this manner one or more philosophies of history will evolve.

Having employed empirical methods involving experiment and experience, scientists in many of the more exact sciences have been able to predict future developments. In this respect historians are fighting against a handicap but they have made progress nevertheless. By attempting to meet the exacting requirements of the more empirical sciences, it has been possible to develop at least one type of philosophy of history. As a result, many kinds of history may be examined using present criteria for adequacy and accuracy. Many historians make a stout effort to define the future. Any such definitions can't help but reflect the mood of the times and the predispositions of the historian. People will presumably continue to strive, of course, and it appears that they must also continue to act on faith (Zeigler, 1979, pp. 230-231).

PHILOSOPHY OF HISTORY

What, then, is philosophy of history? At this time we will not discuss what may be called analytical or *critical* philosophy of history. This typically treats the logical, conceptual, and epistemological description of what it is that the historian actually does-that is, a philosophic analysis of the critical and constructive intellectual processes by which history is written and the subsequent results. This approach to philosophy of history also involves a criticism of the sources employed and their development to form the base of knowledge upon which the historian builds the historical narrative. (See Curti et al., 1946 for a discussion of these issues; see also Nevins, 1962, p. 14 for a discussion of the "lantern-like, tri-directional rays" thrown out by the historian.)

There is always a subjective element present when the historian decides what

what facts, half-facts, and opinions he will weave into the subsequent narrative developed after analysis and synthesis have occurred. Are the facts correct; are they wrong? Time may provide the answers to these questions. The larger interpretation given to the material is truly indeterminate, and "theories of interpretation are peculiarly dependent on the needs and values of the age which produces them." (Handlin, et al., 1967, p. 15.)

In the 20th century there were a number of approaches to historical interpretation. For example, there were interpretations where historians treat the rise and fall of separate civilizations with an accompanying analysis of the rationale presumably underlying such development in civilizations (e.g., Toynbee, Spengler). In similar fashion, but somewhat differently, Hegel and Marx sought to develop sets of rules or principles explaining the continuous change that occurs in all civilizations. Other historians (e.g., F.J. Turner) have uncovered hitherto uncovered factors that moved a society's development in one direction or another. Still others argued that historical research should (and could) be more objective and scientific (e.g., Ranke).

A fifth approach was taken by historians who believed almost the opposite-that history could never obtain true objectivity and should therefore be as contemporaneous as possible. Finally, there have been those who were pragmatic and pluralistic in their historical endeavors. These scholars typically believed that a multiplicity of causative factors underlay historical development. Accordingly, they assumed an intermediate position, avoiding dogmatic theories and agreeing generally that perfect objectivity was not possible. In this last approach, there has been a tendency to employ ad hoc any general theory that appeared to explain a historical point or occurrence (Handlin, 1967, pp. 15-21)

One of the most interesting, insightful, and readable discussions about "ideas in history" came from the pen of the late Allan Nevins. In his *The Gateway to History* (1963), he stated that society has been controlled in the past by both practical and philosophical ideas. *Practical* ideas, as he explains it, express "immediate mundane aims" and are brought to fruition by certain human beings exerting their will upon others. Examples of this would be the idea of nationalism, the divine right of kings, the idea that a religious leader should have greater control than a temporal power over people's lives, or even the idea that the people should decide their own destiny at the ballot box.

Philosophical ideas, conversely, are theoretical and may typically not be judged by any pragmatic test. People in a society tend to believe or accept that a specific doctrine is true. The ancient Greeks, for example, believed that Fate (*Moira*) ruled the destinies of both gods and men. With ideas of this type there was no effort to validate the thought by practical results. Another example of this, Nevins explained, would be the devastating result that would occur if people (in the western world at least) gave up on the idea that there might be an afterlife. A further example of an important, relatively modern philosophical idea is that of progress as a concept or belief (pp. 261-262).

It is both interesting and significant that only two of the principal philosophies of history were expounded before 1700-the Greek/Roman philosophy of history that Fate ultimately ruled all, and the Christian philosophy of history in which St. Augustine declared that there was a divine purpose for God's creatures. In modern times, however, there has been a succession of philosophic interpretations of history beginning with Voltaire's belief that the past can be interpreted rationally. This was followed by Hegel's promulgation that an epoch is typically dominated by an idea (thesis) which is rebutted (antithesis), and after a "theoretical struggle" a new idea (synthesis) is formed.

Then, in the 1850s, Darwin announced his theory of natural selection, and the field of history has not been the same since. This is not to say that the concept of progress in the sense of some sort of evolution had not been thought of earlier, but there can be no denying that Darwin gave the idea more definite direction. This idea has been challenged, of course, by Marxist historians who may be said actually to be espousing a philosophic stance-that the theory and practice of economic production actually determines the other characteristics of the entire political and social system. Others have subsequently carried this doctrine to the extreme, far beyond the designation of the means of production as the dominant factor in a society social condition. Marx and Engels did not deny the influence of ethical or spiritual factors on society, or the possible influence of great leaders; they simply argued that morality emanates from the "social engagement" of men and women, and that economic factors impact greatly upon all aspects of a culture (Nevins, pp. 261-275).

We can now begin to understand more clearly how complex philosophy of history is or can be. This is why there is good, bad, and indifferent history. This is also why students should read excellent, well-written history at all levels of their education and throughout their lives. The best history is more than the recounting of innumerable facts and events in sequential order. It is the interpretation and synthesis of the facts that are gathered that can make history vital or dull and almost useless. However, even if step one (fact-gathering) is well done, and step two (interpreting and synthesizing the data) is carried out by a discerning mind, it is still essential that the historian has the ability to write interestingly, well, and vividly.

How a particular person arrives at his or her own approach to historical interpretation is not easy to explain. As noted above, there are indeed many different philosophies of history and, at present, it hardly seems possible to state that one philosophy of history is paramount. Further, it seems logical that a person develops an implicit "sense of life" very early that is "a pre-conceptual, emotional, subconsciously integrated appraisal of existence, mankind, and that individual's emotional responses and character essence" (Rand, 1979, p. 31). The hope is, of course, that the person will have the opportunity to develop his/her rational powers, and that subsequently reason will act as the programmer of the individual's "emotional computer" (i.e., a rational philosophy will be developed). The relationship of one's implicit sense of life and/or explicit philosophy of life should be reasonably consistent, of course, with the values and norms of the society in which an individual is functioning. If not, serious difficulties of one type or another may arise (Zeigler, 1980. pp. 14-15).

What the 21st century will hold in this regard remains to be seen. The 20th century witnessed the emergence of a variety of treatises in which the development of civilization has been characterized as being shaped by almost rhythmic phases. Without denying that evolutionary forces were involved, theoretic formulations have been postulated in which, to a greater or lesser extent, supernatural power may be directly or indirectly involved (e.g., Spengler, Toynbee, Sorokin, Pareto). On this topic the late Will and Ariel Durant (1961) stated simply that "History smiles at all attempts to force its flow into theoretical patterns or logical grooves; it plays havoc with our generalizations, breaks all our rules; history is baroque." (p. 267)

TOYNBEE'S PHILOSOPHY OF HISTORY

"Toynbee's has been by far the most arresting and influential [force"] stated Nevins (1963, p. 271). Without committing ourselves (the writer or the readers) to any particular philosophy of history, let us follow this recommendation about the work of the late, eminent British historian. Thus, the remainder of this chapter will offer a brief summary of Toynbee's historical analysis. Toynbee (1947) postulated that the story of humankind may be told through the life of 21 major "civilizations"

(p. 34). We learn that five of these civilizations are still alive, but that only Western civilization is still relatively healthy (p. 8). The other four--Far Eastern, Hindu, Islamic, and Orthodox Christian (largely U.S.S.R.)--are weakening and are being incorporated into a "Great Society" with a Western shading (Zeigler, 1989, pp. 10-13). (This view has been challenged strongly by Huntington [1997] who envisages a "clash of civilizations" as the world enter the 21st century.)

Civilization's Pattern of Growth. Most civilizations seem to have gone through a fairly identical pattern of birth, growth, breakdown, and disintegration. A society is but a group of individual humans with an infinite number of interrelationships. It could go on indefinitely, although none has to the present day. Toynbee parted company with Spengler, who believed that a civilization is an organism whose life path is predetermined. Toynbee denied also the theory that a superior race is necessary to found a civilization (p. 55), or that a civilization is created only by a most favorable environment (p. 57).

Themes of Action. Toynbee endowed history with the possession of certain "themes of action." They all seem to have a one-two rhythm such as "challenge-and-response" as the society develops, then "withdrawal-and-return" or "rout-and-rally" as it begins to disintegrate (p. 67). Humans answered the right challenge presented by the environment and thereby are started forward on the path to civilization. This does not mean that people have the help of a favorable or easy environment. Conversely, they are confronted with many difficulties that stimulate them (p. 87). Humans develop as they respond to the various stimuli. Subsequently, the developing society faces a number of other stern challenges such as war, unfavorable environmental conditions, and other conceivable moral or physical pressure.

Breakdown of Civilization. If a civilization meets its challenges, it survives. Its life is measured by the number of challenges that are met successfully. Trouble comes when an incorrect response is made to a specific challenge or stimulus. Then the society is faced with what Toynbee calls a *Time of Troubles.* This period in the civilization's development is not necessarily a catastrophic fall to oblivion; it may go on for hundreds of years. It does, however, usually result in a *Universal State* (p. 12). This occurs when the conflicting countries have order imposed on them by some stronger force. An example of this would be ancient Rome's Augusta dictatorship. Such a Universal State may extend over what seems to be a very long period of time, such as the 2,400 years of Egypt's two empires.

Characteristics of the Universal State. Actually, the beginning of the Universal State appears to some as the foundation of a stable society. In reality it is a symptom of the disintegration of the society, since the people no longer follow the rulers of their own accord. This period of decline is accompanied by a "wanderings of peoples," as occurred in Europe when the Roman Empire waned.

One of the characteristics of such a period may be the adoption of a new religion by the proletariat. For example, consider the growth of the Christian Church, which developed into a Universal Church (p. 24). Subsequently, it served as a basis of a second or "affiliated" civilization. Thus we are told that western civilization grew out of the Greek/Roman society via the Universal Church of Christianity. In like manner, it may be reasoned that the Far Eastern civilization of China-Japan-Korea developed from earlier Since civilization via Buddhism. Toynbee stated, in essence, that these are the broad outlines of the 21 civilizations that the world has seen. (This theory of the development of civilizations is obviously not agreed upon by all historians. Some feel that it does not fit all civilizations exactly, while others assert that it is derived too exclusively from an analysis of the Greek/Roman civilization.)

Progress of Civilizations. Although we are concerned primarily with an analysis of so-called civilization, as stated above it should not be forgotten that the mutation of sub-man into man took place in a social environment more than 300,000 years ago. We should consider the idea that this transformation may well be a more significant amount of growth and development than has taken place yet under the banner of civilization.

The concept of progress, as we think of it, is considered by most to be relatively new historically, although there are some who argue that the ancient Greeks thought of it in just about the same way as we do today. Similarly, the concept of civilization, indeed the word itself may have first been used by the Marquis of Mirabeau in 1757 in his work *L'Ami des Hommes ou Traite sur la Population.* Nef (1979) stated that the term was use to describe "a condition of humane laws, customs, and manners, of relatively tender human relations, and of restraints on warfare which the Europeans supposed had raised them and their kinsmen overseas . . . to a higher level of temporal purpose and of conduct than had been reached before on this planet." (p. 2)

Almost 200 years later Toynbee (1947) used the term less specifically yet with his interesting metaphor of civilizations having arrived at various ledges on the way up a rocky mountainside (p. 49). Each civilization is depicted by a man of that particular society at some level. Most of these "men" are lying dead on a ledge situated at a fairly low level. These include the Egyptiac, Sumeric, Hittite, Babylonic, Indic, Minoan, Hellenic, Syriac, Since, Andean, Mayan, Yucatec, and Mexic civilizations. Five other civilizations appear to have been halted on nearby ledges. Of these five, the Spartan and Ottoman civilizations are dead. The remaining three-Polynesian, Nomadic, and Eskimo-are represented by individuals in a sitting position; they are the arrested civilizations (p. 16).

The Status of Western Civilization. As mentioned above, five civilizations are still climbing up the mountain, but only the Western civilization is relatively healthy. The other four-Far Eastern, Hindu, Islamic, and Orthodox Christian-appear to be "weakening" because of Western influences. To continue with the suggested metaphor, we may ask the question, "How much farther will the Western human climb?" Conceivably it could be argued that our *Time of Troubles* started during the religious wars of the 16th century? (p. 245). Proceeding from this premise, it might be argued that both Napoleon and Hitler failed to create a Universal State. It could be that the United States, the world's only superpower, has now become that "conqueror" through the promotion of democracy, capitalism, technology, and Christianity. Will it be considered as an example of a Universal State (p. 239)? Of course, futurologists or science fiction writers must now give full consideration to whether any country would be in a position to exert such influence if nuclear warfare were to begin.

Interestingly, in 1987, ABC Television's controversial presentation *Amerika* depicted the onset of decay in the United States to such an extent that the Soviet Union merely stepped in and took over with the assistance of an international armed force representing the United Nations. (How ill conceived that prognostication turned out to be!) This appeared to be different from Toynbee's "schism of the body social" postulated as symptoms of such decline in which there were three parts known as the *dominant minority*, the *internal proletariat*, and the *external proletariat*. What Toynbee was describing basically was a situation in which there was "a failure of creative power in the minority, an answering withdrawal of mimesis [limitation] on the part of the majority, and a consequent loss of social unity in the society as a whole" (p. 26). (Often in the past a "creative minority" had degenerated into a "dominant minority," which then used force to rule because the group no longer merited respect.) Certainly in our democratic society we do not find the internal proletariat becoming ascetic and ready to secede or "wander off" because a creative minority has degenerated into a dominant minority. Thus it would appear that our civilization is not very far advanced on its way to disintegration (based on Toynbee's theory anyhow).

SPECULATION ABOUT THE FUTURE

The world continues its evolutional processes. Those who have studied the past with high degrees of intelligence and diligence have offered us a variety of philosophies about humans' history on what we call Earth. It would seem inaccurate, or at least excessive narrowness of definition, to deny a degree of scientific status to the discipline of history. We can indeed argue that with each succeeding generation the study of history, broadly defined, is becoming more of a science (as that term is generally understood).

We can't be sure about what the future holds. However, if the study of the past is credible, we can surmise that there will be continuing uncertainty. In defense of such a condition, we can argue that uncertainty is both dynamic and stimulating as it concomitantly provides a challenge to us all. What should concern us also is the amount of individual freedom we are permitted living within a type of political state known as a democracy. We still have to prove that democracy is possible over a period of centuries. The prevailing trend toward an increasing number of full-time politicians and an overwhelming percentage of indifferent citizens does not bode well for the future.

The various political communities in the Western world that are democratic political states must stress the concept of political involvement to their citizens and promote this ideal whenever and wherever possible to so-called Third World countries as they become ready to make a choice. In addition to reviving and reconstructing the challenge to people within these countries, we must continue to work for the common good-for freedom, justice, and equality-for people all over the world who aspire to better lives for themselves and their children.

If people learn to live with each other in relative peace, the world may not see devastating nuclear warfare with its inevitable results. As McNeill (1963) stated, "The sword of Damocles may therefore hang over humanity indefinitely" (p. 804). However, it could be that the West and the East will no longer be reacting to each other by C.E. 5000. Perhaps the world may be united into a single civilization through the agency of the ideology of political democracy. Toynbee suggested that religions may be the "intelligible field" of historical study rather than the investigation of civilizations. A possibly better approach could well be *the search for consensual values,* values that are delineated but free from the strictures of narrow and often dogmatic formalized religions. To help us in this direction, McNeill looks for "worldwide cosmopolitanism" and "a vastly greater stability" (p. 806).

No matter what we may believe about these conjectures, there is every likelihood that the goal is still a long distance away-especially if a nuclear holocaust is avoided. After all, Earth is somewhat more than 4 billion years old, more or less. According to Sir James Jeans' calculation for the habitability of this planet, men and women, having survived at the rate of 21 civilizations in 6,000 years, still have 1,743 million civilizations ahead of them.

REFERENCES

Commager, H.S. (1961). A quarter century--Its advances. *Look, 25* (10), 80-91.

Cooke, J., Jones, J.S., & Rowland-Entwhistle, T. (1981). *History's timelines.* NY: Crescent.

Curti, M.E. (ed.).(1946). Theory and practice in historical study (*Bulletin 54*). NY: Social Science Research Council.

Durant, W., & Durant, A. (1961). *The age of reason begins.* NY: Simon & Schuster.

Handlin, O. (ed.). (1967). *Harvard guide to American history.* NY: Atheneum.

Huntington, S.P. (1997). *The clash of civilizations and the remaking of world order.* NY: Touchstone.

McNeill, W.H.(1963). *The rise of the West.* Chicago, IL: The University of Chicago.

Melnick, R. (1984). *Visions of the future.* Croton-on-Hudson, NY: Hudson Institute.

Murray, B.G. Jr., (Dec. 10, 1972). What the ecologists can teach the economists. *The New York Times Magazine*; 38-39, 64-65, 70, 72.

Nef, J.U. (1979), The search for civilization. *The Center Magazine,* (an occasional paper): 2-6.

Nevins, A. (1963). *The gateway to history.* Garden City, NY: Doubleday

Rand, A. (1960). *The romantic manifesto.* NY: World.

Toynbee, A.J. (1947). *A study of history.* NY: Oxford University.

Zeigler, E.F. (1979). *Issues in North American sport and physical education.* Washington, DC: American Alliances for Health, Physical Education and Recreation.

Zeigler, E.F. (1980). Issues and problems facing the developing researcher in sport and physical education history. In R. Day & P. Lindsay (Eds.), *Sport*

History Research Methodology (pp. 11-24). Edmonton, AB: Dept. of Physical Education, University of Alberta.

CHAPTER I

HISTORICAL FOUNDATIONS
IN THE UNITED STATES:
SOCIAL AND EDUCATIONAL[1]

THE COLONIAL PERIOD (17TH CENTURY)

Conditions in the American colonies in the 17th century were difficult to say the least. The finer elements of so-called civilized life were possible for only a relatively few wealthy individuals. The culture itself had been transported from Europe with its built-in class distinctions. Slavery was general practice, especially in the south, and the right to vote was typically restricted to property owners. Religion was established legally. The rules of primogeniture and entail served to strengthen the social distinctions. Cultural contrasts were marked, and it may be assumed that geography had a great deal to do with the differences that were evident. There was considerable feeling against democratic principles both from a social and political standpoint. Any consideration of educational practice must, therefore, be viewed in the light of these conditions described above.

Most of the American colonies established between 1607 and 1682 were guided in their educational outlook and activities by England's contemporary practices, the influence of other countries was negligible at first. Thus, education was thought to be a function of the Church and not the State. Judging by today's standards, the provisions made for education were extremely inadequate. In a pioneer country limited by a hazardous physical environment, the settlers were engaged in a struggle for their existence. These differing environments influenced largely the social orders of the North and the South; yet, there were many points of similarity in the traditions and experiences of the people as a whole. They all possessed a common desire for freedom and security, hopes that were to be realized only after a desperate struggle.

The church was the means by which means the religious heritage, and also most of the educational heritage, was preserved and advance. The first schools can

---

[1]Space does not permit, nor does reason support, any more historical material about America than is included at this point. A brief review of the social and educational foundations only did seemed to be required.

actually be regarded as the fruits of the Protestant revolts in Europe. The settlers wanted religious freedom. Nevertheless the reformers among them insisted that a knowledge of the Gospel was required for personal salvation. The natural outcome was to create schools so that children might learn to read. Thus it was the dominant Protestant churches that brought about the establishment of the elementary schools. It is true further that so-called localism, before the advent of the district school, meant that such schools would be randomly located. This was accomplished just as soon as the homes, the churches, and some form of civil government were established. The everyday needs of the citizens, of course, soon made the provision of elementary education even more essential.

Three types of attitudes toward education developed. The first was the compulsory-maintenance attitude of the New England Puritans who established schools by colonial legislation in 1642 and 1647. The second attitude was that of the parochial school which was represented best in Pennsylvania where private schools were made available for those who could afford it. The pauper-non-state-interference attitude was the third. It was best exemplified by Virginia and the southern colonies. It can be appreciated, of course, that many of these people had come to America for profit rather than for religious freedom. Hence there was a strong tendency to continue school practice as it had existed in England. In all of these schools, discipline was harsh and sometimes actually brutal. The curriculum consisted of the three R's and spelling. The books were few, and the teachers were generally unprepared for such a responsibility. Although the school hours were long, there was no place for play and recreation.

The pattern of secondary education had been inherited from England, also; so, Latin grammar schools appeared in most of the colonies. This type of school was developed more significantly in New England. It can be stated further that higher education was not neglected. Nine colleges were founded mainly through the philanthropy of certain individuals and groups. In all of these institutions, except the Academy and College of Philadelphia fostered by Benjamin Franklin, theology formed an important part of the curriculum.

GROWTH AND DEVELOPMENT (EIGHTEENTH CENTURY)

With the advent of the 18th century, fervent religious interest slackened somewhat. The government developed a more civil character, and the schools accordingly became characterized by a "native vein or spirit." This was accompanied by a breakdown in some of the former aristocratic customs. The settled frontier expanded; new interests in trade and shipping grew; and the population increased. A trend toward individualism characterized this period. Several American industries date back to this time, notably the iron mills.

Particularly disturbing were the restrictions placed by England on the use of money by the colonists. There was sufficient prosperity, however, to bring about a change in the appearance of the established communities. Social status was very important to a number of these people. "Colonials" felt that they "had arrived" when they held office and land. In the third decade there was a revival of religious interest. From 1733 on to 1763 the colonies were involved in a series of small wars with the Spanish and the French. These struggles were interspersed by periods of "cold-war" maneuvering. The Seven Years War (1755-1763) ended with the colonies consolidated as a fairly political and economic unit. It was also becoming apparent that the British were failing in their method of governance of the new society. A separatist and nationalistic movement had really begun to develop at mid-century.

Thus, from the middle of the 18th century onward, economic, political, and nationalistic forces were stirring. These influences were felt increasingly in the promotion of elementary education. This change was probably due to a growing religious tolerance, as well as a broader interest in national affairs. Both of these factors served to take the emphasis away from the earlier, strictly religious domination of elementary education.

Secondary education was still provided by the so-called grammar school. These schools, generally located in every large town, were supported by the local government and by private tuition. The curricula were non-utilitarian and were designed to prepare boys for college entrance. Insofar as higher education was concerned, the pattern had been established from the beginning (i.e., Harvard College in 1636) after the European university type of liberal arts education with a strong emphasis on mental discipline and theology.

It should be kept in mind that there were very few heavily populated centers, relatively speaking, even at this time. In the main, frontier life, and life in the small villages, was still very rigorous. Such conditions were simply not conducive to the "intellectual life" characterized by higher educational standards. Educational theorists had visions of a fine educational system, of course, but the states did not have many definite constitutional provisions regarding education--and the Federal Constitution didn't say anything about it at all. There was promise, however, in he many newer social forces at work. Then came the period of unrest and, with the outbreak of the War of Independence, education of the formal type came almost to a complete standstill.

The last 25 years of the 18th century saw a great many changes in the life of the United States. In the first place, many of the revolutionaries who started the war lived to tell about it, and also to help with the sound reconstruction of the nation. This was no small feat by any standard. They began the process of writing state and federal constitutions. Furthermore, it was very important to the early success of the country that commerce be revived. This was accomplished sooner by the south because of the nature of the commodities they produced. New lines of business and trade were established with Russia, Sweden, and the Orient. The Federal Convention of 1787 managed to complete what has been the most successful document in all of history--the Constitution of the United States of America. Then George Washington's administration began, and in retrospect it can be called successful both at home and abroad. The French Revolution then became an issue in American politics, but Washington wisely declared a position of neutrality. However, he was hard pressed to keep in effect.

As soon as America's war was over, considerable attention was turned to education. In the remaining years of the 18th century, development of both secondary and higher education was significant. In the North both Phillips Andover and Phillips Exeter Academies were established. However, the colleges of the North seemed to have suffered more than those in the South. There an imposing list of both private, religiously-endowed and state institutions were founded.

NATIONALISM AND GROWTH (NINETEENTH CENTURY)

The stage had now been set for the United States to enter a most important period in her history. Thomas Jefferson was in office from 1801 to 1809. His period of office was followed by a second war with Great Britain, the War of 1812. In the ensuing period of nationalism, a number of adjustments in the relationships with Britain and other nations were necessary. The Monroe Doctrine declared to the world that countries in this hemisphere should be left alone to develop as they saw fit and were not to be used by outside powers for colonization. Obviously, this was a period in which the United States was finding itself. The pattern was being set for future developments. Unfortunately the North and the South were becoming increasingly divided. The North was being changed by virtue of the Industrial Revolution along with many educational and humanitarian movements. The South, on the other hand, was nurturing a different type of society, one that was regulated by what has been called a "slave and cotton economy."

In the realm of education, the first 50 years of new national life was a period of transition from the control of the church to that of the state. Federal control and support gradually seemed more feasible, although the change was seemingly somewhat slow in coming. Political equality and religious freedom, along with changing economic conditions, finally made education for all seem a necessity. This period was characterized by the introduction of a number of semi-private, philanthropic agencies such as the Sunday School Movement, the city school societies, the Lancastrian Movement, and the infant school societies. The Lancastrian Movement was highly regarded for a time, since it made the education of all seem financially possible because of the use of student monitors as instructors. However, people soon realized the inefficiency of this approach with resultant discussion provoked a situation in which the necessary cost for adequate teaching and facilities was borne by all of the citizens.

By 1825 a tremendous struggle for the creation of the American state school, so to speak, was underway. The field of public education during the years from 1830 to 1860 is often called "The Architectural Period." Educational leaders and a number of leading citizens were calling for public schools that were tax-supported, publicly-controlled, and non-sectarian. The problems of getting tax support, of eliminating the pauper-school idea, and of doing away with pro-rated tuitions were all difficult in themselves to solve. The elimination of sectarianism as a controlling factor and the appointment of public officials to administer school affairs were major problems. Then came the establishment of the first public high school, and thereafter the establishment of state universities. The first compulsory school attendance law was passed in Massachusetts in 1852. The various types of schools had been gradually amalgamated into state systems, also. By 1860 the American educational ladder was fairly complete. Federal support didn't come until 1862 when the Morrill Act was passed. Public land was granted to each state for the founding of a college of agriculture and mechanical arts.

With the development of the public school system, it was natural that attention turned to the quality and type of teacher hired for so important a task as the education of the coming generation. Educational journalism actually had its beginning in America as early as the 1920's. Then, because of interest in concurrent European educational advancements, other subject-matters were added. Before the establishment of the first (what were called) normal schools, the status of common-school teachers was very poor. Secondary school teachers in the Latin grammar schools and academies evidently were significantly better. Specific professional preparation of teachers in any formal way was almost unknown. Today one can be critical of the teachers of this era, of course, but they were probably living up to the demands of the times reasonably well.

Certification of teachers, after a fashion, began early in the 19th century. Town authorities and ministers usually assured themselves that the candidates for teaching positions had a minimum knowledge of the subject matter included in the curriculum and were also "strong in the faith." In the Dutch schools of the New Netherlands, license requirements were gradually taken out of ecclesiastical hands by the civil authorities, but the standard were still low everywhere in 1839, fort example. Is it true that legal requirements were being developed, but the examinations themselves were evidently poorly administered. The agencies issuing certificates were completely local and thus had only local validity.

The advances made in the training of American teachers in teaching techniques took place first in elementary education. This effort began around the time of the War of 1812. Private academies, private normal schools, state-subsidized academies or teachers seminaries, and state-controlled and state-supported normal schools were the first institutions that prepared teachers in any specific fashion. Those leaders who recommended teacher preparation during the first two decades of the 19th century actually knew very little about foreign normal schools until about 1825. It was at this time that travelers abroad reported about the German normal schools. It was these accounts that gave impetus to the movement just getting underway in America. The German pattern was adopted, but with some modifications. The Reverend Samuel R. Hall is generally accepted as the founder of the first normal school in the United States at Concord, Vermont in 1823. The first state normal school was established for a three-year experimental period by Massachusetts legislation in 1839. This normal school was started at Lexington with Cyrus Pierce as principal. The second such school was authorized in 1839, but it was not opened until 1840 at Bridgewater in Plymouth Colony.

During the next quarter century the growth of similar institutions was actually not very significant. The advances were small and made only after a struggle wherever such training schools arose. However, with the rise of the public-school movement, it became obvious that teacher-training would of necessity assume a larger role. The country's population was increasing sharply and, although it remained largely rural, ti city populations were growing at a great rate.

THE CIVIL WAR AND RECONSTRUCTION

The "War between the States" or "the Civil War" wrought tremendous changes in the lives of the people. Teacher education, for example, remained a problem largely of preparing elementary school teachers. This can be explained by the fact that, of the 6,871,532 students enrolled in public schools in 1870, only 80,277 of them were at the secondary level of education. State support and control of these schools was increasing steadily, a fact made possible because national wealth was increasing much more rapidly in proportion to the size of the population itself. Four states had established boards of education by 1850. This trend was important, because the magnitude of the development seemingly required a strong, centralized department of education in each state.

Practically speaking, of course, federal control of education would have brought about the unification of the school systems much more readily and expediently. However, this was not to be the pattern, because control of education from the beginning was to be left in the hands of individual states. This development can be characterized as haphazard. Public school officials at the state level were subject to popular elections in a number of state. Yet, it is argued by many, such development is necessary in a democratic, pluralistic system.

Difficult days were in store for the American people after the Civil War--a war that had actually wrought a tremendous change in the lives of all citizens. Interestingly enough, despite their defeat, the South was able to return to its former national allegiance quickly, although there has been continuing evidence that the South "won the peace" in a sense because change toward equality of opportunity for all has come very slowly. The economic plight was extremely serious, of course, but the people were aided greatly by being allowed to restore normal trading relations. What is called the Reconstruction Period is generally regarded as an unfortunate part of United States history. Lincoln had possessed the wisdom to meet the critical situation, but his life had been taken through assassination. Of course, many in the North felt that strict justice should be employed to punish a now seemingly ungrateful "loser." All in all, however, despite the fact that Lincoln and Johnson were followed by a twenty-four year series of Republican presidents who had all been military men of varying importance, the South was treated reasonably well.

The period from 1870 to 1890, therefore, was marked by steady expansion and development. "Big business" became a reality; the country continued its march westward; organized labor made definite progress; and significant social and cultural developments took place. The development of urban society brought about a greater interest in social affairs than heretofore. Politer society became interested in music and literature, although in retrospect the literature did not achieve great acclaim. Several fine art galleries and museums were founded, but the majority of people had little understanding of the aesthetic in life. The architecture of the period was eclectic, the simple beauty of the earlier Colonial home was seemingly lost. Formal religion as expressed by its leaders was challenged strongly by evolutionary theories and the philosophy of pragmatism with the result that the church was hard pressed.

In the field of education, the idea of equality of educational opportunity made great strides as the educational ladder gradually extended upward. The number of high schools increased fivefold between 1870 and 1890. The state was assuming the position of prime importance in public education. State universities turned their attention to advancing the welfare of their respective states. The result was a marked increase in revenue and attendance. Southern states lagged behind the rest of the country due to the aftereffects of the War, reconstruction, racial conflict, and a continuing fairly aristocratic theory of education. Yet even in the North, President Eliot of Harvard called for educational reform in 1888. One of his main points was the need for better training of teachers.

Insofar as the improvement of general teacher training was concerned, the status of teachers came along slowly during this period. New Pestalozzian procedures had been introduced by Edward Sheldon in Oswego, New York in the 1860's, an approach that quite completely reshaped elementary education. Many state normal schools started during this era and were well distributed over the country as a whole. Although the faculties and curricula of these institutions were poor at first, there has been a steady improvement down through the years. Professional courses of the time were not too effectual as to course content and teaching methodology employed. Scientific method had yet to be applied to educational research. In addition to the state normal schools, there was a significant growth of city normal schools and classes that paralleled the enlargement of the cities. During this period the college and university normal departments of the period, as they were called, were still not very good, even though interest in teaching as an art had been started by New York University in 1832, by Brown University in 1850, and by The University of Michigan in 1860. After 1879 departments of pedagogy began to develop with the aim of preparing secondary school teachers. The growth of in-service teacher education agencies began in this period of educational history. By 1890 such activities as reading circles, professional teachers' organizations and institutes, and summer schools and extension work were contributing to the gigantic task of raising the level of preparation of teachers in service.

Criticism of the educational system in the 1870's and 1880's had been present, but it assumed large-scale proportions in the final decade of the 19th century. All sorts of innovations and reforms were being recommended from a variety of quarters. This social movement in education undoubtedly had a relationship to political progressivism. In the universities, also, the formalism present in psychology, philosophy, and the social sciences was coming under severe attack. Out in the public schools other conflicts were raging. Citizens were demanding that the promise of American life should be realized through the broadening of the school's purposes. Although the seeds of this educational revolution were sown in the 19th century, the story of its accomplishment belongs to the 20th century. That much progress has been made along these lines is self-evident; yet, the promise of the future is ever so much greater still.

THE FIRST HALF OF THE TWENTIETH CENTURY

Looking back on the history of the 20th century in the United States is frightening because so much has happened--and it has all happened so quickly. The very tempo of life is increasing, and one can't but wonder where it will all end up. The phenomenon of change was apparent at every turn of the road. For example, think back to Teddy Roosevelt and his "Big Stick," or to Taft, Wilson and World War I. Then there was the "Roaring Twenties" with booming prosperity, only to be followed by the Stock Market Crash of 1929 and the Great Depression of the 1930's. The rebuilding process seemed slow, but it was actually very rapid thanks to Franklin Roosevelt and the New Deal. The future looked brighter again, but a "small" war in Europe could not be confined. Then, after Japan allied with Germany and Italy, the attack on Pearl Harbor placed the United States squarely in the middle of World War II. Eventual victory came for the Allies, but the period of peace was again short-lived. The Iron Curtain, the Korean War. the Cold War, the War in Vietnam, and the Collapse of the U.S.S.R. followed in quick succession--quite a century by any standards!

In the political arena, social legislation and political reform made truly significant changes in the lives of the people despite the ever-present struggle between conservative and liberal forces. Industry and business assumed gigantic proportions, as did the regulatory controls of the federal government. The greatest experiment in political democracy in the history of the world was grinding ahead slowly. The ideals behind such a plan were being challenged from all quarters. Wars and financial booms and "busts" (or depressions) weren't the type of developments that made planning a simple matter. It seemed conceivable that democracy might be made to work at home, but what about the political systems of the other world countries?

Laissez-faire capitalism had produced the "highest standard of low and mediocre living" for most people that the world had ever seen, but what was "the good life"? Was unmodified capitalism and vast technological expansion and so-called "progress" the answer? Some people were beginning to wonder. Organized labor, through the valiant efforts of its leaders, set about to get what it felt was the common man's fair share of the wealth. In the meantime population growth seemed to decline, but then it spurted upward again. The traditional status of the family was disturbed as women entered the labor market in increasing numbers in World War II. There were so many different "racial groups" and religious denominations and sects that understanding among peoples became extremely difficult. The concept of the "WASP"(white, Anglo-Saxon, Protestant) as the typical American was shattered into bits and pieces--undoubtedly never again to return.

The conservatives fought the liberals, and they both fought the Socialists and the Communists. Then they all turned again the fascism of Hitler, Mussolini, and Hirohito. Nevertheless there still remained the "inscrutable Oriental, an unreasonable fear of any type of Socialism or Communism, the "doves" and the "hawks"--and what have you? For a while at that point the United Nations appeared to be the hope of the world, but slowly people began to wonder whether it could fulfill its promise of world peace and the advancement of humankind.

All of these social developments mentioned immediately above had their influence on the subject at hand--education. Educational opportunity had been equalized considerable, but there was still much work to be done. The Federal Government had participated increasingly in education, but where should it stop? The struggle between the state and the church in regard to education had been reasonably well resolved, but what does he future hold in this regard? The schools are quite democratically administered, but have we truly decided what the term "democracy" means? Or is it an evolving concept that will change as the society changes? The school has traditionally reflected the social and cultural heritage.

Would it--could it--ever lead the way in educational reconstruction?

Now let us return to the beginning of that remarkable 20th century and trace the educational development somewhat more specifically. The goals of American education were that it would be (1) free, (2) non-sectarian, (3) universal, (4) publicly supported, (5) obliquely controlled, and (6) compulsory up to a specified age.

The First Decade (1900-1910). What was the educational situation like in 1900? In the first place, the United States had a population of about 70 million people (62,947,714 in 1890), and 32 states had compulsory school attendance. Approximately 16,000,000 pupils were enrolled in elementary schools. From 1890 to 1900, secondary school attendance had increased from 202,963 to 519,251--a remarkable increase! The higher education enrollment was 250,000, and the predominantly institution was the four-year college. Seventy percent of the public school teachers were women. The average annual salary of teachers was 325 dollars.

The elementary curriculum was typically eight years in length. It was centered around what has been called the "traditional, subject-matter curriculum" including reading, writing, and arithmetic, as well as spelling, grammar, geography, history, and civics. There was great variation in emphasis on such subjects as drawing, music, nature study, and physical education. However, times were changing, and there is evidence that the center of gravity had shifted somewhat from the subject-matter of instruction to the child who was being taught. A new understanding of the nature of a child was developing through the strong influence of such authorities as William James, G. Stanley Hall, John Dewey, and Edward L. Thorndike. The scientific revolution and the growing complexity of American economic life was forcing the educational curriculum to be modified to meet the needs of the day.

At the secondary level of education, a rather thoroughgoing revision of the curriculum was taking place due to several significant factors. The very character of the population was changing, and the needs and interests of their offspring were becoming different from that of the former "college-bound" group in secondary education. Consequently there was a continued multiplication of sub subjects and courses accompanied by a trend permitting greater freedom of election. This trend was coupled with the introduction of a variety of surveys and problems courses. It can be said, nevertheless, that the need for a common background of educational experience was not neglected.

In higher education the influences mentioned above brought about similar changes as well. There were those who wished to preserve the traditional concept of a liberal education. However, a broader general education was being considered seriously as a supplement. The elective system seemed to be the answer to an American way of life characterized by individualism, capitalism, and industrialism. Course requirements were altered; subject-matter fields were grouped into larger bodies of knowledge; and the individual generally received greater attention.

The normal school was a well-established part of the American school system by this time. These schools admitted students of secondary rank and usually scaled their offerings to the ability of the student population. The program was designed to give the students a command of elementary subject-matter, academic secondary studies, and professional education study. The education courses included the history and science of education, as well as instruction in teaching methodology. The normal school has become the main agency for the preparation of elementary school teachers and was beginning to enter the field of training secondary teachers as well. However, it was some time before the normal school was accepted generally as being qualified for this latter endeavor. Simply put, the length of the program had to be increased and the quality of this preparation had to be improved. The transformation of the normal schools to college status was absolutely necessary because of the vast growth of the number of public high schools.

Interestingly, professional education, teacher-training courses in the college and universities of the time were in most cases no better than the normal-school training. Some 30 or 30 different courses in professional education were offered. Many people would now argue that this n umber of courses should have remained fairly constant. Then research could have been directed at improving the scientific base and quality of these efforts. Unfortunately, by 1934, the number of differently named courses in professional education had increased to about 600, and few would argue that this increase was justified. Also, it was interesting to note that college and university educators of the time were concerned that the normal schools were moving into "territory" far beyond their capability.

These first years of the new century certainly held great import for the field of education. In 1902, for example, the township high school at Joliet, Illinois became the first public junior college. This happened because William Rainey Harper, the first president of the University of Chicago, encouraged the idea. Also, in 1902, the distinguished school administrator and later U.S. Commissioner, William T. Harris, passed away, ending a notable career of service to the field. Of passing interest, in 1904, John Dewey was selected as a professor of philosophy at Columbia University.

In 1907, Dean Alexis F. Lange, of the University of California, encouraged the state to enact the first junior college law. The result was that the establishment of public junior colleges began there in 1910. Just one year before, California had taken the lead in another direction with the inauguration of the first junior high school at Berkeley. Another significant development of the time, but in New York State, was the organization of the first class for speech defectives. In addition, at this time, Abraham Flexner was proclaiming his sweeping criticisms of medical education in particular and college education in general.

It is now recognized that somewhere between 1890 and 1910 what was called a "fourth period" in American higher education has begun. The need had arisen for opportunities for greater specialization, and also the free elective system had evidently gone too far. So an attempt was made to bring some order into the large, confusing group of subjects that frequently characterized higher education of the time. This is when the concept of the "major program system" began.

The Second Decade (1910-1919). By 1910, with public high school enrollment at a new high of 1,000,000 students, the beginning can be traced of a movement that was to result in a significant reorganization of the educational ladder. The change was to a six-year elementary school, a three-year junior high school, a three-year senior high school, and a two-year junior college (i.e., 6-3-3-2) as compared to the former 8-4 plan. By 1917, for example, there were 46 junior colleges, and one year later it was estimated that there were 557 junior high schools. Other developments included the passage of the Smith-Lever Act in 1914 that stimulated agricultural extension service in education; the publication of Dewey's Democracy in Education in 1916; and the Smith-Hughes Act in 1917 providing secondary vocational education. (It must be mentioned parenthetically that Dewey's work has been generally recognized as the most through presentation of the implications for education in a democratic society.) Lastly, by 1918 compulsory school attendance laws had been passed in all states of the union.

The Third Decade (1920-1930). The rate of educational change did not slacken in the 1920's after a slight economic depression in 1921-1922. Public high school enrollment reached 2,000,000 pupils, and the junior high school movement continued on unabated. The years just prior to 1920 had been an incubation period for the Progressive Education Association, but it wasn't long before members were speaking of the "child-centered school," aided undoubtedly by Dewey's rapidly spreading philosophy of democratic education. The new science of education produced strong interest in individual development, primarily because of the growing power of the psychology of individual differences. Testing and measuring of students and their various capacities expanded sharply. One result of this movement was the idea of classifying students according to abilities in "homogeneous groups." One widely heralded innovation at this time was the Dalton Plan involving a series of contracts or projects as developed in Massachusetts by Helen Parkhurst.

With the introduction of educational and intelligence testing, a need was revealed for various types of instruction for many different types of people. This represented the beginning of what was to become a vast lateral expansion of the public educational system. Various state and national curriculum committees were established; there was a movement to establish a federal department of education; adult education activities were increased; and a Carnegie Survey was conducted to assess the in-service education of teachers. Additionally, the Vocational Rehabilitation Act of 1920 subsequently exerted a strong influence.

Education benefited great from the economic prosperity of the 1920's. Building programs were soon in evidence all over the country. The development of the junior high school was rapid. and by 1925 some 16,000 public high schools were established as well. From 1920 on, the Junior College Movement grew rapidly, especially in the West. There were, for example, 46 teachers colleges in 1920, and this trend toward "expanded" normal schools was gaining momentum. For those who may, or may not, have had the benefits of a formal education, adult education activities were being sponsored increasingly. Interest grew to a point where the American Association for Adult Education was formed in 1926.

Thus, educational developmentalism and the increasing emphasis on social education brought about a great many changes and innovations during this decade of material prosperity. All types of what were called "extra-curricular" activities were added to the program of the school. Within the curriculum itself a variety of special classes were made available for the handicapped and atypical student. The trend toward equalization of educational opportunity was provided with a stimulus by restrictions against child labor, as well as by more stringent compulsory, school-attendance laws. Although it was pointed out that federal aid of much greater magnitude was necessary for full realization of this social ideal, such backing really did not come to any appreciable extent. The George-Reed Act of 1929, however, did allow secondary vocational education to be increased.

Dewey's influence aided greatly in bringing about what has been referred to as an "educational transformation." a movement toward aiding children to realize greater social efficiency. G. Stanley Hall and Edward L. Thorndike, two most important educational developmentalists, made unique contributions as well. Hall stressed race perpetuation, the basic need for early sound emotional experience, and a well-balanced personality development in accordance with the child's own nature. Thorndike emphasized the uniqueness of each individual, which meant that individual differences should be recognized, and that opportunities for creative experiences should be provided. The breadth of the "new school curriculum" was caught in the now-famous Commission Report of 1918. These aims were stated as the Seven Cardinal Principles of Education:

1. health and safety
2. mastery of tools, techniques and spirit of learning
3. worthy home membership
4. vocational and economic effectiveness
5. citizenship
6. worthy use of leisure
7. ethical character

The Fourth Decade (1930-1939). The 1930's, conversely, were very difficult for the United States. The 1930's were very difficult years for the United States. When the stock market had collapsed in 1929, this event had signaled the beginning of a most severe financial depression. It was inevitable that education would suffer from the necessary budgetary curtailment. This meant that the educational programs itself would have to be assessed most carefully yo determine at which points money could be saved. Educational conservatives demanded that the "essentials" be retained, and that the "frills" had to go. The teaching profession suffered greatly as well, since salaries were cut and the field became overcrowded. This happened because so many returned to a field that offered security, albeit at a low salary.

All of this resulted in a strong reaction against the aims of progressive education by both educators and laymen alike. Even some of the liberal spirits criticized it for too great stress on individualism and insufficient emphasis on a theory of social welfare. It was stated that the real basis for curriculum organization should be the experience of the learners. Still further it was argued that the educational process should become a social process. From the depression onward, therefore, education assumed a new social emphasis.

In the area of higher education, a variety of occurrences were taking place. Alexander Meiklejohn had started an "Experimental College" at the University of Wisconsin. It was designed to help the student focus study on a particular cultural epoch and resultantly to bring integrated knowledge to bear on social needs. Along with this and other educational experiments, there was a separation generally of junior and senior colleges. To the former was assigned a general education function, while the latter was to emphasize specialization to a point. In retrospect, that point was a program in which there was a limited major in a subject-matter field and several minor subjects in related disciplines.

A further trend was to place greater responsibility on the individual student in acquiring his/her own education. From another standpoint, however, colleges and universities were faced with severe financial problems during this decade. The depression tended to curtail, and in many cases eliminate, significant private contributions to higher education, which forced an increasing amount of public money into this level of education. An interesting sidelight to this latter development was a resurgence of interest in the social sciences, especially economics, because of a desire to understand the reasons underlying the economic crisis. It was during this period that a gradual development of the University of Chicago's "aristocratic wing" of higher education was taking place under Hutchins. Another "sign of the time" was a reassertion of the need for academic freedom because of a number of "red scares" on various campuses.

In addition, the 1930's was a time when there were more than 4,000,000 students enrolled in public high schools. It was estimated in 1930 that there was a grand total of 24,000,000 students in elementary schools as well. The percentage of women teachers had risen to 80 percent in the public schools. During this decade, at least in some systems, teachers began to gain a voice in policy-making. In elementary education there was increased emphasis on the experience of the learners as providing the fundamental basis for curriculum organization. Kilpatrick, of Columbia Teachers College, was a foremost exponent of the "learning by doing" dictum. A significant eight-year study at the secondary level involving 30 public and private high schools preparing for university entrance, with significantly altered curricula prior to guaranteed admittance, indicated that the students in the experimental curriculum made slightly higher grade point averages during their period of higher education.

The effects of the Depression were in many ways unfortunate, but there were some benefits as well. The educational and certification requirements for teachers were strengthened. The problem of unemployed youth forced the Federal Government to devote considerable attention and money to the solution of their difficulties as best possible under the circumstances. This was accomplished through such agencies as the Civilian Conservation Corps, the National Youth Administration, and the Works Progress Administration. The George-Deen Act in 1936 provided federal assistance to instruction at the secondary level related to occupations concerned with selling and marketing. Careful scrutiny and assessment of the purposes of education in American democracy resulted in the 1938 Educational Policies Commission statement that (1) self-realization, (2) human relationships, (3) economic efficiency, and (4) civic responsibility were the desired educational objectives.

The Fifth Decade (1940-1949). The year 1940 found the United States returning to normalcy again. However, it should be recognized that the word "normal" doesn't doesn't have a very precise meaning in a rapidly changing world. There were approximately 650,000 children enrolled in kindergartens, but the elementary school enrollment had decreased to under 20,000,000 because of a declining birth rate and restrictive immigration laws during this decade. However, public high school enrollment had climbed to 7,000,000, and there were approximately 1,500,000 students in higher education. The average teacher salary was $1.350, but New York's average was $2,600 and Mississippi's was $526. These figures are the extremes, of course, and need to be related to the cost of living to understand them best. The average expenditure per pupil for education was $80.00 annually, but this figure needs further interpretation as well.

Then, of course, World War II arrived on the doorstep of the United States with the Japanese attack on Pearl Harbor in December of 1941. The resultant, necessary war production exerted a great variety of influences on the educational structure. With the entire nation mobilized for war, so many needed changes and improvements simply could not be implemented. However, federal funds were made available throughout the U.S. Office of Education to train defense workers in schools and colleges. This governmental subsidization, of one type or another, saved many colleges and universities from financial ruin. A great many teachers were asked to serve their country in the several branches of the armed forces.

THE SECOND HALF OF THE TWENTIETH CENTURY

The Third Quarter of the 20th Century (1950-1975). It is now becoming possible to achieve some historical perspective on the period after the cessation of the hostilities in World War II. It has been difficult for those, such as the present author who was "part of these times." to have a clear vision while seeking to bring trends into focus. The population figures are now soaring. The Cold War and the "hot wars" became part of the way of life. Nevertheless, now that the Cold War is itself history, the world has still not managed to rid itself of so many skirmishes and smaller wars still occurring globally. The future in this regard does not look bright.

Basic science marched on, and those involved in the social sciences and humanities were striving mightily, but struggling, to keep apace. New terms like "urban sprawl" and "multiversity" became part of the languages. Yet the older terms, juvenile delinquency and racial unrest, were still present as well and were expressed more frequently. Living costs continued to rise in uneven spurts, and school boards and boards of trustees within the educational establishment were faced with the ongoing struggle to provide adequate teachers and facilities to get the job of education done properly. The standard of living is higher for many, but it is miserable low for so many others ("rich richer, poor poorer"). The United States was literally facing the greatest experiment in democratic living in the history of the world, while the threat of non-militant and militant communism moved alongside with its own aims, ideals, and practices.

None can deny that it was an interesting period in education. There was a return to the aims of social efficiency after the Global War. There was also a renewed emphasis upon the inculcation of moral values through the school. However, it seems that no one knew how to do this efficiently and effectively keeping in mind that church and state were to be kept separate. The Cold War proceeded to bring insecurity. A demand arose to place major emphasis on the development of the human's rational powers. Education for international understanding was promoted as a "must," but somehow there remained an ever-present nationalistic influence on education both at home and abroad.

At the elementary level in education, the prevailing social and political influences tended to bring about a return to what may be called the more traditional pattern of education with renewed emphasis on drill and fundamentals. Reappraisal is usually quite helpful. It is probably inevitable that public confidence in the educational enterprise is disturbed at such time. However, it was unfortunate that the attacks brought to bear on "professional education" were quite so bitter.

At the secondary level, similar attacks centered on what their proponents believed to be the anti-intellectualism of the high school. This minority group of malcontents appeared to be telling all Americans that they knew what was best. They argued most vigorously that the end of democracy (in a republic!) would be served best by a return to a really essential curriculum including "solid" subjects that had been time-tested. It now appears to be very fortunate that a respected educator such as James Bryan Conant of Harvard was available to survey the situation with the financial backing of the Carnegie Corporation. His report gave substantial support to the American comprehensive high school that was serving as a medium where the needs and interests of all might be served. In addition, he recommended special emphasis on the needs of the academically gifted young person.

Higher education in the century's third quarter faced many similar problems. Enrollments shot up sharply after the war and were continuing unabated. Junior and community colleges sprang up practically overnight in many communities. State colleges became state universities, and state universities steadily emerged as state multiversities. Private colleges and universities grew, also, but they usually managed to keep such growth under control. Graduate education swelled enormously with federal support for research exerting great influence on the programs involved. Great strain was placed on the various professional schools within universities as they sought to maintain quality while only partially meeting the increased enrollment demands. In all of this, there was a note of urgency due to the world situation that seemed to require a resultant "pursuit of excellence." However, professors gradually became less available for teaching because of research demands, and often less interested in that phase of their work as well. Demands on the time of many for service to state and nation increased. The three goals of many universities have been teaching, research, and service, but the question is raised continually as to the order of priority, if any, in the attainment of these goals.

The Fourth Quarter of the 20th Century (1975-2000). Although it is impossible to gain true historical perspective about the final quarter of the 20th century in the United States, it is important to keep in mind the significant developments of the decades immediately preceding the 21st century. For example, Naisbitt (1982) outlined the "ten new directions that are transforming our lives," as well as the "megatrends" apparent because of women's evolving role in societal structure (Aburdene & Naisbitt, 1992). Here the reference is to:

1. the concepts of the information society and Internet,
2. "high tech/high touch,"
3. the shift to world economy,
4. the need to shift to long-term thinking in regard to ecology,
5. the move toward organizational decentralization,
6. the trend toward self-help,
7. the ongoing discussion of the wisdom of participatory democracy as opposed to representative democracy,
8. a shift toward networking,
9. a reconsideration of the "North-South" orientation, and
10. the viewing of decisions as "multiple option" instead of "either/or"

Add to this the ever-increasing, lifelong involvement of women in the workplace, politics, sports, organized religion, and social activism. Then it becomes possible to understand that a new world order has descended upon humankind during this 25-year period. Moving ahead in time slightly past Naisbitt's first set of *Megatrends*, as well as the 1992 set of Aburdene & Naisbitt, a second list of 10 issues facing political leaders was highlighted in the mid-1990s in the *Utne Reader* titled "Ten events that shook the world between 1984 and 1994" (1994, pp. 58-74). Just consider the following:

1. the fall of communism and the continuing rise of nationalism,
2. the environmental crisis and the "green movement,"
3. the AIDS epidemic and the "gay response,"
4. many continuing wars and the peace movement,
5. the gender war,
6. religion and racial tension,
7. the concept of "West meets East" and resultant implications,
8. the "Baby Boomers" came of age and "Generation X" has started to worry and complain because of declining expectation levels,
9. the whole idea of globalism and international markets, and, finally,
10. the computer revolution and the specter of Internet.

The Impact of Negative Social Forces Has Increased. In seeking to "live the good life" a the end of the 20th century, people are finding that the human recreational experience will have to be earned typically within a society whose very structure has been modified. For example, the concept of the traditional family structure has been strongly challenged by a variety of social forces (e.g., economics, divorce rate); many single people are finding that they must work longer hours; and many families need more than one breadwinner just to make ends meet. Also, the idea of a steady surplus economy may have vanished, temporarily it is hoped, in the presence of a substantive drive to reduce a budgetary deficit by introducing major cutbacks in so-called non-essentials.

Additionally, many of the same problems of megalopolis living described in 1967 still prevail and are even increasing (e.g., declining infrastructure, crime rates (some of them anyhow), transportation gridlocks, overcrowded schools). Interestingly, also, even though the United States is one of the best places in the world to live, the work week is not getting shorter and shorter--and earlier predictions about four different types of leisure class still seemed a distant dream for the large majority of people.

Further, the situation has developed in such a way that the presently maturing generation, so-called Generation X, is finding that fewer good-paying jobs are available and the average annual income is declining. What caused this to happen? This is not a simple question to answer. For one thing, despite the rosy picture envisioned in the mid-1970's, one in which humankind was supposedly entering a new stage, the society is unable today to cope adequately with the multitude of problems that have developed. This is true whether inner city, suburbia, exurbia, or small-town living are concerned. Transportation jams and gridlock, for example, are occurring daily as public transportation struggles to meet rising demand for economical transport within the framework of developing megalopolises.

Megalopolis living trends have certainly not abated and will probably not do so in the predictable future. More and more families, where that unit is still present, need two breadwinners just to survive. Interest rates fluctuate but remain reasonably high, thereby discouraging many people from home ownership. Pollution of air and water continues despite efforts of many to change the present course of development. High-wage industries seem to be "heading south" in search of places where lower wages can be paid. Also, all sorts of crime are still present in society, a goodly portion of it seemingly brought about by unemployment and rising debt at all levels from the individual to the federal government. The rise in youth crime is especially disturbing. In this respect, it is fortunate that municipal, private-agency, and public recreation has received continuing financial support from the increasingly burdened taxpayer.

What Character Is Sought for Americans? Americans, functioning within a world that has become a "Global Village" communications-wise, need to think more seriously than ever before about the character and traits for which they should seek to develop in people. People can only continue to lead or to strive for the proverbial good life if children and young people develop the right attitudes (psychologically speaking) toward education, work, use of leisure, participation in government, various types of consumption, and concern for world stability and peace. Make no mistake about it: if Americans truly desire "the good life," education for the creative and constructive use of leisure, as a significant part of ongoing general education, should have a unique role to play now and forever more.

The Old World countries all seem to have a "character." It is almost something that they take for granted. Does America have what can be called a character? Americans were thought earlier to be heterogeneous and individualistic as a people as opposed to Canadians, for example. However, the Canadian culture has changed significantly in recent decades as people, feeling welcome because of Canada's planned multiculturalism, began to arrive from many different lands. And, of course, Canada was founded originally by two distinct cultures, the English and the French.

Schlesinger (1998), in his revised analysis of the American situation, writes with considerable concern about "the disuniting of America." Speaking about Canada, also, he asks, "If one of the top five developed nations on earth can't make a federal, multi-ethnic state work, who else can?" His response: "The answer to that increasingly vital question has been, at least until recently, the United States" (p. 14). What he is saying is that Canada has been going about multi-culturalism the wrong way for some time, and that the United States had presumably been working earlier toward a "melting-pot" development. But America somehow is now moving in the same direction as Canada!

In retrospect, shortly after the middle of the 20th century, Commager (1966), the noted historian, enumerated what he believed were some common denominators in the American character. These, he said, were:

1. carelessness;
2. openhandedness, generosity, and hospitality;
3. self-indulgence;
4. sentimentality, and even romanticism;
5. gregariousness;
6. materialism;
7. confidence and self-confidence;
8. complacency, bordering occasionally on arrogance;
9. cultivation of the competitive spirit;
10. indifference to, and exasperation with laws, rules, and regulations
11. equalitarianism; and
12. resourcefulness (pp. 246-254).

What Happened to the Original Enlightenment Ideal? This "new scientific knowledge and accompanying technological power was expected to make possible a comprehensive improvement in all of the conditions of life, social, political, moral, and intellectual as well as material. This idea did indeed slowly take hold and eventually "became the fulcrum of the dominant American world view" (Marx, p. 5). By 1850, however, with the rapid growth of the United States especially, the idea of progress was already being dissociated from the Enlightenment vision of political and social liberation. Then, by the turn of the twentieth century, "the technocratic idea of progress [had become] a belief in the sufficiency of scientific and technological innovation as the basis for general progress" (Marx, p. 9). This came to mean that if scientific-based technologies were permitted to develop in an unconstrained manner, there would be an automatic improvement in all other aspects of life! What has happened, because this theory became coupled with onrushing, unbridled capitalism, was that the ideal envisioned by Thomas Jefferson has been turned upside down. Instead of social progress being guided by such values as justice, freedom, and self-fulfillment for all people, rich or poor, these goals of vital interest in a democracy were subjugated to a burgeoning society dominated by supposedly more important instrumental values-that is. those values that would be useful or practical ones for advancing a capitalistic system!

So the fundamental question still today is, "which type of values will win out in the long run?" In the United States, it seems that a gradually prevailing concept of cultural relativism will be increasingly discredited. This appears to be true because the 1990s witnessed a sharp clash between (1) those who uphold so-called Western cultural values and (2) those who by their presence are dividing the West along a multitude of ethnic and racial lines. This occasioned strong efforts to promote fundamentalistic religions and sects, either those present historically or those recently imported. These numerous religions, and accompanying sects, are characterized typically by decisive right/wrong morality.

The Economic Situation. The economic situation in America is creating a great many problems as well. Massive budget deficits at the national and state or provincial levels, with occasional efforts to become solvent, are bringing forth all sorts of "creative" solutions, solutions basically promulgated as a result of conflicting economic theories. Tax burdens on consumption will no doubt tend to increase tax revolts throughout America as household wealth declines, credit-card debt mounts, and the number of personal and business bankruptcies rises.

Unemployment is proving most difficult to bring under control. Yet any undue protectionism would undoubtedly retard economic free trade. In Canada free trade really doesn't even exist among the various provinces! Since NAFTA was approved, the need for job creation at the governmental level has grown as the "free trade concept" moves from north to south proceeding from Canada to Mexico (and who knows where else in the world). As indicated above, social entitlements to citizens (e.g., social security, Medicare, Medicaid), including the "welfare state concept" will evidently continue to be challenged severely.

Also, as the United States seeks to develop healthcare standards for all, and Canada struggles to retain those that it has, citizens will eventually face higher taxes of varying types in an effort to pay the healthcare bill as well as to reduce the debt at all levels at the same time. Some say a two-tier healthcare system is inevitable in Canada. At present in the USA, the Republican-dominated Congress, with the help of certain Democrats, is holding back the growth of a public healthcare system and other entitlements while at the same time offering a tax cut. How this will play out in the long run is anybody's guess.

These developments all have import for older citizens; retirement at age 65, especially early retirement at 55, may still be available (e.g., the "Golden Handshake"), but government, businesses, and people themselves will find it necessary to keep people working longer to pay the requisite taxes required to pay all of the bills. Yet, statistics reveal that the rich are still getting richer, and the poor are still getting poorer! "Workfare" seems destined for greater implementation. However, for those who can escape, the migration away from the big cities will continue as the various types of infrastructures continue to deteriorate along with the other negative aspects of urban living.

The Status of Education. Shifting the focus momentarily from the economic problems of society in general, and the direct relationship of prosperity to the general availability of leisure, to that of education in particular. If the status of public education is not sound, how can America ever expect to promote "education for the creative use of leisure?" Depending on one's educational philosophy, the revised picture that we see in education today is complex and is also definitely disheartening to many. The clamor of the early 1960s for improvement that followed the U.S.S.R.'s first Sputnik was followed by the passivity of the 1970s. The situation heated up again to a considerable degree in the 1980s at the various educational levels mainly because of competitive demands for the tax dollar. However, despite the clamor for higher educational standards in the 1990s, an analysis of the situation points to the answer that America has simply lost track of—if she ever knew—what the best type of education is. That is, what curriculum and what teaching methodology should be employed in keeping with the democratic ideals that are so glibly espoused.

Note, also, what could well be an unwise thrust toward school privatization caused by declining scores in typically narrowly defined tests. Yet, it is understandable that people are justifiably concerned about the provision of safer environments for their children as the breakdown of public order continues in this basic social institution. Since it is now legal to carry a concealed weapon in more than half of the states in the United States, keeping weapons out of schools has becoming a highly vexing problem.

Granting the presence of pluralistic philosophies of education in democratic countries, the deficiencies of the educational system, often based on inadequate curriculum content and instructional methodology, point up the present inability to provide people with a lifelong educational pattern. This statement applies both to the results of the provision of general education to all, as well as to the best type of professional education. Assuredly, some of the complaints of the 1960s have been rectified to an extent, but now—as so often happens—the pendulum has again swung in the wrong direction. This appears to be true (1) because the evident "return to essentials" is based completely on what has been called a "logical" as opposed to a "psychological" order of learning; (2) because in the present environment social science and humanities-oriented subjects tend to be downgraded along with music and art in the curriculum; and (3) because music, art, and developmental physical activity in sport, exercise, and related activities are relegated by many to a tertiary level.

A "Return-to-Essentials" Approach Prevails. As stated, this "return-to-essentials" educational philosophy is undoubtedly prevailing, especially insofar as the hard sciences and mathematics are concerned. Of course, Americans must do better in these areas, but this improvement should also be spread across the humanities, social sciences, and natural sciences relatively evenly. In each area, educators, with advice, need to spell out precisely what knowledge, competencies, and skill are required for optimum living in today's world. Once this is done, laboratory experiences should be provided in each area to guarantee that minimum achievement has been attained at the various levels along the way.

Approaching the situation from a broader perspective, it could be argued that much of the current problem stems from the fact that education is faced with almost insurmountable problems. This may well be true, because other basic societal institutions (e.g., the church, the family) are floundering. The school's burden is being increased to fill these gaps, deficiencies that could be made up largely if America had the funds and the attitudinal support to implement a competency-based approach to the needed knowledge and skills required for adequacy in life mastery in the 21st century.

Additionally, the educational infrastructure needs approximately 200 billion dollars (plus!) put into it to bring it up to par. This situation is well known by those primarily involved. Americans should be most concerned about the stupidity, illogicality, greed, and lack of foresight evident all around them, not to mention what appears to be ever-present evil! However, it is assuredly true that individuals must work these things out for themselves by being more vigorously melioristic, and not by displaying blind pessimism or "Polyannish" optimism. It is indeed going to be unbelievably difficult—i.e., dragging literally billions of people "kicking and screaming in all directions" through the first quarter of the 21st century.

In addition to education at all levels taking a beating—often undeserved—within this structure, sound physical education and truly recreational sport are, in turn, once again facing crises from without and within. Overemphasized, commercialized sport carried out by misguided administrators, players, coaches, and officials in professional leagues, the programs in a significant percentage of misguided universities (including too many high schools!), and the Olympic Games, each viewed typically by seemingly bewitched spectators, deserve whatever oblivion may eventually befall it! A social institution such as this dubious type of sporting competition, one that actually does more harm than good, should be eliminated. Competitive sport that is not "sportspersonlike" and uplifting has no legitimate place in society, much less in the educational system or community recreation programming. Sport must not be used to enable ever-more aggressive capitalism!

SUMMARY

Americans, generally speaking, still do not fully comprehend that their unique position in the history of the world's development may well change radically in the 21st century. The years ahead will be most difficult ones for all. The United States, as the one major nuclear power, will have the ongoing, overriding problem of maintaining large-scale peace at least. (Of course, other countries may or may not have nuclear arms capability, and that is what is so worrisome.) Additionally, along with other leading countries, there are severe ecological problems, a worldwide nutritional problem, the ebbs and flows of an energy crisis, and a situation where the rising expectations of the underdeveloped nations, including their staggering debt, will somehow have to be met, to name just a few of the major concerns.

Indeed, although it is seemingly more true of the United States than any other country, history is going against her in several ways. This means that previous optimism must be tempered to shake people loose from delusions, some of which Americans still have. For example, despite the presence of the United Nations, the United States has persisted in envisioning itself, the world's only superpower!—as almost being endowed by the "Creator" to make all crucial political decisions. Such decisions, often to act unilaterally with the hoped-for belated sanction of the United Nations, have resulted in United States-led incursions in a variety of directions.

Accordingly, there should soon be reason to expect selected U.S. retrenchment brought on by its excessive world involvement and staggering debt. Of course, any such retrenchment would inevitably lead to a decline in the economic and military influence of the United States. But who can argue logically that the present uneasy balance of power is a healthy situation looking to the future. Norman Cousins appears to have sounded just the right note a generation ago when he stated that perhaps "the most important factor in the complex equation of the future is the way the human mind responds to crisis" (1974, 6-7). The world culture as we know it must respond adequately to the many challenges with which it is being confronted. The societies and nations must individually and collectively respond positively, intelligently, and strongly if humanity as we have known it is to survive.

REFERENCES AND BIBLIOGRAPHY

Aburdene, P. & Naisbitt, J. (1992). *Megatrends for women*. NY: Villard Books.

Brubacher, J.S. (1966). *A history of the problems of education* (2nd ed.). New York: McGraw-Hill.

Butts, R.F. (1947). *A Cultural History of Education* (NY: McGraw-Hill, 1947)

Commager, H.S. (1966). *Freedom and order*. NY: G. Braziller.

Durant, W. & A. (1968). *The lessons of history*. NY: Simon & Schuster.

Frazier, B. F. (1933). Bulletin No. 10. In *National Survey of the Education of Teachers* (Washington, DC: U.S. Govt. Printing Office. 1933. (In Volume Five of this survey, part one dealt with the "History of the Professional Education of Teachers in the United State."

Kateb, G. (1965). Utopia and the good life. *Daedalus*, 24, 2:454-473.

Kekes, J. (Jan. 1987). Is our morality disintegrating? *Public Affairs Quarterly*, 1, 1:79-94.

Lenk, H. (1994). Value changes in the achieving society: A social-philosophical perspective. In *Organisation for Economic Co-operation and Development* (Ed.), OECD societies in transition (pp. 81-94).

Lipset, S.M. (1973). National character. In D. Koulack & D. Perlman (Eds.), *Readings in social psychology::Focus on Canada* (Chap. 1). Toronto: Wiley.

Marx, L. (1990). Does improved technology mean progress? In A.H. Teich, (Ed.), *Technology and the future* (5th Ed.) (pp. 3-14). (1990). NY: St. Martin's.

Melnick, R. (1984). *Visions of the future*. Croton-on-Hudson, NY: Hudson Institute.

Mesthene, E.G. (1990). The role of technology in society. In A.H. Teich, (Ed.). *Technology and the future* (5th Ed.) (pp. 77-99). (1990). NY: St. Martin's.
27, 3:21-22, 30-31.

Naisbitt, J. (1982). *Megatrends*. New York: Warner.

Reid D. & Mannell, R. (1990). Changing patterns of work, non-work and
  leisure. In *The Changing Patterns of Work and Leisure*. Burlington,
  Ontario: Society of Directors of Municipal Recreation of Ontario.

Schlesinger, A.M., Jr. (1998, Rev. & Enl. Ed.). *The disuniting of America:
  Reflections on a multicultural society..* NY; W.W. Norton.

Simpson, G.G. (1949). *The meaning of evolution.* New Haven & London:
  Yale University Press.

Spencer, H. (1949; orig. publ. in 1861). *Education: Intellectual,
  moral, and physical.* London: C.A. Watts.

Teich, A.H. (1990). *Technology and the future.* NY: St. Martin's Press.

Ten events that shook the world between 1984 and 1994. (Special
  Report). *Utne Reader,* 62 (March/April 1994):58-74.

Utne Reader. (July-Aug. 1993). "For love or money," 46:66-87.

Zeigler, E.F. (1988). *History of physical education and sport* (Rev.
  ed.). Champaign, IL: Stipes. (Selected chapters were written by
  M.L. Howell, R. Howell, R. G. Glassford, G. Redmond, R.K. Barney,
  and G.A. Paton.)

Zeigler, E.F. (1990). *Sport and physical education: Past, present,
  future.* Champaign, IL: Stipes.

Zeigler, E.F. (2003). *Socio-cultural foundations of physical education and
  educational sport.* Aachen, Germany: Meyer and Meyer Sports.

CHAPTER II

PHYSICAL EDUCATION IN THE UNITED STATES: AN HISTORICAL PRÉCIS

According to Norma Schwendener (1942), the history of physical education in the United States was divided into four distinct periods: (1) The Colonial Period (1609-1781); (2) The Provincial Period (1781-1885); (3) The Period of the Waning of European Influence (1885-1918); and (4) The Period of American Physical Education (1918-). Although this classification will not be followed here, the reader can get some perspective from Schwendener's earlier outline. However, a similar "longitudinal approach" is followed as opposed to the "horizontal" or "vertical" one that will be followed in Chapter III.

THE COLONIAL PERIOD

Living conditions in the American colonies in the 17th and 18th centuries were harsh, the finer elements of then civilized life being possible for only a relatively few wealthy individuals. The culture itself had been transported from Europe with its built-in class distinctions. The rules of primogeniture and entail served to strengthen such status. Slavery, and near-slavery, were general practice, especially in the South, and the right to vote was typically restricted to property owners. Cultural contrasts were marked. Religion was established legally. Geography, differences between the environment in the North and South, had a great deal to do with many differences that were evident. Actually, there was even considerable feeling against democratic principles both from a political and social standpoints. Any consideration of educational practice must, therefore, be viewed in the light of these conditions.[1]

Most of the American colonies established between 1607 and 1682 were guided in their educational outlook and activities by England's contemporary practices, the influence of other European countries being negligible at first. Education was thought to be a function of the Church, not the State. By today's standards, the provisions made for education were extremely inadequate. In a pioneer country characterized by a hazardous physical environment. the settlers were engaged in a daily struggle for their very existence. Early colonists migrated into different regions relatively close to the eastern coastline almost by chance. These differing environments undoubtedly influenced the social order of the North and the South; yet, for several generations there were many points of similarity in the traditions and experiences of the people as a whole. They all possessed a common desire for freedom and security, hopes that were to be realized only after a desperate struggle.

The church was the institution through which the religious heritage, and also much of the educational heritage, was preserved and advanced. The first schools can actually be regarded as the fruits of the Protestant revolts in Europe. The settlers wanted religious freedom, but the traditionalists among them insisted that a knowledge of the Gospel was required for personal salvation. The natural outcome was the creation of schools to help children learn to read; thus, it was the dominant Protestant churches that brought about the establishment of the elementary schools.

Three types of attitude developed toward education. The first was the compulsory-maintenance attitude of the New England Puritans, who established schools by colony legislation of 1642 and 1647. The second attitude was that of the parochial school, and this was best represented by Pennsylvania where private schools were made available for those who could afford it. The pauper-school, non-State-interference attitude was the third; it was best exemplified by Virginia and the southern colonies. Many of these people had come to America for profit rather than religious freedom, the result being that they tended to continue school practice as it had existed in England. In all these schools, discipline was harsh and sometimes actually brutal. The curriculum consisted of the three R's and spelling, but the books were few and the teachers were generally unprepared.

The pattern of secondary education had been inherited from England too. In most of the colonies, and especially in New England, so-called Latin grammar schools appeared. Also, higher education was not neglected. Nine colleges were founded mainly through the philanthropy of special individuals or groups. In all of these institutions, theology formed an important part of the curriculum. A notable exception that began a bit later was the Academy and College of Philadelphia where Benjamin Franklin exerted a strong influence.

EARLY GAMES, CONTESTS, AND EXERCISE

What about physical training and play for the young? What were the objectives for which people strove historically in what later was called physical education in the United States? We will now take a look at the different roles that such development physical activity played (or didn't play!) in the educational pattern of the States over a period of several centuries down to the present day. This entire time period covering the history of physical education in the United States could be divided logically into four distinct periods: the Colonial Period (1609-1781); the Provincial Period (1781-1885); the Period of the Waning of European Influence (1885-1918); and the Period of American Physical Education (1918-   ).

Because the population of the colonial United States was mostly rural, one could not expect organized gymnastics and sports to find a place in the daily lives of the settlers. Most of the colonies, with the possible exception of the Puritans, engaged in the games and contests of their motherlands to the extent that they had free time. Even less than today, the significance of play and its possibilities in the educative process were not really comprehended; in fact, the entire educational system was opposed to the idea of what would be included in a fine program of sport and physical education today.

THE 18TH CENTURY

With the advent of the 18th century, the former religious interest began to slacken. The government gradually developed more of a civil character with an accompanying tendency to create schools with a native vein or character. This was accompanied by a breakdown in some of the former aristocratic practices followed by a minority. The settled frontier expanded, new interests in trade and shipping grew, and the population increased. An evident trend toward individualism characterized this period as well. Several American industries date back to this time, the establishment of iron mills being most noteworthy.

Although the colonists were typically restricted by the financial practices placed by the English on the use of money, there was sufficient prosperity to bring about a change in the appearance of the established communities. An embryonic class structure began to form, with some colonials achieving a certain amount of social status by the holding of land and office. However, there were other concerns such as a series of small wars with the Spanish and the French extending from 1733 to 1763. These struggles were interspersed by period of cold war maneuvering. What was called the Seven Years' War (1755-1763) ended with the colonies as a fairly solid political and economic unit. However, the British method of governance over the colony was a constant source of annoyance and serious concern with the result that a strong nationalistic, separatist feeling emerging about 1775.

Beginning in the third decade of the eighteenth century, a revival of religious interest was apparent. This occasioned a recurring strong emphasis on religious education in the elementary schools. However, with the stirring of economic, political, and nationalistic forces from approximately 1750 onward, a period of relative religious tolerance resulted. This was accompanied by a broader interest in national affairs by many. The result was a lesser emphasis on the earlier religious domination of the elementary curriculum.

Secondary education was still provided by the grammar schools. These schools, generally located in every large town, were supported by the local government and by private tuition. The curricula were non-utilitarian and were designed to prepare boys for college entrance. Insofar as higher education was concerned, the pattern had been established from the beginning (Harvard College in 1636) after the European university type of liberal arts education with a strong emphasis on mental discipline and theology.

Despite the above, the reader should keep in mind that there were still very few heavily populated centers. In the main, frontier life especially, but also life in small villages, was still most rigorous. Such conditions were simply not conducive to intellectual life with high educational standards. Educational theorists had visions of a fine educational system, of course, but state constitutional provisions regarding education were very limited, and the federal constitution didn't say anything about educational standards at all. The many new social forces at work offered some promise, but with the outbreak of the War of Independence formal education came to almost a complete standstill.

The last 25 years of the 18th century saw a great many changes in the life of the United States. In the first place, many of the revolutionaries who started the war lived to tell about it and to help in the sound reconstruction of the young nation. State and federal constitutions had to be planned, written, and approved. Also, it was very important to the early success of the country that commerce be revived, a process that was accomplished sooner by the South because of the nature of the commodities they produced. New lines of business and trade were established with Russia, Sweden, and the Orient. The Federal Convention of 1787 managed to complete what has turned out to be possibly the most successful document in all of history, the Constitution of the United States of America. Then George Washington's administration began, and it was considered successful both at home and abroad. Interestingly, the concurrent French Revolution became an issue in American politics, but Washington persuaded his government to declare a position of neutrality (although he was hard pressed to maintain it).

As soon as the War of Independence in the U.S. was over, considerable attention was turned to education with the result that higher and secondary education improved. The colleges of the North took longer to recover from the War than those in the South where soon an imposing list of both private, religiously endowed, and state-sponsored institutions were founded.

EARLY SUPPORT FOR PHYSICAL TRAINING

At the secondary level, the institutions that succeeded the Latin grammar schools became known as the academies. Their aim was to prepare youth to meet life and its many problems, a reflection of the main influences of the Enlightenment in America. With such an emphasis, it is natural that the physical welfare of youths gradually was considered to be more important that it had been previously. Some of the early academies, such as Dummer, Andover, Exeter, and Leicester, were founded and incorporated before 1790. This movement reached its height around 1830 when there was said to be approximately 800 such schools throughout the country.

Many of the early American educators and statesmen supported the idea that both the body and the mind needed attention in our educational system. Included among this number were Benjamin Franklin, Noah Webster, Thomas Jefferson, Horace Mann, and Henry Barnard. Further support came from Captain Alden Partridge, one of the early superintendents of the United States Military Academy at West Point, who crusaded for the reform of institutions of higher education. He deplored the entire neglect of physical culture.

THE 19TH CENTURY

With the stage set for the United States to enter a most important period in her history, the 19th century witnessed steady growth along with a marked increase in nationalism. There was a second war with Great Britain, the War of 1812. In the ensuing nationalist era, many political changes or "adjustments" were carried out in relations with Britain and other nations where necessary. The Monroe Doctrine declared to the world that countries in this hemisphere should be left alone to develop as they saw fit and were not to be used by outside powers for colonization. However, at home dissent was growing as the North and the South were being divided. The North was being changed by virtue of the Industrial Revolution taking place, along with many educational and humanitarian movements. The South, conversely, continued to nurture a different type of society regulated by what has been called a slave and cotton economy.

In the realm of education, the first 50 years of the new national life was a period of transition from the control of the church to that of the State. State control and support gradually seemed more feasible, although the change was seemingly slow in coming. Political equality and religious freedom, along with changing economic conditions, finally made education for all a necessity. By 1825, therefore, a tremendous struggle for the creation of the American State School was underway. In the field of public education, the years from 1830 to 1860 have been regarded by some educational historians "The Architectural Period."

North American Turners. In the early 19th century German gymnastics (Turnen) came to the United States through the influx of such men as Charles Beck, Charles Follen, and Francis Lieber. However, the majority of the people were simply not ready to recognize the possible values of these activities imported from foreign lands. The Turnverein movement (in the late 1840s) before the Civil War was very important for the advancement of physical training. The Turners advocated that mental and physical education should proceed hand in hand in the public schools. As it developed, they were leaders in the early physical education movement around 1850 in such cities as Boston, St. Louis, and Cincinnati.

Other leaders in this period were George Barker Win(d)ship and Dioclesian Lewis. Windship was an advocate of heavy gymnastics and did much to convey the mistaken idea that great strength should be the goal of all gymnastics, as well as the notion that strength and health were completely synonymous. Lewis, who actually began the first teacher training program in physical education in the country in 1861, was a crusader in every sense of the word; he had ambitions to improve the health of all Americans through his system of light calisthenics--an approach that he felt would develop and maintain flexibility, grace, and agility as well. His stirring addresses to many professional and lay groups did much to popularize this type of gymnastics, and to convey the idea that such exercise could serve a desirable role in the lives of those who were weaker and perhaps even sickly (as well as those who were naturally stronger).

The Civil War between the North and the South wrought a tremendous change in the lives of the people. In the field of education, the idea of equality of educational opportunity had made great strides; the "educational ladder" was gradually extending upward with increasing opportunity for ever more young people. For example, the number of high schools increased fivefold between 1870 and 1890. The state was gradually assuming a position of prime importance in public education. In this process, state universities were helpful as they turned their attention to advancing the welfare of the individual states. The Southern states lagged behind the rest of the country due to the ravages of War with subsequent reconstruction, racial conflict, and continuing fairly "aristocratic theory" of education. In the North, however, President Eliot of Harvard called for education reform in 1888. One of his main points was the need for greatly improved teacher training.

After the Civil War, the Turners through their societies continued to stress the benefits of physical education within public education. Through their efforts it was possible to reach literally hundreds of thousands of people either directly or indirectly. The Turners have always opposed military training as a substitute for physical education. Further, the modern playground movement found the Turners among its strongest supporters. The Civil War had demonstrated clearly the need for a concerted effort in the areas of health, physical education, and physical recreation (not to mention competitive sports and games). The Morrill Act passed by Congress in 1862 helped create the land-grant colleges. At first, the field of physical education was not aided significantly by this development because of the stress on military drill in these institutions. All in all, the best that can be said is that an extremely differentiated pattern of physical education was present in the post-Civil War of the country.

BEGINNING OF ORGANIZED SPORT

The beginning of organized sport in the United States as we now know it dates back approximately to the Civil War period. Baseball and tennis were introduced in that order during this period and soon became very popular. Golf, bowling, swimming, basketball, and a multitude of other so-called minor sports made their appearance in the latter half of the nineteenth century. American football also started its rise to popularity at this time. The Amateur Athletic Union was organized in 1888 to provide governance for amateur sport. Unfortunately, controversy about amateurism has surrounded this organization almost constantly ever since. Nevertheless, it has given invaluable service to the promotion of that changing and often evanescent phenomenon that this group has designated as "legitimate amateur sport."

THE YOUNG MEN'S CHRISTIAN ASSOCIATION

The YMCA traces its origins back to 1844 in London, England, when George Williams organized the first religious group. This organization has always stressed as one of its basic principles that physical welfare and recreation were helpful to the moral well-being of the individual. Some of the early outstanding physical education leaders in the YMCA in the United States were Robert J. Roberts, Luther Halsey Gulick, and James Huff McCurdy.

EARLY PHYSICAL ACTIVITY AT THE COLLEGE LEVEL

It was toward the middle of the 19th century that the colleges and universities began to think seriously about the health of their students. The University of Virginia had the first real gymnasium, and Amherst College followed in 1860 with a two-story structure devoted to physical education. President Stearns urged the governing body to begin a department of physical culture in which the primary aim was to keep the student in good physical condition. Dr. Edward Hitchcock headed this department for an unprecedented period of fifty years until his death in 1911. Yale and Harvard erected gymnasiums for similar purposes in the late 1800s, but their programs were not supported adequately until the warly 1900s. These early facilities were soon followed elsewhere by the development of a variety of "exercise buildings" built along similar lines.

Harvard was fortunate in the appointment of Dr. Dudley Allen Sargent to head its now-famous Hemenway Gymnasium. This dedicated physical educator and physician led the university to a preeminent position in the field, and his program became a model for many other colleges and universities. He stressed physical education for the individual. His goal was the attainment of a perfect structure--harmony in a well-balanced development of mind and body.

From the outset, college faculties had taken the position that games and sports were not necessarily a part of the basic educational program. Interest in them was so intense, however, that the wishes of the students, while being denied, could not be thwarted. Young college men evidently strongly desired to demonstrate their abilities in the various sports against presumed rivals from other institutions. Thus, from 1850 to 1880 the rise of interest in intercollegiate sports was phenomenal. Rowing, baseball, track and field, football, and later basketball were the major sports. Unfortunately, college representatives soon found that these athletic sports needed control as evils began to creep in and partially destroy the values originally intended as goals.

AN IMPORTANT DECADE FOR PHYSICAL EDUCATION

The years from 1880 to 1890 undoubtedly form one of the most important decades in the history of physical education in the United States. The colleges and universities, the YMCAs, the Turners, and the proponents of the various foreign systems of gymnastics all made contributions during this brief period. The Association for the Advancement of Physical Education (now AAHPERD) was founded in 1885, with the word "American" being added the next year. This professional organization was the first of its kind in the field and undoubtedly stimulated teacher education markedly. An important early project was the plan for developing a series of experiences in physical activity--physical education--the objectives of which would be in accord with the existing pattern of general education. The struggle to bring about widespread adoption of such a program followed. Early legislation implementing physical education was enacted in five states before the turn of the 20th century.

The late 19th century saw the development also of the first efforts in organized recreation and camping for children living in underdeveloped areas in large cities. The first playground was begun in Boston in 1885. New York and Chicago followed suit shortly thereafter, no doubt to a certain degree as a result of the ill effects of the Industrial Revolution. This was actually the meager beginning of the present tremendous recreation movement in our country. Camping, both that begun by private individuals and organizational camping, started before the turn of the century as well; it has flourished similarly since that time and has been an important supplement to the entire movement.

Although criticism of the educational system as a whole was present between 1870 and 1890, it really assumed large scale proportions in the last decade of the 19th century. All sorts of innovations and reforms were being recommended from a variety of quarters. The social movement in education undoubtedly had a relationship to a rise in political progressivism. Even in the universities, the formalism present in psychology, philosophy, and the social sciences was coming under severe attack. Out in the public schools, a different sort of conflict was raging. Citizens were demanding that the promise of American life should be reflected through change and a broadening of the school's purposes. However, although the seeds of this educational revolution were sown in the 19th century, the story of its accomplishment belongs to the present century.

THE 20TH CENTURY

The tempo of life in the United States seemed to increase in the 20th century. The times were indeed changing as evidenced, for example, by one war after another. In retrospect there were so many wars--World War I, World War II, the Korean War, the Vietnam War, and the seemingly ever-present "cold war" after the global conflict of the 1940s. They inescapably had a powerful influence of society along with the worldwide depression of the 1930s. Looking back on 20th century history is frightening; so much has happened, and it has happened so quickly. The phenomenon of change is as ubiquitous today as are the historic nemeses of death and taxes.

In the public realm, social legislation and political reform made truly significant changes in the lives of people despite the leavening, ever-present struggle between conservative and liberal forces. Industry and business assumed gigantic proportions, as did the regulatory controls of the federal government. The greatest experiment in political democracy in the history of the world was grinding ahead with deliberate speed, but with occasional stopping-off sessions while "breath was caught." The idealism behind such a plan that amounted to "democratic socialism" was at times being challenged from all quarters. Also, wars and financial booms and depressions (or later recessions) weren't the types of developments that made planning and execution simple matters. All of these developments mentioned above have had their influence on the subject at hand--education (and, of course, physical education and sport).

In the early 20th century, United States citizens began to do some serious thinking about their educational aims or values. The earliest aim in U.S. educational history had been religious in nature, an approach that was eventually supplanted by a political aim consistent with emerging nationalism. But then an overwhelming utilitarian, economic aim seemed to overshadow the political aim. The tremendous increase in high school enrollment forced a reconsideration of the aims of education at all levels of the system. Training for the elite was supplanted by an educational program to be mastered by the many. It was at this time also that the beginnings of a scientific approach to educational problems forced educators to take stock of the development based on theory and a scholarly rationale other than one forced on the school simply because of a sheer increase in numbers.

Then there followed an effort on the part of many people to consider aims and objectives from a sociological orientation. For the first time, education was conceived in terms of complete living as a citizen of an evolving democracy. The influence of John Dewey and others encouraged the viewing of the curriculum as child-centered rather than subject-centered--a rather startling attempt to alter the long-standing basic orientation that involved the rote mastery of an amalgam of educational source material. The Progressive Education Movement placed great emphasis on individualistic aims. This was subsequently countered by a demand for a theory stressing a social welfare orientation rather than one so heavily pointed to individual development.

The relationship between health education and physical education grew extensively during the first quarter of the 20th century, and this included their liaison with the entire system of education. Health education in all its aspects was viewed seriously, especially after the evidence surfaced from the draft statistics of World War I. Many states passed legislation requiring varying amounts of time in the curriculum devoted to the teaching of physical education. National interest in sports and games grew at a phenomenal rate in an era when economic prosperity prevailed. The basis for school and community recreation was being well-laid.

Simultaneously with physical education's achievement of a type of maturity brought about legislation designed to promote physical fitness and healthy bodies, the struggle between the inflexibility of the various foreign systems of gymnastics and the individual freedom of the so-called "natural movement" was being waged with increasing vigor. Actually the rising interest in sports and games soon made the conflict unequal, especially when the concept of "athletics for all" really began to take hold in the second and third decades of the century.

CONFLICTING EDUCATIONAL PHILOSOPHIES

Even today the significance of play and its possibilities in the educative process have not really been comprehended. In fact, until well up in the 1800s in the United States, the entire educational system was opposed to the entire idea of what would be included in a fine program of sport and physical education today. It was the organized German-American Turners primarily, among certain others, who came to this continent from their native Germany and advocated that mental and physical education should proceed hand in hand in the public schools. The Turners' opposition to military training as a substitute for physical education contributed to the extremely differentiated pattern of physical education in the post-Civil War era. Their influence offset the stress on military drill in the land-grant colleges created by Congress passing the Morrill Act in the United States in 1862. The beginning of U.S. sport as we know it also dates to this period and, from the outset, college faculties took the position that games and sport were not a part of the basic educational program. The colleges and universities, the YMCAs, the Turners, and the proponents of the various foreign systems of gymnastics all made contributions during the last quarter of the 19th century.

In the early 20th century Americans began to do some earnest thinking about their educational aims and values. Whereas the earliest aim in U.S. educational history had been religious in nature, this was eventually supplanted by a political aim consistent with emerging nationalism. But then an overwhelming utilitarian, economic aim seemed to overshadow the political aim. It was at this time also that the beginnings of a scientific approach to educational problems forced educators to take stock of the development based on a rationale other than the sheer increase in student enrollment.

Then there followed an effort to consider aims and objectives from a sociological orientation. For the first time, education was conceived in terms of complete living as a citizen in an evolving democracy. The influence of John Dewey and others encouraged the viewing of the curriculum as child-centered rather than subject-centered. Great emphasis was placed on individualistic aims with a subsequent counter demand for a theory stressing more of a social welfare orientation.

The relationship between health and physical education and the entire system of education strengthened during the first quarter of the 20th century. Many states passed legislation requiring physical education in the curriculum, especially after the damning evidence of the draft statistics in World War I (Van Dalen, Bennett, and Mitchell, 1953, p. 432). Simultaneous with physical education's achievement of a type of maturity through such legislation, the struggle between the inflexibility of the various foreign systems of gymnastics and the individualistic freedom of the so-called "natural movement" was being waged with increasing vigor. Actually the rising interest in sports and games soon made the conflict unequal, especially when the concept of athletics for all really began to take hold in the second and third decades of the century.

The natural movement was undoubtedly strengthened further by much of the evidence gathered by many natural and social scientists. A certain amount of the spirit of Dewey's philosophy took hold within the educational environment, and this new philosophy and accompanying methodology and techniques did appear to be more effective in the light of the changing ideals of an evolving democracy. Despite this pragmatic influence, however, the influence of idealism remained strong also, with its emphasis on the development of individual personality and the possible inculcation of moral and spiritual values through the transfer of training theory applied to sports and games.

EMBRYONIC EMERGENCE OF THE ALLIED PROFESSIONS

School health education was developed greatly during the period also. The scope of school hygiene increased, and a required medical examination for all became more important. Leaders were urged to conceive of school health education as including three major divisions: health services, health instruction, and healthful school living. The value of expansion in this area was gradually accepted by educator and citizen alike. For example, many physical educators began to show a concern for a broadening of the field's aims and objectives, the evidence of which could be seen by the increasing amount of time spent by many on coaching duties. Conversely, the expansion of health instruction through the medium of many public and private agencies tended to draw those more directly interested in the goals of health education away from physical education.

Progress in the recreation field was significant as well. The values inherent in well-conducted playground activities for children and youths were increasingly recognized; the Playground Association of America was organized in 1906. At this time there was still an extremely close relationship between physical education and recreation, a link that remained strong because of the keen interest in the aims of recreation by a number of outstanding physical educators. Many municipal recreation centers were constructed, and it was at this time that the use of some-- relatively few, actually--of the schools for "after-hour" recreation began. People began to recognize that recreational activities served an important purpose in a society undergoing basic changes. Some recreation programs developed under local boards of education; others were formed by the joint sponsorship of school boards and municipal governments; and a large number of communities placed recreation under the direct control of the municipal government and either rented school facilities when possible, or gradually developed recreational facilities of their own.

PROFESSIONAL ASSOCIATIONS FORM AN ALLIANCE

The American Association for Health, Physical Education, and Recreation (now the American Alliance for Health, Physical Education, Recreation, and Dance) has accomplished a great deal in a strong united effort to coordinate the various allied professions largely within the framework of public and private education. Despite membership losses during the 1970s, its success story continues with those functions which properly belong within the educational sphere. The Alliance should in time also gradually increase its influence on those seeking those services and opportunities that we can provide at the various other age levels as well.

Of course, for better or worse, there are many other health agencies and groups, recreational associations and enterprises, physical education associations and "splinter" disciplinary groups, and athletics associations and organizations moving in a variety of directions. One example of these is the North American Society for Sport Management that began in the mid-1980s and has grown significantly since. Each of these is presumably functioning with the system of values and norms prevailing in the country (or culture, etc.) and the resultant pluralistic educational philosophies extant within such a milieu.

We have seen teacher education generally, under which physical education has been bracketed, and professional preparation for recreational leadership also, strengthened through self-evaluation and accreditation. The dance movement has been a significant development within the educational field, and those concerned are still determining the place for this movement within the educational program at all levels. A great deal of progress has been made in physical education, sport, and (more recently) kinesiology research since 1960.

ACHIEVING SOME HISTORICAL PERSPECTIVE

It is now possible to achieve some historical perspective about the second and third quarters of the 20th century as they have affected physical education and sport, as well as the allied professions of health education, recreation, and dance education. The Depression of the 1930s, World War II, the Korean War, and then Vietnam War, and the subsequent cold war with the many frictions among countries have been strong social forces directly influencing sport, physical education, health education, recreation, and dance in any form and in any country. Conversely, to what extent these various fields and their professional concerns have in turn influenced the many cultures, societies, and social systems remains yet to be accurately determined.

It would be simplistic to say that physical educators want more and better physical education and intramural-recreational sport programs, that athletics-oriented coaches and administrators want more and better athletic competition, that health and safety educators want more and better health and safety education, that recreation personnel want more and better recreation, and that dance educators want more and better dance instruction--and yet, this would probably be a correct assessment of their wishes and probably represents what has occurred to a large degree.

PROFESSIONAL PREPARATION AND DISCIPLINE SPECIALIZATION IN AMERICAN PHYSICAL EDUCATION & KINESIOLOGY

In 1988, Zeigler (pp. 177-196) reported the results of a comparative investigation of the undergraduate professional preparation programs in physical education in the United States and Canada based on his own investigation of both the theoretical and the practical aspects of training programs in both countries. Hypothesizing that there have been significant changes, some similar and others in markedly different directions in the past quarter century (from approximately 1960 to 1985), he further hypothesized that, if and when changes did occur, they tended to come about in the United States first. This latter hypothesis was based on the author's personal experience in both countries, and also on the results of a study by Lipset (1973). Lipset had pointed out that there has been reluctance on the part of Canadians "to be overly optimistic, assertive, or experimentally inclined." Based on the results of this investigation, however, such has not necessarily been the case in the field of physical education and sport (see also Zeigler, 1980).

To report more accurately on this subject for the 1980s, and also to gain a better perspective on the the United States' scene, seven members of the American Academy of Physical Education, distributed geographically across the country, each who have been involved in professional preparation for periods up to 40 years, were asked to describe what they believe took place in the United States over three different time periods (i.e., during the 1960s, the 1970s, and the 1980s). What follows here, then, is delimited to their responses for the period covering the 1980s and also to the investigation and analysis carried out personally by the author.

Five problems, phrased as questions, were included in the questionnaire as follows: (1) what have been the strongest social influences during the current decade? (2) what changes have been made in the professional curriculum? (3) what developments have taken place in instructional methodology? (4) what other interesting or significant developments have occurred (typically within higher education)? (5) what are the greatest problems in professional preparation currently?

STRONGEST SOCIAL INFLUENCES

During the 1980s, a number of strong social influences were indicated on the United States scene. Worldwide communication was improving greatly as ever more satellites were put into service. Nevertheless, the seemingly ever-present concern with the several violently conflicting world ideologies remained at a high level of intensity as the decade began. The Reagan administration displayed an aggressive "proud to be American" leadership style, along with emphasis on strong offensive and defensive military concerns, in an ongoing struggle to combat spreading communism at numerous points around the globe. Others were worried that the United States was overextending itself through "imperial overstretch" in its zeal to make the world safe for democracy (Kennedy, 1987, p. 515).

A variety of new and continuing problems and issues were apparent on the home front as well, some having both positive and negative implications for the future. The impact of high technology (e.g., computers, software--the entire "knowledge industry" for that matter) was felt increasingly. Certain large industries were suffering greatly from cheaper foreign competition (e.g., steel production), but fortunately the North American car market held up (to some extent through wise partial mergers with foreign competitors).

The cost of education soared at all educational levels, while concurrently funding from the federal level was decreasing. Greater cooperation between the public schools and higher educational institutions was apparent. With an enrollment decline beginning to have an effect on many colleges and universities, there was increased competition for top students. A presidential task force on the state of education was proclaiming a "prevalence of mediocrity" in the secondary schools. This demand for accountability at a very high level brought about a steady call throughout the decade for a "back to basics" movement in education. It was argued that "teachers can't teach," but others were promoting the idea of "mastery teaching" (an idea that makes sense upon first examination). However, some wanted students promoted anyhow because age differentials were creating more disciplinary problems. Developments that impacted on physical education were (1) the federal government easing off on Title IX enforcement that took some pressure off state legislatures to provide equal opportunity for girls and women in sport, and (2) there was evidence that less than one-third of the total school population (ages 10-17) received daily physical education.

THE PHYSICAL EDUCATION/KINESIOLOGY CURRICULUM

Along with the continued expansion of non-teaching options or areas of concentration within the physical education/kinesiology major program, there was a concurrent decline of interest in undergirding liberal education and an evident increase in the importance of job orientation. Many felt there was a need to eliminate what they regarded as superfluous courses, while stressing the need for improved scholarship within those that remained. The feeling was that students were typically more serious and goal-oriented, but the concern and pressure for high numerical grades was disconcerting to some observers.

Interestingly, and unfortunately, there has been an increased number of students with relatively poor physical skills in the professional/disciplinary programs. Whether this trend was counteracted by an improvement in theoretical understanding remain debatable, however. In the final analysis, however, it should be recognized that each university can't be "all things to all people" with its program offerings.

The 1980s witnessed also a new emphasis on special physical education because of state legislation, but such specialization within professional preparation programs was still not sufficiently available. There was also continued concern, but not much concrete action, for improved standards as evidenced by state certification for alternate career graduates and/or voluntary national accreditation for such programs related to ongoing teacher education programs. One promising note was the establishment of a National Association for Sport and Physical Education (NASPE) Task Force working on a revision of accreditation standards for undergraduate physical education teacher preparation.

Along with declining enrollment in professional curricula, there was a need to generate increased revenue. Faculty positions were being lost due to inadequate funding, and intra-institutional research funding was drying up.

INSTRUCTIONAL METHODOLOGY

Several definite observations can be safely made in connection with instructional methodology. The weakening financial situation brought about a collapsing of course sections into larger lecture groups. This created a problem, however, because there was also been continued concern for teacher/coach effectiveness. Many faculty members began to take their teaching responsibilities more seriously, and there appeared to be an improved level of innovation and creativity in their efforts. This trend was accompanied by the retooling of certain faculty members to improve their instructional competency, thereby making them more valuable to their faculty units. There is no doubt but that course content has been based somewhat more on research findings and improved theory. Computer instruction is gradually being incorporated into the instructional pattern in a variety of ways, as is increased use of videotaping. The need to somehow streamline the learning experiences was expressed, as was a concern that there be greater stress on education for "human fulfillment" with the teacher as facilitator.

OTHER CAMPUS DEVELOPMENTS

At the beginning of the 1980s, the continuing, bleak financial picture brought about a considerable degree of faculty pessimism and cynicism. Requirements for promotion and tenure were ever more stringent, while at the same time faculty positions were threatened because of continued economic pressures. Salary schedules did not keep pace with many other professions and occupations.

Sub-disciplinary specialization of faculty members increased steadily in the larger universities. In the broadly based (i.e., less research and publication, heavier teaching/coaching workloads). Thus, prevailing dictum seemed to be: Get the research grant no matter whether there is time to complete the project. Early retirement schemes appeared, but they were often not sufficiently creative or rewarding to encourage faculty departure. All in all, there was the feeling that the environment was too stressful.

THE GREATEST PROBLEMS OR NEEDS
IN PROFESSIONAL PREPARATION AND
DISCIPLINE SPECIALIZATION

As the field entered the final decade of the 20th century, a number of problems expressed as needs were identified as follows:

1. Need to develop consensus about a disciplinary definition from which should evolve a more unified, much less fractionated curriculum (i.e., a greater balance among the bio-scientific aspects, the social-science & humanities aspects, and the "professional aspects" of our field).

2. Need to develop a sound body of retrievable knowledge in all phases of the profession's work.

3. Need to implement the educational possibilities of a competency approach within the professional preparation curriculum.

4. Need to develop a variety of sound options for specialization within a unified curriculum (extending to a 5th year of offerings?). This involves the expansion of alternate career options in keeping with the profession's goal of serving people of all ages and all abilities.

5. Need to develop a format whereby regular future planning between staff and students occurs.

6. Need to graduate competent, well-educated, fully professional physical educator/coaches who have sound personal philosophies embodying an understanding of professional ethics.

7. Need to seek recognition of our professional endeavors in public, semi-public, and private agency work through certification at the state level and voluntary accreditation at the national level.

8. Need to help control or lessen the impact of highly competitive athletics within the college and university structure so that a finer type of professional preparation program is fostered.

9. Need to recognize the worth of intramural recreational sports in our programs, and to make every effort to encourage those administering these programs to maintain professional identification with the National Association for Sport and Physical Education.

10. Need to continue the implementation of
patterns of administrative control in educational institutions
that are fully consonant with individual freedom within the
society.
11. Need to work for maintenance of collegiality
among faculty members despite the inroads of
factors that are tending to destroy such a
state: lack of adequate funding, faculty
unionization, pressure for publication and the
obtaining of grants, and extensive
intra-profession splintering.
12. Need to develop an attitude that will permit
us to "let go of obsolescence." Somehow we
will have to learn to apply new knowledge
creatively in the face of an often discouraging
political environment.
13. Need to work to dispel any malaise present
 within our professional preparation programs
in regard to the future of the profession.
If we prepare our students to be certified and
accredited professionals in their respective
options within the broad curriculum, we will
undoubtedly bring about a service profession
of the highest type within a reasonable period
of time (Zeigler, 1986).

CONCLUDING STATEMENT

As these words are being written, there is obviously a continuing value
struggle going on in the United States that results in distinct swings of the
educational pendulum to and fro. It seems most important that a continuing
search for a consensus be carried out. Fortunately, the theoretical struggle fades a
bit when actual educational practice is carried out. If this were not so, very little
progress would be possible. If we continue to strive for improved educational
standards for all this should result in the foreseeable future in greater understanding
and wisdom on the part of the majority of North American citizens. In this regard
science and philosophy can and indeed must make ever-greater contributions. All
concerned members of the allied professions in both the United States and Canada
need to be fully informed as they strive for a voice in shaping the future

development of their respective countries and professions. It is essential that there be careful and continuing study and analysis of the question of values as they relate to sport, exercise, dance, and play. Such study and analysis is, of course, basic as well to the implications that societal values and norms have for the allied fields of health and safety education, recreation, dance, and sport management.

NOTE

1. The information about the United States has been adapted from several sources, sections or parts of reports or books written earlier by the author. See Zeigler, 1951, 1962, 1975, 1979, 1988a, 1988b, 1990, 2003.

REFERENCES AND GENERAL BIBLIOGRAPHY

American Alliance for Health, Physical Education, Recreation and Dance (1962) *Professional preparation in health education, physical education, recreation education.* Report of national conference. Washington, DC: Author.

American Alliance for Health, Physical Education, Recreation and Dance. (1974). *Professional preparation in dance, physical education, recreation education, safety education, and school health education.* Report on national conference. Washington, DC: Author.

Bennett, B.L. (1962). Religion and physical education. Paper presented at the Cincinnati Convention of the AAHPER, April 10.

Bookwalter, K.W., & Bookwalter, C.W. (1980). *A review of thirty years of selected research on undergraduate professional preparation physical education programs in the United States.* Unionville, IN: Author.

Brubacher, J.S. (1966). *A history of the problems of education* (2nd ed.). New York: McGraw-Hill.

Brubacher, J.S. (1969). *Modern philosophies of education* (4th ed.). New York: McGraw-Hill.

Bury, J.B. (1955). *The idea of progress.* New York: Dover.

Butts, R.F. (1947). *A cultural history of education.* New York: McGraw-Hill.

Commager, H.S. (1961). A quarter century--Its advances. *Look*, 25, 10 (June 6), 80-91.

Conant, J.B. (1963). *The education of American teachers* (pp. 122-123). New York: McGraw-Hill.

Elliott, R. (1927). *The organization of professional training in physical education in state universities.* New York: Columbia Teachers College.

Flath, A.W. (1964). *A history of relations between the National Collegiate Athletic Association and the Amateur Athletic Union of the United States (1905-1963).* Champaign, IL: Stipes. (Includes a Foreword by E.F. Zeigler entitled "Amateurism, semiprofessionalism, and professionalism in sport: A persistent historical problem.")

Hayes, C. (1961). *Nationalism: A religion.* New York: Macmillan.

Heilbroner, R.L. (1960). *The future as history.* New York: Harper & Row.

Hershkovits, M.J. (1955). *Cultural anthropology* (pp. 33-85). New York: Knopf.

Hess, F.A. (1959). *American objectives of physical education from 1900 to 1957 assessed in light of certain historical events.* Doctoral dissertation, New York University.

Johnson, H.M. (1969). The relevance of the theory of action to historians. *Social Science Quarterly,* (June), 46-58.

Kennedy, P. (1987). *The rise and fall of the great powers.* NY: Random House.

Kennedy, J.F. (1958). Address by the President in Detroit, Michigan. (At that time he was a U.S. Senator.)

Leonard, F.E., & Affleck G.B. (1947). *The history of physical education* (3rd ed.). Philadelphia: Lea & Febiger.

Lipset. S. M. (1973). National character. In D. Koulack & D. Perlman (Eds.), *Readings in social psychology: Focus on Canada.* Toronto: Wiley.

McCurdy, J.H. (1901). Physical training as a profession. *American Physical Education Review,* 6, 4:311-312.

Morris, V.C. (March, 1956). Physical education and the philosophy of education. *Journal of Health, Physical Education and Recreation,* (21-22, 30-31.

Muller, H.J. (1954). *The uses of the past.* New York: New American Library.

Murray, B.G. Jr. (1972). What the ecologists can teach the economists. *The New York Times Magazine,* December 10, 38-39, 64-65, 70, 72.

Naisbitt, J. (1982). *Megatrends.* NY: Warner

Nevins, A. (1962). The gateway to history. Garden City, NY: Doubleday.

Oberlin College Catalogue (1894).

Reisner, E.H. (1925). *Nationalism and education since 1789.* New York: Macmillan.

Sigerist, H.E. (1956). *Landmarks in the history of hygiene*. London: Oxford University Press.

Sparks, W. (1992). Physical education for the 21st Century: Integration, not specialization. *NAPEHE: The Chronicle of Physical Education in Higher Education*, 4, 1:1-10-11.

Wellesley College Catalogue (1910).

Zeigler, E.F. (1951). *A history of undergraduate professional preparation in physical education in the United States, 1861-1948*. Eugene, OR: Oregon Microfiche.

Zeigler, E.F. (1962). A history of professional preparation for physical education in the United States (1861-1961). In *Professional preparation in health education, physical education, and recreation education* (pp. 116-133). Washington,, DC: The American Association for Health, Physical Education, and Recreation.

Zeigler, E.F. (1968). *Problems in the history and philosophy of physical education and sport*. Englewood Cliffs, NJ: Prentice-Hall.

Zeigler, E.F. (Ed. & author). (1973). *A history of physical education and sport to 1900*. Champaign, IL: Stipes.

Zeigler, E.F. (1975). Historical perspective on contrasting philosophies of professional preparation for physical education in the United States. In *Personalizing physical education and sport philosophy* (pp. 325-347). Champaign, IL: Stipes.

Zeigler, E.F. (Ed. & author). (1975). *A history of physical education and sport in the United States and Canada*. Champaign, IL: Stipes.

Zeigler, E.F. (1979). The past, present, and recommended future development in physical education and sport in North America. In *Proceedings of The American Academy of Physical Education* (G.M. Scott (Ed.), Washington, DC: The American Alliance for Health, Physical Education, Recreation, and Dance.

Zeigler, E.F. (1980). An evolving Canadian tradition in the new world of physical education and sport. In S.A. Davidson & P. Blackstock (Eds.), *The R. Tait McKenzie Addresses* (pp. 53-62). Ottawa, Canada: Canadian Association for Health, Physical Education and Recreation.

Zeigler, E.F. (1983a). Relating a proposed taxonomy of sport and developmental physical activity to a planned inventory of scientific findings. *Quest*, 35, 54-65.

Zeigler, E.F. (1986). Undergraduate professional preparation in physical education, 1960-1985. *The Physical Educator*, 43 (1), 2-6.

Zeigler, E.F. (1986). *Assessing sport and physical education: Diagnosis and projection.* Champaign, IL: Stipes.

Zeigler, E.F. *et al.* (1988a). *A history of physical education and sport.*
  Champaign, IL: Stipes. See the excellent chapter on American physical education
  and sport by R.K. Barney, pp. 173-219).

Zeigler, E.F. (1988b). A comparative analysis of undergraduate
  professional preparation in physical education in the United States
  and Canada. In Broom, E., Clumpner, R., Pendleton, B., & Pooley, C.
  (Eds.), *Comparative physical education and sport,* Volume 5.
  Champaign, IL: Human Kinetics.

Zeigler, E.F. (1990). *Sport and physical education: Past, present, future.*
  Champaign, IL: Stipes.

Zeigler, E.F. (2003). *Socio-Cultural Foundations of Physical Education
  and Educational Sport.* Aachen, Germany: Meyer & Meyer Sports.

CHAPTER III

A PERSISTENT PROBLEMS APPROACH
TO THE HISTORY OF PHYSICAL EDUCATION
AND SPORT (WITH SPECIAL REFERENCE
TO THE UNITED STATES)

In just about every physical education and educational sport history book available, the reader will find a unilateral historical narrative in which the author takes the reader through a chronological treatment of the subject with relatively little effort at interpretation. (I call it the "just give me the facts, ma'am" approach.) This approach was followed here briefly in the previous chapter. Now a second, supplementary approach is being recommended, one that I believe leads to a truer understanding of the field's history. I believe that it is more insightful and interpretive for the mature student.

Here, then, the subject is placed into a different historical perspective. The unilateral historical narrative of Chapter 2 has been recast into an approach to the teaching of physical education and sport history that delineates the persistent, recurring problems that have emerged throughout recorded history in sufficient quantity for intelligible qualitative analysis. Within this more pragmatic approach, an inquiry is conducted to ascertain, for example, what influence a type of political system in a culture had on the structure and function of the culture's educational system--and perhaps concurrently on the program of sport and physical education offered. All history can be viewed, therefore, with an eye to the persistent or perennial problems (social forces or professional concerns) that seem to reveal themselves as a result of a searching, in-depth analysis. (In a sense, this historical technique is similar to that followed descriptively in the well-known Megatrends volume where issues that appeared more regularly in the literature were carefully assembled over a period of years. Here this approach was employed with sport and physical education literature for several decades.)

Thus, no matter which of a number of historical theories or approaches is employed, such a "persistent problems" approach almost directs one to search for the interpretive criterion, to seek out underlying hypotheses, to ask how a particular historical approach aids in the analysis of past problems, and to inquire whether new insight has been afforded in the search for solutions to perennial problems that people will perhaps always face. (Or, at least, problems that they will face until they learn how to cope with them!)

Delineation and description of these problems as they might relate to this field has been one of my more important investigative goals. How this idea came to me may be traced to an early period of study at Yale University with the late John S. Brubacher, eminent, longtime professor of the history and philosophy of education at Yale and Michigan to whom the credit for this unique approach in educational history must go. However, many of the ideas for the specific problems in the field of sport and physical education listed below in Figure 3-1 originated with me (and with some of my colleagues and graduate students). Thus, Brubacher's approach has been adapted to this specialized field (Brubacher, 1966; Zeigler, 2003).

Such an approach as this does not really represent a radically different approach to history. The typical major processes are involved in applying historical method to investigation relating to sport and physical education as follows: (1) the data are collected from primary and secondary sources; (2) the collected data are criticized and analyzed; and (3) an integrated narrative is presented, with every effort made to present the material interestingly and yet based solidly upon tentative hypotheses established at the outset.

This approach does differ markedly, however, in the organization of the collected data: it is based completely on a presentation of individual problem areas-- persistent, perennial, recurring problems of the present day that have been of concern to people over the centuries. The idea in this instance, of course, is to illuminate these problems for the student of sport and physical education. A conscious effort is thus made to keep the reader from thinking that history is of antiquarian interest only. The student finds himself or herself in an excellent position to move back and forth from early times to the present as different aspects of a particular subject (persistent problem) are treated. A problem used in this sense (based on its early Greek derivation) would be "something thrown forward" for people to understand or resolve. This technique of "doing" history may be called a "vertical" approach as opposed to the traditional "horizontal" approach--a "longitudinal" treatment of history in contradistinction to a strictly chronological one.

These persistent problems (or influences) of the past and the present will in all probability continue to occur in the future either as social forces that influence all

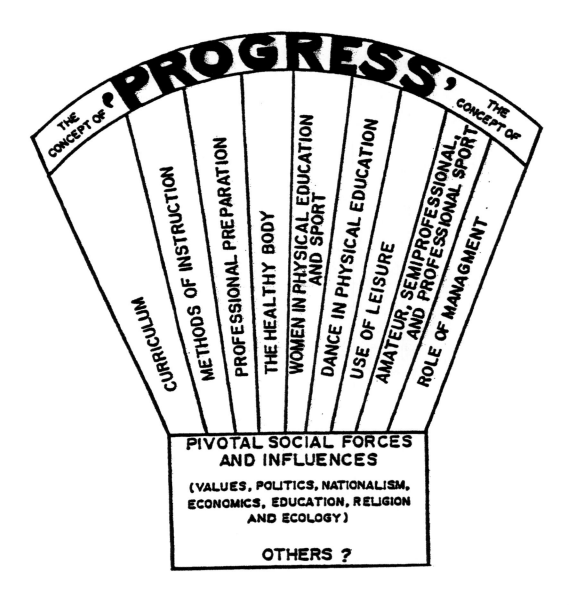

Figure 3.1

**Persistent, Historical Problems of
Physical Education and Sport**

*Others?
- Science & Technology
- Peace Movement
- Commercialized Sport

Earle F. Zeigler
(design advice from
Glenda Dillon)

aspects of the society or as different sets of professional concerns that have a strong effect on a specific profession or aspect of the culture. Thus here we are concerned with influences that have affected the developmental physical activity in sport, dance, exercise, and play of the various societies. Further, we must keep in mind that there are other persistent problems that may appear in a society or culture from time to time (e.g., the current environmental crisis that has stimulated the development of a science of ecology).

THE SOCIAL FORCES (OR INFLUENCES)

Values and Norms. The persistent problem of value and norms, the first social force or influence we will discuss, seems to possess a "watershed quality" in that an understanding of those objects and/or qualities desired by people through the ages can evidently provide significant insight into this particular problem-and also into most if not all of the other recurring problems (social forces or professional concerns) that will be discussed. (A problem used in this sense is based on the Greek derivation that means "something thrown forward" for people to understand and to resolve if and when possible.)

Axiology, or the study of values, is one of four subdivisions of the discipline of philosophy. The nature and theory of value is considered, as are the various kinds of value. Some believe that values exist only because of the interest of the valuer (the interest theory). The existence theory, on the other hand, asserts that values exist independently--that they would be important in a vacuum, so to speak. They are essence added to existence. Pragmatic theory (the experimentalist theory) views value quite differently. Values which yield practical results that have "cash value" bring about the possibility of greater happiness through the creation of more effective values in the future. One further theory, the part-whole theory, is explained by the idea that effective relating of parts to the whole bring about the highest values.

There are various domains of value that must be examined under the subdivision of axiology. First and foremost, we must be concerned with ethics which considers morality, conduct, good and evil, and ultimate aims in life. There are several approaches to the problem of whether life as we know it is worthwhile. A person who goes around all the time with a smile looking hopefully toward the future is, of course, an optimist (optimism). On the other side of the fence is the individual who gets discouraged easily and soon decides that life is probably not worth the struggle (pessimism). In between these two extremes we find the (not always easily achieved) golden mean (meliorism), which would have us facing life squarely and striving constantly to improve our situation.

There is, of course, much more to the subject of axiology than is mentioned here (e.g., what is most important in life). Also, there are other areas of value over and above ethics that treat moral conduct. One of these has to do with the "feeling" aspects of the individual's conscious life (aesthetics). Aesthetics may be defined as the theory or philosophy of taste, and people have inquired down through the ages whether there are principles that govern the search for the beautiful in life.

Over time, a need has developed gradually for people to define additional, more discrete values in the life of man and woman. Thus, we now have specialized philosophies of education and religion--and, more recently, even a philosophy of sport and physical education. Also, speaking somewhat more generally, we often refer to a person's social philosophy. What is meant here is that people make decisions about the kind, nature, and worth of values that are intrinsic to, say, the political process, the educational process, or whatever is deemed important to them.

Naturally, there have been innumerable statements of social and educational values or aims throughout history, and such declarations have been quite often directly related to the hierarchy of explicit and/or implicit values and norms present in the society being considered. Keeping the above ideas in mind about some of the ways in which values and norms have been viewed from different perspectives, value determinations have undoubtedly also influenced developmental physical activity historically in those activities that today we call exercise, sport, dance, and play.

In this chapter, then, each of what we have called "persistent historical problems" (the social forces and the professional concerns) will be treated briefly. Based on the many statements of aims and objectives down through the centuries from earliest recorded history, we can state that physical culture has been roughly classified as either curricular, co-curricular, or extra-curricular. By this is meant that physical activity, either in informal education, in the schools or in social life generally was considered to be of greater or lesser value to men or women based on the needs, interests, and level of development of the culture in question. Thus, each culture developed its own hierarchy of educational values to be transmitted to the young either implicitly or explicitly.

A study of history indicates that there has been a complete range of physical culture activities available from the almost unbelievably stringent physical training of the Spartan male in ancient Greece to a situation such as that "enjoyed" by many youngsters today where vigorous physical activity is really not understood by most young people and almost deplored by some students and parents alike. Or another extreme viewed in today's context might be the (in some ways) glorious period when a balance or harmony of body and mind was sought in ancient Athens. The opposite of this might be that period in the early Middle Ages when asceticism (or subduing the desires of the flesh) was looked upon by many early Christians as the type of life people should seek to emulate. In between these two sets of opposites, there were all kinds and levels of games, sports, self-testing activities, dancing, exercise routines, remedial gymnastics, and combat training either recommended or implemented for youth in the various societies about which we know. In most instances until recently, these activities have been provided largely for boys and young men, since women in our so-called civilized countries have been considered historically to be the weaker sex. How women managed to survive the rigorous labor enforced upon them in the less civilized cultures seems to have rarely crossed the minds of males down through the centuries. What has been explained here briefly is that throughout history people have made decisions about the kind, nature, and worth of values and norms that are intrinsic to the process of involvement in exercise, sport, games, and all types of expressive physical activity.

The United States. In the United States it was the organized German-American Turners primarily, among certain others, who came from their native Germany and advocated that mental and physical education should proceed hand in hand in the public schools. The Turners' opposition to military training as a substitute for physical education contributed to the extremely differentiated pattern of physical education in the post-Civil War era. Their influence offset the stress on military drill in the land-grant colleges created by Congress passing the Morrill Act in the United States in 1862. The beginning of U.S. sport as we know it also dates to this period and, from the outset, college faculties took the position that games and sport were not a part of the basic educational program. The colleges and universities, the YMCAs, the Turners, and the proponents of the various foreign systems of gymnastics all made contributions during the last quarter of the 19th century.

In the early 20th century Americans began to do some earnest thinking about their educational aims and values. Whereas the earliest aim in U.S.

educational history had been religious in nature, this was eventually supplanted by a political aim consistent with emerging nationalism. But then an overwhelming utilitarian, economic aim seemed to overshadow the political aim. It was at this time also that the beginnings of a scientific approach to educational problems forced educators to take stock of the development based on a rationale other than the sheer increase in student enrollment.

Then there followed an effort to consider aims and objectives from a sociological orientation. For the first time, education was conceived in terms of complete living as a citizen in an evolving democracy. The influence of John Dewey and others encouraged the viewing of the curriculum as child-centered rather than subject-centered. Great emphasis was placed on individualistic aims with a subsequent counter demand for a theory stressing more of a social welfare orientation.

The relationship between health and physical education and the entire system of education strengthened during the first quarter of the 20th century. Many states passed legislation requiring physical education in the curriculum, especially after the damning evidence of the draft statistics in World War I (Van Dalen et al., 1953, p. 432). Simultaneous with physical education's achievement of a type of maturity through such legislation, the struggle between the inflexibility of the various foreign systems of gymnastics and the individualistic freedom of the so-called "natural movement" was being waged with increasing vigor. Actually the rising interest in sports and games soon made the conflict unequal, especially when the concept of athletics for all really began to take hold in the second and third decades of the century.

The natural movement was undoubtedly strengthened further by much of the evidence gathered by many natural and social scientists (p. 423). A certain amount of the spirit of Dewey's philosophy took hold within the educational environment, and this new philosophy and accompanying methodology and techniques did appear to be more effective in the light of the changing ideals of an evolving democracy. Despite this pragmatic influence, however, the influence of idealism remained strong with its emphasis on the development of individual personality and the possible inculcation of moral and spiritual values through the transfer of training theory applied to sports and games.

The Influence of Politics. The second social force or influence to be considered is that of politics. The word "politics" is used in its best sense-as the theory and practice of managing public affairs. When we speak of a politician, therefore, the intent is to describe a person interested in politics as a most important profession, and not one who through maneuverings might attempt to amass personal power, influence, and possessions.

Political government may be defined as a form of social organization in which the politician functions. This organization became necessary as a means of social control to regulate the actions of individuals and groups. Throughout history, every known society has developed some measure of formal control. The group as a whole has been termed the state, and the members known as citizens. Thus, the state is made up of territory, people, and government. If the people eventually unified through common cultural tradition, they were classified as a nation. The pattern of living they developed was called its social structure. Of course, political organization was but one phase of this structure, but it exercised a powerful influence upon the other phases. A governmental form is usually a conservative force that is slow to change. Inextricably related to the rest of the social structure, the political regime found it necessary to adapt to changing social organization; if it didn't, anarchy resulted. The three major types of political state in the history of the various world civilizations have been (1) the monarchy, (2) the aristocratic oligarchy, and (3) the democracy or republic.

Aristotle's classification of the three types of political states, mentioned above, holds today largely as it did then. The kind and amount of education offered to young people has indeed varied throughout history depending upon the type of political state extant. In a society where one person ruled, for example, it would seem logical to assume that he or she should have the best education so as to rule wisely. The difficulty with this situation is that there is no guarantee that a hereditary ruler is the best-equipped person in the entire society to fulfill this purpose. Where the few ruled, they usually received the best education. These people normally rose to power by demonstrating various types of ability. That they were clever cannot be doubted; it is doubtful, however, that the wisest and most ethical people always became rulers in any oligarchy that developed.

If the many rule through the power of their votes in democratic elections, as has been the case in some states in the past few hundred years, it is imperative that the general level of education be raised to the highest degree possible. It soon becomes part of the ethic of society, to a greater or lesser extent, to consider the worth of human personality and to give each individual the opportunity to develop his or her potential to the fullest. In return, to ensure smooth functioning of the democracy, the individual is asked to subjugate extraordinary personal interests to the common good. Since democratic states are relative newcomers on the world scene, harmony between these two antithetical ideals will undoubtedly require a delicate balance in the years ahead.

All of this raises a very interesting question: Which agency--the school, the family, or the church--should have control? In a totalitarian state there is but one philosophy of education permitted, whereas other types of government, once again to a greater or lesser degree, allow pluralistic philosophies of education to flourish. Under the latter arrangement, the state could conceivably exercise no control of education whatsoever, or it could take a greater or lesser interest in the education of its citizens. When the state does take an interest, the question arises as to whether the state (through its agency the school), or the family, or the church shall exert the greatest amount of influence on the child. When the leaders of the church feel strongly that the central purpose of education is religious, they may decide to take over the education of the child themselves. In a society where there are many different religious affiliations, it is quite possible that the best arrangement is for the church and the state to remain separate.

The implications of state involvement in education concerns both the person who would call himself an educational progressivist, as well as the person who could be classified as an educational essentialist. The progressivist, who has typically been concerned with social reform, has favored a democratically oriented state in which the individual could choose social goals on a trial-and-error basis. The basic question mentioned above has remained. Which agency--the school, the family, or the church--should exert the greatest amount of influence on the child? In a totalitarian state the answer is obvious because the government automatically exerts the strongest influence. Thus physical training is often an important part of the curriculum up to and including the university level (e.g., Russia). When the church has been able to educate the child--and has decided to do so because it believed the central purpose of education was primarily religious--the role of physical education, sport, health education, and dance has tended to decline for both philosophic and economic reasons. Matters of the spirit and the mind take precedence over the body and, where funding is limited, money is spent for that which is essential. In a totalitarian state, the church has typically been restrained in the achievement of its objective--except that in modern times the role of competitive sport has not been denied. In societies where pluralistic philosophies existed, and where the federal government has perhaps adopted a laissez-faire attitude, the resultant educational product in our specialized area has tended to be quite uneven. The matter is that simple and yet that complex!

The United States. The United States Congress from the beginning showed concern for youth fitness but did not enact legislation to provide funding for physical training in the schools. In this democratic republic, education was a responsibility of the individual state. However, it was until 1866 that the first state physical education law was enacted in California, to be followed by Ohio in 1892 and North Dakota before the turn of the century. Sport and physical recreation had been popular down through the years, but were typically not considered to be part of the educational system.

The Influence of Nationalism. In the English language the word "nation" is generally used synonymously with country or state, and we think of human beings who are united with a type of governmental rule. These individuals, members of a political community, are usually considered to possess a certain "nationality" within a definable period of time. The word "people," having a broader and somewhat more ambiguous connotation, normally refers to the inhabitants of several nations or states as an ethnological unit,

The word "nationalism" itself might apply to a feeling, attitude, or consciousness that persons might have as citizens of a nation-citizens who hold a strong attitude about the welfare of their nation, about its status in regard to strength or prosperity. Carlton J. Hayes in Nationalism: A Religion (1961) offers what have become classic definitions: (1) patriotism as "love of country," and (2) nationalism as a "fusion of patriotism with a consciousness of nationality." Nationalism might also be defined as a political philosophy in which the good of the nation is supreme. The word is often used incorrectly as a synonym for chauvinism.

Thus defined, nationalism (the third social force discussed here) has been evident throughout the history of civilization from the relatively simple organization of the tribe to the complex nation-states of the modern world. Some scholars regard nationalism as a term of relatively recent origin (i.e., since the French and American revolutions). They argue that until the modern period no nations were sufficiently unified to permit the existence of such a feeling. However, it could also be argued that the European heritage reveals many examples of "nationalism." We have only to think of the Greek and Roman cultures with their citizenship ideals and desires to perpetuate their culture. Then, too, the Hebrews believed that they were a people selected by God for a unique role in history, and the Roman Catholic Church developed great power within certain states over a significant period of time, often creating far-reaching loyalties.

At various times throughout history, "city-statism" (e.g., ancient Sparta) and/or nationalism (e.g., Hitler's Germany) have undoubtedly had a strong influence on the developmental physical activity pattern of the citizens, and especially on the young people who were eligible to fight in the many wars and battles.

The United States. In the United States, we find a "mixed bag," so to speak. As VanderZwaag (1965) pointed out, for example, in examining the historical background in the United States, people did eventually call for and accept an "American system" of physical education and sport. From an overall standpoint, he came to the conclusion, however, that physical education had not been cultivated as greatly for nationalistic purposes in the United States as it has been in many other countries.

The Influence of Economics. Broadly interpreted, economics as a field is concerned with what people produce and the formal and informal arrangements that are made concerning the usage of these products. Economists want to know about the consumption of the goods that are produced and who takes part in the actual process of production. They ask where the power lies, whether the goods are used fully, and to what ends a society's resources are brought to bear on the matter at hand.

For thousands of years people lived in small, relatively isolated groups, and their survival depended on a subsistence economy. Early civilizations had to learn how to create surplus economies before any class within the society could have leisure for formal education or anything else that might be related to "the good life."

Educational aims tended to vary depending upon how people made their money and created surplus economies. There was not much time for "schooling" in the typical agrarian society. When commerce was added to the agrarian base, education advanced as people asked more from i64t to meet the needs of the various classes involved. Modern industrial economy has made still further demands on education and has produced the moneys whereby it might be obtained.

In summary, therefore, education has prospered when there was a surplus economy and declined when the economic structure weakened. Thus, it may be said that "educational cycles" of rise and decline seemed to have coincided with economic cycles. Despite these developments, formal education has traditionally regarded vocational areas of study with less esteem than the liberal arts or humanities. However, in recent years the esteem in which these two aspects of the educational system are held seems to have almost completely reversed--in the eyes of the general public at least.

The United States. Professionals in physical education and educational sport rarely give much consideration to the influence of economics until they begin to feel the pinch of "economy moves" at certain times. Then they find--and have found in the past--that some segments of the society considered their subject matter area to be less important than others. When people in positions of power decide that school physical education, or varsity athletics, should be eliminated or at least sharply curtailed, such a move often comes as a distinct shock. Interestingly, even though athletics is typically regarded as being extracurricular, this aspect of our program is often used as a lever to force more funds from a pleasure-seeking public that tends to view competitive sport as a cultural maximizer. Also, people do not wish to see their "spectacles" discontinued!

Physical education, especially as it connotes education of the physical--as opposed to the concept of education through the physical--has a good chance for recognition and improvement under any type of economic system. In largely agrarian societies of the past, physical fitness resulted automatically through hard work. An industrial society, on the other hand, has often had to prescribe programs to ensure a minimum level of physical fitness for all, either through manual labor or some other type of recommended physical activity. When the distribution of wealth has been markedly uneven, the more prosperous groups have achieved their desired level of physical fitness through a variety of means, artificial or natural. In a welfare state, where people typically enjoy a relatively longer period of educational opportunity, society has had to decide to what extent it can or should demand physical fitness of all its citizens and how to achieve this end. Thus the value structure of the society dictates what rank is accorded to sport and physical education within the educational hierarchy.

The Influence of Religion. Religion, the fifth social force to be discussed, may be defined very broadly as "the pursuit of whatever a man [person] considers to be most worthy or demanding of his devotion" (Williams, 1952). To be completely religious, therefore, a person would have to devote himself or herself completely to the attainment of that person's highest aim in life. The more usual definition of religion in the western world explains it as a belief in a Supreme Creator who has imparted a spiritual nature and a soul to a person and who may possibly guard and guide that person's destiny. Because there are so many types of religion in the world, and these are in various stages of development, it is well nigh impossible to present a definition that would be meaningful and acceptable to all.

In all probability the nature of the universe has not changed at any time in the conceivable past and will not change in the predictable future. Nevertheless, people's attitudes toward the world in which they live has changed, albeit gradually, a number of times. Theology has occasionally forged somewhat ahead of the political institutions, however, and we may theorize that there is a definite relationship between these two sets of phenomena. Originally, the primitives were filled with fear and apprehension about the world. They could not understand adverse natural phenomena and attributed their misfortunes to devils and evil spirits. Somewhat later, people looked upon God as a type of all-powerful king, potentially benevolent, but certainly a power to be feared. Approximately 3,000 years ago the concept of "God, The Heavenly Father looking after his children" began to develop. We were to obey His laws, or else we would be punished. Certain orthodox religions today hold this position.

Now we find that a fourth position has emerged clearly. People look at reality (which they may call God) and conceive that some sort of partnership is in process. Some consider God to be a friendly partner, if we proceed according to His physical laws. As a result of this belief, many churchmen, and some scientists, too, are expressing a relatively new theological approach, offering us the concept of a democratic, cooperative God as a foundation for a new and improved world order. Religious liberals are finding considerable difficulty reaching common agreement on this fourth position. While recognizing--in the Western world--their debt to Judaism and Christianity, they appear to be uniting on a "free-mind principle" instead of any common creed. The ideal of the liberal is, therefore, a free spirit who gives allegiance to the truth as he or she sees it (Zeigler, 1965, based on Champion & Short, 1951).

Certain others have taken another interesting position, an existential approach, which has emerged as a somewhat significant force during the past 100 years or so. Kierkegaard, prior to 1850, had become concerned about the number of influences within society that were taking away one's individuality. Originally, existentialism probably started as a revolt against Hegel's idealism, a philosophy affirming that ethical and spiritual realities were accessible to one through reason.

Kierkegaard decided that religion would be next to useless if one could simply reason one's way back to God. Then along came Nietzsche who wished to discard Christianity since science had presumably shown that the transcendent ideals of the Church were nonsense. A person's task was, therefore, to create his or her own ideals and values. After all, in the final analysis, one was only responsible to oneself. Twentieth-century existentialists, such as Sartre, furthered such individuality, and these efforts have met with a fair amount of acceptance both abroad and in North America.

The Christian contribution to the history of education in the Western world has been most significant. Actually, the basis for universal education was laid with the promulgation of Christian principles emphasizing the worth of the individual. The all-powerful position of the Catholic Church was challenged successfully by the Protestant Reformation in that the authority of the Bible was substituted for that of the Church. Accordingly, individual judgment was to be used in the interpretation of the Scriptures and Christian duty. This outlook required the education of the many for the purposes of reading and interpreting God's word. Thus the groundwork was paid for democratic universal education.

The United States. In the mid-19th century in the United States, as the educational ladder extended upward, religious education was removed from school curricula because of many conflicts. Catholics began their own system of education, whereas Protestants went along with the secularization of the schools. This was a great boon for the country if not for the Protestant religion. The home has done reasonably well in the inculcation of morals, but with ever-rising materialism and the recent decline of the traditional family as an institution, a number of problems have arisen. And so discussion continues to revolve around two questions: (1) which agency shall educate the individual--the home, the church, the state, or some private agency; and (2) whether any agency is capable of performing the task alone. An argument can be made that in a democracy each of the agencies mentioned above has a specific function to perform in completing the entire task.

Although the historical influence of religion on physical education and sport (or developmental physical activity in sport, exercise, and related expressive activities such as dance) has been significant, relatively few studies have been conducted within our field relative to this matter. It is true that in the early cultures the so-called physical and mental education of the people could not really have been viewed separately. For example, many ancient rituals and ceremonies included various types of dance and physical exercise that may well have contributed to physical endurance and skill.

However, a number of early religions placed great stress on a life of quiet contemplation, and this philosophy appears to have contributed to the denigration of certain bodily activities. Continuing emphasis on intellectual attainment for certain classes in various societies must have strengthened this attitude, a position that still holds in many quarters to the present. Yet the harmonious ideal of the Athenians had aesthetic and religious connotations that cannot be denied, and physical education and highly competitive sport ranked high in this scheme. (The same cannot be said for the Romans, however, whose "sound mind in a sound body" concept attributed to Seneca meant that the body was to be well-trained for warlike pursuits and similar activities.)

Many have argued that the Christian church was responsible historically for the low status of physical education and athletics in the Western world, but lately some evidence has indicated that the criticism of the church applied more to the pagan sporting rituals and the barbarity of the arena in early times. The fact still remains, however, that physical culture and "the physical" generally did fall into disrepute until certain humanistic educators strove to revive the earlier Greek ideal during the Renaissance. Once again, though, this improvement was not general, and in most cases was short-lived. Considering everything up to the present in the United States, it seems reasonable to say that Christianity had undoubtedly hampered the fullest development of sport, exercise, and related expressive movement in the past, but it appears that the situation has changed to a considerable degree. There has evidently been some revamping of earlier positions as church leaders belatedly realized the potential of these activities as educational and spiritual forces in our lives. Many church leaders now envision the family both "praying and playing together!"

The Influence of Ecology. The six and last of what are claimed to be the major or pivotal social forces is that of ecology. (Keep in mind that the influence of the concept of progress is treated both as a social force and a professional concern in this chapter, but its presentation has been delayed to the end of this chapter because it is also regarded as a type of persistent problem that I have categorized as a professional concern. (Other persistent problems to add to this category that I have classified as social forces or influences are now looming on the horizon for analysis in the near future. For example, the influence of science and technology has become very strong, and the influence of a concern for world peace is gathering strength at the present.)

Ecology is usually defined as the field of study that treats the relationships and interactions of human beings and other living organisms with each other and with their natural environment. As a matter of fact, the influence of ecology--called "conservation of natural resources" earlier--was only felt significantly by a relatively few cognoscenti 20 years ago. Since 1975 interest in this vital subject has increased steadily and markedly with each passing year. Nevertheless, the "say-do" gap in relation to truly doing something about Earth's plight in this regard is enormous.

What, then, is the extent of the environmental crisis in modern society? Very simply, we have achieved a certain mastery over the world because of our scientific and technological achievement. We are at the top of the food chain because of our mastery of much of Earth's flora and fauna. However, because of the explosion of the human population, increasingly greater pressures "will be placed on our lands to provide shelter, food, recreation, and waste disposal areas. This will cause a greater pollution of the atmosphere, the rivers, the lakes, the land, and the oceans" (Mergen, 1970). This bleak picture could be expanded, yet perhaps the tide will soon turn. Certainly the gravity of prevailing patterns of human conduct is recognized by many, but a great many more people must develop attitudes that will lead them to take positive action in the immediate future. It is time for concerted global action, and we can only hope that it is not too late to reverse the effects of a most grave situation.

The United States. We can all appreciate the difficulty of moving from a scientific "is" to an ethical "ought" in the realm of human affairs. There are obviously many scientific findings within the environmental sciences that should be made available to people of all ages whether or not they are enrolled in an educational institution. Simply making the facts available, of course, will not be any guarantee that strong and positive attitudes will develop on the subject. It is a well-established fact, however, that the passing of legislation in difficult and sensitive areas must take place through responsible political leadership, and that attitude changes often follow behind, albeit at what may seem to be a snail's pace.

The field of education should play a vital role now, as it has never done before, in the development of what might be called an "ecological awareness." (It can be seen why it is impossible to state that this problem has been a historical persistent problem. Never before has the overwhelming magnitude of poor ecological practices been even partially understood, much less fully comprehended.

Now some realize the urgency of the matter, but others are telling them that further study is needed, that they are exaggerating, and that they are simply pessimistic by nature.) This is obviously much broader than it was earlier in the conservation movement within forestry and closely related fields. Now ecology places all of these individual entities of Earth in a total context in which the interrelationship of all parts must be thoroughly understood.

If the field of education has a strong obligation to present the various issues revolving about the newly understood need for the development of an ecological awareness, this duty obviously includes physical educators and sport coaches, as well as men and women in our allied fields (e.g., health and safety education), who also happen to be employed within the educational system, have a certain general education responsibility to all participants in their classes or programs. Moreover, all people who are serving outside of schools in society as professionals in some aspect of developmental physical activity in sport, exercise, dance, and play are also directly concerned with our relationship with ourselves, our fellow human beings, other living organisms, and the physical environment.

We must keep in mind that ecologists are concerned with the relationships and interactions of human organisms with themselves and with their environment. As matters stand now, therefore, the "relationships and interactions of human organisms with their environment" has not resulted in a fit population in the United States (or perhaps anywhere else either). Our "army" of experts in human motor performance (physical educators) are confronted daily with the fact that, for a variety of reasons, modern, urbanized, technologically advanced life in North America has created a population with a very low level of physical fitness, with a resultant decrease in overall total fitness. We have somehow created a ridiculous situation in which people on this continent are to a large extent overfed and poorly exercised. It is the profession of sport and physical education that is uniquely responsible for the exercise programs that will enable men and women to withstand the excessive wear and tear that life's informal and formal activities may demand (Zeigler, 1989).

In addition, people at all stages of life show evidence of a variety of remediable physical defects, but there is an unwillingness on the part of the public to make exercise therapy programs readily available through both public and private agencies. Often physiotherapy programs are available after operations or accidents, but they are typically not continued until full recovery has been achieved. Our concern here is with the unavailability of exercise therapy programs in the schools and certain private agencies under the supervision of specially qualified physical educators after the physiotherapist has served his or her function, and the physician prescribes further maintenance exercise. This should include a program in which the circulo-respiratory condition is raised to a desirable level along with necessary stretching and strengthening exercises.

THE PROFESSIONAL CONCERNS

The Curriculum. The seventh persistent historical problem, and the first problem designated as a "professional concern," is the curriculum in sport and physical education. In primitive and preliterate society, physical education, like all education was typically incidental, a byproduct of daily experience. Nor was physical culture in early Egypt part of a formal educational system. Sports and dancing were poplar with the nobility, but the masses simply had to master the many physical skills necessary to earn their living. As was often the case throughout history, fishing, hunting, and fowling were engaged in for pleasure by some and as business by a great many. Much the same can be said about the other early civilizations. Soldiers trained to fight in a variety of ways, and the masses had occasional opportunities for dancing, music, informal games, and rudimentary hunting and fishing activities. Thus any informal educational curriculum, of physical culture activity, has been and still is influenced by a variety of political, economic, philosophical, religious, scientific, and technological factors. Those areas included for the education of youth are selected because of their recurring interest and use among educators and the public. The persistent problem, therefore, is: On what basis is the formal or informal curriculum to be selected? The Cretans were surrounded by water, so they learned to swim; the Spartan Greeks emphasized severe physical training, but they only stressed competitive sport as it related to warfare; the Athenians, on the other hand, believed that harmonious development of body and mind was most important; the Roman ideal was based on the preparation of a citizen to bear arms for his nation; and so on up through the various ages. Basically, the values that are held in a society will be reflected directly and indirectly in the curriculum (informal or formal).

The United States. In the United States the task of the physical educator/coach within educational circles today is to ascertain the values that are uppermost in the society and to attempt to implement them to the greatest possible extent through the medium of sport, exercise, dance, and play. In the wider society, the goals of the professional in developmental physical activity should be essentially the same for people of all ages whether they be categorized as accelerated, normal, or special populations. To accomplish this aim effectively and efficiently based on high professional standards, principles, and rules is obviously a most important professional concern (and, in a larger sense, a persistent problem as defined in this volume).

Methods of Instruction. The second "professional concern," and the eighth persistent historical problem, is that of methods of instruction in sport and physical education. Keeping in mind that curriculum and methods should go hand in hand as they usually have in the past if effective education is a desired end product, it is quite logical to consider methods at this point.

Primitive and preliterate people undoubtedly learned through imitation and through trial and error. When writing was invented in the early civilizations, memorization played a large part in the educational process. Tradition and custom were highly regarded, and precept and proper example were significant aspects of both physical and mental culture. In the Near East we are told that Jesus, for example, was a very fine teacher, and undoubtedly the same might be said about other great religious leaders who originated their specific religions. The religious leaders who followed the initiators evidently often employed less exciting teaching methods with an emphasis on formality and dogmatism. Toward the end of the Middle Ages (c. 1400-1500), educational methodology is said to have improved considerably. For example, with the onset of the Renaissance, there was greater recognition of individual differences, and the whole spirit of the period is said to have gradually become more humanistic.

The United States. Physical activity professionals in the United States need to understand that the concept of a mind-body dualism has prevailed in many quarters down to the present day. A physical educator/coach should determine what influence that content has on method, and whether they go hand in hand on all occasions. Shall sport and physical education be taught formally, semi formally, or informally? The persistent problem remains: How can the student or activity participant be so motivated that learning will occur most easily, that it will be remembered and retained, and that it will change attitudes and produce beneficial change in all who become involved?

Professional Preparation. Preparation for professional service is the third professional concern to be considered. Although professional preparation had its origins in antiquity, professional preparation of teachers of teachers is a relatively recent innovation. In early times the most important qualification for the teacher was a sound knowledge of the subject (and it's still that way in the colleges and universities of North America, but not the public schools). In the Middle Ages there was no such thing as professional education (through departments of education) to be a teacher, as least in the sense that certification is needed today to teach in most public institutions. In Prussia, much headway was made in improving teacher education in the late 18th and early 19th centuries, and this system was copied extensively elsewhere. Significant advances in the theory of pedagogy occurred through the influence of Pestalozzi.

The United States. In the United States, the "normal school" became a well-established part of the educational system. In the 20th century, this type of school progressed to college or even university status. Professional education eventually achieved status at the college and university level as a subject to be taught, but it has not been regarded as highly as it might be.

Generally speaking throughout the world, professional preparation for physical education and sport has been offered at the normal and/or technical school level. Despite what was said immediately above, university recognition has been achieved at many institutions in the United States with the first doctoral degree (Ph.D.) being awarded in 1924 (Columbia Teachers College).

The Healthy Body. The concept of "the healthy body" is the fourth professional concern (and the 10th persistent problem). The condition of our bodies has undoubtedly always been of concern to men and women throughout history and presumably for different reasons at different stages of people's lives. Early peoples found that a certain type of basic fitness was necessary for life. Physical fitness was absolutely essential for survival. Interestingly, a study of past civilizations indicates that the states of war or peace have had a direct bearing on the emphases placed on personal and/or community health. Strength, endurance, and freedom from disqualifying defects are important to people who want to win wars. When a war has ended, a society may then be able again to focus greater attention on a healthful environment at home.

Modern people in the developed countries have been more successful than their forebears in making an adjustment to their environment, and consequently they live significantly longer on the average. Their success, however, is dependent on complicated procedures, and it is profoundly disturbing that so many people in the world are not able to profit from the outstanding progress that has been made in public health science. The big problem for society, with those who are living longer, is finding ways to occupy these older men and women who still have the ability and the desire to serve their communities.

The United States. Much of the disagreement over the role of health education, in the schools, or outside in the community, stems from different educational philosophies and the various resultant concepts of health. There is the ever-present question as to which agency--the home, the school, or the community agency--should play the greatest role in this area. Early in this century Jesse Feiring Williams (of Columbia Teachers College) offered a broadened concept of health in which he define it as "the quality of life which enables the individual to live most and serve best." According to this interesting definition, the ultimate test of health is the use to which it is put for individual and social service.

Women, Ethnic Minorities, and the Handicapped. The place of sport, exercise, and related expressive activity in the lives of women, ethnic minorities, and the handicapped or special populations is the fifth so-called professional concern and the 11th persistent problem. It may seem odd to list these three segments of the population under one heading, but it has been done because each--for one reason or another--have been denied equal opportunity to the benefits that may be accrued from full participation in physical education and educational sport. Throughout history, these groups have been hampered not only by people's ideas of the place of such physical activity in a particular society, but also by the place that the members of these groups themselves have held in most societies.

It has been believed by both sexes, for example, that a woman had severe limitations because of her anatomical structure and because of her role in the reproductive process. Aristotle felt that women were generally weaker, less courageous, and less complete than men, and they therefore had been fitted by nature for subjection to the male. (Conversely, Plato believed that women should have all types of education similar to the pattern that he prescribed for men (including the highest type of liberation, and even preparation for warfare). Throughout history, with notable exceptions in the cases of Crete, Sparta, later ancient Rome, and certain other individual instances, practically all women were considered inferior.

The United States. It is now fully apparent that one of the significant social trends of the 20th century has been women's "emancipation." Women are now more likely to be evaluated in terms of intellectual function and individual qualifications, even though there is still a struggle going on in regard to the "equal pay for equal work" concept. However, both the democratic and socialistic theories of state have fostered equalitarianism. As a result, many people now feel that men's and women's physical education and educational sport programs should more nearly approximate each other. There is still much to be done in regard to the norm projected by society for women (e.g., excessive concern about external appearance). Thus if the profession of physical education and educational sport has advantages to offer to women (and also to ethnic minorities and the handicapped), society should see to it that they receive these opportunities to the greatest extent possible and desirable.

Dance Within HPER Programs. The sixth professional concern, and the 12th persistent historical problem, is the role of dance within programs of health, physical education, and recreation.

In all ages people have danced for personal pleasure, for religious and social purposes, for expression of the gamut of emotions, and for the pleasure of others. An analysis of the dance forms of a civilization can frequently tell a qualified observer much about the total life pattern therein. In primitive societies, various types of rhythmic expression were "instinctive satisfiers" of people. Dance was most often serious in nature and only incidentally served as physical fitness, health, or recreation.

Dance served a purpose in Roman civilization, but its status was below that accorded to it by the Athenian Greeks. During the Middle Ages, dance and some other fine arts had very low status, probably because of their corruption in the later Roman era and their subsequent rejection by the Catholic Church. However, the place of dance began to rise again during the Renaissance. Since then, different types and forms of dance have waxed and waned over the centuries in Europe, England, and North America.

The United States. The 20th century has witnessed truly remarkable development in dance, the body gradually being rediscovered as a means of communication through the dance medium. Yet there is still much room for development and progress (keeping in mind the difficulty of defining the latter term adequately). For example, a significant body of scholarly research organized in the form of ordered principles or generalizations is not yet available. Furthermore, better interaction between dance within educational circles and dance within professional circles has added, and is continuing to add, further strength to the overall development of the field.

Certainly a more accurate and open-minded view of the role of dance within the overall curriculum at the various educational levels is needed. For example, on the North American continent what was called "modern dance" gradually received acceptance with the majority of male physical education teachers and coaches, but it was definitely an uphill struggle with the result that many negative attitudes are still conveyed--directly or indirectly--to the boys and young men in their classes. However, such opinions and attitudes should change as adequate support and accurate understanding comes from both people in dance and those in physical education and educational sport.

In the late 1970s dance was added as the fourth "allied profession" within the AAHPER, and it is now AAHPERD. In a number of universities, the people concerned with dance have made efforts to be switched from the physical education unit to that of fine arts. Some universities (e.g., the University of Wisconsin) resisted this trend.

There is some justification for efforts to separate dance from physical education particularly when it loses its significance as an "art" form. However, it seems that dance somehow should maintain close relationships with three units on campus--fine arts, physical education, and (professional) education. Yet dance should probably be located where it is wanted and best received on any particular campus. It may be the attitudes of physical educators that determine if dance should be able to function best within programs of health education, sport and physical education, recreation, and dance. Finally, beyond the struggle of determining the best home for dance in education, dance will probably always be with us as both an art and a social function. Also, it will undoubtedly reflect the dominant influences of the age in which it is taking place.

The Use of Leisure. The use of leisure has been designated as the seventh professional concern (and the 13th persistent historical problem). Citizens in the industrialized world (and now the post-industrial world) are said to have more leisure than ever before in history, but the promotion of the concept of "education for leisure" depends a great deal on whether the prevailing educational philosophy will support such programs. As we can appreciate, there has been a hue and cry relatively recently about the failures of public education and a demand for a "return to essentials." Thus it remains to be seen how this swing toward educational essentialism will influence the time spent on avocational living. An unfortunate development in many ways also is that economic inflation has forced many men to take second or part-time jobs, and has forced many women out of the home to seek employment (whether they wanted to have this opportunity or not). Such pressures have undoubtedly affected leisure patterns significantly.

Throughout history the use of leisure has been strongly influenced by the economic status of society. Both education and recreation have prospered in times when there was a surplus economy. However, in most past and present civilizations the average man has had to work very hard to earn a meager living. Certain classes--rulers, priests, and nobles--were the first to enjoy anything like extended leisure. Even in the Middle Ages life still held many inequalities for the masses, although recreation did begin to take on a broader significance. Persistent war-making, the fact that times change slowly, and the power of the Church prevented political democracy and socialistic influences from taking hold. Then, too, the natural sciences had to be advanced sufficiently so developing technology could direct men to what was called the Industrial Revolution, a development that in time has lowered people's working hours markedly.

The United States. We can all appreciate today that there are about five different types of recreational activity: (1) physical recreational interests, (2) social recreational interests, (3) communicative recreational interests, (4) aesthetic and creative recreational interests, and (5) so-called learning recreational interests (e.g., educational hobbies). When people do earn leisure, how should they spend this time? Obviously, in a free society there can be no such thing as recreational standards--norms but not standards. Thus the choice of recreational pursuits by a person is a highly individual matter. Where developmental physical activity in sport, exercise, and related expressive movement fits into the life pattern of a person (i.e., how much time should be spent on which pursuits) cannot be mandated in this society. This means that the profession of physical education and educational sport is confronted with a challenge to get its message across adequately to people of all ages.

Now we hear about increased automation and the possibility of cybernation, and this reminds us again that "education for leisure" remains a serious responsibility that we can't shunt to the side for long. The term "recreation" has assumed a broader meaning than that of "play," although many people use both interchangeably. We need to articulate within our concept of leisure a definition of recreation that embodies all those types of recreational/educational experiences indicated above. We used to talk about "the good life," but now improvement of the "quality of life" seems to have supplanted this earlier idea. Sound, diverse recreational experiences in their leisure can provide people of all ages with pleasure, satisfaction, and an even more rewarding life. Healthful physical activity deserves serious consideration in the lifestyles of all as they choose from the recreational kaleidoscope that America is now providing for citizens of all ages.

Amateur, Semiprofessional, and Professional Sport. The eighth professional concern, and the 14th persistent historical problem, is the matter of amateur, semiprofessional, and professional sport The relationship of these three subdivisions within competitive sport to one another, to the educational system, and to the entire culture must be fully understood before improvements can be made in the light of changing circumstances. The motivation for people to participate in sports and games through the ages has been so complex that there is really no general agreement on the matter. People have taken part for fun, for re-creation, for self-expression, for self-arousal and adventure, for health, for exercise, for competition, for money, and probably for still other reasons not readily discernible. There was an important early relationship of sporting competition to religious observances. Even in the earlier days the aspect of overspecialization because of the desire to win, and presumably the desire for material reward, soon "tarnished the luster" of what has become known as "the amateur ideal."

The United States. There were so many different definitions of an amateur that it became next to impossible for one person to comprehend them fully--in fact, no one seems to bother anymore. We steadily but surely re-evaluated some of the treasured, basic assumptions about the amateur code in sport, a position that categorizes the matter on the basis of polarities (i.e., if you "take a nickel," you're a "dirty pro"). There is an urgent need for the full recognition of a semiprofessional category in which the athlete will not be viewed as a lesser person by many of the older amateur sportspersons. There is a further need for professional athletes (often called "sportsmen") who will be taught somehow to comprehend that a truly professional person in this culture presumably devotes his or her life to a social ideal--that is, to serve their fellow human beings through their contributions to the many phases of sports' development. The assumption is that all types of sport can hold value for people under the finest auspices with the best professional leadership (i.e., that which develops a fine set of professional ethics not dominated primarily by the thought of financial gain). The theory is that competitive sport can (and should!) be employed as a socially useful servant. If it doesn't fulfill this function, it should either be made to do so or abandoned as an activity!

The Role of Management. The role of management or administration is the ninth professional concern and the 15th persistent historical problem. As our society continues to grow in complexity, amazing social changes are taking place. The continuing Industrial Revolution, and now with the advent of a so-called post-industrial society to a certain degree, has placed our most modern societies in a highly difficult situation. Because of these factors, along with the exploding population, the resultant development of immense urban and suburban areas, and the fantastic advances in science and technology, a steadily growing percentage of available human resources has been necessary to manage the efforts of a large majority of the people. Eventually this development became known as the "Administrative Revolution."

Social organizations of one type or another are inextricably related to people's history as human and social animals. Superior-subordinate relationships evolved according to the very nature of things as people produced goods, fought wars, politically organized society, formed churches, and developed a great variety of formal and informal associations. As societies became more complex, role differentiation increased greatly. A central theme seems to have been that of change, such change being made presumably to strengthen the organization administratively. It was only recently, however, that "administrative thought emerged as a differentiated field of sustained writing, conscious observation, abstract theory, and specialized terminology" (Gross, 1964, p. 91).

The United States. The management of developmental physical activity in sport, exercise, or related expressive movement is needed in society generally in many different types of public and private organizations. Education, for example, has become a vast public and private enterprise demanding wise management based upon sound administrative theory. The "organizational revolution" meant that educational administrators were forced to create a greater amount of bureaucracy. Educational traditionalists have tended to believe that there are valid theoretical principles of administration that should not be violated. Many with a more pragmatic orientation view management as a developing social science. If and when a truly definitive inventory of management theory and practice arranged as ordered generalizations or principles becomes available, such knowledge could then be of great use to all administrators and managers.

In many educational institutions the administration of physical education and athletics is "big business within big education," and the same can be said, of course, for the management of professional sport and private exercise establishments. Unfortunately, there is practically no tenable theory or ongoing research about the administrative task taking place. For example, the professional preparation of physical education and athletics administrators had long been carried out almost universally in a relatively haphazard and poorly articulated fashion. The people responsible for these programs at the university level should be engaged in pure and applied research themselves, but very few are fulfilling this function. Where possible, and seemingly when necessary, athletics administrators are receiving token assistance from seminars in which knowledgeable people from other disciplines are recruited as ad hoc leaders. Thus changes in professional preparation for administrative leadership are coming about slowly. Fortunately the North American Society for Sport Management was inaugurated in 1986 and now gives significant hope for the future. However, there is concern whether it will offer the results of research and scholarly endeavor in all aspects of sport and physical activity management. By that is meant that there is an ongoing need for a balanced approach that serves the needs of the administrator in educational, recreational, and private enterprise settings, as well as the needs of the more commercialized sport enterprises. We can only hope that this and other developments will enable the administrator's practice in this field to be based increasingly on sound knowledge available from our endeavor and that of the several behavioral sciences.

Progress As A Concept. The concept of progress is considered here as both a social force and a professional concern. With everything that has been "happening to" physical education and educational sport in the past 50 years, can we really say that progress has been made? In the remainder of this chapter, I will try to answer this question by giving consideration to this concept. I will also discuss progress in education generally and conclude with a statement about the need for consensus on this topic in the field of physical education and sport. Any fusion of the past and present, which this effort undoubtedly is, cannot escape the element of controversy and struggle. Of course, I recognize that it is literally impossible for any one person or group to be infallible with a topic that involves historical perspective.

Furthermore, you may find that you (1) have already made a number of judgments for yourself; (2) are currently in the process of making these judgments; or (3) will make these judgments for yourself once you understand the problems and issues more fully. One's judgment could well be determined by one's mood or by the prevailing mood of the times. The man or woman who thinks profoundly in the light of the occurrences of the recent transitional 20th century deserves praise, not blame. Also, he or she cannot be blamed for being pessimistic or skeptical at best. If pessimistic, this person will probably feel that our future prospects on this Earth are not good at all. Perhaps you are an optimist, however. At any rate, your considered philosophy (both personal and professional) will have much to do with your plans and the way you go about executing them. Keep in mind, also, that thoughts expressed in words are just that and nothing more. Others will ultimately judge you and your efforts by your deeds as a professional person--not by what you say you believe. You can only hope that they won't prejudge you (the ever-present "judging the book by the cover" fallacy). For better or worse, you live your philosophy every day of your life. That is why it is so important to determine where you are going and how you want to get there. It is for this reason this particular persistent problem (i.e., the concept of progress) has been placed at the end of this section.

A Definition of Progress. Any study of history inevitably forces a person to conjecture about human progress. I first became truly interested in the concept of progress in the work of the world-famous paleontologist, George Gaylord Simpson (1949, pp. 240-262). After 25 years of research, Simpson offered us his assessment of the vital question as to whether evolution represented progress. His study convinced him that humankind reject "the over-simple and metaphysical concept of a pervasive perfection principle." That there had been progression he agreed, but he inquired whether this could really viewed as progress. The difficulty arises, Simpson argued, when we seek to maintain that change is progress; we must ask ourselves if we can recommend a criterion by which progress may be judged.

We are warned that it may be shortsighted for us to be our own "judge and jury" in this connection. It may well be an acceptable human criterion of progress to say that we are coming closer to approximating what we think we ought to be and to achieving what we hold to be good. It is not wise, according to Simpson, however, to automatically assume that this is "the only criterion of progress and that it has a general validity in evolution." Thus, throughout the history of life there have been examples of progress and examples of retrogression, and progress is "certainly not a basic property of life common to all its manifestations." If it is a materialistic world, as Simpson would have us believe, a particular species can progress and regress. There is "a tendency for life to expand, to fill in all the space in the livable environments," but such expansion has not necessarily been constant, although it is true that human beings are now "the most rapidly growing organism in the world."

It is true also that we have made progress in adaptability and have developed our "ability to cope with a greater variety of environments." This is also progress considered from the human vantage point. The various evolutionary phenomena among the many species, however, do not show "a vital principle common to all forms of life," and "they are certainly inconsistent with the existence of a supernal perfecting principle." Thus, Simpson concludes, human progress is actually relative and not general, and "does not warrant choice of the line of man's ancestry as the central line of evolution as a whole." Yet it is safe to say that "man is among the highest products of evolution . . . and that man is, on the whole but not in every single respect, the pinnacle so far of evolutionary progress" on this planet.

With the realization that evolution (of human and other organisms) is going on and will probably continue for millions of years (indefinitely?), we can realize how futile it is to attempt to predict any outcome for the ceaseless change so evident in life and its environment. We can say that we must be extremely careful about the possible extinction of our species (humankind) on Earth, because it is highly improbable, though not absolutely impossible, that our development would be repeated in the same way here or on any other planet. Some other mammal might develop in a similar way, but this will not happen so long as we humans have control of our environment and do not encourage such development. Our task is to attempt to modify and perhaps to control the direction of our own evolution according to the highest goals that we can determine. It may be possible through the agency of education, and the development of a moral sense throughout the world, to ensure the future of our species. One way to accomplish this would be to place a much greater emphasis on the social sciences and humanities while working for an ethically sound world-state at the same time.

Societal Progress. Next it seems advisable to transfer our attention from Simpson's broader concept of evolutionary progress to the more immediate problem to the type of society that North Americans, for example, wish to have on their own continent in their hemisphere. At the same time we can't forget or neglect the rest of the world. Here in North America we find a culture in which the people have developed a great faith in material progress. Because technology has advanced so rapidly in the past 70 years, leaders in the various walks of life are devoting a great deal of time and money planning for the years immediately ahead. Specific industries in both the United States are spending untold millions of dollars investigating the possibilities of the future, as are branches of the armed forces, many non-profit foundations, universities, and professional associations. The United States now has a population of over 300 million people. People have to be housed, fed, transported, cared for medically, entertained, and educated, and superannuated in even larger super cities and their environs. The threat of increased stress and strain looms large, unless greater "creature comforts" can be provided, along with the need to help people make life more meaningful. It seems imperative to devise better uses of leisure, because there seems to be some likelihood that a percentage of the population may have to be paid to be idle (i.e., the types of work as we know it presently may not be sufficiently available). And yet those who are brighter and more energetic, and who desire responsibility, recognition, and power, will seemingly gain such rewards only through work. Where does education for the best use of leisure fit into this picture?

Progress in Education. At present there are upwards of 90 million young people enrolled at some level of the vast education system, along with more than 30 percent of the total population engaged similarly in Canada. More than 100 billion dollars is spent annually in the United States alone to finance this gigantic enterprise. The enormity of the structure is staggering and almost incomprehensible to any one individual or group. Of course, debate about what should comprise a fine education is entirely healthy. Naturally enough, many of the same questions raised today have been asked and debated since so-called educational progress began: How can we determine what is indeed a good education. That is, what criteria shall we employ? How should present educational practice be modified? What type of environment should be provided to guarantee the best educational outcome? And, specifically, what is the function of the school?

Throughout the course of history until the golden age of Greece, a good education had been based on the transmission of the cultural heritage and the society's particular methods of survival. The Greeks, however, became so prosperous that for the first time it was possible for a relatively few, at least, to depart from previous educational norms. Plato proposed an educational scheme in The Republic in which the Greeks might look forward to an ideal society. But the populace was not ready to try to put this utopian scheme into practice, or even to accept Socrates' critical approach to current educational practice. Plato's best-known pupil, the great Aristotle, took sides against his master in this respect. In his Politics he called for an educational pattern conforming to the actual political state in existence.

Throughout the Roman Empire and the Middle Ages such practices continued, despite the fact that from time to time certain educational theorists offered proposals of greater or lesser radical quality. Thus, when a society declined, those involved in the educational system had no idea about societal rejuvenation and were in no position to be of significant assistance. During the Renaissance, however, new ideas and practices developed outside the traditional educational pattern. Then, later, after humanism had made itself a strong force and had brought about the introduction of a special school to foster its spirit, the introduction of science into the curriculum faced the same barriers all over again.

As the late John Brubacher, a leading educational historian, pointed out, this pattern continued in the 18th through the 20th centuries as political and economic revolutions took place (1966, pp. 584-87). The school always played "the secondary rather than the primary role . . . in periods of social transition." This was true in the French Revolution, the American Revolution, the Industrial Revolution in England, the Russian Revolution, and the several upheavals in Germany and Italy-- to even a great degree. It even continued in the so-called period of progressive education in the United States in the 20th century. All of which leads to the conclusion that political leaders have never in world history viewed the school as an agent of social reconstruction.

Yet in modern history there have been a number of educators who believed strongly that the school was not living up to its potential in the preparation of the young for future leadership roles. Such people as the Marquis de Condorcet, Adrien Helvetius, Immanuel Kant, Jean Jacques Rousseau, Johann Pestalozzi, Wilhelm Froebel, Horace Mann, John Dewey, George S. Counts, and Theodore Brameld have seen the need for the schools to serve a more creative function--to provide young people with the knowledge, understanding, and attitudes whereby they could more effectively lead the way. Such an approach would require great understanding on the part of an enlightened citizenry and complete academic freedom. The most controversial of issues would be the order of the day in such a school environment, and infinitely greater respect and confidence would have to be accorded to the teaching profession. This is not to say, of course, that great progress has not been made in regard to the matter of academic freedom. However, such freedom has been gained for the most part at great personal loss to individual teachers who led the way.

The question whether our educational institutions have made progress insofar as quantity and quality are concerned must be considered briefly. The almost self-evident answer is "yes," even in those countries that have not provided educational opportunities for more than a selected minority. In the United States from 40 to 50 percent are presently going on to some form of higher education. In the United States, there are those who contend that it is wrong to have approximately five "levels" of higher education ranging from community colleges to the select Ivy

League-type of institution. When this question is raised, the emphasis in the discussion necessarily shifts from quantity to quality--to a degree at least. With societies changing their economies, and often their political regimes, from one type to another, the body of knowledge has grown and the curriculum has expanded immeasurably. Knowledge about the teaching and the learning processes has also expanded, but not to the same measure. The cost of new facilities and equipment now comprises more than half of the community's operational budget. In the final analysis, the taxpayer is called upon to make crucial decisions.

Even with all this advancement there are typically many who are not satisfied with the quality of education being offered to our young people. As these words are being written, for example, there is a significant hue and cry about the need to improve the learning environment so higher standardized test scores will result. The complainants' main argument is that the school's end product is not the most "desirable." Enter the question of educational philosophy! The matter is so simple, yet so complex--determining a hierarchy of educational values is almost unbelievably difficult in a pluralistic society such as ours. As encouraged as we might be by the fact that the individual counts for more in the United States today than perhaps ever before in human history, for example, we are still confronted by the ever-present struggle between what has been called traditionally educational essentialism and educational progressivism. The one thing that we can really be thankful for is that our type of society allows us the freedom for such continuing debate.

The Need for Consensus. A determination of qualitative progress would depend upon the extent to which educational practice approximated a particular philosophical ideal. Therefore, your personal decision about progress that our field may have made in solving the specific persistent problems enumerated in this volume cannot help but be highly subjective. Your personal evaluation should be based on the philosophical tendency or stance to which you subscribe. Naturally it will be conditioned by your personal background and experiences--including the scientific evidence available--that have caused you to develop a set of attitudes. Professional maturity depends upon a sound philosophical base.

Philosophical investigation of a metaphysical, normative, and analytical nature over the past 50 years within this and related fields has convinced me of the vital importance of a continuing search for, and the possibility of, consensus among the conflicting philosophies of physical education and sport in the Western world. Frankly, we have been proceeding amoeba-like for so long with our own biased and eclectic statements of philosophical position that almost any attempt to delineate our individual positions represents a vast improvement. Philosophical ineptitude is actually characteristic of the large majority of practitioners in the educational world. These words are not meant to be overly critical of any one individual or group of individuals--only those "sport philosophers" who have denigrated the wisdom of so-called amateur philosophizing by professional practitioners and who thereby discourage any efforts along these lines unless unless they conform to the practices of the analytic movement only.

As a result, the difficulty of achieving consensus is now more complex than ever. However, I have come full circle in my opinion about whether the American Alliance for Health, Physical Education, Recreation, and Dance can hope to achieve true consensus by the conferences that are held periodically. I now believe that we have no choice but to proceed on this basis and work for consensus on controversial issues and problems. I say this even though these groups usually contain a significantly higher percentage of progressivists than essentialists. The result is that, although the outcome is largely predetermined, the chances of implementing the recommendations back on the home front are typically slim. Nevertheless, these reports do provide the practitioner with ammunition to do battle with more conservative elements on the local level.

We are fortunate that there is more agreement in practice than in theory among the conflicting positions. From another standpoint, also, a certain amount of agreement in theory is required in order to disagree. To make any progress there must be agreement on the issues and on an interpretation of the rules for debate.

There are actually a number of methods available by which greater consensus can be achieved. A formidable task, but perhaps not an impossible one, is to attempt to break down communications barriers. The study of semantics, the language analysis movement in philosophy, and the developing social science of management or organizational behavior should help expedite this matter. The development of a truly international language (which English seems somehow to be becoming), one taught in all countries in conjunction with the mother tongue, would be an enormous aid to communication as well.

It is interesting and important to note that there are some common presuppositions among the various conflicting philosophical stances about education. In fact, there are definite points of agreement, as well as large areas in which many points are somewhat similar and often overlapping. In the field of education, for example, some of the areas of practical agreement are that (1) the safety of the child is basic; (2) the school has the responsibility to provide a health service unit; (3) teachers need a certain educational background and experience; (4) boys and girls should be educated for at least a specific period of time; and (5) there are certain cardinal principles of education. Statements explaining principles such as these have been published regularly by the National Education Association of the United States. The development of the ability has been continually reaffirmed as a central purpose of education.

The extent of class involvement in the discussion of controversial issues is one area where there is a difference of opinion. Many would argue that students should be free to arrive at a solution, but it is recognized that they will have to be careful in many situations about how they express themselves in certain areas of politics, religion, or problems of a particular social nature. It could be stated further that study of racial heritage ought to be the common heritage of all, but the difficulty comes when we get down to the specifics of how much race experience should be included in the curriculum, or what should be emphasized, or how it should be taught. And so it goes as increasingly less consensus is apparent.

Possible Common Denominators. What common denominators may be found--or perhaps should be found--in physical education and educational sport and, to an extent, in health and safety education? Can these "denominators" be expressed as standards. The answer to this question might be as follows:

1. What a desired level of physical vigor and fitness is.
2. Whether we believe that a reasonably standardized program of sport and physical education should be required and, if so, to what educational level.
3. What attitudes toward health and ecological problems are needed for survival and, further, for optimal living.
4. What developmental physical activity is desirable in relation to other leisure activities.
5. Who is responsible, and to what extent, for therapeutic exercise for remediable physical defects.
6. What type of competitive sport experience is desirable for both sexes.

7. To what extent sport and developmental physical
   activity can contribute to character and
   personality development (Zeigler, 2003)

Having stated these possible common denominators that should be expressed as professional standards, it would appear that the time for consensus on what it is that we do and to what extent we do it is long overdue.

The potentialities for pure and applied research in developmental physical activity in sport, exercise, and related expressive activities are limitless. The unique nature of the field, and its role throughout people's lives in all aspects of society, relates to:

(1) the field's background, meaning, and intercultural
    significance;
(2) the functional effects of physical activity;
(3) the socio-cultural and behavioral aspects;
(4) motor learning and development;
(5) mechanical and muscular analysis of motor skills;
(6) management theory and practice;
(7) program development, including curriculum and
    instructional methodology; and
(8) measurement and evaluation (Zeigler, 1982a, p. vii)

Accordingly we have our related disciplines in the humanities, social sciences, and natural sciences (e.g., philosophy, psychology, and physiology, respectively). To achieve our long-range goals as a field that is quasi-professional and quasi-disciplinary, we need help from these related disciplines and our allied professions (e.g., health and safety education). However, we also must have our own fully qualified researchers, people who possess what I call "physical educator and educational sport hearts." By that I mean people with professional preparation in physical education and sport, with sound ancillary or supplementary backgrounds in one of the related disciplines, with an understanding of research methods and techniques as they might apply to our field's problems, and who in the final analysis are really interested in this field and its future. Many more bright, idealistic young people should seek admittance to our professional programs, while at the same time we should concurrently improve the quality of these programs at both the undergraduate and graduate levels. Time is running short!

The United States. In concluding we can say that the field of physical education and educational sport within education has often been buffeted by prevailing social forces. We have rarely witnessed significant change from within. Today we have reached a point where we would be well-advised to continue with diligence a search for increasing consensus among the conflicting philosophical stances and positions extant today. The profession--to the extent that it is one and not simply a "partner" within the profession of education--has been proceeding amoeba-like for far too long. I say this considering the body of knowledge that has been amassed concerning the effects of regular, purposeful physical activity. Other specialized groups are encroaching on what was traditionally regarded as the responsibility of physical education and educational sport. The 21st century will undoubtedly be a crucial era for the field.

REFERENCES AND BIBLIOGRAPHY

American Alliance for Health, Physical Education, Recreation and Dance (1962) *Professional preparation in health education, physical education, recreation education.* Report of national conference. Washington, DC: Author.

American Alliance for Health, Physical Education, Recreation and Dance. (1974). *Professional preparation in dance, physical education, recreation education, safety education, and school health education.* Report on national conference. Washington, DC: Author.

Ballou, R.B. (1965). *An analysis of the writings of selected church fathers to A.D. 394 to reveal attitudes regarding physical activity.* Unpublished doctoral dissertation, University of Oregon.

Bennett, B.L. (1962). Religion and physical education. Paper presented at the Cincinnati Convention of the AAHPER, April 10.

Bereday, G.Z.F. (1964). *Comparative method in education* (pp. 11-27). New York: Holt, Rinehart and Winston.

Bereday, G.Z.F. (1969). Reflections on comparative methodology in education, 1964-1966. In M.A. Eckstein & H.J. Noah (Eds.), *Scientific investigations in comparative education* (pp. 3-24). New York: Macmillan.

Berelson, B. & Steiner, G.A. (1964). *Human behavior.* New York: Harcourt Brace Jovanovich.

Bookwalter, K.W., & Bookwalter, C.W. (1980). *A review of thirty years of selected research on undergraduate professional preparation physical education programs in the United States.* Unionville, IN: Author.

Brubacher, J.S. (1966). *A history of the problems of education* (2nd ed.). New York: McGraw-Hill.

Brubacher, J.S. (1969). *Modern philosophies of education* (4th ed.). New York: McGraw-Hill.

Bury, J.B. (1955). *The idea of progress.* New York: Dover.

Butts, R.F. (1947). *A cultural history of education.* New York: McGraw-Hill.

Canadian Association for Health, Physical Education and Recreation. (1966). *Physical education and athletics in Canadian universities and colleges* (pp. 14-21). Ottawa: Author.

Champion, S.G. & Short, D. (1951). *Readings from the world religions.* Boston: Beacon.

Commager, H.S. (1961). A quarter century--Its advances. *Look,* 25, 10 (June 6), 80-91.

Conant, J.B. (1963). *The education of American teachers* (pp. 122-123). New York: McGraw-Hill.

Cosentino, F. & Howell, M.L. (1971). *A history of physical education in Canada.* Don Mills, Ont.: General Publishing Co.

Cowell, C.C. (1960). The contributions of physical activity to social development. *Research Quarterly,* 31, 2 (May, Part II), 286-306.

Durant, W. & Durant, A. (1968). *The lessons of history.* New York: Dover.

Elliott, R. (1927). *The organization of professional training in physical education in state universities.* New York: Columbia Teachers College.

Flath, A.W. (1964). *A history of relations between the National Collegiate Athletic Association and the Amateur Athletic Union of the United States (1905-1963).* Champaign, IL: Stipes. (Includes a Foreword by E.F. Zeigler titled Amateurism, semiprofessionalism, and professionalism in sport: A persistent historical problem.)

Fraleigh, W.P. (1970). Theory and design of philosophic research in physical education. *Proceedings of the National College Physical Education Association for Men,* Portland, OR, Dec. 28.

Glassford, R.G. (1970) *Application of a theory of games to the transitional Eskimo culture.* Unpublished doctoral dissertation, University of Illinois, Urbana.

Good, C.F., & Scates, D.E. (1954). *Methods of research* (pp. 255-268). New York: Appleton-Century-Crofts.

Gross, B.M. (1964). *The managing of organizations.* 2 vols. New York: Crowell-Collier.

Hayes, C. (1961). *Nationalism: A religion.* New York: Macmillan.

Heilbroner, R.L. (1960). *The future as history.* New York: Harper & Row.

Hershkovits, M.J. (1955). *Cultural anthropology* (pp. 33-85). New York: Knopf.

Johnson, H.M. (1969). The relevance of the theory of action to historians. *Social Science Quarterly,* (June), 46-58.

Kennedy, J.F. (1958). Address by the President in Detroit, Michigan. (At that time he was a U.S. Senator.)

Kennedy, P. (1987). *The rise and fall of the great powers.* NY: Random House.

Kennedy, W.F. (1955). *Health, physical education, and recreation in Canada: A history of professional preparation.* Unpublished doctoral dissertation, Teachers College, Columbia University.

Lauwerys, J.A. (1959) The philosophical approach to comparative education. *International Review of Education,* V, 283-290.

LaZerte, M.E. (1950). *Teacher education in Canada.* Toronto: W.J. Gage.

Leonard, F.E., & Affleck G.B. (1947). *The history of physical education* (3rd ed.). Philadelphia: Lea & Febiger.

Lipset. S. M. (1973). National character. In D. Koulack & D. Perlman (Eds.), *Readings in social psychology: Focus on Canada.* Toronto: Wiley.

Marrou, H.I. (1964). *A history of education in antiquity.* Trans. George Lamb. New York: New American Library.

McIntosh, P.C. et al. (1957). *History of physical education.* London: Routledge & Kegan Paul.

Martens, Rainer. (1971). Demand characteristics and experimenter bias. Paper presented at the AAHPER Convention, Detroit, April 5.

Martens, Rainer. (1970). A social psychology of physical activity. *Quest,* 14 (June), 8-17.

Meagher, J.W. (1958). *A projected plan for the re-organization of physical education teacher-training programs in Canada.* Unpublished doctoral dissertation, Pennsylvania State University.

Meagher, J.W. (1965). Professional preparation. In M.L. Van Vliet (Ed.), *Physical Education in Canada* (pp. 64-81). Scarborough, Ont.: Prentice-Hall of Canada.

Mergen, Francois. (1970). Man and his environment. *Yale Alumni Magazine,* XXXIII, 8 (May), 36-37.

Morris, V.C. (1956). Physical education and the philosophy of education. *Journal of Health, Physical Education and Recreation,* (March), 21-22, 30-31.

Morrow, L.D. (1975). *Selected topics in the history of physical education in Ontario: From Dr. Egerton Ryerson to the Strathcona Trust (1844-1939).* Unpublished doctoral dissertation, The University of Alberta.

Muller, H.J. (1954). *The uses of the past.* New York: New American Library.

Murray, B.G. Jr. (1972). What the ecologists can teach the economists. *The New York Times Magazine,* December 10, 38-39, 64-65, 70, 72.

Nevins, A. (1962). *The gateway to history.* Garden City, NY: Doubleday.

Nevins, A. (1968). The explosive excitement of history. *Saturday Review,* April 6.

Paton, G.A. (1975). The historical background and present status of Canadian physical education. In E.F. Zeigler (Ed.), *A history of physical education and sport in the United States and Canada* (pp. 441-443). Champaign, IL: Stipes.

Proceedings of the 6th Commonwealth Conference. (1978). *Sport, physical education, recreation proceedings* (Vols. 1 and 2). Edmonton, Alberta: University of Alberta.

Reisner, E.H. (1925). *Nationalism and education since 1789.* New York: Macmillan.

Roberts, J.M. & Sutton-Smith, B. (1962). Child training and game involvement. *Ethnology, 1.*

Royce, J.R. (1964). Paths to knowledge. In *The encapsulated man.* Princeton, NJ: Van Nostrand.

Sigerist, H.E. (1956). *Landmarks in the history of hygiene.* London: Oxford University Press.

Simpson, G.G. (1949). *The meaning of evolution.* New Haven & London: Yale University Press.

Van Vliet, M.L. (Ed.). (1965). *Physical education in Canada.* Scarborough, Ontario: Prentice-Hall.

Von Neumann, J. & Morgenstern, O. (1947). *The theory of games and economic behavior.* (2nd ed.). Princeton: Princeton University Press.

Williams, J. Paul. (1952). *What Americans believe and how they worship.* New York: Harper & Row.

Woody, T. (1949). *Life and education in early societies.* New York: Macmillan.

Zeigler, E.F. (1951). *A history of undergraduate professional preparation in physical education in the United States, 1861-1948.* Eugene, OR: Oregon Microfiche.

Zeigler, E.F. (1962). A history of professional preparation for physical education in the United States (1861-1961). In *Professional preparation in health education, physical education, and recreation education* (116-133). Washington,, DC: The American Association for Health, Physical Education, and Recreation.

Zeigler, E.F. (1964). *Philosophical foundations for physical, health, and recreation education.* Englewood Cliffs, NJ: Prentice-Hall.

Zeigler, E.F. (1965). *A brief introduction to the philosophy of religion.* Champaign, IL: Stipes.

Zeigler, E.F. (1968). *Problems in the history and philosophy of physical education and sport.* Englewood Cliffs, NJ: Prentice-Hall.

Zeigler, E.F. (Ed. & Au.)). (1973). *A history of physical education and sport to 1900.* Champaign, IL: Stipes.

Zeigler, E.F. (1975). Historical perspective on contrasting philosophies of professional preparation for physical education in the United States. In *Personalizing physical education and sport philosophy* (pp. 325-347). Champaign, IL:

Stipes.

Zeigler, E.F. (Ed. & Au.). (1975). *A history of physical education and sport in the United States and Canada.* Champaign, IL: Stipes.

Zeigler, E.F. (Ed. & Au.). (1979). *A history of physical education and sport.* Englewood Cliffs, NJ: Prentice-Hall.   (A revised edition of this work was published in 1988.)

Zeigler, E.F. (1980). An evolving Canadian tradition in the new world of physical education and sport. In S.A. Davidson & P. Blackstock (Eds.), *The R. Tait McKenzie Addresses* (pp. 53-62). Ottawa, Canada: Canadian Association for Health, Physical Education and Recreation.

Zeigler, E.F. (1986). Undergraduate professional preparation in physical education, 1960-1985. *The Physical Educator,* 43(1), 2-6.

Zeigler, E.F. (1988). A comparative analysis of undergraduate professional preparation in physical education in the United States and Canada. In Broom, E., Clumpner, R., Pendleton, B., & Pooley, C. (Eds.), *Comparative physical education and sport, Volume 5.* Champaign, IL: Human Kinetics.

Zeigler, E.F. (1988). (Ed. & Au.) *History of physical education and sport. (Rev. ed.).* Champaign, IL: Stipes. (See the excellent chapter on U.S. physical education and sport by R.K. Barney, pp. 173-219.)

CHAPTER IV

AN HISTORICAL ANALYSIS
OF
UNDERGRADUATE PROFESSIONAL PREPARATION
FOR PHYSICAL EDUCATION IN AMERICA (1861-1961)

Although professional training had its origins in antiquity, professional preparation of teachers is a relatively recent innovation. In early times the most important qualification for the teacher was a sound knowledge of the subject, an essential which is once again being reiterated today. In the Middle Ages there was no such thing as professional education to be a teacher, at least in the sense that certification is needed today to teach in most public institutions. In Prussia (early Germany), much headway was made in improving teacher education in the late 18th and early 19th centuries, and this system was copied extensively elsewhere. Significant advances in the theory of pedagogy occurred through the influence of Pestalozzi. In the United States, for example, the "normal school" became a well-established part of the educational system. In the 20th century this type of school progressed to college and university status. Professional education eventually achieved status at the university level as a subject to be taught--but interestingly not within the general education aspect of a university curriculum. Also, university-level teachers are not required to take a certain number of courses in it--a number that varies from state to state or province to province) as are those who wish to teach at earlier educational levels.

Generally speaking throughout the world, professional training to prepare for the teaching of physical education has been offered at the normal and/or technical school level. University recognition at the undergraduate level was achieved in the United States, however, with the first doctoral degrees being awarded in 1924. Developments at this highest level began in both the Federal Republic of Germany and Great Britain in the 1970s (although Germany had a degree program briefly before World War II). Japan has made significant progress in the field of physical education and now does award the doctoral degree in physical education at several universities (e.g., Tsukuba University). There has been an extensive development along these lines in the Soviet Union and several other formerly USSR communist countries.

The years from 1830 to 1860 were sometimes called the "Architectural Period" of American public education. It was during this period that the struggle for state-supported school took place. The problems of getting tax support, of eliminating the pauper-school idea, and doing away with pro-rated tuitions were all difficult in themselves to solve. Other major problems of the period included the elimination of sectarianism as a controlling factor in the schools and getting public officials appointed to run school affairs.

However, by 1860 the American educational ladder as a one-way system was fairly complete. The first compulsory school-attendance law was passed in Massachusetts in 1852. With this development of the public school system, it was quite natural that attention turned to the type and quality of teacher hired for so important a task as the education of the coming generation.

SCHOOL PHYSICAL EDUCATION IN THE U.S.A.

The history of physical education in the United States may be divided into four relatively distinct periods: (1) the Colonial Period from 1609 to 1781; (2) the Provincial Period from 1781 to 1885; (3) (the Period of the Waning of European Influence; and (4) the Period of American Physical Education from 1918 on (Schwendener, 1942).

In the field of physical education in this so-called Provincial Period, gymnastics was introduced at the Round Hill School in Northampton, MA in 1823. Next physical training was introduced as one of a number of innovations in the school curriculum of New York City in 1825. Harvard College started the first American college gymnasium in 1826. Not to be outdone, Yale followed Harvard's lead and established grounds for gymnastics during the same year. One year later Amherst, Brown, and Williams developed such areas as well, also. However, because competent instructors were not available to carry out the aims of this type of physical training, the whole movement quickly waned a few years after its beginning (Van Dalen, Bennett, and Mitchell, 1953).

Although physical education was generally not yet part of the school curriculum, interest was developing in exercise and recreation. Many elementary schools were springing up in the newer parts of the country, and the older public schools in the eastern and middle states were being greatly improved in both organization and administration. Insofar as hygiene and health instruction were concerned, some early educators showed an interest in the health and comfort of their students. There were many articles and resolutions in the literature of the time discussing physical education in the sense of personal and school hygiene. This resulted in the publication of a number of textbooks of physiology as well as many manuals describing calisthenics.

THE PERIOD FROM 1860 TO 1890

Difficult days were in store for the American people after the Civil War, a conflict that had wrought a tremendous change in the life of the entire country. Industrial capitalism became increasingly powerful, and the nation's population doubled rapidly. However, it wasn't very long before rampant, unbridled capitalism created a situation where most of the wealth reside in the hands of the few.

As urban society developed, it was natural that a greater interest in social affairs would appear. Polite society began to show a growing interest in music and literature, but the majority of the people had yet to acquire an understanding of the aesthetic as there had been relatively few art galleries and museums established. The architecture of the period could be described as eclectic. Orthodox religion was still a strong social influence despite the fact that the theory of evolution had become common knowledge to the more educated. In the realm of philosophy, pragmatism challenged more traditional philosophic thought.

There was evidence of considerable life and vigor in the colleges and universities of the time in the areas of sport and gymnastics. Athletic clubs and associations of all types started. This development caused a subsequent increase in newspaper publicity. Harvard, Yale, and Amherst erected new gymnasia in 1860, and their example was followed extensively by other institutions after the close of the War.

In education the idea of equality of educational opportunity had made significant strides. The educational ladder was gradually extending upwards, For example, there was a fivefold increase in the number of high schools between 1870 and 1890. The state eventually assumed the primary role with accompanying responsibility for public education. Developing state universities turned their attention to advancing the welfare of their own states with a resultant increase in their revenues and attendance. In 1888 President Eliot of Harvard felt the time had come to call for educational reform. One of his main points was that there was a need for better training of teachers.

In the area of general teacher training, improvement in the status of teachers came slowly in this period. Many state normal schools started at this time and were soon well distributed over the country as a whole. Although the facilities and courses of instruction were poor at first, there had been a gradual improvement down through the years. Professional courses of the time were not too effectual, mainly because scientific method in educational research was still at a low level. Similarly there was a rapid growth of city normal schools and classes, but the normal departments of these institutions were quite inadequate by present standards. It wasn't until after 1879 that so-called departments of pedagogy began to spring up with the aim of developing qualified secondary school teachers. However, a demand for these people was not yet present to a large degree.

However, there was some growth in the area of in-service teacher education at this time. By 1890 such activities as reading circles, professional teachers' organizations and institutes, and summer schools and extension work were contributing to the gigantic task of raising the level of teachers in service.

In schools the main emphasis in hygiene centered around the environment provided for the students. Cleanliness and ventilation were primary concerns, and the increasing possibility of communicable disease was a most important consideration. In school health education a dull pedagogical system which, combined with the social taboos of the time, made progress very difficult. Medical science had not achieved the necessary status to overcome these difficulties. The American Public Health Association had only held its first meeting in 1872.

THE BEGINNING OF PROFESSIONAL PREPARATION FOR PHYSICAL EDUCATION

Professional preparation for physical education in the United States didn't start actually until the later years of what Schwendener (1942) identified as the Provincial Period in the history of physical education (1781-1885). The years from 1885-1918 was given the title the Period of the Waning of European Influence, and from 1918 on was called the Period of American Physical Education. So it was toward the end of this "Provincial Period," around 1860 that the gymnastic revival of 1860 grew out of the movement to disseminate knowledge of the laws of health (Hartwell, 1960, p. 750). Subsequently the desire grew to have these "laws" included in the program of school instruction. Dio (clesian) Lewis gave great impetus to this movement when he lectured before the American Institute of Instruction in Boston on August 21, 1860.

Lewis' Normal Institute of Physical Education was the first attempt to prepare teachers of physical education in the United States. The first course opened July 5, 1861 and ran for a ten-week period (Lewis, 1861, p. 663). Instruction was provided in anatomy, physiology, hygiene, and gymnastics. Special work was given explaining Ling's methods for treatment of chronic diseases. It was planned that each student would be able to use 200 different exercises by the end of the 10 weeks. Another feature was a type of student teaching with each participant having the opportunity to lead a small class. During the seven years of the school's existence, 421 men and women graduated (Eastman, 1891). These people met much of the demand for instructors in the "new gymnastics" that came first from New England cities, and later from all over the country.

The second such program began through the efforts of leaders in the societies of the North American Turnerbund. In 1856 the Turners at their convention in Pittsburgh, PA. actually recommended the inauguration of such a teacher-training school. However, for several reasons, including the outbreak of the Civil War, the normal school was not opened until November 22, 1866 in New York City with an enrollment of 19 men (Metzner, 1924). It was a traveling school and was conducted subsequently in Chicago, Milwaukee, and Indianapolis (Brosius, 1896, pp. 165-168).

The course offered by the Turnerbund included lectures on the history and aims of the German Turners. anatomy and esthetics in their relation to gymnastics, and first aid. Other course work included gymnastic nomenclature, the theory of the different gymnastic systems, and practical instruction with special attention to the training of boys and girls. By 1885 this curriculum had expanded to include the history and literature of physical training, a bit of the history of civilization, the essentials of physiology, some of the principles of education, and something about the German and English languages and literature. A little time was spent also on fencing and wrestling (Rathmann, 1886, pp. 22-27).

Although the first schools for the training of physical educators started in Boston and New York City, respectively, California was the first state in the United States to pass a statewide mandatory physical education provision in 1866. With the adoption of a new constitution in 1879, this provision was abolished. However, it is important to note that the worth of physical education was recognized as far west as early as the post-Civil War era (Degroot, 1940, pp. 63-65).

Very little information has been published about the early effort of the various state normal schools in training teachers of physical education. Although the beginnings seem unimpressive today, they are worthy of mention. The Mankato State Teachers College of Minnesota offered a type of teacher-training course in physical training in 1868. West Chester State Teachers College in Pennsylvania is said to have had a two-year normal course (a minor for a select group!) in physical training in 1871. However, the first gymnasium was not erected at West Chester until the early 1890's with Dr. & Mrs. Ehinger in charge (Bramwell and Hughes, 1894, pp. 130-131).

THE FIRST IMPORTANT DECADE (1980-1990)

Actually the first important decade in physical education, from many standpoints, was the period from 1880 to 1890. It was especially significant because so many sound teacher education programs were established. A growing conviction had developed that teachers of physical education needed to be carefully and thoroughly prepared for their work. Hartwell spoke of the measure of success attained by a few normal and training schools for the teaching of the principles and practice of physical education (Hartwell, 1899, p. 550).

In this connection he mentioned (1) Sargent's Normal School at Cambridge (1881); (2) Anderson's Normal School at Brooklyn (1886); (3) The Physical Department of the International Young Men's Christian Association Training School at Springfield, Mass. (1887?); (4) The Boston Normal School of Gymnastics (1889); and (5) the Posse Normal School of Boston (1890)--as well as the Turnlehrer Seminar in Milwaukee (discussed previously above). Each of these schools, at the time of Hartwell's report, offered a course of theoretical and practical work that extended for two years. There were summer schools as well; especially prominent were those of (1) the American Gymnastic Union (Turners), (2) the Chautauqua School of Physical Education (1886), (3) the Harvard Summer School of Physical Training (1887), and (4) the summer course of the International Young Men's Christian Association Training School (later named Springfield College).

In considering the the first normal school mentioned above, for example, the Corporation of Harvard College had appointed Dudley Allen Sargent, M.D., as director of the recently completed Hemenway Gymnasium and assistant professor of physical training in 1879 (Van Dalen et al., 1953, p. 392). Two years later Sargent began to train teachers of physical training. Oddly enough, this did not take place with men or with Harvard College. The beginning was in the "sanatory

Gymnasium" opened for the benefit the young women studying in the "Harvard annex," which is now called Radcliffe College. From 1882 until 1904 a total of 261 women completed the regular course in theory and practice.

A prominent early leader. Delphine Hanna, closed out her own program of studies at Sargent's Normal School and went to teach at Oberlin College in Ohio. She is reported as taking with her a deep conviction that the teaching of gymnastics should be founded in science with resultant genuine body-building. Her first teacher-training courses in physical education began at Oberlin in 1866 (Zeigler, 1950, p. 40). Although Luther Halsey Gulick, later of Springfield College. had known her but a short time, her friendship and influence became the determining spark of his life. He left Oberlin right away to study under Sargent in Boston.

The developing interest in physical education resulted in the founding of the Association for the Advancement of Physical Education at Adelphi Academy, Brooklyn, NY on Nov. 15, 1885. William G. Anderson, M.D., later under of what was eventually called Arnold College, and also Director of the early Yale Gymnasium, had the inspiration to start the organization that added the word "American" to its title in the following year. This is the professional group that is today designated as the American Alliance for Health, Physical Education, Recreation, and Dance. Among those present at this first meeting were Anderson, Sargent, Edward Hitchcock of Amherst College, William Blaikie (author of How to Get Strong), Dio Lewis, R.J. Roberts (later of Springfield College), W.L. Savage (found of another training school), J.W. Seaver of Yale, and other interested people making a total of sixty (Proceedings of the AAPE, 1885, pp. 2-3). The succeeding meetings of this group until 1890 were characterized by reports from various members of the Association. The topics of these reports ranged from a discussion of military drill to the use of the sphygmograph (Leonard, 1915, p. 115).

The problem of special certification for the teaching of individual subject-matters arose after the Civil War as well. The early California school teachers, for example, taught all subjects. In 1881 the California State Board of Education legalized the issuance of the first special subject certificates in city high schools. It was under such provisions that a number of cities there first employed special teachers of physical education. It wasn't until later that California adopted the policy of accrediting properly qualified institutions to prepare and recommend their own graduates for teaching credentials (Degroot, 1940, pp. 436-437).

Carl Betz proposed the introduction of physical education into the public schools of Kansas City in 1885, also. Betz, a graduate of the Normal School of the North American Gymnastic Union (NAGU), directed the work there during the next 13 years. Actually, in the period from 1886 to 1896, physical training was introduced into the public schools of many cities by graduates of the Turnerbund school. Whereas the Turnvereine were reported to have provided classes for 13, 161 boys and 3,888 girls of January, 1866, this figure doubled only two years later (Leonard, 1915, p. 115).

Another milestone in the history of physical education in this period was the organization of the historically noteworthy "Conference in the Interest of Physical Training" by Mrs. Mary Hemenway (and her colleague, Miss Homans). Four sessions were held in Boston on November 29-30, 1899 (Barrows, 1889), Several thousand interested persons attended these meeting that were presided over by William T. Harris, United States Commissioner of Education. Representatives of the various physical training systems extant at the time presented papers. For example, Heinrich Metzner. one of the first instructors in the Normal College of the American Gymnastic Union. discussed the German system of gymnastics. Baron Nils Posse explained the Swedish system's chief characteristics in the second session. This was followed by Edward Hitchcock's discussion of the essential principles for the direction of a college department of physical education and hygiene. The third session was highlighted by Dudley A. Sargent's presentation of the system of physical training that he was instituting at Harvard's Hemenway Gymnasium. It was reported that spirited discussion followed all four addresses.

THE PERIOD FROM 1890 TO 1920

Introduction. The standard of living made considerable progress during the period from 1890 to 1920. Although 20 percent of the population was foreign born, the culture was gradually becoming more Americanized in keeping with the "melting pot" concept. In the process both organized religion and education were finding it necessary to renew their claims for recognition and acceptance. In the case of religion the impact and validity of Darwin's theory of evolution was considerable. This had an effect on Sabbath observance generally.

In the field of general education of the public, American educators were becoming more critical of both the content of the curriculum as well as the methods of instruction employed. John Dewey led the way in socializing the school program more than had been possible previously. Since the programs offered were changing at all three educational levels, physical educators were struggling to find their field's place in the curriculum. Leaders such as Sargent, Hartwell, and Anderson gave continued impetus to the field's efforts.

By 1890 there was a variety of institutions offering preparation for teaching. There were the normal schools, either state or private; selected high schools that maintained classes to train teachers; and departments of pedagogy (or so-called normal departments) in certain colleges and universities. The normal school was a well-established part of the American school system by the end of the 19th century, The normal schools admitted students of secondary rank and usually scaled their offerings to the ability of the students. The program aimed to give command of elementary school subject-matter, academic secondary studies, and professional education work. This latter area included the history and science of education along with courses in methods. As it turned out, the normal school had become the main agency for preparing elementary school teachers. It was also entering the field of training teachers for secondary education. However, this move was not readily accepted by all, because the length and quality of the academic programs had to be raised. In 1890 it was the rare normal school program that extended beyond two years. Hence the eventual transformation of this institution to full collegiate status really only started at the beginning of the 20th century,

In this early period, teacher training in the colleges and universities was in most cases evidently no better than the normal school training. Over a period of time, chairs of pedagogy had been introduced to provide college level instruction for beginning teachers. Unfortunately these programs were almost completely theoretical in nature with no provision for practice teaching. It seems that the colleges and universities were uncertain about the role they should play in teacher education. Many of these institutions had traditionally neglected the technical phases of teaching since this subject was considered unscientific, and consequently unnecessary. [This belief still exists to a considerable extent in the minds of many college and university professors--especially those instructors who are not connected to departments or schools of professional education.] However, a demand for these services had come about because of the tremendous growth in the number of public high schools. By this time many normal schools devoted solely to producing "gymnastics teachers" had sprung up, but they could not solve the problem for long. Thus, with concern, certain colleges and universities authorized departments of physical training to offer teacher education courses in this decade from 1890 to 1900.

It was during this period that a number of different, but related, developments took place. For example, the Swedish gymnastics movement began. Organized camping for children and young people started, as did the playground movement in cities. Sports continued their rapid rise to popularity with a consequent lessening of interest in the more formal gymnastics. Such activities as golf, tennis, and handball were introduced. American football and baseball, as team games, enjoyed increasing popularity both as games to be played and as spectator sports. Basketball, invented in 1891 at Springfield College, was started on its way to achieving a high goal--the country's foremost indoor team sport.

Physical education, probably because of its supposedly non-academic nature, became identified with the movement that included vocational training and household arts in the school curriculum. Physical education could attribute a surge in interest in gymnastics because of the onset of the Spanish-American War. At the beginning of the 20th century, this position was strengthened by the impact of such leaders as Thomas Dennison Wood, Luther Halsey Gulick, and Clark Hetherington.

Entrance Requirements (1890-1920). Selective admission, guidance, and placement were unheard of in the period from 1861 to 1890. No mention was made of any entrance requirements in the programs of the normal school of the American Gymnastic Union or that of Oberlin College. The catalogue of the School of Christian Workers (Springfield College) did state that its course was open only to Christian young men who had already "shown some ability" (Catalogue of School for Christian Workers, 1886-1887). Also, at least a fair education in English was necessary, and business experience was desirable (but not absolutely essential).

However, from 1890 to 1920, a great change took place in the entrance requirements of the various schools, colleges, and universities offering professional training. Simply put, they were no longer vague and provincial. By 1910 most institutions specifically required that the applicant be a graduate of an approved high school, or at least be able to score satisfactorily in the required entrance subjects. Entrance requirements for the University of Wisconsin, which started a professional program in 1911, mentioned also the necessity of sound health, organic vigor, aptitude for a high degree of motor efficiency, and evidence of strong leadership (Catalogue, University of Wisconsin, 1911-1912).

Methods of Instruction (1890-1920). Important changes were evident, also, in regard to the aims and methods of the various curricula. In the 1890s some leaders were predicting great happenings for the future, even though the curricular aims were evidently only loosely formed. The general aim was simply to provide a normal course in physical training for persons interested in this "new crusade." In some instances, as in the case of the International Young Men's Christian Association Training School (later Springfield College), a distinct Christian emphasis was evident throughout this entire second period. The University of Wisconsin's stated aim was to train teachers of physical education and directors of playgrounds for service in educational institutions, clubs, playgrounds, and municipal recreation systems.

The methods employed in the programs continued to vary greatly in this second period with the influence of the foreign systems upon the United States' program waning considerably. Some leaders claimed that their teaching methodology was the "eclectic system," while others with pride clung to what they knew and appreciated the most.

Length of Programs (1890-1920). As stated above, the first course inaugurated in 1861 extended for a 10-week period with the student receiving a diploma upon successful completion of the experience. Approximately at the middle of the period from 1920 to 1961, the professional student in physical education/kinesiology (or some similar title) may be awarded the doctor of philosophy degree (Ph.D.) or the doctor of education degree (Ed.D.) upon successful completion of a program extending three years or more beyond the bachelor's degree. In a few instances the degree awarded is called the doctor of physical education degree (either P.E.D or D.P.E.).

In this period from 1890 to 1920, the length of the different undergraduate curricula varied greatly. From 1890 to 1900 the programs extended over a two-year period on the average with certain normal schools still offering a one-year program. Summer-course "wonders" were causing distress in some quarters, because they were taking positions on the strength on one or two six-week summer sessions. Springfield College, to cite one example, discontinued its summer course because many of these relatively inexperienced people were passing themselves off as "Springfield men."

It was in the final decade of the 19th century that a few of the four-year programs leading to baccalaureate degrees began. However, in the first decade of the new century four-year programs were introduced in all sections of the country. Teachers on the faculties of these institutions began to appear with various degrees, although many possessed only diplomas from one or another of the better-known normal schools of physical training. Perhaps the outstanding innovation of this era was the farsighted program introduced at Wellesley College after the Boston Normal School of Gymnastics had been transplanted to that campus. This program extended over a five-year period with the student receiving the traditional bachelor of arts degree at the end of four years, and then a certificate bespeaking competence in physical education after the successful completion of the fifth year.

Curriculum (1890-1920). During this period from 1890 to 1920, the subject-matter of the various curricula continued to expand. The normal courses were seemingly organized very well from the standpoint of emphasis in the sciences and also in the practice and theory of professional physical education. At Oberlin College, for example, no formal work whatsoever was given in professional education, but practice teaching was required of all in both college and local schools. Instruction in the "academic" courses was almost completely lacking before the baccalaureate degree course began. In another instance, because of its Christian sponsorship, the curriculum at Springfield College included a good amount of religious training over and above the usual courses of the period.

Around the turn of the century, the courses of study began to take on a broader aspect. In the final (second) year at the Boston Normal School of Gymnastics, professional courses in educational psychology and in the history of education were offered. In 1910 after the affiliation with Wellesley, the curriculum included a broad general education. The only professional education course offered in this curriculum was one called "Education and Physiology (for Physical Education students)." The Oberlin physical education curriculum was designed with a similar educational philosophy behind it. It too was extended to four years in 1898 and was quite extensive in scope since the A.B. degree was awarded upon graduation. The student received a diploma certifying the physical education specialization, also. No other courses in professional education were included at this time. Practical work in a variety of physical activities was required throughout the four years of study. Interestingly the University of Nebraska was the first state university to graduate a woman from a four-year major curriculum in 1900.

In 1911 the University of Wisconsin gave evidence that it was abreast of the most advanced thinking in the preparation of teachers in general, and physical education teachers in particular. A degree program was offered that extended over a four-year period. The curriculum was well rounded and included a reasonable distribution over the general academic, basic science, professional education, and professional physical education courses. Along with the theoretical work, a sound succession of practice courses was integrated into the overall curriculum. Both a major unit (40 credits) and a minor unit (14 credits) were available to interested students.

In summarizing curriculum development during this period, the academic program ranged from a one-year course of study, in one instance, to a quite well-rounded program extending over a five-year period--with the successful student in the latter instance receiving he A.B. degree at the end of the fourth year and a certificate in physical education at the end of the fifth year. The struggle for sound professional training for all prospective physical educators was far from over, of course, but it is possible to say that immeasurable progress had been made during the period from 1890 to 1920.

Faculty (1890-1920). The teachers in this new field gradually received more academic preparation and earned advanced degrees as time went by in the period from 1890 to 1920. It was common practice for the director of the normal school or department to hold the M.D. degree at the beginning of this period, but by the end of the second decade of the 20th century this practice had been changed dramatically. Typically, the director would gather about him either graduates holding diplomas from his own program or from other well-known normal schools of the time. Gulick, during his 14 years at Springfield College, practiced inbreeding to an extreme with his staff--but with good results seemingly. Sargent, of the Harvard Summer School of Physical Education, invoked a system whereby he made available to his students the best instruction to be found in the entire United States. To cite one case, Miss Homans of the Boston Normal School of Gymnastics (which later joined with Wellesley College) added six science courses to the curriculum in 1893. These courses were taken at the Massachusetts Institute of Technology and were taught by regular members of the Institute's faculty.

As the various programs grew and developed, it became necessary to add many new faculty members to the different departments and schools. It became increasingly important that these teachers have better preparation and hold baccalaureate degrees rather than just diplomas from two-year normal courses. Thus, it can be reported that teaching personnel during this period had grown from one in certain teacher education institutions to fifteen or twenty full-time and part-time instructors by 1920. The usual procedure had been for an institution to hire one person for this new "experimental" program. This person would then urge the school to hire an assistant of the opposite sex to work with students on that gender. The private normal schools and the summer schools followed the practice of engaging visiting professors or lecturers who were proficient in specialized areas of instruction. This lent prestige to the programs and also saved the expense of hiring permanent people, an expense they could ill afford.

To summarize, a tremendous growth took place during the period from 1890 to 1920 in the number of institutions offering professional preparation for teachers of physical education. Whereas seven private normal schools of physical education, several summer schools, and a small number of state normal schools, colleges, and universities had offered professional training from 1861 to 1890, the period from 1890 to 1920 witnessed the establishment of professional preparation programs of all types in all kinds of educational institutions. This was the period when the colleges and universities became aware of the great need for trained teachers in all fields, this mainly because of the growth of the American high school. All together approximately 175 training programs, ranging from 15 or twenty six-week summer courses to a five-year program granting a baccalaureate program and a certificate in physical education, began within this span of 30 years (Zeigler, 1850, p. 136).

THE PERIOD FROM 1920 TO 1961

Introduction. The years from 1920 to 1930 were filled with great changes in the way of life for many Americans. After a brief period of unemployment and depression in 1921-1922. the years immediately following were very prosperous. Education benefitted greatly from this as evidenced by building programs all over the country. The educational philosophy of John Dewey had considerable weight in determining a more child-centered aim for the educational curriculum in this decade. In general there was an increasing interest in individual development because in the field of psychology significant stress was placed on the psychology of individual differences. Testing and measurement assumed great importance in education as efforts were made to classify students in groups based on their abilities. By 1929 some 70% of the United States cities followed some form of homogeneous grouping.

A number of new types of experimental schools developed at this time with such names as The Dalton Plan, The Country Day School, the Child Center School, the Play School, the Winnetka Plan, and many others. California legislation reduced the number of elementary subjects in the curriculum from 27 to 15, with 12 prescribed and three optional. It is interesting to note that 85% of the public school teachers were women. The development of the junior high school movement (i.e., grades seven through nine) was rapid. Overall there were 16,000 public high schools established by 1925. From 1920 on the junior college movement grew rapidly in the western part of the country. Farther up the educational ladder the trend toward teachers' colleges--and away from the normal schools--became apparent. For those who may (or may not) have had the benefits of formal education, adult education activities were being sponsored increasingly. In 1926 the American Association for Adult Education was formed.

The trend toward equalization of educational opportunity was given further momentum by restrictions against child labor and a stronger set of laws about compulsory school attendance. Although it was pointed out that federal aid was necessary for full realization of America's educational ideal, such backing did not come to the extent desired by its proponents. After the stock market crash of 1929, and depression set in, college and university endowment funds were severely drained in many instances. Thus the need for increased public funding became much more significant for the successful operation of higher education.

After what some considered the excesses of the 1920s, a rather strong reaction against the aims of progressive education set in. Developing industry and technology were causing many educators to think of democracy in social rather than individual terms. The progressive school movement of the preceding decade was "reined in" to a degree by the influence of counteracting conservative opinion, but the ideal of education as a "social process" appeared to be increasingly acceptable to many. Experimental school experience, employing the term "conservatively progressive," often described innovations as "regard for the whole child." Teachers became more concerned with the development of attitudes and the importance of accompanying emotions. Curricula continued to expand bolstered by greater emphasis on "activity" or laboratory experience. Even though the matter of individual differences had become a concern in the 1920s, from the depression onward the social emphasis within formal education seemed assured. By way of contrast, President Robert M. Hutchins, of the University of Chicago, was concurrently organizing and administering what was to become known as the "aristocratic wing" of higher education.

Expanding Programs of Physical Education. In the period after the first World War and before the subsequent Global War, physical education found its scope increasing in many ways. Individual, dual, and team sports had been accepted almost universally, and various types of dance had become very popular too. Actually a considerable struggle was being waged between the proponents of an informal program of physical education as opposed to a more formal system.

Due in large measure to the changing American scene, and probably also to the greater functional aspects of the seemingly more natural program, the more formal systems continued to wane. The possibility of greater learning both direct and concomitant, the opportunities for use of such learning during leisure, and "cultural background" of the informal program made the battle very unequal.

It was at this time that a new idea appeared in connection with sports participation. The element of competition, long accepted for varsity squads, now became available on a modified scale for a larger number of students through the intramural athletic program. This additional phase, added to the concept of a total physical education program, grew faster in colleges and universities than it did at the high school level. Yet, although the idea found a favorable reception with both teachers and administrators at all levels of the educational system, unfortunately the necessary facilities and staff required had only slowly and marginally caught up with the impetus of the movement. Remedial or corrective physical education (also designated various as "therapeutic," "individual," "adapted," or "adaptive" physical education), aquatics and water safety, and health education were also recommended as being basic to the newer program. Still later, safety education, and then later driver education, were added to the responsibility of the field of physical education.

"Flushed" with the growth of the field's various added responsibilities, the financial depression of the early 1930s nevertheless brought a marked change to the field of physical education. Many schools actually discontinued the teaching of this subject, while others combined physical education teachers' duties with the teaching of other subjects with resultant overload to many teachers. Also, few new people were hired, and this soon resulted in an oversupply of physical education teachers. The only good that this produced was the careful revision of curricula of teacher-education institutions, as well as the raising of admission requirements. Several states also revised their certification requirements during this trying period. So the "bad" news also resulted in some "good news" as the caliber of teacher preparation improved to a degree.

The need for a broader cultural or general education for physical education teachers became apparent at this time as well. Although increased emphasis was placed on this phase of the major curriculum in some institutions, the field as a whole had not caught up. In 1934 Peik and Fitzgerald pointed out this deficiency in their analysis of the curricula of 21 universities and six colleges. Their conclusion was that "Physical education majors stood at the bottom of all teaching fields in the range and depth of their academic training" (1934, pp. 18-26). Since then there has been a continuing emphasis on the importance of a more sound general education along with a more thorough training in the foundation sciences and the professional physical education courses. Because of the expanding university curriculum generally, there was undoubtedly still room for improvement in this matter of "cultural heritage" in respect to all teachers including those preparing for the physical education field.

World War II and Its Aftermath. After the entry of the United States into World War II following the Japanese attack on Pearl harbor, the entire nation was soon mobilized. Federal funds were made available through the U.S. Office of Education to train military and defense workers in schools and colleges. Governmental subsidization actually brought many institutions through the war period. Obviously, an all-out effort was demanded to wage war successfully.

Physical training programs with a broader scope were initiated in the several branches of the armed forces. and there were improved rehabilitation programs for injured service men. Draft statistics again pointed up the need for improved programs of school health, physical education, and recreation. Since the beginning of what was called the "Cold War" about 1947, there was an increased emphasis on health and physical fitness that grew in intensity. Health programs improved considerably, and many leaders and other citizens recognized the need for leisure education n to meet society's growing problem of automation in industry.

The Korean War of the early 1950s also reemphasized the need for improved physical fitness of youth. Then in 1954 President Eisenhower heard about a set of "motor fitness" tests that were given to some American children with an accompanying comparison to a relatively small group of European children. Since he was shocked at the evident disparity of the results, he called a meeting in Washington, D.C. that resulted in a conference titled the President's Conference on Fitness of American Youth. One of the positive outcomes of this undertaking was the establishment of the President's Council on Physical Fitness and Sport (PCPFS), an office that is still in existence at the turn of the 21st century. One publication of this office is a highly useful quarterly newsletter titled Research Digest that keeps physical educators and coaches apprised on the latest research findings. This digest is co-authored by Drs. C.B. Corbin, R.P. Pangrazi, and B.D. Franks.

The American Association for Health, Physical Education, and Recreation (as it was then called), voice of more than 25,000 teachers in the profession, moved rapidly also after Mr. Eisenhower expressed his concern. From September 12-15, 1956 a National Conference on Fitness was held in Washington, D.C. At this meeting, after considerable preparation and with the help of its Research Council, the AAHPER sponsored a national youth fitness study under the direction of Dr. Paul A. Hunsicker, The University of Michigan. For the first time a reliable sampling of American youth was obtained, and a set of norms--not standards--was established in such tests as pull-ups (chins), sit-ups, and the 600-yd. run, to mention just a few. Some international comparisons with these United States' norms were made. and the evidence seemed to indicate that American youngsters were indeed deficient in many of these test items.

Immediately after his election in 1960, President John F. Kennedy published an article explaining his belief in the importance of physical fitness for youth. He followed this statement with action, and the President's Council guided itself by these words taken from a "Presidential Message to the Schools on the Physical Fitness of Youth":

> The strength of our democracy is no greater than
> the collective well-being of our people. The vigor of
> our country is no stronger than the vitality and
> will of all our countrymen. The level of physical, mental,
> moral, and spiritual fitness of every American citizen
> must be our constant concern.

> The need for increased attention to the physical fitness
> of our youth is clearly established. Although today's
> young people are fundamentally healthier than the
> youth of any previous generation, the majority have
> not developed strong, agile bodies. The softening process
> of our civilization continues to carry on its persistent
> erosion.

> It is of great importance, then, that we take immediate
> steps to ensure that every American child be given the
> opportunity to make and keep himself physically fit--fit to
> learn, fit to understand, to grow in grace and stature, to
> fully live (Kennedy, 1961, inside cover).

Following this directive, the American Association for Health, Physical Education, and Recreation started "Operation Youth Fitness" at this time.

Entrance Requirements (1920-1961). Returning to a consideration of one of the persistent problems in the history of undergraduate professional preparation for physical education (i.e., entrance requirements), it can be reported that it was during this period that the concept of selective admission, guidance, and placement originated during this period. By 1920 a "new plan" had been instituted at Wellesley College, for example, combining the best elements of the certificate of graduation system and of the examination system. Columbia Teachers College, as another example, had made some changes in its entrance requirements as follows: a student could be admitted by (1) examination of Columbia or the College Entrance Examination Board; (2) certificate from an approved secondary school including the diploma and the principal's statement about the requisite 15 units and his health, character, and general scholarship; or presenting credentials from the Education Department of the State of New York listing the approved entrance units. However, the need for teachers at this time (early 1920s) was so great that the admission procedures could often not be too strictly enforced.

Toward the end of the 1920s, the supply was beginning to catch up with the demand. The need for immediate raising of entrance requirements became apparent. Such qualifications as (1) background experience in athletics, (2) recommendations, (3) ability and proficiency tests, (4) an intelligence test, (5) a medical examination, and (6) a probationary period of one year was recommended for each prospective student (Neilson, 1930, p. 9). In 1933 the National Survey of the Education of Teachers report recommended that teacher-preparing institutions should agree on a set of principles. It was evident that research was needed to develop more accurate measuring instruments of teaching success. personal traits, and scholarship attainment. It was recommended further that "a progressive program of selection, admission, elimination, and final recommendation for teaching should begin with matriculation and carry through to certification" (Rugg. 1933, pp. 29-31).

By 1940 many colleges and universities had indeed showed a definite trend toward consolidation of entrance requirements in an effort to standardize the situation across the country. Springfield College, for example, selected 160 men each year who gave evidence of possessing the greatest promise for success. It was stated that admission officers obtained their evidence regarding the candidate from application forms, school officers, the examining physician, personal and character references, personal interviews, and aptitude tests. Of the 15 units still required for admission, nine had to be from English (3), history and social studies (2), algebra and plane geometry (2), and science (2), while four of the remaining six elective units could be in non-academic subjects (Springfield College Catalogue, 1940-42).

There was also a gradual tendency to include student guidance and subsequent placement, along with selective admission, as an important phase of the total preparation effort (Zeigler, 1951, p. 182). This approach seemed fundamental to the production of superior teachers of physical education. However, down to the present day there is still disagreement as to the most accurate bases upon which prospective teachers should be admitted because of the difficulty of securing valid criteria. A noticeable trend toward generalization of entrance requirements is readily apparent upon examination of college and university announcements from 1950 on. The lack of standardization for entrance into the physical education field appears to have been unfortunate (At this time in the subsequent hiring process, administrators were considering of prime importance such qualities as personal integrity and sincerity, moral influence over pupils, willingness to cooperate with superiors and associates, personal health and vigor, knowledge and understanding of the nature of pupils, initiative, and self-reliance [Graybeal, 1941, pp. 741-744].)

Curriculum (1920-1961). The aims, methods, and content of the various undergraduate curricula underwent many changes in the period from 1920 to 1961. Leaders in the teacher education area of physical education began to envisage the physical educator as a person of more professional stature (Hines, 1920, pp. 52-56). Initially, the results of the army draft medical examinations during World War I had come as a distinct shock to the American people. Because of this, legislation soon appeared for improved school health education, as well as for more physical education. Woods' strong leadership helped to bring the status of a special subject field to the teaching of health, knowledge that had previously been considered the same as that of physical education (Williams, 1927, pp. 330-340). Concurrently the "natural" program of physical education, as so admirably propounded in the 1920s by Wood and Williams, began to make itself felt, but not without a struggle and considerable misunderstanding in relation to the earlier more formal approach to physical training.

It can be argued further that a unique American philosophy of physical education was developing as well, and it gradually but steadily exerted its influence on teacher preparation in the field. Sports, athletics, and team games had been fostered strongly by the several war experiences. They were then laid at the door of the profession of physical education for better or worse. It was inevitable that these various developments within the field as a whole would soon make themselves felt in the various professional curricula.

During the period from 1920 to 1925 alone approximately 75 institutions started four-year degree programs in physical education, although some colleges still held out for a three-year course. As the field continued to broaden in scope, such programs gradually succumbed (Zeigler, 1950, p. 227). In 1926 statistics showed a definite trend away from medical training for those who would direct college programs in the field. There were two distinct types of physical directors in colleges: (1) those who administered intercollegiate athletics, and (2) those who were concerned with the required physical education program and the teacher preparation program. A tendency toward a centralized department including all aspects of field was becoming more evident (Metcalf, 1926, pp. 45-47).

The most prevalent specialized curriculum in physical education for men was that of athletic coaching! It was evidently felt that, due to the broadening scope of the field to include coaching of sports and health services, such an opportunity for specialization would help to fulfill the need for qualified men as directors of physical education, athletic coaching, and health education. On the other hand, professional preparation for women teachers was offered largely in separate departments. In this connection the Division of Girls and Women's Sports of the American Association for Health, Physical Education, and Recreation was exerting a strong and beneficial influence on professional preparation for women since its inception as the Standing Committee on Women's Athletics of the American Physical Education Association in 1916. This contribution ranged from the maintenance of high standards for the conduct of girls and women's sports to the development of sport guides and other publications relating to this area. Examination of the literature revealed a conflict between the philosophy of sport held by men and women in the field who had responsibilities for sport competition.

As early as 1925 a conference of institutions offering professional training in physical education was arranged by the United States Bureau of Education at which time the aims and objectives of professional training were discussed. Committees were appointed to consider various topics and then report at a future meeting. The second conference of the group of college and university personnel assembled in Washington, D.C. on March 30, 1927. The problem of the "coach" versus the "physical educator" came in for much discussion at the time. Some felt that one person could not be both an athletic coach and a physical educator at the same time. The majority opinion seemed to favor the idea of selling the concept of a broader physical education training--including all aspects of the field--to the professional schools in existence (U.S. Bureau of Education, 1927, pp. 38-41).

In a comprehensive doctoral study by Elliott--one of the first completed in the field in 1927--five "outstanding developments in professional training" were listed as follows: (1) the philosophy of physical education has undergone a change; (2) educators took the place of physicians as directors; (3) academic degrees are granted for major units in physical education; (4) specialized curricula in physical education are offered in schools of education; (5) the organization has become very complex (pp. 16-23). In the process of this investigation, however, Elliott found that many interesting problems presented themselves for further study:

1. An investigation of the qualifications and functions of the physical educator.
2. The need of a selective process in the admission of students to professional curricula that will not only determine mental and physical fitness, but personality and leadership qualifications as well.
3. The organization of a professional curriculum, with a greater freedom of election than is now in practice, which will provide the necessary and desirable professional preparation in physical education, as well as a cultural background.
4. The organization of courses, especially in the foundation sciences, anatomy, physiology, etc. that are adapted to satisfactorily meet the needs of students majoring in physical education.
5. Creating a standardized nomenclature in physical education.
6. Devising a means of coordinating the several department, schools and colleges that contribute to the professional curriculum.
7. The determination of the minimum essentials for the preparation of teachers.
8. The organization of graduate work in physical education for specialists, administrators, and directors of physical education (pp. 56-57).

At this time, also, leaders were urging the establishment of a standardized course nomenclature that they felt would result in progress toward a standardized curriculum. A committee, with J. H. McCurdy of Springfield College as chairman, was appointed to study the terminology and to construct a list of the most suitable generic terms for curricular subjects.

Those in attendance at the two successive conferences had also requested unanimously that a committee study the existing curricula in the field. After the death of the committee chair, W.P. Bowen of Michigan State Normal School in Ypsilanti, McCurdy was asked to take over the this committee too. This study group's report was published in 1929 (U. S. Bureau of Education, 1929). It gave detailed information about the hours required in all courses in each of 139 institutions. The study made clear that the terminology attached to courses often gave no idea of the course content. The committee also recommended a definite distribution of courses that totaled 136 semester hours.

An attempt to bring order into the existing situation originated within the profession itself. At a meeting of the Department of School Health and Physical Education of the National Education Association held in Los Angeles, CA in July, 1931, a resolution was passed authorizing the appointment of a national committee with N. P. Neilson (California) as chairman for the purpose of establishing standards to be used in evaluating teacher education institutions preparing health and physical education teachers. The entire problem was subdivided with subcommittees to recommend the following: (1) basic characteristics of the secondary school program, (2) general standards, (3) standards for selection of students to be trained, (4) course standards, (5) standards for staff, and (6) standards for facilities. In 1935 this National Committee Report on Standards was published in the Research Quarterly of the American Physical Education Association. The standards recommended by Sub-committee A4 (Course Standards) divided the courses comprising the total curriculum into basic areas, a plan that has been used extensively since that time for the classification of subject-matter necessary to prepare a physical education teacher adequately. These basic areas were: (1) academic courses required by the institution (other than foundation sciences), (2) foundation sciences required, (3) courses in general professional education required, and (4) courses in health and physical education required. A standard four-year curriculum was recommended. In addition, a complete seven-year program was listed (Neilson, 1935, pp. 48-68).

Other recommendations were being made during this period as well. For example, in 1934 a five-year integrated curriculum had been recommended, one in which general education, specialization in physical education, a second teaching field, thorough orientation in professional education and psychology, and training at the elementary school level was included. Another interesting recommendation was that of H.A. Scott, of the Rice Institute, who in 1935 urged the adoption of a unit plan of instruction as employed at his school. Basically he urged that techniques of scientific method should be employed to determine the nature of the professional curriculum in the future. Scott suggested further that the major student should be encouraged to start thinking professionally as soon as possible. He argued further that the nature and importance of the subject matter should determine the length of the unit, not the traditional semester and semester-hour format (Scott, 1935).

To summarize, those physical educators who administered the curricula of the various teacher-training programs in physical education began to realize that a gradual shift in emphasis had come about in relation to the place of the biological sciences in the curriculum (i.e., zoology and physiology). They were to be taught as tool subjects rather than as ends in themselves. Other leaders, such as J. F. Bovard, advised the revamping of the curriculum in the direction of a greater affiliation with the social sciences (Bovard, 1933).

Length of Curriculum (1920-1961). The various trends evident in relation to the aims and methods of the professional physical education curriculum were not peculiar to the overall field of health education, physical education, and recreation. The teachers colleges generally wished to provide adequate scholarship to the various other fields of the entire teaching profession. Requirements in professional education had been decreased slightly and had also been more carefully defined. A trend away from formal academic courses seemed to be developing with increases in functional courses stressing contemporary life. The professional objectives of teaching itself were becoming more clearly defined with a resultant increase in course prescription. Inasmuch as more inclusive, broader majors for specialization purposes were conceived, more time became necessary for the entire program. When the time elements involved under the different sub-curricula headings were totaled, it became obvious that teachers colleges were tending toward a five-year program for the realization of broad and adequate preparation of secondary school teachers (Sprague, 1940).

While this move for a five-year curriculum resulting in either a teaching credential or a master's degree had been gathering momentum with evident support from the experience of colleges and universities, there had also arisen a minority in in the field who inquired whether the lengthening of the curriculum would really provide the answer to the problem. Some felt that a new approach to the problem of the curriculum was needed. This group working within the structure of the College Physical Education Association recommended further experimentation. The plan recommended was first to improve what was being done currently--and then to lengthen the curriculum if necessary (Fredericks, 1938, p. 123).

Raising Standards. The Cooperative Study in Physical Education, sponsored by the American Council of Education from 1938 to 1943, devoted considerable time to the matter of procedures and conditions conducive to improved teacher education. Four basic conclusions of this study were:

> (1) Schools made most progress when there was a conscious and studied effort by the faculty to become more democratic in their relationships,
> (2) By and large, the most successful programs were those that started with problems that teachers believed important,
> (3) Teachers and administrators work together most effectively when they work on problems on which they can make progress, and
> (4) Adequate resources and materials should be available (Troyer, 1945, pp. 542, 582-584).

Although two major attempts to improve the quality of professional education in physical education had been to a certain degree unsuccessful, the objective was still not considered hopeless. National standards had not been realized, but further efforts were to be made. After the Global War was over, the College Physical Education Association revived an earlier Cooperative Study Committee of the American Association for Health, Physical Education, and Recreation that had been curtailed because of the War. The original idea had been to include representatives from the national association, the College Physical Education Association, the National Association of Directors of Physical Education for College Women, The City Administrative Directors Society, the Society of State Directors of Health and Physical Education, and others at the discretion of the committee and the president of the national association (AAHPER). This group established its purpose at the outset, but decided to take no definite stand on the question of ideal standards for teacher preparation. It decided that it would be unwise to try to rate institutions as has been recommended by the earlier national study in the 1930s. The main objective was to seek out "desirable practices" for teacher education institutions (Scott, 1947, pp. 97-101).

As a sign of the times, the organized teaching profession sent its leadership from all parts of the country to Miami University in Oxford, Ohio for the National

Conference on the Improvement of Teaching in 1947. In presenting a list of the desirable qualifications of a good teacher, twelve abilities, attributes, and understandings were listed which the excellent teacher should possess. In addition, a very high standard was set in regard to specialized professional training as well as in general education and in the personal and social qualities required (The NCTEPS, 1947, p. 51).

Still further, the American Association of Teachers Colleges completed an extensive study that called attention to the lack of a well-organized, overall program for the training of teachers. This was some consolation to the field of physical education, because it once again demonstrated that the criticism physical educators were leveling against themselves could actually be made about the teaching profession as a whole. Again the need for a broad background of general education was emphasized. It was stated that student teaching possibilities were not being fully utilized in many institutions. The charge was made also that many teacher education programs focused attention on preparing teachers as technicians to the exclusion of developing them as responsible society members. It was suggested that students need the opportunity to share to a greater extent in the development of plans to be used in their own guidance. Some students need more preparation along certain lines than others. Such factors as intelligence, mental and physical health, social development, and emotional maturity should be taken into consideration when programs for the individual are planned (AATC, 1948).

The "Jackson's Mill Conference" of 1948. The physical education field continued to make progress toward improving the aims and methods of teacher preparation. The Committee on Teacher Education of the College Physical Education Association (that became the NCPEAM and later NAPEHE) cooperated with 18 organizations in sponsoring and participating in the National Conference on Undergraduate Professional Preparation in Health Education, Physical Education, and Recreation held at Jackson's Mill, Weston, West Virginia in May, 1948. The Athletic Institute, located in Chicago, financed this important venture. This group of professionals reemphasized the necessity of a cultural background for successful teaching. It was asserted that many teachers of physical education entering the field without a "frame of reference" upon which to base their lives professionally and socially. It was generally accepted that this was true because many institutions were allowing their students to over-specialize. It was agreed that the exact amount of time required to produce a competent teacher will vary with individuals and with institutions. A general curriculum was considered essential. It was stressed further that competency in achieving the objectives of the curriculum should be the criterion for graduation rather than a definite number of years or a certain number of specific courses (Nat. Conf. on UPP in HPE&R, 1948}.

Those attending the conference at Jackson's Mill placed the burden on the teacher preparation institutions to develop teachers who are masters of many "knowledges" and skills. To accomplish this aim, superior instruction is needed under conditions where facilities and equipment are excellent. An unusually large number of colleges and universities had entered the field recently, but they couldn't possibly have adequate staffs and facilities for the task at hand. Many leaders felt that standards for accrediting would come as an aftermath of the Jackson's Mill report. Some states (e.g., Pennsylvania) had already acted to prevent colleges with inadequate facilities and staffs from offering major programs in the field.

A Call for Accreditation of Professional Programs. The American Association of Colleges for Teacher Education had served as one of the sponsoring agencies of the Jackson's Mill conference. This body was formed at that time by a merger of the American Association of Teachers Colleges, schools of education in universities, and municipal universities engaged in teacher preparation. Its primary purpose was to improve the quality of teacher education. In his report on this movement, Nordly explained how the association had "assumed the role of a voluntary accreditation agency, developed evaluation schedules for that function, and held a series of evaluations of teacher education programs to familiarize college representatives with the schedules. . . ." (1959, p. 4).

Evaluative criteria for the rating of professional programs in physical education were developed in the 1950s, and a number of institutions expressed willingness to have their programs rated. These criteria were made available inexpensively by the American Association for Health, Physical Education, and Recreation. Professional leaders called for all departments of physical education to undertake self-evaluation of major programs as a first step.

The newly founded American Association of Colleges for Teacher Education relinquished its embryonic accreditation functions to the National Council for Accreditation of Teacher Education in 1954. In 1957 the AAHPER held a workshop to revise the evaluative criteria for physical education in light of the changes made by the NCATE to the earlier criteria developed by the AACTE. Nordly reported that it was evident that "General public respect for our profession and the effectiveness of our unique to education are dependent upon the standards attained through cooperative efforts" (1959, p. 7).

Numbers of Program (1920 to 1961). In the period from 1920 to 1961, the growth in the number of institutions offering professional preparation for physical education was phenomenal. In the decade after World War I, a conflict that exerted a tremendous influence on the field forcing a flood of state physical education laws, some 137 colleges and universities began to offer teacher preparation in health and physical education. From 1930 through 1939, despite the severe financial depression that affected he entire education field greatly, approximately 97 more institutions entered the field. As had its predecessor, World War II exerted a further very strong influence. From 1940 to 1950 over 100 colleges and universities decided to offer programs to prepare physical education teachers. An exact figure for the 1950-1960 decade is not available, but a safe estimate would be that all together by 1961 there were more than 635 colleges and universities offering teacher education in physical education (Undergraduate and Graduate Professional Preparation in Health Education, Physical Education, and Recreation, 1954).

SUMMARY

In the 100-year period from 1861 to 1961, starting with the first "roving" program offered by the North American Gymnastic Union (NAGU or the Turners) in 1861, the total number of professional preparation programs in physical education grew to more than 635 such programs in the colleges and universities of the United States of America. In many instances the early schools were actually owned by the individual or society sponsoring them. Subsequently these so-called normal schools underwent a marked transformation. Names were changed; curricula were expanded; staffs were increased in number greatly; baccalaureate degrees were offered, and eventually affiliation with colleges and universities took place.

The field was influenced by a variety of social forces as the American scene changed Foreign traditions and customs held sway initially, but gradually a distinct American philosophy of physical education and athletics emerged. Such occurrences as wars and periods of depression and/or prosperity brought about significant changes when they took effect.

In the period from 1900 to 1920, professional educators began to take the place of physicians as directors of professional programs. Many publicly supported colleges and universities entered the field. A significant development was the awarding of academic degrees upon the completion of major programs in physical education. Specialized curricula were developed usually within, or affiliated with, departments or schools of education. In many instances the subsequent establishment of separate schools and colleges of physical education within universities had a notable influence of the field's overall development.

Down through the years of the 20th century many educators urged a stronger "cultural" component for the physical education teacher. (However, although some progress was made, the demands being made on this person "in the field" limited the extent to which this objective could be reached.) A further demand made was for an improved background in the foundation sciences. Until the mid-1950's at least, there was a definite trend to increase the number of semester hours required for professional education courses. A number of studies indicated a lack of standardization in course terminology within the developing specializations of the overall field of health education, physical education, and recreation.

There were many attempt to improve the quality of professional preparation through studies, surveys, research projects, national conferences, and accreditation plans. A very significant text recommending a "competency approach" to the preparation of teachers was published (Snyder and Scott, 1954). The field continued to move toward ongoing self-evaluation and improvement. The American Association for Health, Physical Education, and Recreation (subsequently "the Alliance") was a great influence in this historic development. They were aided significantly by such affiliated groups as the College Physical Education Association (later the NCPEAM) and the National Association of Physical Education for College Women, both of which subsequently merged to form the National Association for Physical Education in Higher Education.

REFERENCES

American Association of Teachers Colleges. (1948). *Report on teacher education, 1948*. Washington, DC: The Association.

Barrows, I. C. (1899). *Physical training*. Boston: Press of G. H. Ellis. (This is a full report of a ground-breaking conference held in 1899).

Bovard, J. F. (1935). Some trends in teacher training curricula. *Journal of Health and Physical Education*, VI (4).

Bramwell, A. B. & Hughes, H. M. (1894). *The Training of Teachers in the United States of America*. London: Schwann, Sonnschein & Co.

Degroot, D. S. (1940). *A history of physical education in California (1848-1939)*.

Unpublished doctoral dissertation, Stanford University, CA.

Fredericks, J. W. (1938). Final report of the committee on the professional curriculum. *Proceedings of the College Physical Education Association*, USA.

Graybeal, E. (1941). A consideration of qualities used by administrators in judging effective teachers of physical education in Minnesota. *Research Quarterly*, 12 (4), 741-744.

Gulick, L. H. (1892). Professor T. D. Wood. *Physical Education*, V (1), 25-26.

Hartwell, E. M. (1899). Physical training. In *Report of the Commissioner of Education, 1899*. Washington, DC: Government Printing Office.

Hartwell, E. M. (1903). On physical training. In *Report of the Commissioner of Education, 1903*. Washington, DC: Government Printing Office.

Hines, L. N. Personal and professional qualifications of the physical training teacher. *American Physical Education Review*, XXV (2), 52-56.

Kennedy, J. F. (1961). A presidential message. In *Youth physical fitness, 1961*. Washington, DC: U. S. Government Printing Office.

Leonard, F. E. (1915). *Pioneers of physical training*. NY: Association Press.

Metcalf, T. N. (1926). Professional training for directors of physical education. In *Proceedings of the Society of Directors of Physical Education in Colleges*, USA.

National Commission on Teacher Education and Professional Standards. (1947). *The improvement of teaching*. Washington, DC: National Education Association of the U.S.A.

National Conference of Undergraduate Professional Preparation in Physical Education, Health Education, and Recreation. Chicago, IL: The Athletic Institute, 40 p.

Neilson, N. P. (1930). Job-analysis technique should be applied to physical education. *Journal of Health and Physical Education*, 1 (1), 9.

Neilson, N. P. (1935). National study of professional education in health and physical education. *Research Quarterly*, VI (4), 48-68.

Nordly, C. L. (1959). The development of the standards and guide. In *Evaluation standards and guide*. Washington, DC: AAHPER.

Peik, W. E. & Fitzgerald, G. B. (1934). The education of men teachers of physical education for public school service in selected colleges and universities. *Research Quarterly*, 5 (4), 18-26.

Proceedings of the Association for the Advancement of Physical Education. (1885). Brooklyn, NY: Rome Brothers.

Proceedings of the American Association for the Advancement of Physical Education for 1886, 1887, and 1888. Brooklyn, NY: Rome Brothers.

Rathmann, C. G. (1886). German system of training teachers at the Milwaukee Normal School. In *Proceedings of the American Association for the*

Advancement of Physical Education, Brooklyn, NY.

Rugg, E. U. et al. (1933) *Teacher education curricula (No. 10, Vol. III, 29-31).*
  Washington, DC: National Survey of the Education of Teachers

School for Christian Workers Catalogue (Springfield College) for 1886-1887,
  Springfield, MA.

Scott, H. A. (1935). The unit plan of instruction as employed in professional
  preparation of teachers in health and physical education at Rice Institute.
  Research Quarterly, VI (4).

Scott, H. A. (1947). Report of the committee on teacher education. *Proceedings of
  the College Physical Education Association,* USA.

Schwendener, N. (1942). *A history of physical education in the United States.*
  NY: A.S. Barnes.

Snyder, R. & Scott, H. A. *Professional preparation in health, physical education,
  and recreation.* NY: McGraw-Hill.

Sprague, H. A. (1940). *A decade of progress in the preparation of secondary
  school teachers.* NY: Teachers College, Columbia University.

Springfield College Catalogue. (1940-1942). Springfield, MA: Author.

Troyer, M. E. (1945). Trends in teacher education. *Journal of Health and Physical
  Education,* XVI (10), 542, 582-584.

*Undergraduate and graduate professional preparation in health education,
  physical education, and recreation.* (1954). Washington, DC: U. S. Department
  of Health Education and Welfare, Office of Education, Circular No. 403.

U. S. Bureau of Education (1928). *Professional training in physical education.*
  Physical Education Series No. 9. Washington, DC: Author. (This is a report of
  a conference held on March 20, 1927.)

U. S. Bureau of Education. *Professional courses in physical education for teachers.*
  Circular. Washington, DC: Author.

Van Dalen, D. B., Mitchell, E. D., & Bennett, B. L. (1953). *A world history of
  physical education.* NY: Prentice-Hall.

Williams, J. F. (1927). Nature and purpose of health education and physical
  education viewed from the standpoint of general education. *American Physical
  Education Review,* XXXII (5), 330-340.

Zeigler, E. F. (1950). *A history of professional preparation for physical education in
  the United States, 1861-1948.* Ann Arbor, MI: University Microfilms.

CHAPTER V

AN HISTORICAL OVERVIEW OF GRADUATE STUDY IN AMERICAN PHYSICAL EDUCATION (1891-1975)

This overview of the history of graduate study in physical education in the United States was originally conceived in the mid-1960s at a time when the field had presumably arrived at a very low point. In 1963, James Conant, president of Harvard University, and his associates had condemned all graduate work in the field of physical education (1963, p. 201). How the field arrived at this presumed low point will be described in this paper.

The specific headings to be discussed are as follows: (1) Early Development of Graduate Study, (2) Graduate Study in Physical Education to World War I, (3) World War II and the 1950s, (4) The Assessment and Disciplinary Thrust of the 1960s, (5) Status in the 1970s, and (6) Concluding Statement (Including Recommendations for the Future).

EARLY DEVELOPMENT OF GRADUATE STUDY

The master's degree, taken as the second degree, became available at Harvard College only six years after Harvard was founded in 1636. The "graduate" student was required to take an additional year of study beyond the bachelor's degree, prepare a thesis or "synopsis" for presentation prior to the commencement ceremony, and pay the additional tuition fee for the academic year in question. These academic disputations were usually unscientific efforts and often theological in nature.

Interestingly, however, it wasn't until the middle of the 19th century that more formal graduate work was offered to students in the United States. Also, truly earned degrees under reorganized academic councils didn't appear until the 1870's (Knight, 1940, pp. 1-8). At the undergraduate level the United States had borrowed the English system. At the graduate level, however, it was the graduate school pattern of Germany that was superimposed on the university academic structure (Ryan, 1939, pp. 1-8). The German approach involved basic change, one characterized by the adoption of a newer philosophy based on significant advances in science and mathematics introduced at the University of Halle. Such an interest in research and scholarly endeavor had caught the imagination of American university educators who had traveled abroad. It was in 1876 that John Hopkins University became the first institution to pattern itself directly after the model that had been adopted by certain of the German universities. (p. 28).

Although many universities awarded more or less honorary master's degrees well up into the 1800's, Yale University had actually offered the first Ph.D. program in 1860 (Rosenberg, 1966, p. 34). This number grew rapidly, so that at the beginning of the 20th century 50 universities were offering the doctoral degree-- the earned Ph.D. There was an effort to standardize and accredit these institutions, but only approximately 20 of this number seemed to be really concerned with such improvement (Good, in Henry, 1951, p. 6). In both 1908 and 1916 1016, committees representing associations of universities made recommendations about the maintenance of standards. In 1932 a similar statement was made concerning the status of the master's degree (Knight, 1940, pp. 436-437).

Graduate programs in the United States developed steadily and appeared to have been built on a sound base. The attempts to meet the needs of the time were sincere; the quality of faculty and students was quite high; and the administrative leaders of the institutions involved gave every evidence of being qualified. From a most modest beginning of only 198 graduate students in 1871-72, a total of 47,255 men and women were reported in 1930 (Edwards, 1935, pp. 569-570). Obviously, such an expansion must have involved many considerations and a great many problems. One recurrent problem, repeated time and again in the literature, revolved around the concept of "research"--as opposed to what was called "teacher preparation"--as the basic responsibility of the graduate school (Dale, 1930, pp. 198-202).

Certain social developments between 1920 and 1940 influenced graduate study significantly. Enrollments were rising sharply, and many of the characteristics of a considerable percentage of these students were changing. Graduate degree programs were established in a great many professional schools, and it became difficult to maintain high standards of scholarship. A break with the tradition of "scholarship and research only" became inevitable. The recommended change in emphasis involved a broadening of the objectives of the graduate program for teachers and administrators was considered justifiable, according to Edwards in the mid-1930's, because of the demand for large numbers of practitioners. Also, it appeared impossible to demand intensified preparation for scholarly endeavor and research specialization on the part of so many people. As Edwards pointed out, there were 3,000 Ph.D.'s and 25,000 master's degree graduates being produced annually (1935, pp. 469-470).

Many different types of master's degree programs were started as well. It is generally accepted that within this divergent group of study patterns there was a "wide diversity of standards relating to entrance and degree requirements. . . ." (Snyder and Scott, 1954, p. 205). Thus, it is understandable why the Council of Graduate Schools in the United States recommended that a master's degree program should be inaugurated only when the "resources and special traditions available" would seem to make such a degree program desirable (n.d., p. 4).

It should be noted further that the master's degree in education-- and it should be kept in mind that that physical education programs were typically affiliated with schools of education--was offered initially in the latter part of the 19th century. In the year 1900, some 31 master's degrees were awarded by a total of 12 leading universities. To demonstrate clearly the growth of graduate study in professional education--for these same universities--some 134 degrees were awarded in professional education in 1910, 678 by 1920, and 3,231 in 1930 (John, 1935, p. 450). By 1949-1950, this number had grown six fold to 18,311 master's degrees in education by all colleges and universities in the country offering such programs (Story, 1950, p. 78).

While this development was taking place at the Master's level, graduate education generally was Berelson had designated as a "growth and diversification" phase from World War I to World War II. Thereafter began another period that he called "revival and reappraisal" that was still in force as he wrote (1960, pp. 24-42). It was during the former period that the doctoral program was made available in many more fields within the traditional arts and science component of the university--but also in a great many professional fields (one of which was education; see p. 27). The recurring problem of "purpose and quality" was considered time and again (p. 28). According to Berelson,

> The demand for training and the supply of students, the
> institutions offering graduate work, the body of knowledge
> to be communicated, the professionalization of graduate
> study, the debate over the entire enterprise--all of these
> familiar trends were back in high gear by 1950 . . . (p.
> 32).

About this time, also, both general and special professional education, as units related to schools and colleges of education within universities, were confronted with what to many seemed a most serious problem. (General professional education refers to those courses in schools of education that were required typically for professional certification. This might have included history, philosophy, and international education; educational psychology; educational administration and supervision; teaching methodology, and others. Special professional education referred to professional preparation for the teaching of any specialized subject-matter approved for the school curriculum: (i.e., English, art, physical education, health education, mathematics, sciences, etc.). Teachers were being urged routinely to obtain a master's degree, and subsequently the eventual possession of a second degree became mandatory for job permanence and maximum salary attainment.

Thus, if the teacher elected to pursue the master's degree in education--and especially if the undergraduate degree has been in education, also--there was every likelihood that he teacher would not have a sufficient quantity of more substantive courses in what were called "academic" subject-matters in the total program of study. Conversely, if the teacher elected the M.S. degree in--say--chemistry, he or she might well be criticized because of inability to provide evidence (either on a transcript or in actuality) of "master-teacher" qualifications. These two examples were unfortunately more representative of the norm than the extreme. They did, and continued to, represent a serious problem in graduate education in the United States.

Then, in the 1960's, this dilemma was brought even more sharply into focus by the fact that the arrival of Sputnik on the scene brought immediate pressure upon the entire educational enterprise. There was a demand for the upgrading of the "body of knowledge" in each subject-matter that presumably had a place in the total curriculum of schools and universities. Many knowledgeable people were recommending a fifth year of undergraduate preparation. Some state actually implemented this extra work as a requirement for permanent certification. This development served to heighten the concern about the articulation present between undergraduate programs and those of the professional and graduate schools. The basic question seemed to be: Should the program of study in this fifth year be advanced undergraduate work, or should it be what many call true graduate study involving the development of scholarly and research competency? At that point there appeared to be no definitive answer to this question that was acceptable to the large majority of those concerned.

GRADUATE STUDY IN PHYSICAL EDUCATION
TO WORLD WAR II

To comprehend why and how graduate study in physical education got its start, one must understand that undergraduate professional preparation in this field began first in the United States in 1861 when Dio Lewis organized the first 10-week diploma course. In the first 100 years after this inauspicious beginning, some highly significant changes and developments took place. Foreign traditions held sway initially, but gradually--because of a variety of social influences--a fairly distinct American philosophy of physical education emerged. This "philosophy" has since been blurred considerably.

Actually, very little graduate study of a scientific or scholarly nature was conducted prior to the third decade of the 20th century. This statement is true even though a number of colleges and universities had entered the field--or were planning to do so. As far back as 1891, Springfield College had offered the first "graduate" course, although it must be admitted that it was only a one-year program superimposed on the regular two-year undergraduate curriculum. The catalog of the International Y.M.C.A. Training School (Springfield College!) offered four courses in what was called a "graduate year." They were Physiological Psychology, History and Philosophy of Physical Education, Anthropometry, and Literature of Physical Education (Catalogue of International YMCA Training School, 1890-1891). The "seminary method" was used in these classes which began in the fall of 1891. A thesis of at least 3000 words involving original investigation was required.

This embryonic graduate program was discontinued in 1895 when the undergraduate program was lengthened to three years (Doggett, 1943, p. 80), but it started up again in the fall of 1900 when a graduate course was listed in the catalogue (Catalogue of International YMCA Training School, 1900-1901). Although only three men completed the requirements for the graduate diploma in the Physical Department (as it was called) between 1891 and 1900, it does represent the first graduate work of any type in United States physical education. (It must be admitted, however, that the question of a graduate degree did not come up until 1905. In this year the Massachusetts Legislature authorized the college to confer the degrees of Bachelor of Physical Education [B.P.E.] and Master of Physical Education [M.P.E.}. Also, the M.P.E. degree represented only a fourth year of of collegiate study, since the four-year undergraduate program didn't go into effect until 1916 (?). Thus, a graduate department in every sense of the word, as represented today, began in 1927 under the direction of Dr. J. H. McCurdy (Doggett, 1943, p. 130). (Three other sources gave the date as either 1905 or 1907.)

In 1901, Columbia University, under the auspices of its educational unit known as Columbia Teachers College, is reported to have established the first graduate program in physical education that was preceded by a full-fledged baccalaureate degree. (This claim needs further investigation, because catalogues at that time do not list such a program. Mention was made in the 1910 catalogues of the possibility of students pursuing graduate curricula leading to the degrees of M.A. and Ph.D. in education with specialization in the area of physical education.)

It was reported that Oberlin College instituted a major in physical education leading to the master's degree in the early 1900's. The first student to receive this degree presumably did so, although he was said to have held a B.A. degree in Greek (Clarke in Nash, 1935, p. 332). However, the catalogues of the College (1930 and 1940) state that no graduate work was available until some time between 1930 and 1940. Further, the catalogue for 1948-49 included only two courses under graduate work.

Other institutions that entered the field of graduate study in physical education were, for example, the Normal College of the American Gymnastic Union in 1907, Wellesley College in 1917. the University of Southern California in 1918, and the University of Oregon in 1920 (Zeigler, 1951, pp. 275-276).

As it developed, a most important step was taken by both Columbia Teachers College and New York University in 1924 with the establishment of programs leading to the doctor of philosophy degree with a major or concentration in physical education. This pioneering effort saw Ethel J. Saxman receiving the first Ph.D. from Columbia Teachers College in 1926 and, in the same year, James G. Bliss completed the program for the doctorate at New York University, Interestingly, Welch uncovered the fact that four doctor of physical education degrees (D.P.E.) were awarded at the Y.M.C.A. Graduate School of Nashville, Tennessee between the years of 1925 and 1929 (1968, pp. 9-10).

Interestingly, Clark Hetherington, the organized of graduate study in physical education at New York University, spoke on the subject of graduate study in physical education at the 1924 sessions of the Society of Directors of Physical Education in College. (This is now the National Association for Kinesiology and

Physical Education in Higher Education.) He expressed the fear that many universities would merely list their undergraduate courses as graduate ones while the transition to the offering of legitimate courses and programs was taking place. If the undergraduate curriculum was well planned, integrated, and articulated from year to year, he believed that in the graduate program a prospective teacher could be prepared to perform the full task adequately. This included some opportunity for specialization (1925).

In 1934 and 1935, Clarke reported on the status of master's degree programs in physical education in the United States. This work was followed by Norris and Sweet's survey to determine that status of graduate work in the field (1937, pp. 3-10). Between 1926 and 1949, some 54 colleges and universities began master's degree programs in physical education with approximately an equal distribution between the nomenclature of master of arts and master of science. In the late 1940's, however, the large majority of institutions reporting new programs offered the master of science degree in physical education (M.S.) (Zeigler, 1949). Viewed somewhat differently, Hewitt, in his assessment of graduate study, reported that in 1942 that "56 institutions offer major work in physical education" (p. 255).

The basic difference in the mid-1930's between undergraduate and graduate courses revolved around greater emphasis on problems courses the concept of "seminar," the introduction to methods of research course, and a thesis based on original research (Norris and Sweet, 1937, pp. 3-10). In 1938, Lloyd reaffirmed the need for increased effort along the lines of research (pp. 73-77). The literature on the subject of graduate study in physical education was sparse, but there were several studies employing descriptive analysis of existent programs carried out as doctoral projects at this time. Frederick developed principles that might be used as guidelines for the reformulation of requirements for the master's program (1938). Her study related to programs for women, and Shaw followed with a similar project that applied to men (1939).

FROM WORLD WAR II UP THROUGH THE 1950'S

In addition to a detailed listing of institutions offering a variety of graduate programs in physical education, Hewitt raised some interesting questions about the graduate program itself (many still pertinent at the time this present study concluded). For example, he inquired whether physical education at the graduate level with schools of education because it truly belonged there as an integral part of professional education. Then, as a corollary question, he inquired whether physical education must (should?) continue to align itself with professional education schools because it is "such a new and growing profession" and because it lacked "the respect of an old established profession." He asked further whether the pattern being established would hinder physical education's future growth and might prevent it from "becoming an upstanding body comparable to other established professions" (1942, pp. 252-256).

> (Note: Dr. Hewitt would be surprised to learn that in 2004 the profession is still called "physical education," and that the discipline is becoming known as "kinesiology" or "exercise science." Of course, it can be argued, also, that the profession is "education," and that physical education is simply a subdivision of the "teaching profession.)

Hewitt also reported specifically on the various requirements for the master's degree in physical education. In 45 of the 56 institutions studied, an undergraduate major in physical education was required for entrance to graduate study. Thirty-six of these institutions required no skill competence test for admission to the graduate level. This might mean that the majority viewed graduate study as being more theoretical and research oriented. It is not known to what extent the remaining 20 universities did exact a level of skill in physical activity from its applicants. Five years was the maximum of time allowed (on the average) for completion of the degree requirements. Forty of the 56 universities studied required some sort of a final comprehensive examination. A sharp division of opinion was expressed as to the need for a thesis requirement. Also, the majority of program that did require a thesis did not insist that it had to be a "contribution to knowledge" (1945a).

The status of the graduate faculty was reviewed in another article by Hewitt in 1945. The majority of universities offering graduate study in the field did not specify any prerequisites for inclusion as a member of the graduate faculty. Only seven of the 56 studied required graduate instructors to hold the rank of assistant professor at least. Eight listed that a person should hold a master's degree before being permitted to teach at this level, while eight others required the possession of a doctoral degree. One of Hewitt's conclusions was that, if the possession of a higher degree-- or working for an advanced degree--is an indication of an adequate background to instruct at this level, the average graduate staff member was, or would soon be, well prepared for the task. However, at that time the existing "standards" for graduate faculty teaching physical education fell below those recommended by the various national professional associations and also the various accrediting agencies. Of course, the situation was not unique to the subject of physical education. (1945b).

Shortly thereafter, Hewitt made a further contribution to knowledge available about graduate study in physical education. This time it was a presentation about the status of the doctoral program in the field. There were some 20 universities offering specialization in physical education. Proceeding alphabetically by state they were as follows:

1. California (Stanford and the University of Southern California)
2. Indiana (Indiana University)
3. Iowa (State University of Iowa)
4. Kentucky (University of Kentucky)
5. Louisiana (Louisiana State University)
6. Massachusetts (Boston University)
7. Michigan (The University of Michigan)
8. Missouri (University of Missouri).
9. New York (Columbia Teachers College, New York University, Syracuse University)
10. Ohio (University of Cincinnati, The Ohio State University)
11. Oregon (University of Oregon).
12. Pennsylvania (Pennsylvania State College, University of Pittsburgh)
13. Tennessee (George Peabody College for Teachers)
14. Texas (University of Texas)
15. Wyoming (University of Wyoming) (1946)

Typically, there were three types of doctoral degrees available with specialization in physical education in these 20 universities: (1) the Ph.D. degree in physical education; (2) the Ph.D. degree in education (with specialization in physical education); and (3) the Ed.D. degree in education (with specialization in physical education). Indiana University had traditionally offered the P.E.D. degree (doctor of physical education), and subsequently Springfield College offered the D.P.E. degree. Hewitt felt that the standards recommended for advanced degrees by the professional associations were being met reasonably by the 20 institutions surveyed. For example, the programs were uniform in that at least one year in residence was required, and three years beyond the bachelor's degree comprised the total program requirement. All of the universities required a qualifying examination of some type to determine the candidate's ability to proceed forward into actual candidacy for the degree. Typically the Ph.D. program emphasized research competency in an area of specialization, while the doctor of education degree (Ed.D.) stressed development of professional competence and scholarship. It is questionable whether such competence has ever been evaluated validly.

A reading knowledge of two foreign languages was required in almost all instances of the Ph.D. program, whereas standards concerning language background for the Ed.D. degree were less stringent and not uniform. A comprehensive test on measurement in education was required in almost all cases. In all universities the candidate had to defend his/her thesis or project before a faculty committee. Interestingly, Hewitt recommended that the field of physical education sever its basic connection with schools of education to aid in the achievement of fundamental recognition.

In 1947 at the meeting of the Teacher Education Section of the College Physical Education Association (then known as the CPEA), the program was designed to improve understanding of the status of graduate programs in physical education. Meredith, of the University of Pennsylvania, discussed the five-year program begun there in 1933, an effort that was dropped subsequently to the detriment of the field. Scott, of Columbia Teachers College, chaired a panel which decided that there were at least eight characteristics of graduate-level instruction (as over against undergraduate study) that were as follows: (1) the development of the ability to think critically; (2) a broader field of preparation emphasizing expansion of one's knowledge both horizontally and vertically; (3) development of research tools for independent investigation; (4) the ability to do independent thinking; (5) specialization; (6) an opportunity to sense and apply relationships among the various areas of knowledge and human experience; (7) a greater amount of individualized instruction; and (8) a period of at least one academic year beyond the bachelor's degree should be required for the master's degree (Nordly, 1947, pp. 58-61).

Further discussion at this meeting was directed to the possible unique characteristics of the doctoral program over and above the program for the master's degree. There was agreement that the student was both "broadened" and "sharpened" with this further preparation, and also that "maturation" was important to the candidate for the doctoral program. Still further, it was explained that it had never been completely decided that a Ph.D. program should concentrate on so-called sharpening only, as opposed to broadening--and indeed that exactly the opposite is the case in the basic design of the Ed.D. program. Generally speaking, the program leading to the doctorate was thought to be more leisurely than an intensive 30-week master's program of a more "professional" nature. In many of the these programs, course work could be substituted for the thesis project, and the succeeding summer was therefore not needed to complete the write-up of such a project. Because of the doctoral program's "more leisurely approach," it presumably afforded a greater opportunity for individual investigation and independent study.

In 1948 Jones reported on the question of minor subjects elected by graduate majors in physical education. In his study he investigated, also, that status of minors in physical education taken by students not specializing in physical education. There was no uniformity among the various universities surveyed as to their administration of such programs. A minor in physical education was available in only 60% of the universities responding, with a large percentage of the people electing such a program officially registered in departments or schools of education. Only four institutions required that graduate students in physical education elect a minor in a second field, Professional education, sociology, and biology were indicated most frequently as the minors selected by those students (pp. 18-21).

Beginning in 1946, the first of a series of meetings on the topic of graduate study in physical education was called by Seward Staley of Illinois "to discuss ways and means of upgrading graduate study" in the field. (National Conference on Graduate Study in Physical Education, 1950, p. 5). Similarly, larger meetings were convened in 1947 and 1948. At the third conference, standards were considered for the accreditation of universities offering such graduate work. These recommendations were to include such subdivisions as:

1. Minimum standards,
2. History and accreditation of parent institution
     and physical education unit,
3. Financial status of university,
4. Faculty qualifications,
5. Admission requirements,
6. Course offerings,
7. Scholarship standards,
8. Degree requirements,
9. Library facilities, and
10. Laboratory facilities (Staley, 1948).

As a result of these early meetings, it became apparent that a nationally representative conference was needed to begin to answer the many and involved problems facing the profession. The Athletic Institute was asked to finance a meeting of an organizing committee in Chicago on January 15, 1949. Subsequently, the first national conference on graduate study was planned for January, 1950 at Pere Marquette State Park in Illinois. The conference report made it clear that "the function of the master's program was (1) to assist students to become better teachers and administrators, and (2) to prepare qualified students for doctoral programs" (Report of National Conference, etc., 1950, pp. 16-17). The overall purposes for graduate study were listed as (1) the production of teachers, administrators, and creative scholars; (2) the stimulation and improvement of the quality of research and its consumption; and (3) to develop "specialists who have preparation in particular lines of endeavor beyond the bachelor's degree" (p. 7).

The master's degree program was specifically assigned certain broad areas of concentration as follows:

1. That area which is chiefly concerned with the fundamental philosophy on which the profession of physical education is based.
2. That area which deals with the methods and tools of research.
3. That area in which attention is focused on the human organism and how it works.
4. That area which is primarily concerned with the planning and operation of the total physical education program. (This would include study of problems relating to organization, administration, supervision, and instruction. . . .
5. That area which is primarily concerned with the aesthetic phases of physical education (pp. 17-18).

(Note: In retrospect, the importance of careful delineation between the two purposes indicated as "the function of the master's program" (i.e., [1] assisting teachers to become better teachers and administrators and [2] preparing qualified students for doctoral programs) was not fully appreciated by many leaders in the field. It must be explained further that physical educators were not alone in this regard and should not be singled out for special blame in this regard. These programs were situated typically in schools of education that have often--rightly or wrongly--

been criticized for lesser academic standing. Also, this problem perplexed most colleges and universities in connection with their master's programs. Henry, in 1952, explained that many degree patterns in higher education have been confused to say the least (1952, pp. 352-353).

In the 1950's, self-evaluation was urged upon colleges and universities as a means whereby professional programs at all levels might be improved. The American Association of Colleges for Teacher Education had been formed in 1948 and soon assumed the role of a voluntary accrediting agency. In 1954 the accreditation function was transferred to the National Council for Accreditation of Teacher Education. The American Association for Health, Physical Education, and Recreation (now known as AAHPERD) revised its evaluative criteria for professional preparation in 1957 because of changes approved by NCATE (National Commission for the Accreditation of Teacher Education) (1959).

Graduate study in physical education has had its share of criticism over the years--as had graduate study in professional education generally. It is probably true, also that much of the criticism was warranted if one is judging these programs according to the standards set in selected field where either fine scholarly writing or research endeavor of high quality was carried out. In 1957 C. H. McCloy stated that graduate study, in his opinion, was of a poor quality. This outstanding professional leader and scholar was disturbed because the master's thesis was gradually, and steadily, being replaced with six to eight semester hours of additional classwork. Further, he decried the lack of prerequisites for entry into so-called higher level courses. Still further, he expressed deep concern because there was an insufficient number of faculty members available at the university level capable of carrying out quality scholarly endeavor and research (1957, pp. 33-34). As true as these statements might have been, they created no appreciable stir. This is probably the case because they came from someone within the field--even from such a man as Professor McCloy from the State University of Iowa. It remained for certain social influences and the sting of criticism "from outside" the field to create the desire for a certain measure of reform.

ASSESSMENT AND THE DISCIPLINARY THRUST OF THE 1960'S

Very few people in the field, if any, were able to foresee the disciplinary thrust and period of assessment that was to take place in the 1960's and immediately thereafter. In retrospect, McCloy's warning fell on deaf ears, as did the advent of Russia's Sputnik. Hence it took some time for the effect of Conant's devastating criticism about graduate study in 1963 to be felt by those concerned with programs at this level, not to mention the much larger number of people in the profession. This writer can well remember his shock and amazement(and some anger too) when he read he following words for the first time:

> I am far from impressed by what I have heard and read about graduate work in the field of physical education. If I wished to portray the education o teachers in the worst terms, I should quote from the description of some graduate courses in physical education. To my mind, a university should cancel courses in this area. If the physical education teacher wishes to enter into a research career in the field of physiology and related subjects, he should use the graduate years to build on his natural science background. . . . (Conant, 1963, p. 201.

Although such statements as this do have a certain amount of influence on the field of professional education generally, the field of physical education was far too well established under the aegis of responsible graduate schools in most universities to have its very existence threatened by such criticism. The field reacted to this denunciation officially by means of a letter sent to Conant in 1964 from the Professional Preparation Panel of the American Association for Health, Physical Education, and Recreation. The chairman of the Panel, Dean Arthur Esslinger, of the University of Oregon, admitted that there was a certain number of poor graduate programs, but he emphasized that there were some superior programs as well. Fortunately, Esslinger was in a position to know that "the profession is striving to improve conditions related thereto." He indicated that Conant's statement condemned all graduate programs in physical education, and that such blanket condemnation was most unfortunate and quite probably not merited. In addition, he forwarded materials explaining the status of scholarly investigation in the field. Lastly, Conant was urged to discuss the subject personally with the AAHPER Panel. The hope was also expressed that he undertake a more careful investigation in the hope that such an analysis might lead him to revise his statement (Letter to Conant, Aug. 17, 1964.

No matter whether the statement by Conant was generally true, whether it caused a certain amount of ridicule to be leveled against physical education, or whether the reply caused Conant to eventually "recant," it did cause serious analysis by leaders in the area of graduate study. The field had been jarred and became less complacent. A decision was made to hold a national conference on graduate study. In preparation the American Academy of Physical Education devoted its 1966 meeting to a consideration of background papers on various aspects of graduate study. The plan was that these papers would lay the groundwork for the 1967 conference at the AAHPER Headquarters in Washington, DC.

A concurrent development worthy of note was the implementation of the Big Ten Body-of-Knowledge Project by the Western Conference Physical Education Directors in December, 1964 (Zeigler and McCristal, 1967, pp. 79-84). Daniels (Indiana) and McCristal (Illinois) were responsible for the 1964 sessions in Champaign-Urbana, Illinois and decided on the conference theme of "The Body of Knowledge in Physical Education." Speaking at the conference, Daniels said:

> If we are to gain greater recognition in the academic world, we must follow the pathways similar to that traversed by other disciplines. This means a greatly expanded program of scholarly research and development in which the body of knowledge is defined as nearly as possible in terms of its fundamental nature, and in its relationships with other disciplines (p. 80).

In 1966, after reports from the various sub-disciplinary areas had been presented at both the 1964 and 1965 meetings, it was decided to organize the academic content--at least initially--into six specific areas of specialization: (1) exercise physiology, (2) biomechanics, (3) motor learning and sport psychology, (4) sociology of sport education, (5) history, philosophy, and comparative physical education and sport, and (6) administrative theory. Eventually, symposia were conducted on each of these topics, and also a series of substantive publications resulted through the support of The Athletic Institute.

The Conference on Graduate Education, sponsored by AAHPER after a year and a half of planning under the guidance of Ben Miller (UCLA) and Laura Huelster (Illinois, C-U), was held from January 8-13, 1967. The report of this important conference designated the following five purposes of graduate study:

1. To add to the store of human knowledge through basic research.
2, To extend the range of nonverbal expression (dance, games,

sports, etc.) through encouragement of human invention and imagination.

3. To prepare scientific research workers and humanistic scholars.
4. To provide advanced preparation for practitioners (teachers, coaches, supervisers, activity specialists, and administrators) at various levels of competency.
5. To develop leaders who have the ability to think and to employ rational powers in gaining understanding, aesthetic sensitivity, and moral responsibility (Graduate Education Report, 1967, p. 21).

Further, indicating that "the core body of knowledge of physical education concerns human motor performance . . . all of the following areas" were deemed to be "appropriate for scholarly study and research":

1. Meaning and significance of physical education, including philosophical and historical considerations,
2. Social, cultural, and aesthetic aspects of physical education,
3. Behavioral aspects of physical education,
4. Motor learning and motor development,
5. Biomechanics
6. Exercise physiology,
7. Administration
8. Curricular aspects of physical education including supervision, instruction, and curriculum development, and
9. Evaluative aspects of physical education (1967, p. 62).

Unfortunately, just at the time wherein the profession appeared ready to add more of a "disciplinary thrust"--including the humanities and social-science aspects of the field to an already heavily professional-preparation-oriented graduate curriculum--the financial outlook began to darken considerably. Research funds from the main source of supply, the federal government, were cut drastically. Legislators faced with ever-mounting budgets, and also the economic condition known as "stagflation," found that educational spending at the college and university level could be curtailed without fear of any significant reprisal. Further, in many instances higher boards of education within states were created to keep universities from unreasonable program expansion. It was undoubtedly fortunate that some controls were instituted to prevent many more universities from establishing Ph.D. programs in a multitude of subjects (including physical education), because it suddenly became apparent that a "Ph.D. glut" was developing in many different fields. This was a situation that practically no one had predicted.

STATUS IN THE MID-1970'S: FUTURE DIRECTIONS

Writing in the mid-1970's it was obvious to the writer that "the present is too much with us," thus taking note of the impossibility of obtaining true historical perspective. Thus, an effort is made to assess present status and to point out some possible future directions for consideration. This assessment is based on historical analysis over a period of approximately 35 years, as well as a continuing effort to apply descriptive method to the analysis of graduate study in physical education. This investigator believes that the time has come for the introduction of "a competency approach" to graduate study in physical education as one way of improving the curriculum. Such implementation could possibly also strengthen the position of physical education in relation to the other subject-matters in the overall graduate program. What is being recommended affirms the belief that the student needs to come to a full understanding of related problems by gradually moving from (1) a consideration of personal and immediate problems, to (2) the larger social implications of these issues, on to (3) the professional aspects of these problems, and (4) to the application of these situations and issues which are peculiar to his/her subsequent professional endeavor (Snyder and Scott, 1954, pp. 108-176).

Such a recommendation is not made lightly. It seems that so many different approaches have been employed in curriculum revision throughout the history of professional preparation for physical education in the United States. Yet, unfortunately, the end result has not been such that there can be reasonable pride and satisfaction with the outcome. Early curricula were forged by individualistic medical doctors who had turned to physical education. These initial approaches were superseded through curricula change based on others who seemed to be achieving success. A third approach (or stage) was when certain professional programs achieved a level of stature that enticed other institutions to follow their lead.

Then, toward the middle of the 1920's, a type of job analysis was used to decide what curriculum change was needed for the on-the-job demands of the day. Next, during the 1930's and 1940's, many state, regional, and national conferences were held. These sessions resulted in a wide variety of recommendations and proposed standards about curricula and teacher education in general. Subsequently, in the 1950's, self-evaluation was being foisted upon universities in one more effort to bring about improvement of teacher education. Finally, in the 1960's, there was a growing realization that sociological analysis of society and its need might shed some light on the matter of curriculum revision. All of these approaches have undoubtedly served their purposes to a greater or lesser extent at a particular time. They may each have had some merit, but one still wonders whether at this point that a multiple transcending approach is needed.

It is with all of these thoughts and ideas in mind, therefore, that a "knowledge, skills, and competency approach" is recommended for the immediate future at least. The argument being made is that all graduate students should share more fully in the planning and appraisal of their education. The selection of experiences designed to provide the knowledge, skills, and competencies to be obtained through the medium of the graduate program should be an even more cooperative venture of all concerned than hitherto. However, it is not being advocated that the students' experiences should be completely elective. The educational sequence should advance from (1) the selection of problems, to (2) the determination of the competencies to be obtained, to (3) the selection of the planned experiences necessary for the attainment of these competencies, and, finally, to (4) the evaluation of the extent to which the entire plan has been successful when executed. (Note that, with this approach, the typical courses offered as part of the graduate program will be more than "sacrosanct entities" on the way to a diploma or degree (as so often seems to be the case). Their function will be purely and simply as "resource areas" within the total process. Finally, then, the basic question is: "Have the necessary knowledge, skills, and competencies actually been been tested so that a necessary "stamp of approval" can be placed on the individual involved?" If the answer is "yes," this will be just fine, and the department can be pleased and proud of the result.

There is at present a need for both consolidation and innovation in the overall program. This should be achieved before any steps are taken in either direction. This means that a period of intensive self-evaluation is needed most certainly at the local and state levels. and probably also at the regional, national, and international levels. Each university should have its own master plan for graduate work in physical education that has been developed in cooperation with all concerned. Of course, local and regional needs must be served by universities within their respective geographical areas. However, no one will ultimately appreciate a college or university that becomes a "diploma mill for married teachers and coaches." Whether one or more types of degree-program patterns are implemented, it seems highly desirable to preserve a common core experience of physical education and sport knowledge that all must have mastered prior to elective course experiences designed to provide the attainment of selected knowledge, competencies, and skills.

In addition to consolidation (e.g., a graduate program where a disciplinary-oriented program combines its various offerings into two options such as [1] humanities and social-science option and [2] bio-science option), there is a need for at least three different types of master's program to be offered (or available) at universities situated in one region of a state (or geographical region of the nation). The greatest demand would naturally be for a master's program to prepare a more highly qualified teacher and/or coach (i.e., the M.A. T. program or the M.S.T. program). A second type of program or degree pattern that should be available to a considerably smaller group within a state would be the disciplinary-oriented master's program leading to the M.A. or M.S. degree. (People in this program might well have aspirations to acquire a Ph.D. or Ed.D. degree eventually.) A third type of program deserves early consideration as well. This would be a master's degree program where the student would specialize in the theory and practice of some type of human motor performance e.g., gymnastics, aquatics, a team sport, an individual sport). It is past time that the field should move positively to establish sport as a legitimate part of culture that merits scholarly study at the university level.

Finally, if the field is serious about improving graduate study and research in physical education/kinesiology from the standpoint of both quality and breadth, it is being recommended that universities should add the concept of innovation to that of consolidation. It should even be possible to innovate through consolidation, while at the same time making certain that the various needs and interests of graduate students are being met in a particular geographical region. Obviously, most of the help will necessarily come from "within ourselves"--from people already in the field or at some stage in the educational training process. As a field such as physical education/kinesiology seeks recognition within scholarly circles, there is always an effort to draw personnel from respected, related disciplines. The sincerity of the commitment of the related-discipline professor being lured to relate to this field must be examined carefully before a firm offer is made. This person may not have been doing "all that well" in his/her own discipline, and "the grass often seems greener, , , ," Or, as was the case with one example, the person transferring disciplines simply liked the idea of returning to a beloved sport where he could "a major sport" without too much pressure to win. So he soon moved away from his former scholarly research in the related discipline. Conversely, far too many people trained as physical education and still receiving the bulk of their salaries from the physical education/kinesiology unit, are much too anxious to identify themselves with the related discipline and to play down their basic affiliation with the physical education/kinesiology department or school. (This might be designated as the acquisition of a "Judas complex".)

SUMMARY

This study has presented an historical overview of graduate study in physical education in the United States. Further, considering the present status of graduate study and research programs in physical education/kinesiology, several recommendations have been made about what might be done as we look to the future. The internal and external environments in which the profession/discipline operates are, of course, vitally important and cannot be neglected in any future plans. The field will develop properly only if it is based on a sound fund of know provided by dedicated scholars and researchers/ Armed with sound knowledge and developing theory, men and women professional practitioners will be able to teach, coach, administer, supervise, and perform in fine programs of physical education and educational sport according to the highest tradition of a respected profession and discipline.

REFERENCES

American Association for Health, Physical Education, and Recreation. (1959). *Evaluative standards and guide to health education, physical education, recreation.* Washington, DC: The Association.

American Association for Health, Physical Education, and Recreation. (1962). *Professional preparation in health education, physical education, recreation.* Washington, DC: The Association.

American Association for Health, Physical Educaion, and Recreation. (1966). *Directory of professional preparation institutions.* Washington, DC: The Association.

American Association for Health, Physical Education, and Recreation (1967). *Graduate education in health education, physical education, recreation education, safety education, and dance.* Washington, DC: The Association.

American Association for Health, Physical Education, and Recreation. (1969). *Self-evaluation checklist for graduate programs in health education, physical education, recreation education, safety education, and dance.* Washington, DC: The Association.

American Association of Colleges for Teacher Education, The. (1967). *Standards and evaluative criteria for the accreditation of teacher education.* Washington, DC: The Association.

Berelson, B. (1960). *Graduate education in the United States.* NY: McGraw-Hill.

Brubacher, J.S. and Rudy, W. (1958). *Higher education in transition.* NY: Harper and Row.

Carmichael, O.C. (1961). *Graduate education: A critique and a program.* NY: Harper & Row.

Cartwright, H.W. (April 1959). Graduate education of teachers: Proposals for the future. *Educational Record,* 40:148-149.

Clarke, H.H. (April 1934). The extent of graduate study in physical education in the United States. *Journal of Health and Physical Education,* 5:33.

Clarke, H.H. (1935). A survey of the requirements for the master's degree in physical education. In Nash, J.B. (Ed.), *Professional preparation.* NY: A.S. Barnes & Co.

Columbia University. (March 1939). Advanced degree without thesis proposed at Columbia University. *School and Society,* 49:321-322.

Conant, J.B. (1963). *The education of American Teachers.* NY: McGraw-Hill, 1963.

Cooper, R.M. (Jan. 1964). The college teaching crisis: Has the graduate school done right by the college teacher? *Journal of Higher Education,* 35:6.

Council of Graduate Schools in the United States, The. (n.d.). *The master's degree.* Washington, DC: The Council. (This is a pamphlet.)

Council of Graduate Schools in the United States, The. (n.d.). *The doctor of philosophy degree.* Washington, DC: The Council . (This is a pamphlet.)

Council of Graduate Schools in the United States, The. (n.d.) *New doctor of philosophy degree programs.* Washington, DC: The Council. (This is a pamphlet.)

Council of Graduate Schools in the United States, The. (n.d.). *The doctor's degree in professional fields.* Washington, DC: The Council. (This is a pamphlet.)

Dale, E. (1930, No.1). Training of Ph.D.'s. *Journal of Higher Education,* 4, 198-202.

Doggett, L.L. *Man and a school.* NY: Association Press, 1943.

Edwards, N. (1935). The reorganization of graduate study in the United States. *School and Society,* 42, 469-472.

Eells, W.C. (1934). American graduate schools. *School and Society,* 39, 708-712.

Eells, W.C. (1937). Another ranking of American graduate schools. *School and Society*, 46, 282-284.

Frederick, P.M. (1939). *A study of the requirements for the master's degree for women students majoring in physical education.* Unpublished doctor of education dissertation, Columbia Teachers College, New York.

Furniss, E.S. (1934 April). Status of graduate education in the United States. *School and Society*, 39, 440-442.

Good, C.V. (1951). History of graduate instruction in the United States. In Henry, N.B. (Ed.), *Graduate study in education.* Chicago, IL: The National Society for the Study of Education.

Gross, C.E. (1959 April). Rationale for teacher education. *Educational Record*, 40, 137-142.

Henry, N.B. (1951), Summary of reports from 85 universities and colleges. In Henry, N.B. (Ed.), *Graduate study in education.* Chicago, IL: The National Society for the Study of Education.

Hetherington, C. (1925 No. 4). Graduate work in physical education. *American Physical Education Review*, 30, 207-211. (This was continued in the May, 1925 issue, and had been presented earlier as an address to the Society of Directors of Physical Education in Colleges in December, 1924.

Hewitt, J.E. (1942 May). The graduate major in physical education. *Research Quarterly*, 13, 252-256.

Hewitt, J.E. (1945 September). Requirements for the master's degree in physical education. *Journal of Health, Physical Education, and Recreation*, 16:369-370, 410-413.

Hewitt, J.E. (1945 October). Status of the graduate faculty in physical education. *Research Quarterly*, 16, 231-240.

Hewitt, J.E. (1946 May). The doctoral program in physical education. *Research Quarterly*, 17, 82-95).

Horton, B.J. (1940). *The graduate school.* New York: McGraw-Hill.

Illinois Association for Professional Preparation in Health, Physical Education, and Recreation. *Proceedings of the 19th Annual Conference.* Monticello, IL: A.F. Loftin (Ed.).

Illinois Association for Professional Preparation in Health, Physical Education, and Recreation. *Proceedings of the 20th Annual Conference.* Monticello, IL: A. F. Loftin (Ed.).

International Y.M.C.A. Training School (Springfield College), *Catalogue for 1890.*

International Y.M.C.A. Training School, *Catalogue for 1891.*

John, W.C. *Graduate study in universities and colleges of the United States.* Washington, DC: Office of Education Bulletin #20, 1935.

Jones, L.W. (1948 March). The graduate minor in physical education. *Research Quarterly*, 19, 18-21.

Knight, W.W. (1940). *Twenty centuries of education*. Boston: Ginn.

Koerner, J.D. (1963). *The miseducation of American teachers*. Boston, Houghton Mifflin.

Kroll, W. (1965 March) Graduate education: Teacher versus researcher? *The Physical Educator*, 22, 15-18.

Lloyd, F. (1938 December). The research specialist. *Research Quarterly*, 9, 33-37.

Lumiansky, R.M. (1959 April). Concerning graduate education for teachers. *Educational Record*, 40, 143-147.

McCloy, C.H. (1957 November). Current trends in graduate study. *Journal of Health, Physical Education, and Recreation*. 28, 33-34.

McGrath, E.J. (1959). *The graduate school and the decline of liberal education*. NY: Columbia Teachers College.

McIlroy, J. (1950 October), A study of degrees and ranks held and the graduate credit offerings taught by men and women in physical education. *Research Quarterly*, 21, 239-244.

Murray, R.K. (1961 May). The effect of a university's graduate program on its undergraduate curriculum. *Journal of Higher Education*, 12, 260-264.

National Conference on Graduate Study in Health Education, Physical Education, and Education. (1950). *Report on graduate study in health education, physical education, and recreation*. Chicago, IL: The Athletic Institute.

Nordly, C.L. (1947). Teacher education. *Proceedings of the 50th Annual Meeting, College Physical Education Association*, pp. 58-61.

Norris, J.A. and Sweet, D.C. (1937 December). A survey to determine the status of graduate work in physical education. *Research Quarterly*, 8, 3-10.

Piper, J.D. (1969). *A criteria score card for evaluating doctoral programs in physical education*. Unpublished Ph.D. dissertation, The Ohio State University.

Reller, T.L. (1934 April). Survey of the requirements for the degree of doctor of education. *School and Society*, 39, 516-520.

Richardson, L.B. (1930 November). Training for college teachers. *Journal of Higher Education*,1, 425-435.

Rosenberg, R.F. (1966 Spring). The first American doctor of philosophy degree. *Ventures*, 7, 31-37.

Rosenhaupt, H. (1958). *Graduate students' experience at Columbia University, 1940-1956*. NY: Columbia University Press.

Ryan, W.C. (1939). *Studies in early graduate education (Bulletin #39)*. NY: Carnegie Foundation for the Advancement of Teaching.

Shaw, J.H. (1939). *A study of the requirements for the master's degree for men students majoring in physical education at Teachers College.* Unpublished master's thesis, Teachers College , Columbia University.

Snyder, R.A. and Scott, H.A. (1954). *Professional preparation in health education, physical education, and recreation.* NY: McGraw-Hill.

Staley, S.C. (1948 December). Report on the Pere Marquette Physical Education Graduate Study Conference. *Proceedings of the College Physical Education Association.*

Staley, S.C. (1961). Keys to advancement in physical education. *The Physical Educator,* 18, 83-88.

Story, E.C. (1950 December). *Earned degrees conferred, 1949-50. Higher Education,* U.S. Office of Education, 7, 77-78.

Van Dalen, D.B. (1961 April). Evaluating graduate instruction in physical education. *Journal of Health, Physical Education, and Recreation,* 32, 34-35.

Waits, L.A. (1935 June). Significance of the Ph.D. *School and Society,* 45, 837-839.

Walters. E. (Ed.). (1963 October). Graduate programs. *Journal of Higher Education,* 34, 411-412.

Welch, J.E. (1968). The YMCA Graduate School of Nashville. Unpublished paper presented to the Research Section, American Association for Health, Physical Education, and Recreation, St. Louis, MO.

Wilson, D.M. (1958 April) Next problem of articulation: The undergraduate college and the professional and graduate schools. *Educational Record,* 39, 124-128.

Zeigler, E.F. (1951). *A history of professional preparation for physical education in the United States, 1861-1948.* Eugene, OR: Microform Publications, University of Oregon.

Zeigler, E. F. (1962). A history of professional preparation for physical education in the United States (1861-1961). In *Professional preparation in health education, physical education, recreation education.* Washington, DC: The Association, pp. 116-133.

Zeigler, E.F. and McCristal, K.J. (1967 December). A history of the Big Ten Body-of-Knowledge Project. *Quest,* 9, 79-84.

Zeigler, E.F. and Jones, M.L. (1969 March). Common denominators in physical education graduate study in Illinois. *Journal of Health, Physical Education, and Recreation,* 40, 85-87.

Zeigler, E.F. and Penny, W.J. (1969 December). Generalizations about developing graduate programs in physical education. *The Physical Educator,* 26, 169-170.

Zeigler, E.F. (1971 February). A recommended irreducible minimum for graduate study in physical education and sport. *Journal of Health, Physical Education, and*

Recreation, 42, 85-86.

Zeigler, E.F. (1972 No. 2). An historical analysis of the professional master's degree in physical education in the United States. *Canadian Journal of the History of Sport and Physical Education*, 3, 44-68.

Zeigler, E.F. A model for optimum professional development in a field called "x". In *Proceedings of the First Canadian Symposium on the Philosophy of Sport and Physical Activity*, Windsor, Ontario, pp. 16-28.

Zeigler, E.F. and Paton, G.A. (1974). Consolidation and innovation in graduate study in physical education and sport. In *Proceedings of the National College Physical Education Association for Men*, Minneapolis, MN, pp. 101-107.

Zeigler, E.F. (1975 May). Historical perspective on contrasting philosophies of professional preparation for physical education in the United States. *Canadian Journal of History of Sport and Physical Education*, 6, 23-42.

Zook, G.F. (1936 January). Present position of graduate studies in the United States. *School and Society*, 43, 41-49

CHAPTER VI

AMERICAN PHYSICAL EDUCATION
IN THE 20TH CENTURY: AN ANALYTIC REVIEW[1]

20TH CENTURY PROGRAM DEVELOPMENT

A reasonably balanced disciplinary development was envisioned in the 1960s in the field of physical education, but whether this movement will result ultimately in a more significant professional development for the field remains to be seen. Because there have been so many different interpretations with varying and at times conflicting emphases, the aims and objectives of physical education and its allied professions in the 20th century in North America should be reviewed. The goals of the allied professions (AAHPERD) stated here as "common denominators" are to provide (1) movement fundamentals, (2) regular exercise, (3) health and safety education, (4) physical recreation, (5) physical fitness, (6) competitive sport, and (7) therapeutic exercise (when needed). They are probably accepted by the majority in the several allied professions. If this listing of common denominators is reasonably acceptable, then this presumed agreement--having coming about gradually over a period of decades--has offered certain approaches, emphases, and courses of action for our scholars and researchers to pursue in their work over the past 50 years or so (See Figure 6.1 below).

During the first half of this century our leaders have espoused a plethora of objectives for the field as they sought to make a case for our greater or lesser "intrusion" into the school, college, and university curricula. Because of our typical defensive posture--a stance almost automatically assumed still today by the large majority--our leaders have felt it necessary to proclaim that an excellent health and physical education program can produce truly remarkable results in children and young people. However, the evidence to support the arguments for these possible accomplishments has not been readily available in sufficient quantity or quality. Quite often we have used missionary zeal to make up for the lack of supportive scientific data. Be that as it may, these educators were dedicated leaders with a certain amount of vision regarding their chosen profession--and they did actually point the way for the coming generation. Notable among these leaders who have defined a variety of objectives, starting in the early 1920s, were Hetherington (1922), Bowen and Mitchell (1923), Wood and Cassidy (1927), Williams (1927), Hughes (with Williams) (1930), Nash, 1931, Sharman (1937), Wayman (1938),

Figure 6.1

Common Denominators in Physical Education
Program Development in the 20th Century

Statement of Objectives by Leaders (1922-1950s)

Hetherington, Wood & Cassidy, Williams, Hughes,
Bowen & Mitchell, Nash, Sharman, Wayman, Essinger,
Staley, McCloy, Clark, Cobb, Lynn, Bownell, Scott,
Bucher, Oberteuffer, Metheny, N. Shepard, Brightbill,
Sapora

Developing Allied Professions

1. Health Education
2. Safety Education
3. Recreation & Park Administration
4. Dance (Education)
5. Athletics
6. Exercise Therapy

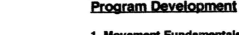

Common Denominators in
Program Development

1. Movement Fundamentals
2. Regular Exercise
3. Health & Safety Education
4. Physical Recreation
5. Physical Fitness
6. Competitive Sport
7. Therapeutic Exercise
8. Others? (Zeigler, 1977)

Hess's Objectives of the 20th Century
in the Field of Physical Education

Hygiene or Health Objective (1900-1919)
Socio-Educational Objective (1920-1928)
Socio-Recreational Objective (1929-1938)
Physical Fitness & Health Objective (1939-1945)
"Total Fitness & International Understanding (1946-1957)
Disciplinary Development; Sport Experience 1960-???

Esslinger (1938), Staley (1939), McCloy (1940), Clark (1943), Cobb (1943), Lynn (1944), Brownell & Hagman, Scott, Bucher, Oberteuffer (all in 1951). (See the top left of Figure 6.1 above.)

There have been many other fine, earlier statements some later ones as well (e.g., the names of Metheny, Shepard, Brightbill, and Sapora are also shown in the figure). One could categorize and then enumerate the various objectives proposed for the field by category, and the resultant list would be really impressive as to our subject matter's potential educational contribution. Our professional task today, of course, is to ascertain in an ever more scholarly and scientific manner what the effects of planned, developmental physical activity are under a myriad of conditions. Additionally, we need to become ever more alert in our interpretation of the various social forces impacting on our work in regard to their effect on acceptable program development for the normal, accelerated, and special populations at all levels for all ages (Zeigler, 2003).

In the late 1950s, Hess (1959) completed a study in which he investigated the objectives of physical education in the United States from 1900 to 1957 in the light of certain historical events. (See Figure 6.1 at bottom left.) While we must grant a certain subjectivity to this type of historical analysis, this investigation does nevertheless offer us a point of departure when we seek to compare (1) the results of Hess' study, (2) the stated objectives expressed by the various leaders listed, (3) the influence of the several (now) allied professions that were growing rapidly during this 50-year period (keeping in mind that many physical educators favored "being all things to all people"), and (4) the ever-present pivotal social forces operative in the society. The major objectives of the various periods, as identified by Hess, are the following :

1. The hygiene or health objective (1900-1919)
2. The socio-educational objectives (1920-1928)
3. The socio-recreational objectives (1929-1938)
4. The physical fitness and health objectives (1939-1945)
5. The "total fitness" and international understanding objectives (1946-1957)

(**Note**: It was next to impossible for Hess to achieve historical perspective for the 1950s, of course, but he could certainly list several "leading" objectives [which he did]. Also, we should not forget the overlapping nature of these objectives from one period to another--or even to the next period beyond that.)

The influence of physical education's allied professions on the objectives of physical education is an interesting question in itself. Each of these professions had dedicated adherents who were working to have their embryonic profession both well and fairly represented within the health and physical education curriculum of the first half century. At the same time they were looking forward to the day when separate, fully independent status might be granted to their particular field (or subject-matter) with resultant increased curricular time allotment. These allied professions have been identified as the following:

1. Health education
2. Safety education (including driver education)
3. Recreation and parks administration
4. Dance (education)
5. Competitive athletics
   (interscholastic & intercollegiate *and*
   intramurals and recreational sports, with the
   latter now striving for its own professional
   identity and with a significant number
   wanting to call it "campus recreation")
6. Adapted or special physical education
   (See left middle of Figure 6.1.)

COMMON DENOMINATORS IN PROGRAM DEVELOPMENT

Interestingly, even as each of these allied professions (listed immediately above) was developing to a point where it saw clearly its own program objectives (and therefore felt it necessary to break free from a direct relationship with physical education), each nevertheless has had a greater or lesser influence on the stated objectives of physical education in the 20th century. These presumably consensual objectives offer an indication of this influence on what toward the middle of the century was designated as physical education at all educational levels. Further, it is highly interesting to note that--even today with only slight modification--these "common denominators" of human motor performance within what is here being called "physical activity education" in sport, exercise, and expressive movement are still intact and we find considerable agreement on them all over the civilized world:

1. That regular physical education and sport periods be required for all children and young people (who are presumably still in school) up to and including 16 years of age.

2. That human movement fundamentals through various expressive activities are basic in the elementary, middle, and high school curricula.

3. That physical vigor and endurance are important for people of all ages. Progressive standards should be developed from prevailing norms.

4. That remediable defects should be corrected through exercise therapy at all school levels. Where required, adapted sport and physical recreation experiences should be stressed.

5. That a young person should develop certain positive attitudes toward his or her own health in particular and toward community hygiene in general. Basic health knowledge should be an integral part of the school curriculum.

> (**Note**: This "common denominator" should be
> a specific objective of the profession of sport and
> physical education only as it relates to
> developmental physical activity.)

6. That sport, exercise, and expressive movement can make a most important contribution throughout life toward the worthy use of leisure.

7. That boys and girls (and young men and women) should have an experience in competitive sport at some stage of their development.

8. That character and/or personality development is vitally important to the development of the young person, and therefore it is especially important that all human movement experience in sport, exercise, and expressive movement at the various educational levels be guided by men and women with high professional standards and ethics. (See right side of Figure 6.1 above.)

(See, also, Zeigler, 1989, pp. 185-186, for an
elaboration of these proposed common denominators.)

A DIAGRAMMATIC REPRESENTATION OF 20TH CENTURY DEVELOPMENT OF PHYSICAL EDUCATION KINESIOLOGY

In an effort to make this historical analysis even more clear, the remainder of this investigation will combine narrative with diagrams dating back to 1900 and concluding with diagrammatic figures and tables indicating what should begin to happen during the remainder of the 1990s. My hope is that physical education/kinesiology will now sharpen its focus and delimit its aims and objectives as it seeks to serve humankind more efficiently and effectively in the 21st century.

Stage 1--Physical Education--circa 1900-1930. In this analysis of the emerging physical education field at the beginning of the 20th century within the public education system primarily, three subdivisions (or categories) of the field will be traced as follows:

1. The *potential body-of-knowledge* as characterized by its
sub-disciplinary areas (e.g., anatomical and physiological aspects)

2. The *concurrent professional components* of the developing
field such as exist in all subject-matter fields (e.g.,
curriculum, methods of instruction)

3. The *potential allied professions* (e.g., health education,
competitive athletics)

(See Figure 6.2 below; note that the sub-
disciplinary names in the diagrams use the
names of other disciplines (e.g., physiology,
psychology), but that toward the end of the
study a recommendation is made to employ
those names only that do *not* "give our field
away" to another established discipline.)

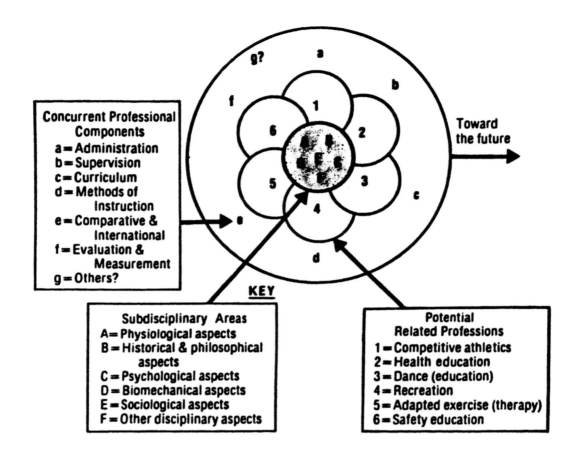

Concurrent Professional Components
a = Administration
b = Supervision
c = Curriculum
d = Methods of Instruction
e = Comparative & International
f = Evaluation & Measurement
g = Others?

Toward the future

KEY

Subdisciplinary Areas
A = Physiological aspects
B = Historical & philosophical aspects
C = Psychological aspects
D = Biomechanical aspects
E = Sociological aspects
F = Other disciplinary aspects

Potential Related Professions
1 = Competitive athletics
2 = Health education
3 = Dance (education)
4 = Recreation
5 = Adapted exercise (therapy)
6 = Safety education

Figure 6.2

Stage One--1900-1930

Figure 6.2 describes the situation for the period extending from app. 1900 to app. 1930 (or Stage 1). It indicates that the sub-disciplinary areas are "blurred" and almost indistinguishable within the center of the circle depicting physical education. It is true that professional students of that time received instruction in anatomy and physiology, as well as in chemistry and physics, prior to the required professional physical education courses identified, for example, as physiology of exercise, kinesiology, anthropometry, physical examination and diagnosis, massage, history of physical training, emergencies, and medical gymnastics (*Oberlin College Catalogue* for 1894). However, the strong point to be made here is that there were (1) basic science courses and (2) professional physical education courses. Instruction in the so-called "academic courses" was almost completely lacking. It was true, very importantly, that certain professors (instructors) had areas of specialization (e.g., Fred Leonard in physical education history; Delphine Hanna in medical gymnastics), but the very large majority of these people *saw themselves as physical educators*--not as specialists in some other disciplinary subject-matter within the college or university.

> (**Note:** We must mention the "M.D. phenomenon" in our
> early history. For example, a person such as James H.
> McCurdy, M.D., recognized that our embryonic
> profession needed people with "scientific ability who will
> increase our knowledge with reference especially to
> bodily growth, to personal hygiene, to physiology of
> exercise, etc." [McCurdy, 1901, pp. 311-312].)

The "potential allied professions" were also "blurred" and almost indistinguishable within the center of the circle depicting physical education in Figure 6.2. For example, in the *Wellesley College Catalogue* for 1910, athletics ((no.1 under potential allied professions) is included in the requirements for the Bachelor of Arts degree in Physical Education under the heading of "Professional Courses" by virtue of a two-hour course in "organized sports," a three-hour course in "athletics" (presumably track and field), and a three and one-half hour course in "outdoor games and athletics."

Health education (no. 2) is included as "Reg. A.B. Hygiene" for one hour, and dance (education) (no. 3) is listed as "dancing" for one or two hours. Recreation (no. 4) could conceivably be regarded as *physical* recreation insofar as sports activities were offered within the physical education curriculum. Adapted exercise (therapy) (no. 5) appeared as "corrective gymnastics and massage" for one hour. Finally, the only reference to safety education (no. 6) was a course experience called "emergencies" for one hour. Thus, if you will check Figure 4 above again, you will note (1) that the sub-disciplinary areas (A, B, C, D, E, and F) are very close together in the center of the core depicting physical education as a field; (2) the potential allied professions (shown as 1, 2, 3, 4, 5, and 6) are firmly attached, or closely spaced next to, the core of the diagram; and (3) the concurrent professional components (a, b, c, d, e, f, and g) are simply indicated as belonging in the larger circle (similar to the way that they will be shown in subsequent diagrams).

Stage 2--Physical Education--circa 1930-1960. In Figure 6.3 below, which represents roughly the period from 1930 to 1960, we find that there has actually been considerable change within the field still known as "physical education." However, in Figure 6.3, the sub-disciplinary areas are beginning to emerge from the core depicted in Figure 6.2 above. The typical tests and measurements course, for example, was gradually characterized by an improved laboratory experience, often largely physical fitness/exercise physiology in nature. These were soon supplemented by motor learning and kinesiological laboratory experiences as well. There was kinematic analysis of human movement in sport and exercise, but the first doctoral study involving kinetic analysis had not yet been carried out. Sport and physical education sociology had not yet appeared on the scene, nor had the social psychological analysis of sport and physical activity surfaced to any recognizable extent.

There were a great many historical and biographical theses, but by and large the historical studies were not characterized by the use of an interpretive criterion to evaluate the evidence that had been gathered. The biographical studies were interesting and usually substantive, but the subject of such an investigation typically emerged with such a large halo around his/her head that one wondered whether there had been "a second coming of the Lord"! Early philosophical studies were not impressive, although in the mid-1940's and the fifties they improved and were similar to studies being carried out in educational philosophy. Occasionally the question was being asked by scholars like C.H. McCloy, and especially about the "softer side" of our field (as it is often unfortunately called), as to how long a field could expect to prosper as a profession when the bulk of its research was carried on through the medium of doctoral study.

Shifting attention to the designated "concurrent professional components," there were a large number of doctoral studies that could be characterized as *administrative* in nature. Many of these were helpful and provided useful information,

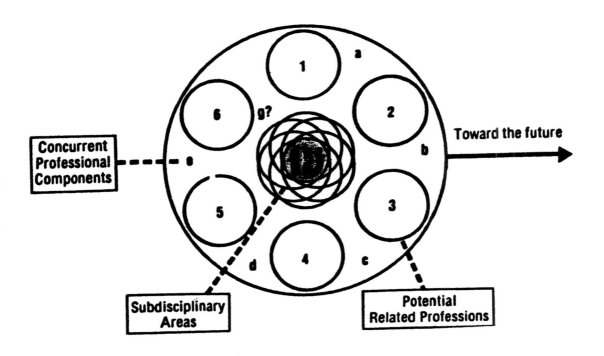

Figure 6.3

Stage Two--1930-1960

but as Spaeth (1975) reported, "there is an almost total lack of theoretical orientation in the design of research and interpretation of the findings in the sample of administrative research studied." She stated further, "the administrative research lacked the methodological rigor necessary for contributions to the development of scientific knowledge about administrative performance" (Zeigler and Spaeth, 1975, p. 44). With exceptions, of course, much the same can probably be said for the studies carried out in the components identified as "supervision," "curriculum," and "instruction."

It is important to keep in mind, however, that these are usually types of investigation employing a variety of techniques under descriptive research methodology. In such cases it is often not possible nor desirable to emerge from these studies with a coefficient of correlation or a multiple correlation--not to mention results available from employment of a factor-analysis technique. International and comparative research in sport and physical education was practically nonexistent from the standpoint of the use of even relatively complex social science methodology and accompanying techniques. The final category listed here ("measurement and evaluation") was viewed more as part of the sub-disciplinary efforts of our scientists. It was therefore tied in with those interested in the physiological, kinesiological, and psychological aspects of physical education. Today it is being used more as a tool subject that may be used by almost any researcher in the field carrying out an investigation based on the natural sciences, the social sciences, or even the humanities.

Finally, then, in this period from 1930 to 1960, the "potential allied professions" will be considered briefly. Examination of Figure 6.3, which is called Stage 2, indicates that the "allied professions," which were firmly attached to (and literally part of) physical education, have now moved out of its inner core. By 1960, these potential allied professions--i.e., competitive athletics, health education, dance (education), recreation, adapted exercise (therapy), and safety education--have clearly established their own identities. Indeed, in some cases they have even established a separate identity within the field of education, not to mention any recognition that had been accorded to them by the public.

Stage 3--Physical Education (and Sport)--circa 1960-1970. Many people can recall vividly the events of the 1960s both within society in general and within physical education specifically. Our graduate study programs were attacked by Conant (Harvard); responded to by Esslinger (Oregon) on our behalf; and the field developed an incomplete understanding of the need for a substantive body-of-knowledge to undergird our professional efforts. A notable undertaking, still operative in an altered format, was the Big Ten Body-of-Knowledge Project as conceived by Daniels and followed through to fruition by McCristal and some of us who were present at the time. The sub-disciplinary areas included in this undertaking were (1) sociology of sport and physical education; (2) administrative theory; (3) history, philosophy, and comparative physical education and sport; (4) exercise physiology; (5) biomechanics; and (6) motor learning & sport psychology (Zeigler, ed., 1975, p. 292).

The sub-disciplinary areas shown in Figure 6.4 below are similar, the only difference being that certain sub-disciplinary areas are indicated as concurrent professional components (e.g., administrative theory). The significant point to be made, however, is that the sub-disciplinary areas themselves have moved from the central core of physical education in the earlier diagrams to a position not unlike the positions held earlier by the potential allied professions. These sub-disciplinary areas (e.g., so-called sociology of sport) were indeed moving strongly away from physical education toward the end of the 1960-1970 decade. The position of sport sociology, soon followed by other sub-disciplinary societies being established. reminded one of the "floating apex" of Peter Principle notoriety. They had gone off to function by themselves without any undergirding organizational support of the mother discipline of sociology. Thus, it was essentially unrecognized by the societal entities that they purported to describe--i.e., sport or sociology.

Further examination of Figure 6.4 in regard to the movement of the potential allied professions shows that all six of the field have moved further in the direction of establishing their own identity even within educational circles. It is impossible to describe *precisely* where each of these professions concerned was located, but it was clear that further movement away from the field of physical education had been taken.

Examination of the concurrent professional components for the period from 1960-1970--components which by their very nature are inextricably linked to the professional development of physical educators--brings to light some interesting developments as well. For example, we saw the introduction of a more theoretical orientation in these topics on the part of a relatively few graduate programs. Typically, the concept of supervision had merged more completely with the larger realm of overall administration. The subject of curriculum (i.e., program development) received somewhat more attention generally, and several scholars led the way in giving this topic a more theoretical orientation than previously. The

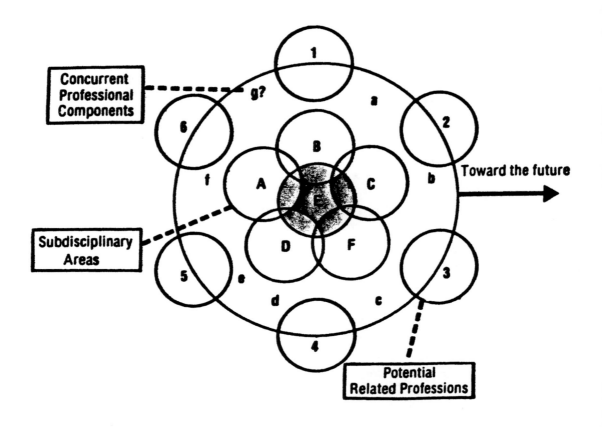

Figure 6.4

Stage Three--1960-1970

same can be said for the topic "methods of instruction," but this professional component did not receive noticeably more attention during this decade. (A few professors reacted to what they considered to be the overemphasis of the sub-disciplinary orientation by a very small segment of the total population of physical educators in the United States. As a result, they cast their lots with what they called a "professional preparation" approach to both undergraduate and graduate education in the field. It could be argued that this "move" was simply an improved, more precise approach to what the large majority of college and universities had been emphasizing for decades.

Stage 4--Physical Education (and Sport--circa 1970-1990. Stage 4, as explained in Figure 6.5 below, treats the period from 1970 to 1990 and, as we can readily appreciate, it is extremely difficult to gain a true perspective on the happenings of this recent 20-year period. Nevertheless, some of the developments that began in previous decades did indeed continue along apace, and so several reasonably accurate observations may be possible.

For example, the sub-disciplinary areas that were moving strongly away from involvement with physical education at the professional- conference level have continued with their movement in the direction of the respective mother disciplines (e.g., sport history and sport philosophy). However the movement of those who called themselves sport philosophers was "sharper" in nature, whereas the North American Society for Sport History still provides a "comfortable atmosphere" for those with an historical interest in physical education to convene. This trend has continued despite the fact that the very large majority of these people received their graduate training in what were called physical education units and--where some money was still available--received their travel funds from the same units as well.

Also, although many within the larger professional associations in both the United States and Canada have been aware of this departure of many scholars, it has been difficult to know whether to ignore this development or to attempt to reverse it. We did witness the inauguration of a number of sub-disciplinary and sub-professional "academies" with the larger professional groupings. In the United States, the professional association (AAHPER), recognizing the impact of the term "sport" established the entity now known as the National Association for Sport and Physical Education. (It should be noted at this point that the large majority of conferences held on other continents, including those with a worldwide orientation, typically employ the word "sport" in their terminology in one way or another along

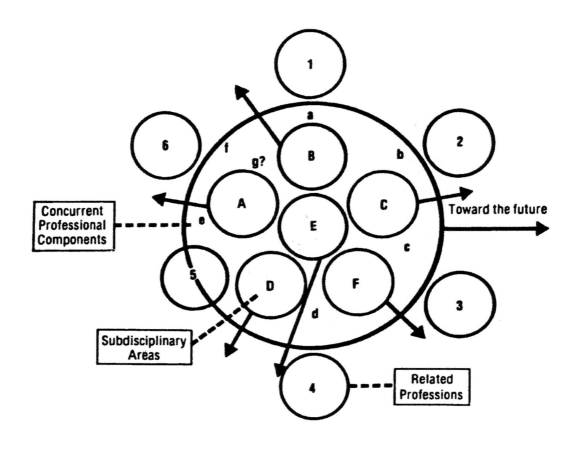

Figure 6.5

Stage Four--1970-1990

with the term "physical education.")

Viewed from an overall basis, it can be argued that the six potential allied professions have almost completely consolidated their positions outside of the domain of physical education at the college and university level, although this has not yet been possible officially at the lower educational levels. The American *Association* for Health, Physical Education, and Recreation recognized this independent growth of the allied professions by changing its name to the American *Alliance* for Health, Physical Education, and Recreation. Then, just before the turn of the 1980s decade, the Alliance Board of Governors officially added the word "dance" to the official title and AAHPER became AAHPERD. This action culminated a period in which a number of dance units within colleges and universities moved, or sought permission to move, out of the physical education unit per se to some other educational entity on campus. Thus, whether the topic is about competitive athletics, health education, dance (education), recreation (education), safety education, or even adapted exercise (therapy), it became obvious that most of those people who came to relate primarily to one or the other of these allied professions want to be free from what they identify as the "fizz ed stigma."

During this recent period, there doesn't appear to have been a considerable amount of change in the concurrent professional components shown in Figure 6.5 as Stage 4. The term "management" began to gain acceptance in the latter half of the 1970s, and then really began to supplant the term "administration" as sport management curricula began to spring up in the 1980s. However, it was only after the establishment of the North American Society for Sport Management (and its official journal) in the latter half of the decade that there was some evidence of the need for improving both the theoretical and practical components of professional preparation in this aspect of the field.

Also, a small, stalwart band of curriculum theorists continued to strive for careful investigation into the intricacies of this aspect of our professional program. Further, and fortunately for those interested in professional preparation, including curriculum or program development and instructional methodology, higher education institutions are continuing their drive for an improved level of instructional competency by all professors, a move that was sparked by the clamor of students in the 1960s and which has been perpetuated by the continuing aim to please occasioned by the ongoing financial constraints that began in the 1970s and the accompanying need to preserve the student head-count, constraints that seem even more constricting at the beginning of the 1990s.

The remaining two professional components to be considered within Stage 4 are "international and comparative" and "measurement and evaluation." There is a relatively small, loyal group of professionals keeping the former area alive within the Alliance, as well as a second small international group functioning within the International Society for Comparative Physical Education and Sport. However, the amount of scholarly investigation carried out in this aspect of our professional endeavor must be categorized as slight throughout the 1970-1990 period. This is truly an indictment of our professional growth at a time when we should be moving toward more not less involvement with our colleagues abroad. However, there is no doubt but that a good deal of cross-fertilization does occur within the sub-disciplinary societies at international meetings. Yet, there is no mechanism for the knowledge engendered at all of these conferences to be transmitted to professionals everywhere in a useable fashion.

Measurement and evaluation, typically packaged earlier in the required tests and measurement course, was still an important part of undergraduate professional preparation in physical education at the end of the 1970s, but during that decade it became diffused in many programs at the graduate level into the various sub-disciplinary or sub-professional streams available. During the 1980s a similar development was occurring at the undergraduate level at well. There are some universities that offer it as an area of specialization at the graduate level, and there are universities who maintain a "measurement and evaluation professor" (i.e., allot a percentage of this person's workload) to service students and/or professors needing advice insofar as research design and statistical techniques are concerned. The feeling seems to be that it is a physical impossibility to do a good job of packaging the research methodologies and the multitude of accompanying research techniques under one specific course. There is some merit in this argument, but I believe that the student is being shortchanged with this approach and resultantly does not understand the "big picture" in regard to scholarly research.

Stage 5--Physical Education/Kinesiology--circa 1990-????. We have finally arrived at the point where we are in a position to conjecture *about*, and possibly prescribe *for*, the future of the field of physical education/kinesiology as we struggle ahead toward the turn of the century. By combining these two terms in this way, the current position seems to be that "physical education" is what the professional practitioner does, and kinesiology (or the study of movement) is where the undergirding knowledge resides.

Before moving ahead, it will be necessary to retrogress for a moment to Figure 6.4 (Stage 3--1960-1970) above where it was explained that the sub-disciplinary movement at that point began to move significantly away from what might be called the "central core" of the physical education profession. It was at that point that Cyril White, an Irish sport and physical education sociologist, offered the idea in a discussion paper that our field might be moving from a *multidiscipline* to a *crossdiscipline* on the way toward becoming an *interdiscipline* (Zeigler, 1975, pp. 350-51). However, he postulated that the profession's "future development to interdisciplinary level will require a far greater degree of sophisticated research abilities and orientations than the field at present possesses." The idea was intriguing, but it simply was not happening that way at that time, and thus seemed completely out of phase with the development taking place. Interestingly, somewhat later in a chance discussion, Philip Sparling (then of Georgia Tech) opined that we were moving in the opposite direction. Time has shown that Sparling was indeed correct in his judgment! (See Figure 6.6 below.)

To compound further what is already a complex situation, we as a field are not moving rapidly enough to what may be called true professional status. Those of us functioning in the public schools probably feel that we will be sheltered indefinitely by the protective arm of the teaching profession. They and others in the field may believe that society will not recognize our field as that profession which should be the leading force in human motor performance in exercise, sport, and related expressive movement. Whatever the facts in the matter may be, there is no escaping one discouraging fact that--despite our *unique* mission--we are, along with art and music typically at the bottom of the totem pole in educational circles. Additionally, we are missing the opportunity to become the profession of which we are capable and along with this omission are thereby deprived of any accompanying social recognition and support.

It is for these reasons, therefore, that a Stage 5 is being postulated here for the profession's consideration. If certain vigorous steps were to be taken by the leading professional associations (e.g., AAHPERD, NAKPEHE), it is conceivable and possible that a strong thrust would lead to a trend that would be recognized and could soon lead to a much stronger profession undergirded by a body-of-knowledge generated by the scholars and researchers of our *crossdiscipline* (that could be well on the way to becoming an *interdiscipline*).

This recommended development is explained in Figure 6.7 below. The reader will notice immediately as the diagram is examined that the *sub-disciplinary areas*,

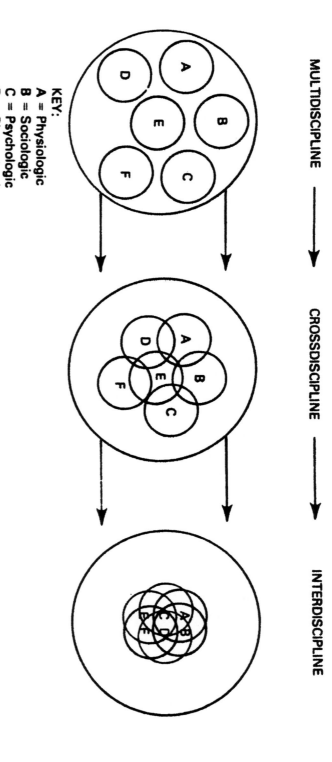

MULTIDISCIPLINE ⟶   CROSSDISCIPLINE ⟶   INTERDISCIPLINE

KEY:
A = Physiologic
B = Sociologic
C = Psychologic
D = Biomechanic
E = Historical, Philosophic,
    Comparative
F = Others?

Figure 6.6

Physical Education: A Multi-Discipline
on the Way toward Becoming a Cross-Discipline

(Courtesy of Cyril M. White, Ph.D.,
Ireland, adapted by Earle Zeigler.)

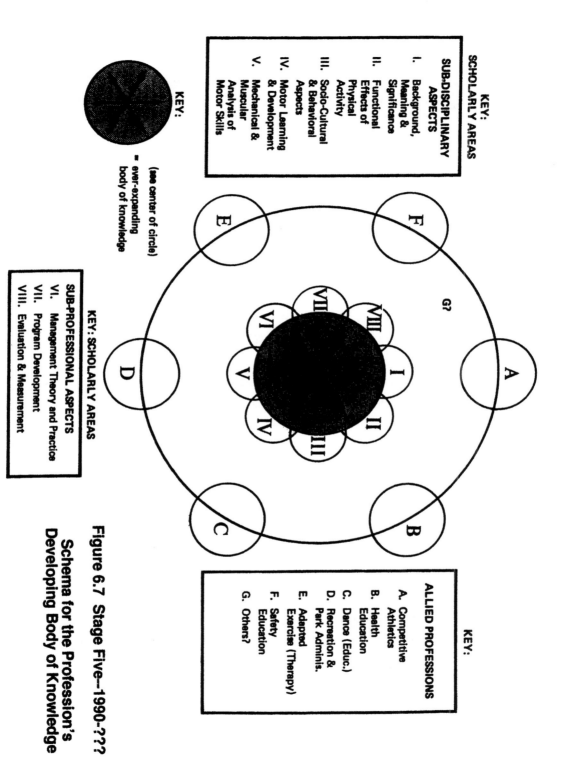

KEY: SCHOLARLY AREAS

SUB-DISCIPLINARY ASPECTS

I. Background, Meaning & Significance
II. Functional Effects of Physical Activity
III. Socio-Cultural & Behavioral Aspects
IV. Motor Learning & Development
V. Mechanical & Muscular Analysis of Motor Skills

KEY:

● (see center of circle)
■ ever-expanding body of knowledge

KEY: SCHOLARLY AREAS

SUB-PROFESSIONAL ASPECTS

VI. Management Theory and Practice
VII. Program Development
VIII. Evaluation & Measurement

KEY:

ALLIED PROFESSIONS

A. Competitive Athletics
B. Health Education
C. Dance (Educ.)
D. Recreation & Park Adminis.
E. Adapted Exercise (Therapy)
F. Safety Education
G. Others?

Figure 6.7 Stage Five—1990-???

Schema for the Profession's Developing Body of Knowledge

instead of continuing along with their movement for greater identification with the *related* disciplines, have been persuaded to function more strongly *within* the field of physical education/kinesiology and are firmly attached to the profession's core-- explained as a developing body-of-knowledge about the theory and practice of movement or physical activity in exercise, sport, and related expressive movement. Obviously, persuading these groupings (NASPE, and NAKPEHE) to move solidly and soundly to a position of direct alliance or affiliation will be a tall order, but it could be done by means of persuasion, encouragement, influence, and even "bribery" if necessary.

The present situation cries out the following to occur: (1) the scholars and researchers of our field identifying and working strongly with the professional associations and (2) the leaders of the professional associations recognizing that the future of the profession *requires* the sound knowledge undergirding that the scholars and researchers can provide. As matters stand now, neither set of groupings (guided by their own leaders) sees the need for such a development clearly. We have done a bit of hand-wringing over the dispersion that is occurring, but the leaders haven't made it clear to all concerned that the profession needs a concerted effort to assure a future that embodies professional status of a higher order. Frankly, as matters stand now, keeping all of the characteristics typically ascribed to a full-fledged profession in mind, the field of physical education is a "glorified trade" with the potential to become a true profession when it organizes itself sufficiently to provide its practitioners with tenable theory about human movement based on ongoing high-level scholarly endeavor. Further, any such resultant body-of-knowledge should be made available in the form of *ordered generalizations* that can be readily understood and applied by our professional practitioners.

If the *sub-disciplinary areas* of our anticipated cross-discipline/interdiscipline can be brought to conform with the proposal made in Figure 6.7, what about the *concurrent professional components*? In this instance we are fortunately not in a position where we will have to retrieve these elements from other professional organizations far removed from our midst. Our task here is to simply follow the lead to a greater extent of those scholarly people who have played leadership roles in curriculum and program development, professional preparation, instructional methodology, measurement and evaluation, comparative physical education and sport, and management theory. If their investigations are well executed, such scholarly efforts need to be recognized equally along with the work of those in the sub-disciplinary areas. Thus, these components have been left importantly within the circle that describes the total field of physical education/kinesiology.

Within AAHPERD we are, of course, faced with the continuing problem of our relationship with what have been described as the (potential) *allied professions*. The Alliance has made steady progress in this regard, and on October 1, 1992 implemented a three-year transition to full implementation of a new organizational model "intended to maximize autonomy of functioning for the national associations (the Alliance program arm), maintain autonomy for the district associations, and at the same time preserve the Alliance umbrella and the potential for synergistic mission accomplishment inherent in such an organization" (*Update*, April, 1993, 1). This plan should insure that these related professions stay firmly allied to us. We can do this best, of course, (1) by making the members of these associations (e.g., the National Dance Association) feel completely at home within the Alliance and by demonstrating through our actions that we are proud of the early role that physical education played in assisting them to develop to the point where separate professional status was the next feasible step for them to take; (2) by improving the quantity and quality of our own scholarly endeavor so that they will feel proud to be allied with us; and (3) by relating in cross-disciplinary fashion to those scholars in each of these related professions at those points where joint research effort can be rewarding to all involved.

SCHOLARLY AND PROFESSIONAL DIMENSIONS OF DEVELOPMENTAL PHYSICAL ACTIVITY IN EXERCISE, SPORT, AND RELATED MOVEMENT

The ongoing, *ad nauseam* struggle involving the search for a name for our field has indeed brought us to a state of utter confusion. The term "sport and physical education" is recommended by NASPE within the Alliance to describe the *professional* entity in the United States. In Canada it is still "physical and health education" in the schools. However, the terms "physical education and sport" and "sport" are now more popular in other countries that identify with the Western world and the European continent, respectively. In my opinion, no one of these names, or combination of names, is going to make it in the long run. For purposes of this discussion, therefore, I have gone along here with the current name democratically arrived at in the (now) American Academy of Kinesiology and Physical Education--"kinesiology and physical education"--but in reverse order.

I believe that (1) agreement about a name, (2) a taxonomy for our subject matter, (3) the steady development of a undergirding body of knowledge, and (4) certification or licensure at the state/provincial level would reasonably soon place our field in a position where a professional practitioner would be recognized as a "such-and-such". I believe this is true, also, no matter what type of position that person held within the field--or for that matter in which state, province, or territory such professional service was carried out. Reaching consensus now at this late date will undoubtedly be extremely difficult. However, it is absolutely essential that we strive for such an objective.

In my opinion, the time is overdue for us to bring our field's image into sharper focus for the sake of our colleagues and students, not to mention the public. I must as well climb right out on a limb by stating my own position about what it is for which we should be responsible. We could call ourselves *human motor performance,* but this may not sound sufficiently academic for some. Movement arts and science has possibilities. The term "*kinesiology*" has been in the dictionary for decades, but we would have to broaden the definition that is there in one sense and narrow it in another. What we are fundamentally involved with is "*developmental physical activity in sport, exercise, and related expressive movement*"--and that's it! The late Elizabeth Halsey recommended it in the late 1950s, but the time was not yet ripe for its acceptance.

Simply put, our profession should be promoting such developmental physical activity for people of all ages and abilities. Further, we should be "professing" our theoretical and applied knowledge to help our practitioners in the field. The time is past due for our field to make our body of knowledge available through computer technology in a variety of ways (e.g., ordered principles, expert systems). In the process we should also convey the understanding to the public that we are not typically qualified to be *recreation directors, health specialists* or *dance specialists* holding undergraduate and graduate degrees in either of these three allied professions. These allied professions are now too highly specialized for us to think that there ever can be *one professional association* again that can serve all four fields. What we do understand is *physical* recreation only, some of the "health aspects" of developmental physical activity, and occasionally some of the social and traditional dances.

In the early 1970s, my late friend and colleague, Laura Huelster, and I decided that one approach would be to "conjure up" a taxonomy that would include both the professional and the scholarly dimensions of our work. With this thought uppermost in our minds, we decided upon a balanced approach between the *subdisciplinary* areas of our field and what might be identified as the *subprofessional* or concurrent professional components as explained above. As part of an effort to close what we regarded as a debilitating, fractionating rift within the field, we developed a taxonomical table to explain the proposed areas of scholarly study and research using *our field's* nomenclature (physical education and sport terms only) along with the accompanying disciplinary and professional aspects. We agreed upon eight areas of scholarly study and research that are correlated with their respective subdisciplinary and subprofessional aspects in Table 1 (see below). Most importantly, you will note that the names selected for the eight areas *do not include terms that are currently part of the names of, or the actual names, of other recognized disciplines* and that are therefore usually identified with these other (related) disciplines primarily by our colleagues and the public.

Thus, our position is that we must promote and develop *our own discipline* of physical education/kinesiology (or whatever it is called eventually) and *our own profession* of physical education and sport as described above, while at the same time working cooperatively with the related disciplines and the allied professions (to the extent that interest is shown in our problems). We maintained that by continuing to speak of *sociology* of sport, *physiology* of exercise, etc., the time is ever closer when these other disciplines and professions will really awaken to the importance of what we believe to be *our* professional task (i.e., the gathering and dissemination of knowledge about developmental physical activity through the media of sport, exercise, and related expressive movement--and the promotion of it to the extent that such promulgation is socially desirable).

The reader can readily understand our concern: the end result of a continuation of this multi-disciplinary splintering of our field of sport and physical education will inevitably result in a "mishmash" of isolated findings by well-intentioned, scholarly people not in a position to fully understand the larger goal toward which our profession is striving. Also--and this is vital for us--we will be destined (doomed?) to perpetual trade status--not *professional* status--as perennial jacks-of-all-trades, masters of none.

What I am arguing for, therefore, is that we call ourselves by a name that bespeaks what it is that we study and what we stand for professionally. Dr. Huelster and I finally decided to recommend "developmental physical activity" as *our field's* term that is similar to such terms as law, medicine, business administration, etc. The understanding would be that it relates to sport, exercise, and related expressive movement. However, physical education and kinesiology as a term could also work at all levels of the educational system, as well as in public, private, and commercial

Table 1
SCHOLARLY AND PROFESSIONAL DIMENSIONS OF DEVELOPMENTAL PHYSICAL ACTIVITY IN EXERCISE, SPORT, AND RELATED MOVEMENT

Areas of Scholarly Study & Research	Subdisciplinary Aspects	Subprofessional Aspects
I. BACKGROUND, MEANING, AND INTERCULTURAL SIGNIFICANCE	-History -Philosophy -International & Comparative Study	-International Relations -Professional Ethics
II. FUNCTIONAL EFFECTS OF PHYSICAL ACTIVITY	-Exercise Physiology -Anthropometry & Body Composition	-Fitness & Health Appraisal -Exercise Therapy
III. SOCIO-CULTURAL & BEHAVIORAL ASPECTS	-Sociology -Economics -Psychology (individual & social) -Anthropology -Political Science -Geography	-Application of Theory to Practice
IV. MOTOR LEARNING & CONTROL	-Psycho-motor Learning -Physical Growth & Development	-Application of Theory to Practice
V. MECHANICAL & MUSCULAR ANALYSIS OF MOTOR SKILLS	-Biomechanics -Neuro-skeletal Musculature	-Application of Theory to Practice
VI. MANAGEMENT THEORY & PRACTICE	-Management Science -Business Administration	-Application of Theory to Practice
VII. CURRICULUM THEORY & PROGRAM DEVELOPMENT	-Curriculum Studies	-Application of Theory to Practice

(General education; professional preparation; intramural sports and physical recreation; intercollegiate athletics; programs for special populations (e.g., handicapped) including both curriculum and instructional methodology)

VIII. MEASUREMENT AND EVALUATION	-Theory about the Measurement Function	-Application of Theory to Practice

agencies. It would simply be up to us to explain further that this title of physical education & kinesiology is an all-encompassing term that refers to the theory of human motor performance in *developmental physical activity* in exercise, sport, and expressive human movement for accelerated, normal, and special populations of all ages. This developing theory is being based increasingly on scholarly and research endeavor of a high order. We are the people in the profession that is concerned with physical activity that is used for some sort of worthwhile development throughout a person's life. Any specializations within the profession could develop further by using this name as a point of departure. However, in the final analysis, we simply must agree on *some* acceptable name and see that it is implemented forever (or at least for decades to come).

The controversy over a name does point up the urgent need for clarity in our use of language, however, not to mention the need to close the "say-do" gap in our professional endeavors. Indirectly it points the way also to bridging the ever-widening gap developing among the professional practitioner, the bio-scientific researcher, the social science and humanities scholar, and the administrator/manager and superviser. I believe most sincerely that increased emphasis on *our own* profession is a truly important point right now, because it is symptomatic of the many divisions that have developed in the past fifty years or so in our field. That is why the taxonomy for the scholarly and professional dimensions of our field is being recommended (Table 1).

A SYSTEMS APPROACH TO DEVELOPMENT AND USE OF THEORY AND RESEARCH IN PHYSICAL EDUCATION/KINESIOLOGY

In Table 1 above a revised taxonomy including both the sub-disciplinary and sub-professional aspects of the field was recommended. It was argued that continuing scholarly investigation grounded in such a taxonomy would result in an inventory of scientific findings arranged as ordered generalizations upon which a practitioner in the field could base his or her professional practice.

The first such inventory developed would obviously have certain gaps or deficiencies. There would be no need for apology, however, because such an effort would represent a meager beginning compared to what may be possible in 10, 20, or 50 years. However, the development will materialize unless substantive change occurs in present practice. To this end, I am recommending the gradual implementation of a systems approach, so that university personnel, professional practitioners in the field, scholars and researchers in other disciplines, and the general public may visualize the development needed to make available a sound, complete body of knowledge about developmental physical activity. Using a systems approach would result in a more rapid development and use of theory and research related to this unique profession. (See Figure 6.8 below.)

Along with many other fields, physical education and sport does not yet appreciate the need to promote the implementation of a "total system" concept. However, there are urgent reasons why this field must take a holistic view if the profession hopes to merit increased support in the future. The promotion of this "evolving entity" of physical education/kinesiology (developmental physical activity) characterized as it is with so many dynamic, interacting, highly complex components in sport, exercise, and related expressive movement--would require the cooperation of innumerable local, state (provincial), national, and international professional associations so that full support for the *total* professional effort could be provided.

The model presented here to help achieve a common purpose for developing and using theory and research explains a system with interrelated components that should be functioning as a unit--admittedly with constraints--much more effectively than they are at present. Although in practice the execution of such an approach would be very complex, the several components of the model are basically simply. As can be observed from Figure 6.7, the cycle progresses from *input* to *thruput* to *output* and then, after sound consumer reaction is obtained and possible corrective action is taken, back to input again (possibly with altered demand or resources).

A MODEL FOR OPTIMUM PROFESSIONAL DEVELOPMENT IN A FIELD CALLED "X", CIRCA 2000-2010

It is now possible to offer for consideration a model that may be employed for the optimum development of our profession as we move into the first two decades of the 21st century. Interestingly, this is the same model I recommended more than 30 years ago in similar form. Even then there was conflict going on about our field's name; so, I called it "A Model for the Optimum Professional Development in a Field Called "X". Selected minor modifications have been made since that time.

The model (see Figure 6.9 below) includes the following six subdivisions: (1)

Figure 6.8

A Systems Approach to the Development and Use of Theory and Research in Sport and Physical Education

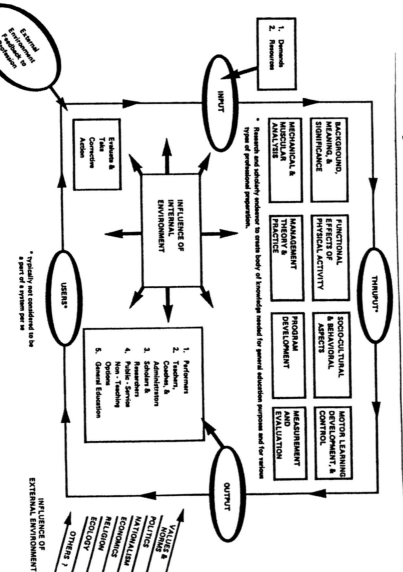

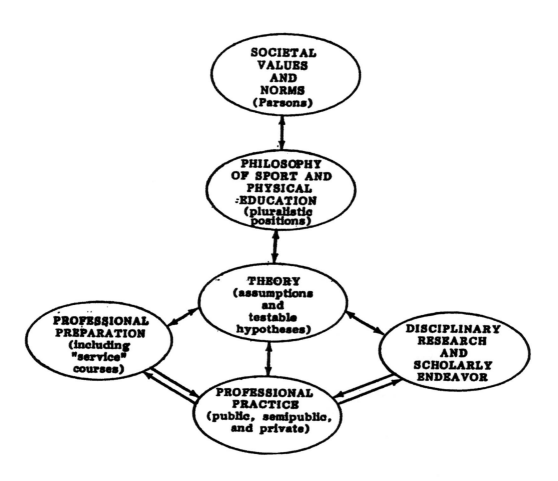

Figure 6.9

A Model for Optimum Development of
a Field Called "X"

professional practice, (2) professional preparation, (3) disciplinary research, (4) a developing theory embodying assumptions and testable hypotheses, (5) an operational philosophy of physical education and sport, and (6) societal values and norms.

Public, semi-public, and private *practice* may be professional, semiprofessional, or volunteer in nature and should be based on tenable theory. Professional preparation could or should involve the education of (1) the performer, (2) the teacher/coach, (3) the teacher of teachers/coaches, and (4) the scholar/researcher. The idea of offering "general education" may be added to enlarge the *professional-preparation circle*, since it seems logical that "introduction" to physical education/kinesiology (or whatever it is eventually called) should be added to the educational curriculum as either a required or elective subject. *Sub-disciplinary research* should be carried out according to the terminology recommended in the left-hand column in Table 1 above. What I call *subprofessional investigation* is subsumed under this heading as well.

The assumptions and testable hypotheses of a steadily evolving *theory*, the circle present in the middle of the model, should comprise a coherent group of general and specific propositions that can be used as principles to explain the phenomena observed in human movement in exercise, sport, and related expressive movement. Next the inclusion of the *philosophy of physical education and sport*--the values and ethics according to which the profession conducts its practice. This is based finally on *the sociological theory that the values and norms of a society* will be realized in the final analysis, albeit gradually and unevenly within the culture (Zeigler and Spaeth, 1975, pp. 407-411).

RECOMMENDATIONS

In drawing this analysis to a close, I would like to make (1) some *specific* recommendations which, if carried out, could insure the future of physical education/kinesiology in the 21st century, and (2) some *general* observations about the culture at large and the international scene:

Specific Recommendations. Based on what has been reported in this historical analysis of physical education/kinesiology in the 20th century, can it be stated that the field through its own efforts is indeed undergoing a significant process of modification? Or are we simply in the unfavorable position of being buffeted about by all of the various social forces? Or do we have more than our share of "that vast majority who either watches things happen, or doesn't even know that anything is going on?" I ask further, "Could we possibly take control of our professional destinies?" Is there a chance that we could soon become somewhat more able to make things happen in our field within education and within the larger society? In other words, are we as a profession capable of accepting a behavioral science image of man and woman as people who are continuously adapting reality to our own ends to the greatest extent possible?

After lengthy consideration of the subject over a period of many years, I feel able to state that we have definitely undergone a process of considerable modification. I use the term "modification" deliberately, rather than the terms "change," "alteration," "variation," "transformation," "conversion," or "transmutation." By this I mean that we are definitely tending to restrict, limit, or qualify what it is that *we*--in what is called sport and physical education by NASPE and kinesiology and physical education by the Academy (AAKPE) and the National Association for Kinesiology and Physical Education in Higher Education (NAKPEHE)--should be doing professionally. We have indubitably reached the point in our professional development where we must sharpen our focus. My fear, however, is that this process of modification is occurring too slowly. In the meantime, other social forces are crowding us; are delimiting us in various undesirable ways; and are, in the process, often buffeting us unmercifully. The following, then, are some of the changes that are occurring.

1. Because in the past the field of physical education has sought to be "all things to all people," *we now don't know exactly what we stand for.* Pretty soon we won't even be certain whether push-ups and jogging still belong to us. What ever happened to the late Arthur Steinhaus's "principal principles" of physical education? Where does our major thrust lie?

2. *All sorts of name changes are occurring* to explain either what people think we are doing or should be doing, not to mention how they can camouflage the "unsavory" connotation of the term "physical education." Thus, we are becoming kinesiology, human kinetics, ergonomics, sport management, sport studies, kinanthropology, or what have you?

3. The advent of Sputnik; the subsequent "race for the moon" and how this affected education, science, and technology; Conant's devastating criticism of

the presumed academic content of our curricula; and the subsequent almost frantic drive for a body-of-knowledge based on solid scientific and scholarly investigation for the field have placed us in a curious position as a profession--*we really don't know where or what our body of knowledge is.* Nowhere is it available to us in a series of ordered principles or generalizations based on an accepted taxonomy of subdisciplinary and subprofessional specializations.

4. *We are not supporting our own professional organizations anywhere nearly sufficiently*, either at the state or provincial, or national levels. As a result, they are struggling with insufficient funding and are thereby incapable of meeting the many demands being made by the practitioners.

5. *An ever-widening gap is developing* between what might be called the related-discipline sport societies and the established profession of physical education. For example, we find the North American Society for the Sociology of Sport, the International Association for Sport Philosophy, the earlier Association for the Anthropological Study of Play, the North American Society for Sport History, the American College of Sport Medicine, and many others who ostensibly could care less, to put it bluntly, what happens to the field of physical education and educational sport. For me it was very interesting to note the plea by Sparks (1992, 1, 10-11) in which he also asked our "specialists" to consider integrating more closely with the profession.

6. Despite the fact that the College Entrance Examination Board in the United States in the early 1970s established a commission that eventually *recommended much greater weight and consideration in entrance requirements be allotted to certain important qualities and attributes over and above the traditional verbal factor and mathematical factor* (e.g., sensitivity and commitment to social responsibility, political and social leadership, ability to adapt to new situations), there is no evidence that we have stressed, or even understand to any degree, whether physical education majors possess originally or subsequently achieve knowledge, competence, or skill in any of the total of nine vital components as recommended by the CEEB.

7. *Another unacceptable series of gaps* has developed among (a) the people in physical education concerned with the bio-science aspects of the field; (b) those investigating the social science and humanities aspects of the discipline; (c) a third group concerned with the professional preparation of physical educators and with investigation concerning what might be called the subprofessional aspects of the field (e.g., curriculum, instructional methodology, supervision, management); (d) a

group of professionals promoting professional training in sport management; and (5) the professional practitioners in the field where divisions often exist among the physical educator, the coach, and the dance teacher.

8. *A further disturbing development is taking place.* For several reasons, at least one of which is our fault, the highly influential and volatile area of competitive sport has become a playground for several of our allied professions, as well as for an increasing number of people in what we call our related disciplines. Many of these people became aware of the ever-increasing popularity of exercise programs and competitive sport, and are tackling "our" problems in a piecemeal fashion, often without a full awareness of sport and physical education's total domain and outlook. Here I am referring to (a) the relatively recent, close identification of the recreation profession with highly competitive sport and fitness, (b) the interest of health educators in exercise science, (c) the takeover by physiotherapists of adaptive or special physical education, (d) the developing relationship between business administration and sport management and/or intercollegiate sport, and, of course, (e) the gradually awakening interest of historians, philosophers, sociologists, psychologists, anthropologists, physiologists, medical professors, biomechanics specialists, etc. in competitive sport. All of these people could readily help our mission without seeming to ignore us or put us out of business at the same time.

9. Steadily, but surely, because physical education has been struggling to acquire an "academic image" since it was criticized so sharply by Conant in the early 1960s, *a larger wedge than ever has been driven between physical education and intercollegiate athletics.* (Of course, that relatively small, but highly visible, segment of intercollegiate sport that may be called "big-time, commercial, intercollegiate athletics" has been subject to all sorts of abuses *throughout this century and is to all intents and purposes out of educational control.*) This has been a highly unfortunate development for us and, I do believe, for them, too. A relatively small group of pressure-driven administrators and coaches has used us and many of their colleagues in other disciplines as well, not to mention the unethical way in which many so-called scholar-athletes have been sacrificed along the way (e.g., the large percentage of black athletes who have not graduated or who take "x" number of years to complete their degrees). This has been most unfortunate for all concerned.

10. Finally, and such a listing as this always seems to include 10 items, *I detect an uneasiness or malaise no doubt brought on by the developments of the past 25 years.* Possibly the most crucial aspects of the modification that I claim we are undergoing are the beliefs of those who seem ready and willing to write off physical education.

Also, there is evidence that many within the field are losing their *will to win*. In the final analysis this latter conclusion could be the most devastating of all the aspects of modification indicated above.

General Intercultural Observations. In addition to including some political and social observations about world development early in this presentation, I felt it necessary to include some "general intercultural observations" with more direct implications for the physical education/kinesiology field before concluding here. There are a relatively small number of physical educators and a minute number of coaches with what I would call an international orientation in relation to their chosen profession. I'm concerned that the vast majority in the United States especially who feel that "if anything worthwhile is going to happen, it will be here." Further, this group is saying "it had better be made available in English if I am to be expected to read it." This may sound harsh, but it is my considered opinion that far too much of this attitude prevails, and it does not bode well for the 21st century.

For this reason it is important that the International Council for Health, Physical Education, Recreation, Sport, and Dance (ICHPER.SD sponsored by AAHPERD) has for decades now continued to strive to broaden our horizons. Also, the inauguration of the International Society for Comparative Physical Education and Sport in 1968 in Israel marked the beginning of a second thrust in this direction. It is through efforts such as this that we in this profession may be able to assist civilization to move a bit faster toward what Glasser (1972) identified as "Civilized Identity Society" in which the concern of humans will again--as he theorizes--focus on such concepts as "self-identity," "self-expression," and "cooperation." Postulating that so-called "primitive society" societies ended in a great many areas several thousand years ago as populations increased sharply and some countries considered it necessary to take essential resources from neighboring societies, he argued that a "civilized survival" situation ensued. Now for the continuation of life on this planet, with ecological dictates and presumed economic requirements clashing sharply, it is possible--but not probable--that humankind may re-enter what Glasser called civilized identity society again.

Encouragement to move in this direction comes from the findings of Kaplan (1961, pp. 7-10) comes from the findings of Kaplan who over three decades ago found even then certain "recurring elements in the various world philosophies." Despite continuing warfare on earth--29 major ones in the current year--Kaplan theorized that there are indeed four recurring themes of rationality, activity, humanism, and preoccupation with values present in the leading world philosophies.

For reasons such as the above, I have been promoting for 20 years the fundamental importance of three concepts as we move toward the twenty-first century: the concepts of "communication," "diversity," and "cooperation." First, the concept of "communication" has now become vitally important because what the late Isaac Asimov (1970, pp. 17-20) called a "fourth revolution" has occurred in this area. We now witness its presence every day! The world has moved from the invention of speech, to writing, to mechanical reproduction of the printed word, and now to relay stations in space creating a blanketing communications network that will make possible a type of international personal relationship hitherto undreamed of by men and women.

Interestingly, this development has fantastic implications for the profession of physical education and sport, making it mandatory that we view this aspect of our task in a new light. Basically, the world *must* "win this race"--that is, this vastly improved means of communication must be employed to foster international goodwill and cooperation rather than as a means to promote global conflict.

Second, the concept of "diversity"--the state or fact of being different, unlike, or diverse--must be fostered as well. We are a diverse lot--now both here *and* abroad, and we simply must come to understand this diversity ever so much better than we do at present. It is at this point that the struggle between the world's leading ideologies comes into focus. Communists--both before the collapse of the U.S.S.R. and still at present in China and elsewhere--argue that humankind in social settings must pass through four stages: from agrarianism to capitalism to socialism and, finally, to ideal communism. Presently, hovering presumably somewhere between between the second and third stages, we can observe that China, for example, has stifled the concept of "diversity" in their culture. So the question is whether we can ever have a world in which all people could be "significantly diverse" if they wish. Must we eventually have a type of operant conditioning (based on B.F. Skinner's theory [1971]) involving behavior modification so that people's actions are regulated more stringently than ever before because of over-population, aggressive tendencies, and many other deterrents? This is the major issue that will have to be addressed in the not-too-distant future, and we can only hope that this crucial issue can be worked out peacefully.

Third, the concept of "cooperation" must be paramount in our planning for the future along with the other two concepts mentioned above. Cooperation implies working together for a common purpose or benefit. As the world grows "smaller," we must pay ever so much more attention to international relations. This will be vital within society generally, as well as between cultures. The field of education can lead the world in this respect. Our specific concern is how this applies to the field of physical education and sport as we develop new plans and extend the horizons for cooperation in the various aspects of endeavor among individuals, groups, and societies on earth--and maybe some day in space.

As we contemplate this "Third Wave" world, what will this mean to us who are interested in developmental physical activity in sport, exercise, and expressive movement for people of all ages who might be classified as "accelerated," "normal," and "special" populations? We have our responsibilities in our own countries, of course, to help people understand the need for, and opportunities in, human motor performance of a correct and desirable nature throughout their lives. Our role is to so guide general education that all will comprehend that healthful and enjoyable physical activity is necessary to promote (1) circulo-respiratory efficiency, (2) joint flexibility, (3) adequate muscular strength, and (4) the development and maintenance of correct, functional segmental alignment of bodily parts to foster health, functional efficiency, and aesthetic movement.

As we look outward to all parts of the world, however, we need to devise a step-by-step approach for the description, interpretation, comparison, and evaluation of prevailing patterns of human movement from a cross-cultural standpoint. As matters stand now in the United States especially, many travelers' tales have been told, but very little educational borrowing has been carried out. A number of other countries have been more cosmopolitan that we in this regard, and their relative progress is significant. Admittedly, a certain amount of international cooperation has occurred, but language barriers, economic shortages, a resurgence of unwise nationalism, and other barriers have hampered development. Many come to North America to learn, but very few of us have the desire to go elsewhere to learn, much less the language capability to profit from such an experience or the funds to support the venture. In summary, what is needed is an international strategy for a worldwide cross-cultural comparison, a step-by-step analysis of the prevailing patterns of human movement in sport, exercise, and expressive movement. Only in this way will it be possible for the profession to reach its potential on a worldwide basis in the future.

CONCLUDING STATEMENT

Above I have argued that the profession is neither dead nor quiescent, but that it definitely went through serious modification throughout the course of the 20th century. I believe it can be further argued successfully further that our profession: physical education and sport (physical education/kinesiology?) has not been growing and developing as rapidly and strongly as it should be in a society where the idea of "change" must now become our watchword. It is difficult to refute the thought that change is here to stay. Our problem seems to be that we are "ill," that many recognize the symptoms, but that they don't appreciate the serious nature of the illness. Thus, are therefore unwilling to take drastic action in an effort to effect a cure.

I wish that I were able to say that I had overstated the 10 developments above that seem so disturbing to me. They indicate that a serious modification of what seemed to be physical education's earlier, embryonic, halcyon state at the turn of the 20th century. Other problems and issues could be recounted by some with a different perspective. I wish that I could simply shout "April Fool" and be done with it. Alas, such is not the case. In my opinion these problems represent accurately the modification that our profession has been undergoing.

What should we do--perhaps what *must* we do--to ensure that the profession will move decisively and rapidly in the direction of what might be called *true* professional status? Granting that the various social forces will impact upon us willy-nilly, we must determine what we can do collectively in the years ahead that will bring about the best possible solution to the continuing efforts of all those men and women who throughout the 20th century had a deep commitment for the future of all that physical education/kinesiology stands for in serving as a highly valuable component of human life.

Without attempting to enumerate specifically where any stumbling blocks might confront us as we strive to move ahead strongly in the 21st century, I would like to propose *four major processes* that could be employed chronologically as we seek to realize our desired objective as follows (March and Simon, 1958, pp. 129-131).\:

> 1. *Problem-solving.* Basically what is being proposed here is a problem for our profession to solve or resolve. We must move as soon as possible to convince others of the worthwhileness of our plans for rejuvenation. Part of our approach includes assurance that the objectives are indeed operational (i.e., that their presence or absence can in most cases be tested empirically as we progress). In this way, even if sufficient funding or unanimous

approval were not available--and it well might not be--the various parties who are vital or necessary to the ultimate success of the field would at least have reached considerable consensus about the field's objectives. However, with a professional task of this magnitude, it is possible, and quite probable, that consensus will not be
achieved at the outset.

2. *Persuasion*. For the sake of argument, then, let us assume that many of our objectives on the way toward the achievement of long-range aims are not shared by the others whom we need to convince, people who are either inside our own profession or are in allied professions or related disciplines. On the assumption that the stance of the others is not absolutely fixed or intractable, then this second step of persuasion can (should) be employed on the assumption that *at some level* our objectives will be shared, and that disagreement over sub-goals can be mediated by reference to common goals.

> **Note:** If persuasion were to work, then the parties concerned can obviously return to the problem-solving level (No. 1 above).

3. *Bargaining* We will now move along to the third stage of a theoretical plan on the assumption that the second step (persuasion) didn't fully work either. This means obviously that there is still disagreement over the operational goals proposed at the problem-solving level (the first stage). Now the profession has a difficult decision to make: do we attempt to strike a bargain, or do we decide that we simply must "go it alone" without the help and approval of--say--our allied professions, related disciplines, or the public?

The problem with the first alternative is that bargaining implies compromise, and compromise means that each group involved will have to surrender a portion of its claim, request or argument. The second alternative above may seem more desirable, but following it may also mean eventual failure in achieving the final, most important objective.

> **Note**: We can appreciate, of course, that the necessity of proceeding to this stage, and then selecting either of the two alternatives, is obviously much less desirable than settling the matter at either the first or second stage.

4. *Politicking*: The implementation of the fourth stage (or plan of attack) is based on the fact that that proposed action of the first three stages has failed.

The participants in the discussion cannot agree in any way about the main issues. It is at this point that the organization (or professional association) involved has to somehow expand the number of parties or groups involved in consideration of the proposed objectives and the overall plan. The goal is, of course, to attempt to include potential allies so as to improve the chance of achieving the final desired objective. Employing so-called "power politics" is usually tricky, however, and it may indeed backfire upon any group bringing such a maneuver into play. However, this is the way the world (or society) works, and the goal may well be worth the risk or danger involved.

> **Note**: Obviously, we hope that it will not be necessary to operate at this fourth stage too frequently in connection with the highest type of development for our profession. Politicking is often divisive and time-consuming and, at time, does more harm than good.

Finally, what we with a humanistic orientation should be thinking is that life has everything to do with succeeding at the level of *doing one's best* as we strive to be "creatures who adapt reality to our own ends, who transform reality into a congenial form, and who make their own reality." This concept of the ideal way to live explains that not everyone catches the brass ring on life's carousel. Most of us had better enjoy the ride for its own sake, or we may end up believing that life has no meaning at all. Finally, in this shrinking world we had better do all that we can to encourage others to control the world population and to live together peacefully-- or else this "noble experiment" of humankind may have well been in vain. . . .

NOTE

1. This chapter has been adapted from the Delbert Oberteuffer Memorial Lecture presented at The Ohio State University, Columbus in 1993. Accordingly, opinions and recommendations offered are in the first person.)

REFERENCES AND BIBLIOGRAPHY

American Alliance for Health, Physical Education, Recreation and Dance (1962) *Professional preparation in health education, physical education, recreation education.* Report of national conference. Washington, DC: Author.

American Alliance for Health, Physical Education, Recreation and Dance. (1974). *Professional preparation in dance, physical education, recreation education, safety education, and school health education.* Report on national conference. Washington, DC: Author.

Berelson, B. & Steiner, G.A. (1964). *Human behavior.* New York: Harcourt Brace Jovanovich.

Bookwalter, K.W., & Bookwalter, C.W. (1980). *A review of thirty years of selected research on undergraduate professional preparation physical education programs in the United States.* Unionville, IN: Author.

Brubacher, J.S. (1966). *A history of the problems of education* (2nd ed.). New York: McGraw-Hill.

Brubacher, J.S. (1969). *Modern philosophies of education* (4th ed.). New York: McGraw-Hill.

Canadian Association for Health, Physical Education and Recreation. (1966). *Physical education and athletics in Canadian universities and colleges* (pp. 14-21). Ottawa: Author.

Commager, H.S. (1961). A quarter century--Its advances. *Look, 25,* 10 (June 6), 80-91.

Conant, J.B. (1963). *The education of American teachers* (pp. 122-123). New York: McGraw-Hill.

Cosentino, F. & Howell, M.L. (1971). *A history of physical education in Canada.* Don Mills, Ont.: General Publishing Co.

Cowell, C.C. (1960). The contributions of physical activity to social development. *Research Quarterly,* 31, 2 (May, Part II), 286-306.

Elliott, R. (1927). *The organization of professional training in physical education in state universities.* New York: Columbia Teachers College.

Flath, A.W. (1964). *A history of relations between the National Collegiate Athletic Association and the Amateur Athletic Union of the United States (1905-1963).* Champaign, IL: Stipes. (Includes a Foreword by E.F. Zeigler entitled Amateurism, semiprofessionalism, and professionalism in sport: A persistent historical problem.)

Hess, F.A. (1959). *American objectives of physical education from 1900 to 1957 assessed in light of certain historical events.* Doctoral dissertation, New York University.

Johnson, H.M. (1969). The relevance of the theory of action to historians. *Social Science Quarterly,* (June), 46-58.

Kennedy, P. (1987). *The rise and fall of the great powers.* NY: Random House.

Kennedy, W.F. (1955). *Health, physical education, and recreation in Canada: A history of professional preparation.* Unpublished doctoral dissertation, Teachers College, Columbia University.

Lauwerys, J.A. (1959) The philosophical approach to comparative education. *International Review of Education,* V, 283-290.

LaZerte, M.E. (1950). *Teacher education in Canada.* Toronto: W.J. Gage.

Leonard, F.E., & Affleck G.B. (1947). *The history of physical education (3rd ed.).* Philadelphia: Lea & Febiger.

Lipset. S. M. (1973). National character. In D. Koulack & D. Perlman (Eds.), *Readings in social psychology: Focus on Canada.* Toronto: Wiley.

McCurdy, J.H. (1901). Physical training as a profession. *American Physical Education Review,* 6, **4**:311-312.

Meagher, J.W. (1958). *A projected plan for the re-organization of physical education teacher-training programs in Canada.* Unpublished doctoral dissertation, Pennsylvania State University.

Meagher, J.W. (1965). Professional preparation. In M.L. Van Vliet (Ed.), *Physical Education in Canada* (pp. 64-81). Scarborough, Ont.: Prentice-Hall of Canada.

Mergen, Francois. (1970). Man and his environment. *Yale Alumni Magazine,* XXXIII, 8 (May), 36-37.

Morris, V.C. (March, 1956). Physical education and the philosophy of education. *Journal of Health, Physical Education and Recreation,* (March), 21-22, 30-31.

Morrow, L.D. (1975). *Selected topics in the history of physical education in*

Ontario: From Dr. Egerton Ryerson to the Strathcona Trust (1844-1939). Unpublished doctoral dissertation, The University of Alberta.

Murray, B.G. Jr. (1972). What the ecologists can teach the economists. *The New York Times Magazine,* December 10, 38-39, 64-65, 70, 72.

Naisbitt, J. (1982). *Megatrends.* NY: Warner

Nevins, A. (1962). *The gateway to history.* Garden City, NY: Doubleday.

Oberlin College Catalogue (1894).

Paton, G.A. (1975). The historical background and present status of Canadian physical education. In E.F. Zeigler (Ed.), *A history of physical education and sport in the United States and Canada* (pp. 441-443). Champaign, IL: Stipes.

Proceedings of the 6th Commonwealth Conference. (1978). Sport, physical education, recreation proceedings (Vols. 1 and 2). Edmonton, Alberta: University of Alberta.

Royce, J.R. (1964). Paths to knowledge. In *The encapsulated man.* Princeton, NJ: Van Nostrand.

Update (April, 1993), 1. (Newsletter of the Alliance for Health, Physical Education, Recreation, and Dance, Reston, VA).

Van Vliet, M.L. (Ed.). (1965). *Physical education in Canada.* Scarborough, Ontario: Prentice-Hall.

Wellesley College Catalogue (1910).

Spaeth, M.J. (1975). Administrative research in physical education and athletics. In *Administrative Theory and Practice in Physical Education and Athletics* (E.F. Zeigler & M.J. Spaeth, eds. & aus.), p. 44.

Sparks, W. (1992). Physical education for the 21st Century: Integration, not specialization. *The Chronicle of Physical Education in Higher Education (NAPEHE),* **4**, 1:1-10-11.

Zeigler, E.F. (1951). *A history of undergraduate professional preparation in physical education in the United States, 1861-1948.* Eugene, OR: Oregon Microfiche.

Zeigler, E.F. (1962). A history of professional preparation for physical education in the United States (1861-1961). In *Professional preparation in health education, physical education, and recreation education* (pp. 116-133). Washington,, DC: The American Association for Health, Physical Education, and Recreation.

Zeigler, E.F. (1968). *Problems in the history and philosophy of physical education and sport.* Englewood Cliffs, NJ: Prentice-Hall.

Zeigler, E.F. (1975). Historical perspective on contrasting philosophies of professional preparation for physical education in the United States. In

Personalizing physical education and sport philosophy (pp. 325-347). Champaign, IL: Stipes.

Zeigler, E.F. (Ed. & author). (1975). *A history of physical education and sport in the United States and Canada.* Champaign, IL: Stipes.

Zeigler, E.F. (1977). *Physical education and sport philosophy.* Englewood Cliffs, NJ: Prentice-Hall.

Zeigler, E.F. (1979). The past, present, and recommended future development in physical education and sport in North America. In *Proceedings of The American Academy of Physical Education* (G.M. Scott (Ed.), Washington, DC: The American Alliance for Health, Physical Education, Recreation, and Dance.

Zeigler, E.F. (1980). A systems approach to the development and use of theory and research in sport and physical education. *Sportwissenschaft,* 10, 4, 404-416.

Zeigler, E.F. (1980). An evolving Canadian tradition in the new world of physical education and sport. In S.A. Davidson & P. Blackstock (Eds.), *The R. Tait McKenzie Addresses* (pp. 53-62). Ottawa, Canada: Canadian Association for Health, Physical Education and Recreation.

Zeigler, E.F. (Ed.) (1982). *Physical education and sport: An introduction.* Philadelphia: Lea & Febiger.

Zeigler, E.F. (1983a). Relating a proposed taxonomy of sport and developmental physical activity to a planned inventory of scientific findings. *Quest,* 35, 54-65.

Zeigler, E.F. & Bowie, G.W. (1983b). *Developing management competency in sport and physical education.* Philadelphia: Lea & Febiger.

Zeigler, E.F. (1986). Undergraduate professional preparation in physical education, 1960-1985. *The Physical Educator,* 43(1), 2-6.

Zeigler, E.F. (1986). *Assessing sport and physical education: Diagnosis and projection.* Champaign, IL: Stipes.

Zeigler, E.F. (Ed. & Au.) (1988). *A history of physical education and sport.* Champaign, IL: Stipes.

Zeigler, E.F. (1988). A comparative analysis of undergraduate professional preparation in physical education in the United States and Canada. In Broom, E., Clumpner, R., Pendleton, B., & Pooley, C. (Eds.), *Comparative physical education and sport, Volume 5.* Champaign, IL: Human Kinetics.

Zeigler, E.F. (1989) *Sport and physical education philosophy.* Carmel, IN: Benchmark.

Zeigler, E.F. (1990). *Sport and physical education: Past, present, future.* Champaign, IL: Stipes.

Zeigler, E.F. (2003). *Socio-Cultural Foundations of Physical Education and Educational Sport.* Aachen, Germany: Meyer and Meyer Sports.

CHAPTER VII

A COMPARATIVE ANALYSIS OF
PROFESSIONAL PREPARATION
FOR PHYSICAL EDUCATION
IN THE
UNITED STATES AND CANADA (1960-1985)

PURPOSE OF THE STUDY[1]

In this study, a preliminary comparative analysis was made of undergraduate professional preparation in physical education in the United States and Canada. I hypothesized that there have been significant changes, some similar and others different, in the undergraduate professional preparation programs of both countries. I further hypothesized that, if changes occurred, they typically tended to come about in the U.S. first. Lipset (1973) pointed out that there has been reluctance on the part of Canadians "to be overly optimistic, assertive, or experimentally inclined." Finally, it should be recognized that it is difficult, if not impossible, to obtain true historical perspective on at least the latter half of this 25-year period.

I have been concerned with both the theoretical and the practical aspects of this historical development of professional development (having spent equal time on an alternating basis in the United States and Canada at both the undergraduate and graduate levels during this period). In addition, I have carried out historical research on the topic of professional preparation and disciplinary scholarship commencing with doctoral dissertation work in the 1940s. These experiences may have equipped me uniquely to make this comparative analysis; nevertheless, highly competent men and women---people who have lived through these 25 years in both countries---have been called upon to buttress and expand upon the facts and opinions that are provided.

Interestingly, most people in my generation thought that progress in life, and accordingly in professional preparation in physical education, would be mostly an unhindered upward growth after World War I. However, such has not been the case, and many changes (some good and some bad) have undoubtedly been brought about by the prevailing social forces or influences that developed in each country (e.g., the influence of values, nationalism, economics) (Zeigler, 1975).

Also, a number of professional concerns (e.g., approach to professional preparation, curriculum content, instructional methodology) have been affected by these social forces. Therefore, I decided in 1984 to investigate developments in the United States since 1960 using descriptive methodology and a questionnaire technique (Good & Scates, 1954). The instrument was sent to a small group comprising 10 members of The American Academy of Physical Education, selected primarily on the basis of geographical and known to have a deep interest in undergraduate professional preparation. The results of this preliminary survey about developments in physical education in the U.S. were reported at the 100th Anniversary Convention of the American Alliance for Health, Physical Education, Recreation, and Dance in 1985 (Zeigler, 1986).

The results of a similar investigation for Canada are now being reported as well. Leaders from across Canada who have been involved in professional preparation during the 1960s, 1970s, and 1980s were asked to describe what they believe took place in Canada during the same 25-year period (see Paton, 1975; Canadian Association for Health, Physical Education and Recreation, 1966). The Canadians were given the results of the earlier U.S. survey with which to begin the statements of descriptive characteristics and some preliminary comparisons.

METHODOLOGY

The investigation employed broad descriptive methodology together with the following techniques to gather and analyze data: (1) a questionnaire distributed to approximately 10 authorities in each country; (2) a comparative approach (recommended by Bereday, 1964, 1969) that included four steps explained as description, interpretation, juxtaposition, and comparison; and (3) selected documentary analysis.

Five problems, phrased as questions, were included in the questionnaire: (1) What have been the strongest social influences during each decade? (2) What changes have been made in the professional curriculum? (3) What developments have taken place in instructional methodology; (4) What other interesting or significant developments have occurred (typically within higher education); and (5) What are the greatest problems in professional preparation currently? Respondents were also asked to make any additional comments that they wished.

DESCRIPTION AND INTERPRETATION

The results of the first two steps of the Bereday technique (description and interpretation) within broad descriptive methodology were assembled according to the various categories of answers. The questionnaires distributed to respondents in the United States and Canada were identical, both asking the five questions relative to each of the three decades. So much detailed material was obtained form the responses to add to the data uncovered by the investigator that it was decided to complete the results in the form of tables. A table for each decade presents the results from the United States and Canada, respectively, for the first four questions. Separate tables were required to list "the greatest problems in professional preparation." Based on these findings, tentative hypotheses were then postulated in the third step (juxtaposition) of the Bereday comparative technique.

Juxtaposition. The third and fourth steps of this approach are juxtaposition and comparison. In 1969, Bereday introduced two possible approaches for each of these steps---tabular or textual juxtaposition and balanced or illustrative comparison. In juxtaposition, the preliminary matching of data textually after a degree of systematization presented an opportunity for the orderly establishment of comparable topics. At this point one or more hypotheses are made "in terms of what the assembled data are likely to permit one to prove" (Bereday, 1969, p. 5).

In regarding this investigation as preliminary because of its extent and complexity, I decided to carry out an illustrative rather than a balanced comparison. Rather than matching each of the many items from one country to the other, a few similar and dissimilar practices or occurrences in each category in each country were selected randomly to illustrate comparative aspects of the two developments. Such an approach obvious has limited effectiveness because no subsequent principles can be reliably established. With this limitation in mind, the data were assembled and juxtaposed textually, 11 broad hypotheses were established, and the data from both countries were compared illustratively in an effort to confirm, disconfirm, or refine the hypotheses established. An analysis of the related literature was helpful at this point.

Based on the textual juxtaposition and analysis of the data obtained for each country, the following 11 tentative hypotheses were made from the categories examined:

Category #1 (Social influences)

1.1 The federal government has had much more influence on physical education and sport in Canada than in the United States.

1.2 Politics influence public higher education more in the United States than in Canada.

Category #2 (Curriculum)

2.1 Canada has developed a greater subdisciplinary orientation in its curriculum than has the United States.

2.2 Non-teaching, alternative-career options in degree programs have developed more rapidly in the United States.

2.3 Enrollment levels in physical education/kinesiology programs have held up better in Canada.

Category #3 (Instructional methodology)

3.1 Development in instructional methodology has been comparable and concurrent in both countries.

3.2 Pressure for improvement in the teaching act arrived somewhat earlier in the United States.

Category #4 (Other campus developments)

4.1 The pattern of rotation for administrators in Canada has tended to preserve their scholarly competence, contrary to the situation in the United States.

4.2 A smaller percentage of women in Canada have been acculturated to become university physical education and kinesiology professors and scholars.

Category #5 (Greatest problem/need)

5.1 The need to control or lessen the impact of highly competitive athletics within the college and university structure is much greater in the United States.

5.2 Different emphases are needed for the development of improved professional training for teacher/coaches in the two countries.

COMPARISON

My decision to carry out an illustrative rather than a balanced comparison of the data assembled in Bereday's Step #4 was made in an effort to tentatively confirm, disconfirm, or refine the broad hypotheses established as the final phase of Step #3 (juxtaposition).

The following similar and dissimilar practices, occurrences, or stated problems were selected randomly to illustrate the broad hypotheses designated above. (See Table 9.)

DISCUSSION AND PRELIMINARY CONCLUSIONS

This comparative analysis of undergraduate professional preparation in physical education in the United States and Canada from 1960-1985 must be recognized as preliminary. I hypothesized generally at the outset that significant changes have occurred in undergraduate programs in the previous 25 years, and that similarities and differences between the two countries exist both because of and despite their contiguity. Also, earlier studies have shown Canadians to be generally more conservative than Americans toward change.

After carrying out the juxtaposition phase (Step #3) of Bereday's comparative technique, I established 11 tentative hypotheses involving the five different categories. Each is based on textual matching of comparable data. When illustrative comparisons were made in Step #4, the tentative hypotheses established were justified preliminarily by the data presented. Although more in-depth comparative analysis of these developments is called for, this investigative technique has provided a good basis for further study.

Table 1   The United States--the 1960s

THE 1960S: Undoubtedly a period where there was considerable social unrest; in higher education the field was being criticized for the lack of academic rigor in its programs (Conant, et al, 1963.).

   a. Strongest Social Influences

      - Aftermath of Sputnik

- Call for fitness for "Soft American"
- JFK's plans for America; LBJ's "Great Society"
- Civil Rights Movement
- Vietnam involvement
- Hippie Movement (a minority "opted out")
- Students prioritized values; eschewed materialism
- Carnegie Study states that teachers don't relate
    subjects to ongoing living

b. The Professional Curriculum

- Many undergraduate requirements opposed
- Beginnings of sub-disciplines (scientific base!)
- Many disciplinary models & names proposed
- Generalist concept challenged
- Academic rigor of programs under question
- Beginnings of individualized, specialized programs

c. Instructional Methodology

- Effort made to improve laboratory experiences
- Token student involvement typically did not result
    in intelligent modifications; faculty still reti-
    cent about allowing basic student contributions
- Improved instructional materials (A-V, etc.)
- Decreased funding beginning to create specter of
    overly large lecture classes
- Mosston's recommendations regarding teaching
    styles (from "command to discovery")

d. Other Campus Developments

- Student demand for input in decision-making
- Greater use of main frame computers
- Beginnings of subdisciplinary societies
- A variety of inputs into proposed disciplinary models
- Increasing demand for academic integrity begins to
    open rift between researchers/scholars & people in-
    volved with teacher training primarily

- Physical education faculty members judged by same
  standards as other disciplines
- Excesses in gate-receipt sports continue
- Assessment of joint arrangements with intercollegiate
  athletics units on campuses
- Spiraling costs of intercollegiate programs
- Many faculty unprepared for new standards of account-
  ability (including research output)
- Faculty on campuses beginning to organize unions

Table 2   The United States--the 1970s

THE 1970S: Aftermath of the 1960s; a Ph.D. glut; the job market slackens generally; "stagflation"; financial cutbacks in education, etc.

a. Strongest Social Influences

- Lingering effect of Vietnam
- Adding of Watergate guilt to scene; increasing
  distrust of politicians
- Taxpayers' revolt against increasing burden
- Slowing down of economy (stagflation)
- Influence of oil cartel
- Carter's leadership style deplored by some; the
  Iranian hostage incident
- Concern about falling birthrate
- Women's Movement (role expectations of men and women
  tended to blend together)
- Professionals began to break away from tradition in
  terms of dress, behavior, and educational values
- Continuing threat of legal suits against teachers
- Enforced busing for racial mix
- Affirmative action hiring
- Legislation regarding education of handicapped
- Promotion of idea of "competency-based curricula"
- Variety of analyses appearing about most notable
  improvements in U.S. undergraduate teaching
  (Change)

b. The Professional Curriculum

- Curriculum becomes more "scientifically" oriented;
  effect of physical fitness thrust
- Growth of opportunities for specialization
  (elective sequences or emerging tracks such as
  athletic training, fitness specialist, sport
  management, special physical education recommended
  as alternate careers)
- Concern for a core program in physical education
  theory & practice (basic requirements)
- Sub-disciplinary areas continue to expand within
  departments (bio-science and social sciences
  & humanities)

c. Instructional Methodology

- More field work opportunities
- Independent course experiences
- Demand for teacher evaluation grows with possible
  improvement in instruction resulting
- Impact at several educational levels of Mosston's
  work on teaching styles
- Courses taught by specialists to greater extent
- Computer-assisted instruction (e.g., PLATO)
- The sport pedagogy thrust in Federal Republic of
  Germany with some later influence in U.S.A.

d. Other Campus Developments

- Merging of men's and women's departments by admini--
  strative fiat
- Title IX legislation (women in sport)
- Improvement shown re faculty professionalism; younger
  faculty definitely a "new breed"--but without a
  definite interest in the broad picture of developmental physical activity in the schools
- Increase in number of graduate students (few jobs!)
- Splintering of departmental faculty, all "doing their

own thing"
- Changing departmental titles reflecting disciplinary
    emphases & continued growth of allied professions
- Concern for licensing & certification (action?)
- Job market grim in higher education; faculty faced
    with few opportunities to move except in highly
    specialized areas
- Opportunity for faculty grievances increases
- Pressure to "publish or perish" in PE too!
- Grant moneys less available
- Re-tooling of faculty a definite concern
- Excesses in gate-receipt sports seem to increase
- Emergence of the "female jock"--a Catch 22 situation!

Table 3   The United States--the 1980s

THE 1980S: Financial recovery of a sort; job market still tight in higher
education, but shortages are predicted at other levels; federal government impact
on education, research funding, etc.

a. Strongest Social Influences

- Conflicting world ideologies; how to combat spreading
    communism without invoking its methodology & tech-
    niques
- Worldwide communication via satellites
- Impact of Reagan's administration at high level;
    many people, including the young, like the leader-
    ship style ("proud to be American," etc.)
- Rise of fundamentalist religious phenomenon (TV)
- Urban population soaring in desirable parts of the
    country; other cities suffering and crime rates
    increase, thus enhancing the problems
    of cities
- Demographic surveys indicate increasing number of
    elderly in the nation
- Enormous increase in health care costs
- Federal government establishes Health Objectives,
    1990 (for all five stages of life)

- Impact of high technology (e.g., computers, software)
  --the "knowledge industry"
- Certain large industries suffering greatly; recovery
  of automobile industry
- Enrollment decline beginning to have an effect in
  many colleges & universities
- Funding from federal level for education decreasing
- Cost of education soaring at all levels
- Presidential Task Force on Education proclaims
  the prevalence of mediocrity in the secondary
  schools
- Continuing concern that "teacher can't teach"
- Demand for accountability at very high level
- Steady call for "back to basics" in education
- Concept of 'mastery teaching' is "catching on"
- Greater cooperation between the public schools and
  higher education
- Competition for top students
- Federal Government eases off on Title IX enforcement
- Less than one-third of the school population (10-17)
  receive daily physical education

b. The Professional Curriculum

- Concern for greater teacher effectiveness
- Continued expansion of non-teaching programs;
  importance of job orientation; decline of
  liberal education
- Continued concern for improved standards (regular
  certification or voluntary accreditation?)
- Stressing of need for improved scholarship
- Need to eliminate superfluous courses
- How to generate increased revenue?
- Declining enrollment in professional curriculum
- Faculty positions being lost due to inadequate funds
- Intra-institutional research funding drying up

c. Instructional Methodology

- Larger lecture groups/combining of sections
- Need to somehow streamline learning experiences
- Introduction of microcomputer into curriculum
- Continued concern for teacher/coach effectiveness
- Continued retooling of faculty to improve level of
    instruction
- Some stress for education for "human fulfillment"
    with teacher as facilitator

d. Other Campus Developments

- Salary schedules still at low ebb at all levels
- Get the grants whether there is time to complete the
    research or not
- Creative "early semi-retirement" schemes are needed
- Faculty members often find outside means to increase
    substandard salary levels
- The environment is definitely too stressful
- Faculty subdisciplinary specialization increases in
    the large universities; in smaller institutions--
    perhaps because of heavy workloads--faculty members
    are still broadly based (i.e. less research and
    publication; heavier teaching/coaching loads)
- NASPE Task Force working on revision of NCATE
    accreditation standards for undergraduate physical
    education teacher preparation

Table 4
The Greatest Problems in
United States' Professional Preparation

- Need to develop consensus about a disciplinary
    definition from which should evolve a more
    unified, much less fractionated curriculum (i.e.,
    a greater balance among the bio-scientific aspects,
    the social-science & humanities aspects, and the
    "professional aspects" of our field).
- Need to develop a sound body of retrievable
    knowledge in all phases of the profession's

work.
- Need to implement the educational possibilities of a competency approach within the professional preparation curriculum.
- Need to develop a variety of sound options for specialization within a unified curriculum (extending to a 5th year of offerings?). This involves the expansion of alternate career options in keeping with the profession's goal of serving people of all ages and all abilities.
- Need to develop a format whereby regular future planning between staff and students occurs.
- Need to graduate competent, well-educated, fully professional physical educator/coaches who have sound personal philosophies embodying an understanding of professional ethics.
- Need to seek recognition of our professional endeavors in public, semi-public, and private agency work through certification at the state level and voluntary accreditation at the national level.
- Need to help control or lessen the impact of highly competitive athletics within the college and university structure so that a finer type of professional preparation program is fostered.
- Need to recognize the worth of intramural recreational sports in our programs, and to make every effort to encourage those administering these programs to maintain professional identification with the National Association for Sport and Physical Education.
- Need to continue the implementation of patterns of administrative control in educational institutions that are fully consonant with individual freedom within the society.
- Need to work for maintenance of collegiality among faculty members despite the inroads of factors that are tending to destroy such a state: lack of adequate funding, faculty unionization, pressure

for publication and the obtaining of grants, and
extensive intra-profession splintering.
- Need to develop an attitude that will permit us to
"let go of obsolescence." Somehow we will have to
learn to apply new knowledge creatively in the face
of an often discouraging political environment.
- Need to work to dispel any malaise present within our
professional preparation programs in regard to
the future of the profession. If we prepare our
students to be certified and accredited
professionals in their respective options within
the broad curriculum, we will undoubtedly bring
about a service profession of the highest type
within a reasonable period of time (Zeigler, 1986).

Table 5   Canada--the 1960s

THE 1960S. Undoubtedly a period when there was some unrest, but rarely as much as in the U.S.A. (except possibly for Quebec). There was considerable expansion within education at several levels in Canada.

a. Strongest Social Influences

- Era of economic "sufficiency"
- Evidence of Canadian nationalism (e.g., concern
for independence from the U.S.A.)
- Social unrest due to world situation
- Beginning of women's "liberation"
- Education more highly valued
- Continued faith in government to solve societal
ills; resulting governmental expansion and
involvement in education
- Developing rift in Canada--a "quiet revolution"
leading toward "Western separatism"
- Growing concern with the use of leisure, with
significant improvement in municipal recreation
offerings
- Lack of fitness of Canadians indicated; poor show-
ing in international competition decried; Bill C.

131 enacted (Fitness and Amateur Sport Act)
- Growth of professional sport

b. The Professional Curriculum

- Aftermath of 1966 Physical Education & Athletics
   Conference in Toronto
- Largely oriented to producing high school teacher/
   coaches
- Gradual expansion of curriculum offerings in the
   late 1960s
- Emergence of the social-science aspects of physical education and sport
- More electives; fewer requirements in curriculum
- Significant growth of the number of professional
   programs
- Division of task in Ontario: physical education
   units adopt a disciplinary approach, while
   teacher education is allotted to professional
   education schools or departments; the arrangement
   in Western provinces is a combined one similar in
   nature to that offered in the U.S.
- Outdoor education and orienteering added to
   curriculum

c. Instructional Methodology

- Quality of teaching mediocre; little effort to
   evaluate performance as faculty members "do their
   own thing"
- Increased use of seminars and laboratories
- Introduction of readings texts
- Audiovisual aids stressed more

d. Other Campus Developments

- Expansive development of universities, community
   colleges, and secondary education
- Student unrest on campuses; but p.e. students'

demands for greater involvement are limited
- Governing boards submitted to variety of pressures
- Only "strongest" top administrators survived
- Physical education develops somewhat higher profile
   in Canadian universities
- Concern for "academic respectability" begins to
   drive wedge between researcher/scholars and
   those concerned mainly with preparation of the
   teacher/coach
- Gradual entry into graduate education in physical
   education/kinesiology in the late 1960s
- Prospective faculty members work toward specialized
   programs for their doctoral degrees
- Very few well-qualified faculty to cope with newer
   disciplinary approach
- Beginning of federal funding to competitive sport--
   and to a lesser extent to physical education
   (e.g., undergraduate scholarships)
- Job market for graduates is open; very difficult to
   predict future developments
- Team sports grow in popularity; gymnastics declines
- Continued struggle to make the Canadian Association
   for Health, Physical Education and Recreation a
   fully viable professional society
- Expansion of facilities (e.g., swimming pools,
   racquet courts)

Table 6   Canada--the 1970s

THE 1970S. Aftermath of the 1960s; beginnings of the Ph.D. glut in higher education (not physical education initially, however); the job market declines at the secondary level; the beginning of financial cutbacks in education at all levels, etc.

a. Strongest Social Influences

- Faith in the "just and rational" society (early
   impact of Trudeau)
- Economic downturn ("stagflation")
- Further development of "The Cold War"; prolifera-

tion of the hydrogen bomb
- Impact of oil shortage (OPEC)
- Sharp increase in Women's Movement
- Separatist Movement in Quebec (FLQ)
- Falling birth rate; predictions of enrollment slump
  at university & community college level
- Developing Western Canada "isolation"
- Physical activity promoted by federal government
  (e.g., Participaction, a crown corporation);
  designed to ultimately reduce health costs
- Federal government's decision to promote elite
  sport nationally and internationally as an aid to
  the promotion of national unity and world status
- Continued struggle between provincial and federal
  governments threatens federal support to higher
  education
- Professionals begin to break away from traditional
  values & behavior patterns (e.g.,dress, grooming)

b. The Professional Curriculum

- Opportunities for greater specialization (including
  fitness options because of governmental
  influence)
- Concern for a core program in physical education/
  kinesiology theory and practice
- Gradually increasing interest in administrative
  theory as a sub-discipline within the field
  (along with accompanying recognition of the
  importance of the "mother disciplines")
- A significant increase in the sophistication of the
  field's knowledge base
- Federal government's attention to elite sport
  brings a demand for training programs for coaches
  and a national certification plan
- Universities feeling pressure to develop high
  performance\athletes (including testing centers
  and various types of laboratories)
- De-emphasis on teacher training per se as

disciplinary based curriculum receives steadily
increasing emphasis (with courses often seemingly
designed to meet the teachers' needs)
- De-emphasis of the activity-based aspect of the
total curricular offerings
- A steady increase in female enrollment in programs
- Departments, schools, and faculties called a
variety of names (e.g., kinesiology, human
kinetics)

c. Instructional Methodology

- Larger classes resulting in fewer seminars and
fewer essays to correct (i.e. less individual
attention)
- Audiovisual emphasis has a big impact on activity
teaching
- Play increasingly recognized as learning
- Greater opportunity for laboratory experiences
(including individual help from teaching/research
assistants)
- Field work opportunities (e.g., internships) are
greater
- Significant decrease in the use of ever more
expensive textbooks as professors increasingly
develop their own texts and study guides
- Demand for teacher evaluation grows with seemingly
greater emphasis on the teaching process
- Courses are being taught typically by professors
with greater specialization (at the upper
undergraduate level at least); typically use a
greater theoretical orientation
- Attempts were often made to use new technologies in
the teaching act, but the profession was
seemingly slow to pick them up

d. Other Campus Developments

- Faculty members gradually developing a larger

number of areas for research and scholarly
investigation
- Earlier altruism and professional dedication
declines significantly
- Some faculty disillusionment due to aging, outmoded
equipment
- Growth typically comes to a halt in the mid-1970s
due to the increasingly stringent financial
situation
- A decrease occurs in the emphasis on health and
safety education within many curricula
- The Sport Administration Centre in Ottawa continues
to grow in size, scope, and influence
- Participaction, as a crown corporation, increases
in influence through sound marketing approach
- Increase in the number of students enrolled in
graduate study; this is to a considerable extent
due to the job market
- Significant change did not occur rapidly enough
when the climate was right for such innovation
- Grantsmanship develops increasingly because of the
need for external funding

Table 7   Canada--the 1980s

THE 1980S. Financial recovery of a sort takes place; nevertheless, education
continues to be underfunded (especially at the university and community college
level); job market still tight; decline of the Canadian dollar, etc.

a. Strongest Social Influences

- Constitution Act becomes law in 1982; includes
Canadian Charter of Rights & Freedoms; will have
tremendous influence in all areas of living
- Heating up of the Cold War (terrorists, Central
America, Middle East conflict, Afghanistan,
Libya, etc.)
- Satellite communication becomes a boon, but

incipient problems for the world loom large
- Impact of high technology (the "knowledge industry")
- Conservative political control at the national level, and also in certain provinces as well
- Gradually increasing financial crises at both the federal and provincial levels despite recovery from recession of the early 1980s
- Unemployment problem (especially with the young); fewer government jobs available
- The "haves" and the "have-nots" grow further apart
- Enormous increase in health care costs
- Increased awareness of the need for preventive medicine
- University and community college enrollments do not drop off as predicted; some actually increase
- The "Computer Age" is upon us

b. The Professional Curriculum

- Curriculum aims and objectives are lacking
- A back-to-basics emphasis (the core courses)
- Concern over which courses should be required and which elective
- Continued expansion of non-teaching options and concentrations with curricula (e.g., sport management, athletic training, fitness testing & aerobics, coaching)
- Continuing decline of teacher education
- Concern for improved program standards and scholarship
- Some recognition that each university can't "be all things to all people" with its program offerings
- Inability to predict what curricular changes should be made to best equip our graduates for job placement
- Students are typically more serious and goal-oriented
- Increased number of students with poor physical

skills in the professional program
- Beginning of a new emphasis on special physical
    education
- Call for lengthening of curricular program in some
    universities

c. Instructional Methodology

- Computer instruction is slowly being incorporated
    into pattern of instruction
- Larger lecture groups/combining of sections
- Instruction based more on research findings and
    improved theory
- Improved research/teaching facilities & equipment
    available
- Continued concern for teacher/coach effectiveness;
    many faculty members taking teaching
    responsibilities more seriously; improved level of
    creativity & innovation
- Some retooling of certain faculty members to
    improve instruction--and to make them more
    valuable
- Increased use of videotaping
- More Canadian educational materials become available

d. Other Campus Developments

- Physical education/kinesiology has achieved greater
    respectability on most campuses
- Some faculty pessimism and cynicism present
- Salary schedules have not kept pace with other
    professions and occupations; pension schemes leave
    something to be desired
- Sharp increase in faculty unionization (more than
    50% of faculty members in country unionized)
- Early retirements schemes appearing, but they are
    not sufficiently creative to encourage faculty
    departure; also, mandatory retirement illegal in
    certain of the provinces

- Requirements for promotion and tenure are ever more stringent; moreover, faculty positions are threatened because of continued economic pressures
- Circumstances have created managers rather than "old style" department heads
- Dedication to the established profession is sorely lacking
- Increased number of students going on for degrees in other fields

Table 8
The Greatest Problems in
Canadian Professional Preparation

- Need regular turnover in faculty to change the "collective staleness" that has developed.
- Need to find more money to carry out an improved level of professional preparation.
- Need to provide a sharper focus to professional preparation programs to counter present "aimless wandering."
- Need to zero in on the best ways of preparing teachers and coaches (i.e., improve the teaching/learning process)
- Need to provide meaningful, relevant, challenging professional preparation for those seeking alternative careers employing purposeful physical activity in sport, exercise, dance, and play.
- Need to graduate competent, well-educated, fully professional physical educator/coaches who have sound personal philosophies and professional ethics.
- Need to develop a more selective admission process to the undergraduate programs in physical education and sport.
- Need to achieve a consensus in regard to what constitutes the core of the curricular sub-disciplines.

- Need to convince qualified women that there is a
place for them at the university level--and
then find it!

Table 9
Comparisons Between the United States and Canada

Note: The illustrative comparisons relate directly
to the 11 hypotheses established above.

	United States	Canada
Category #1 (Social Influences)	1. Federal government has typically been involved financially more directly with higher education	1. Education has been clearly established as belonging to the provinces; influence of federal government more indirect, because funding must be granted through theprovince
	2. State legislatures often become directly involved with state university operations and programs	2. A "hands-off relation-ship has been established traditionally at the provincial level
Category #2 (Curriculum)	1. Teacher education occurs typically within the four-year bachelor's degree program in a school of education	1. In much of Canada teacher education begins after the "disciplinary" degree has been granted
	2. The teacher surplus developed sooner in the U.S., thus creating pressure for alterna-tive career option; more difficult for	2. Pressure for alterna-tive career options came some what later in Canada; difficult to implement within present degree

215

U.S. students to gain admission to degree programs in other fields	because of stronger arts and science and disciplinary orientation
3. The slumping job market caused a sharp drop in enrollment in many colleges and universities; the financial outlook caused retrenchment that affected physical education, also	3. Despite slumping job market, and the predictions of statisticians, the enrollment figures held up; this may have been because of the liberal arts & science nature of the programs (i.e., many students could switch to other fields more easily)

Category #3
(Instructional
Methodology)

1. Responses to the survey in both countries indicated that developments and improvements in instructional have been comparable and concurrent; this finding seems reasonable in that politics and other factors do not appear to have been a consideration here (with the possible exception of inadequate funding for physical education at the local level).

2. The evidence is that the social unrest of the 1960s impacted higher education sooner in the U.S. with resultant demands for more attention to the teaching act on the part of professors	2. Social unrest in Canada was evident in Quebec largely with fewer demands for teacher accountability elsewhere

Category #4 1. In the United States,	1. In Canada there is

(Other Campus Developments)	deans, directors, heads, and chairpersons were rarely appointed for specified periods of time; study or administrative leave was a rarity	typically a specified number of years associated with each category of appointment; study leave was usually available
	2. In the United States graduate study was established during the first 25 years of the century; women typically had separate departments and earned professorial rank at all levels	2. In Canada, graduate study began in the 1960s; women were not acculturated to carry on to the doctoral level in physical education; as a result there are very few full professors in the country
Category #5 (Greatest Problem/ Need)	1. Gate receipts in athletics and the extra-curricular nature of highly competitive sport brought many evils that influenced teacher education in physical education negatively; in many cases it has become necessary to separate athletics from the educational unit	1. The universities and colleges are still in control of their own own destinies in inter-university athletics; it has been fully possible to maintain unified departments & schools including a division of interuniversity athletics
	2. Teacher/coach education in the U.S. requires more selective admission along with a stronger arts and social science background; often more	2. Canadian students have a longer period of training that includes considerable arts and science work the deficiency

professional theory &	is Canada is more
practice is needed as	related to intern-
well	ship experiences for
	the non-teaching
	options

CONCLUDING STATEMENT

Obviously a great deal of progress has been made in physical education and sport in many countries located in all parts of the world. This concluding statement is, however, confined largely to the United States, and, to a slightly less degree, to Canada, countries that have had a fine development in the field in their own right. Undoubtedly very few people still regard physical education and military training as being synonymous. The national interest in all kinds of sport has continued to grow unabated. In a world with an uncertain future, there has been an ever-present demand, admittedly with limited success, for an improved level of physical fitness for citizens of all ages. Despite financial stringencies and overemphasis in certain areas, there is evidence for reasonable optimism while we trust that continuing, sincere efforts will be made by politicians in many countries to strive for healthy, fit populations along with efforts toward world peace.

As these words are being written, there is obviously a continuing value struggle going on in the United States that results in distinct swings of the educational pendulum to and fro. It seems most important that a continuing search for a consensus be carried out. Fortunately, the theoretical struggle fades a bit when actual educational practice is carried out. If this were not so, very little progress would be possible. If we continue to strive for improved educational standards for all this should result in the foreseeable future in greater understanding and wisdom on the part of the majority of North American citizens. In this regard science and philosophy can and indeed must make ever-greater contributions. All concerned members of the allied professions in both the United States and Canada need to be fully informed as they strive for a voice in shaping the future development of their respective countries and professions. It is essential that there be careful and continuing study and analysis of the question of values as they relate to sport, exercise, dance, and play--and, of course, to the implications that societal values and norms have for the allied fields of health and safety education, recreation, and dance.

ACKNOWLEDGMENTS

I wish to express my deep appreciation to the following members of the American Academy of Physical Education for their assistance: Anita Aldrich (Indiana), Ted Baumgartner (Georgia), Jan Broekhoff (Oregon), Charles Corbin (Arizona State), Marvin Eyler (Maryland), M. Dorothy Massey (Rhode Island), and George Sage (Northern Colorado).

In Canada the following colleagues were equally helpful in giving time and knowledge to this undertaking: P.J. Galasso (Windsor), earlier at Waterloo and Queen's), Patricia Lawson (Saskatchewan), Donald Macintosh (Queen's), Fred L. Martens (Victoria), John Meagher (New Brunswick), William Orban (Ottawa, earlier at Saskatchewan), and Garth A. Paton (New Brunswick, earlier at Western Ontario).

NOTE

1. Because of the difficulty of obtaining true historical perspective from 1960 on, at this point the reader will find below the results of an investigation employing a comparative technique of broad descriptive method that was presented in to the Fifth International Symposium on Comparative Physical Education and Sport held at The University of British Columbia, Vancouver, Canada, May 26-31, 1986. The proceedings were edited by E. Broom, R. Clumpner, B. Pendleton, and C. Pooley and published as Comparative physical education and sport, Volume 5. Champaign, IL: Human Kinetics Publishers, 1988.

REFERENCES AND BIBLIOGRAPHY

American Alliance for Health, Physical Education, Recreation and Dance (1962) *Professional preparation in health education, physical education. recreation education.* Report of national conference. Washington, DC: Author.

American Alliance for Health, Physical Education, Recreation and Dance. (1974). *Professional preparation in dance, physical education, recreation education, safety education, and school health education.* Report on national conference. Washington, DC: Author.

Ballou, R.B. (1965). An analysis of the writings of selected church fathers to A.D. 394 to reveal attitudes regarding physical activity. Unpublished doctoral dissertation, University of Oregon.

Bennett, B.L. (1962). Religion and physical education. Paper presented at the Cincinnati Convention of the AAHPER, April 10.

Bereday, G.Z.F. (1964). *Comparative method in education.* New York: Holt, Rinehart and Winston.

Bereday, G.Z.F. (1969). Reflections on comparative methodology in education, 1964-1966. In M.A. Eckstein & H.J. Noah (Eds.), *Scientific investigations in comparative education* (pp. 3-24). New York: Macmillan.

Berelson, B. & Steiner, G.A. (1964). *Human behavior.* New York: Harcourt Brace Jovanovich.

Bookwalter, K.W., & Bookwalter, C.W. (1980). *A review of thirty years of selected research on undergraduate professional preparation physical education programs in the United States.* Unionville, IN: Author.

Brubacher, J.S. (1966). *A history of the problems of education* (2nd ed.). New York: McGraw-Hill.

Brubacher, J.S. (1969). *Modern philosophies of education* (4th ed.). New York: McGraw-Hill.

Bury, J.B. (1955). *The idea of progress.* New York: Dover.

Butts, R.F. (1947). *A cultural history of education.* New York: McGraw-Hill.

Canadian Association for Health, Physical Education and Recreation. (1966). *Physical education and athletics in Canadian universities and colleges* (pp. 14-21). Ottawa: Author.

Champion, S.G. & Short, D. (1951). *Readings from the world religions.* Boston: Beacon.

Commager, H.S. (June 1961). A quarter century--Its advances. *Look, 25,* 10: 80-91.

Conant, J.B. (1963). *The education of American teachers.* New York: McGraw-Hill.

Cosentino, F. & Howell, M.L. (1971). *A history of physical education in Canada.* Don Mills, Ont.: General Publishing Co.

Cowell, C.C. (1960). The contributions of physical activity to social development. *Research Quarterly, 31,* 2 (Part II):286-306.

Durant, W. & Durant, A. (1968). *The lessons of history.* New York: Dover.

Elliott, R. (1927). *The organization of professional training in physical education in state universities.* New York: Columbia Teachers College.

Flath, A.W. (1964). *A history of relations between the National Collegiate Athletic Association and the Amateur Athletic Union of the United States (1905-1963).* Champaign, IL: Stipes. (Includes a Foreword by E.F. Zeigler.)

Fraleigh, W.P. (1970). Theory and design of philosophic research in physical education. *Proceedings* of the National College Physical Education

Association for Men, Portland, OR, Dec. 28.

Glassford, R.G. (1970) *Application of a theory of games to the transitional Eskimo culture.* Unpublished doctoral dissertation, University of Illinois, Urbana-Champaign.

Good, C.F., & Scates, D.E. (1954). *Methods of research.* New York: Appleton-Century-Crofts.

Gross, B.M. (1964). *The managing of organizations.* 2 vols. New York: Crowell-Collier.

Hayes, C. (1961). *Nationalism: A religion.* New York: Macmillan.

Heilbroner, R.L. (1960). *The future as history.* New York: Harper & Row.

Hershkovits, M.J. (1955). *Cultural anthropology.* New York: Knopf.

Johnson, H.M. (1969). The relevance of the theory of action to historians. *Social Science Quarterly*, (June), 21, 46-58.

Kennedy, J.F. (1958). Address in Detroit, Michigan when he was a U.S. Senator.)

Kennedy, P. (1987). *The rise and fall of the great powers.* NY: Random House.

Kennedy, W.F. (1955). *Health, physical education, and recreation in Canada: A history of professional preparation.* Unpublished doctoral dissertation, Teachers College, Columbia University.

Lauwerys, J.A. (1959) The philosophical approach to comparative education. *International Review of Education,* V, 283-290.

LaZerte, M.E. (1950). *Teacher education in Canada.* Toronto: W.J. Gage.

Leonard, F.E., & Affleck G.B. (1947). *The history of physical education (3rd ed.).* Philadelphia: Lea & Febiger.

Lipset. S. M. (1973). National character. In D. Koulack & D. Perlman (Eds.), *Readings in social psychology: Focus on Canada.* Toronto: Wiley.

Marrou, H.I. (1964). *A history of education in antiquity.* Trans. George Lamb. New York: New American Library.

McIntosh, P.C. *et al.* (1957). *History of physical education.* London: Routledge & Kegan Paul.

Martens, Rainer. (1971). Demand characteristics and experimenter bias. Paper presented at the AAHPER Convention, Detroit, April 5.

Martens, Rainer. (1970). A social psychology of physical activity. *Quest,* 14 (June), 8-17.

Meagher, J.W. (1958). *A projected plan for the re-organization of physical education teacher-training programs in Canada.* Unpublished doctoral dissertation, Pennsylvania State University.

Meagher, J.W. (1965). Professional preparation. In M.L. Van Vliet (Ed.), *Physical Education in Canada* (pp. 64-81). Scarborough, Ont.: Prentice-Hall of Canada.

Mergen, Francois. (1970). Man and his environment. *Yale Alumni Magazine,* XXXIII, 8 (May), 36-37.

Morris, V.C. (1956). Physical education and the philosophy of education. *Journal of Health, Physical Education and Recreation,* (March), 21-22, 30-31.

Morrow, L.D. (1975). Selected topics in the history of physical education in Ontario: From Dr. Egerton Ryerson to the Strathcona Trust (1844-1939). Unpublished doctoral dissertation, The University of Alberta.

Muller, H.J. (1954). *The uses of the past.* New York: New American Library.

Murray, B.G. Jr. (1972). What the ecologists can teach the economists. *The New York Times Magazine,* December 10, 38-39, 64-65, 70, 72.

Nevins, A. (1962). *The gateway to history.* Garden City, NY: Doubleday.

Nevins, A. (1968). The explosive excitement of history. *Saturday Review,* April 6.

Paton, G.A. (1975). The historical background and present status of Canadian physical education. In E.F. Zeigler (Ed.), *A history of physical education and sport in the United States and Canada* (pp. 441-443). Champaign, IL: Stipes.

Proceedings of the 6th Commonwealth Conference. (1978). *Sport, physical education, recreation proceedings* (Vols. 1 and 2). Edmonton, Alberta: University of Alberta.

Reisner, E.H. (1925). *Nationalism and education since 1789.* New York: Macmillan.

Roberts, J.M. & Sutton-Smith, B. (1962). Child training and game involvement. *Ethnology,* 1.

Royce, J.R. (1964). Paths to knowledge. In *The encapsulated man.* Princeton, NJ: Van Nostrand.

Sigerist, H.E. (1956). *Landmarks in the history of hygiene.* London: Oxford University Press.

Simpson, G.G. (1949). *The meaning of evolution.* New Haven & London: Yale University Press.

Van Vliet, M.L. (Ed.). (1965). *Physical education in Canada.* Scarborough, Ontario: Prentice-Hall.

Von Neumann, J. & Morgenstern, O. (1947). *The theory of games and economic behavior. (2nd ed.).* Princeton: Princeton University Press.

Williams, J. Paul. (1952). *What Americans believe and how they worship.* New York: Harper & Row.

Woody, T. (1949). *Life and education in early societies.* New York: Macmillan.

Zeigler, E.F. (1951). *A history of undergraduate professional preparation in physical education in the United States, 1861-1948.* Eugene, OR: Oregon Microfiche.

Zeigler, E.F. (1962). A history of professional preparation for physical education in the United States (1861-1961). In *Professional preparation in health education, physical education, and recreation education* (pp. 116-133). Washington,, DC: The American Association for Health, Physical Education, and Recreation.

Zeigler, E.F. (1964). *Philosophical foundations for physical, health, and recreation education.* Englewood Cliffs, NJ: Prentice-Hall.

Zeigler, E.F. (1965). *A brief introduction to the philosophy of religion.* Champaign, IL: Stipes.

Zeigler, E.F. (1968). *Problems in the history and philosophy of physical education and sport.* Englewood Cliffs, NJ: Prentice-Hall.

Zeigler, E.F. (Ed. & author). (1973). *A history of physical education and sport to 1900.* Champaign, IL: Stipes.

Zeigler, E.F. (1975). Historical perspective on contrasting philosophies of professional preparation for physical education in the United States. In *Personalizing physical education and sport philosophy* (pp. 325-347). Champaign, IL: Stipes.

Zeigler, E.F. (Ed. & author). (1975). *A history of physical education and sport in the United States and Canada.* Champaign, IL: Stipes.

Zeigler, E.F. *et al.* (1979). *A history of physical education and sport Englewood Cliffs*, NJ: Prentice-Hall. (A revised edition of this work was published in 1988.)

Zeigler, E.F. (1980). An evolving Canadian tradition in the new world of physical education and sport. In S.A. Davidson & P. Blackstock (Eds.), *The R. Tait McKenzie Addresses* (pp. 53-62). Ottawa, Canada: Canadian Association for Health, Physical Education and Recreation.

Zeigler, E.F. (1986). Undergraduate professional preparation in physical education, 1960-1985. *The Physical Educator, 43*(1), 2-6.

Zeigler, E.F. (1988). A comparative analysis of undergraduate professional preparation in physical education in the United States and Canada. In Broom, E., Clumpner, R., Pendleton, B., & Pooley, C. (Eds.), *Comparative physical education and sport, Volume 5.* Champaign, IL: Human Kinetics.

CHAPTER VIII

A HISTORY OF
MANAGEMENT THEORY AND PRACTICE IN
AMERICAN PHYSICAL EDUCATION AND SPORT

INTRODUCTION

For thousands of years, much thought has undoubtedly been given to the governing of both elementary and complex organizations.[1] It must be assumed, also, that people often learned how to administer by simply observing the errors of others. The great organizational achievements in history belong, of course, to the actual history of administration or management per se. Information and hypotheses about past administrative thought and practice underlying such accomplishment can be gleaned from the work of historians, as well as from such diverse fields as philosophy, political science, economics, and religion. Accordingly, in considering this topic, it is important to distinguish among administrative thought (of which there is considerable evidence throughout the ages), administrative practice (which has been effective and/or efficient to varying degrees since time immemorial), and the more scholarly and scientific administrative theory (that has emerged from various quarters as emerging social science during the twentieth century).

Recognizing that many people have organized and administered all types of enterprises in the past, therefore, what should be understood here is that an "organizational," "administrative," or "managerial" revolution has now taken place, and that it will continue because of the ever-increasing complexity and actual transformation of our evolving society. It is the more complex thought and the concomitant administrative theory that is new in this century. Thus, such theory is now serving us in a similar way to manage our organizations as did earlier, less complex administrative thought and practice enable people of earlier periods to accomplish their goals. Such thought and practice have necessarily been inextricably interwoven with the broad processes of historical evolution within society.

What we are discovering in America, of course, is that everything has become big--almost monstrous--and then even bigger still (witness the relatively fate of AT&T!). Thus there is Big Business, Big Government, Big Labor (now getting a bit smaller), Big Science and Big Technology, Big Agriculture (some problems here too), Big Religion (including the inroads of the fundamentalists in the TV industry), Big Communications Media, Big Education, and now Big Sport and Big Fitness. Of course, Big Sport within Big Education has now become Big Business too, along with mushrooming professional sport, and this means that fine managers and administrators are needed in all of these enterprises if their place in our countries is to continue to grow and prosper.

The record tells us clearly that people desired many changes in the late nineteenth and down through the present century. The social, scientific, and technologic changes that occurred have been such that a term like "managerial revolution" was needed to describe what transpired. Only through the more efficient managing of organizations could these social and technologic developments have created the modern world--a development that occurred often despite--and at times because of--ongoing warfare. Concurrently, significant steps in management theory and practice have been fostered by the gradual development of ordered generalizations (i.e., tentatively agreed-upon theoretical principles) within the behavioral sciences with assistance from the professional and scholarly achievement of public administration, business administration, and educational administration.

To state the current situation boldly, but in an overly simplified manner, if power is required to accomplish a task in a certain way, then people must be organized and programs must be administered to bring about the desired development. Generally speaking, the more formal the organizational structure is, the more power can be brought to bear to effect the desired goals. Actually, however, the necessary power is usually achieved through both formal and informal organization. In this way, human, physical, and monetary resources can be combined to accomplish the tasks necessary for the accomplishment of both immediate objectives and long range goals.

To continue, leaders use money or some other valuable commodity to combine human and physical resources in such a way that the necessary power is mustered to get the job done. Further, as these resources are combined in many different ways to achieve the ultimate goal, improved techniques are often developed that may hasten the end result. Development of such new methods and techniques has proceeded hand in hand with technologic advancement through the ages. And, as a corollary of the above, if people are sufficiently motivated, they will change the administrative structure and thereby mobilize the necessary resources to develop the social power to effect the desired changes.

Before we can discuss what we should be doing right now in our planning for the future in the area of management theory and practice as applied to our field, we would be well advised to review the broader situation historically. How did all this happen? It happened because the knowledge explosion which has affected almost the entire world has also had its impact on the managing of organizations, and more specifically on the individuals managing these organizations. Management tends to be a dynamic process with steady, almost constant, change as a typical pattern of life. The Industrial Revolution of the mid-eighteenth century was the precursor, the effects of which soon spread to all aspects of life including education. Technological change of necessity has been closely related to administrative or managerial change; new methods and techniques of management became part of the technological development itself. With this managerial revolution came "more organization, larger-scale organization, more bureaucracy, and more administrators" (Gross, 1964).

ADVENT OF THE MARKETING CONCEPT

However, in an effort to avoid the presumed fate of the dinosaur, any. organization today must have a stance in regard to what has become known as the marketing concept--that business phenomenon that began to gain some momentum in the 1940s and has hit the stratosphere since that time. Marketing is typically defined as activities that accelerate the movement of goods and services from the manufacturer to the consumer (Rosenberg, 1978, p. 277). Thus it is marketing whether one is talking about advertising, distributing, merchandising, product planning, promotion, publicity, and even transportation and warehousing.

The development of the marketing concept was a response from business to a society that was steadily acquiring more buying power. The personal income of the average family rose steadily so that life's basic essentials used up a smaller proportion of a person's salary. Along the way the nature of the consumer's demands was also changing along with the rising production levels. All of this has brought about a dramatic rise in the demand for services since 1950. As the social environment changed, the business community was affected as well. The variety of demands by the consumer soon brought about the introduction of the concept of market segmentation. With each segment having its own discrete desires, needs, and preferences, businesses found it necessary to develop and maintain individual market-strategy plans. (In this connection sport managers of all types need an ever-improving understanding of marketing orientation so that the needs and interests of the presumed market segment are best served.)

As our culture and North American society continued to grow in complexity, continuing social change is occurring. Such change occurs only, of course, if and when people develop the desire, the physical resources, and the technical know-how to perform the tasks in the most expedient manner possible. Our desires are, of course, closely related to the values and norms of the culture--values that aid in attitude formation so that the leaders can get the support of the people to fulfill the assigned duties and responsibilities. There is now considerable knowledge about human behavior, but obviously much remains to be discovered and passed along to practitioners. Management theory has made great strides, but has not yet developed specifically to the point or level of generalization whereby it can be called systematized knowledge about organizational phenomena in all foreseeable circumstances.

A FORMAL ORGANIZATION DEFINED (PARSONS)

Writing in 1958, Parsons explained that "a formal organization in the present sense is a mechanism by which goals somehow important to the society, or to various subsystems of it, are implemented and to some degree defined." With all of this development as society became increasingly complex, however, there has been a strong trend toward the dehumanization of people. They tended to lose their identities as work tasks became increasingly splintered. The individual became more subordinated to the organization with attendant alienation from other people. A clash of ideological systems is present as well within our increasingly over-organized society. All around us we see examples of inflexibility as totalitarian patterns of management compete with more democratic models. Such models are often subjected to great strain, and the increasing complexity could well be bringing the large modern organization to the point where it too will face what might have been the now legendary fate of the early behemoth.

Three Major Eras of Administrative Thought. During the twentieth century an extensive body of literature on administration has developed, also. An initial review of this data suggests three major eras of administrative thought. First, in the early years of the twentieth century, investigation focused on the formal organization itself and job performance within that structure. Frederick Taylor, for example, was one researcher who looked into the question of efficiency. Others concentrated on the formal structure of organizations. All together, these studies constituted what has been called the "scientific management" era of administration (Gross, 1954, p.

38). As a result of such investigation, various scholars formulated several taxonomies and a number of principles that were widely adopted in government, business, and education.

The so-called "human relations era" arose from studies carried out primarily in industry, investigations that were to have an important influence on administrative thought (Gross, pp. 50-51). These studies, carried out at the Western Electric Company's Hawthorne plant between 1925 and 1933, revealed how important the social aspects of job performance are. As a result, the emphasis in administration began to shift more toward the institution of a human relations approach to management. The evidence seemed to indicate that worker satisfaction would result in greater work productivity (Bedeian, 1985, pp. 493-494).

What may be designated as the third major era of administrative thought in the twentieth century has been called the area of administrative science or theory. The writings of Chester I. Barnard in business and Herbert A. Simon in public administration were important in strengthening this emphasis that was leading to a general theory of administration that could guide professional practice toward implementation of sound research findings.

A FOURTH STAGE IS POSTULATED

Gordon (1966, pp. 6-23), in his assessment of the late nineteenth century and the first half of the twentieth century, traced what he argued were four reasonably distinct, yet overlapping, stages in the history of management thought: the traditional, the behavioral, the decisional, and the ecological. These correspond nicely with the three eras described immediately above, and add a fourth (an "ecological era"). After this, however, it seems impossible to gain historical perspective on what has been occurring during the past two or three decades. Each of the earlier four stages mentioned above were named because some person or group believed in certain generally agreed-upon "truths." Gordon himself was probably on safe ground when he, in conclusion, called for an approach that transcends any one school of management thought.

The mushrooming of the behavioral sciences since has made it literally impossible for a scholar to keep up with the vast quantities of literature in many languages being produced all over the world. As a result those preparing for the profession of management have found themselves facing an impossible task-- keeping up with an information overload, as well as retrieving a great deal of knowledge that helps to form a sound human behavior inventory. Also, the conflicting approaches to management (i.e., the different theories as to "how it should be done") that compete for the attention of the manager in the many books, monographs, and journals are very puzzling. Gordon's recommendation of a flexible framework could well be employed as a synthesis of the four approaches enabling the student of administrative theory to build a conceptual framework that provided a much fuller perspective and a "working model" of the management process.

A SITUATIONAL CONTINGENCY APPROACH AS A COMPOSITE RESEARCH DESIGN?

In a 1979 analysis, however, Hodgetts explained that there is one line of thought that envisions three schools of management thought (i.e., the management process school, the quantitative school, and the behavioral school) merging into a systems school. A second point of view at this time, however, held that we already had a well-established systems school of thought and that it, along with the three approaches just mentioned, are moving in the direction of an overarching situational or contingency school. This had been called a general contingency theory of management by Luthans and Stewart (1977) in which management problems can be encompassed in a theoretical framework that integrates and synthesizes the various schools of thought into a workable research design that has three dimensions--management variables, situational variables, and performance criteria variables. The objective is to integrate tenable management theory into a composite system for ongoing study and investigation.

In the mid-1980s, Harold Koontz of UCLA (now deceased), explained that in the mid-1960's he had decided that there was a "management theory jungle out there," a situation in which academic theorists primarily were seeking to explain the nature and theory of management from six different points of view or "schools." However, instead of the situation becoming clarified in the intervening 20 years between and 1985, he stated that "the jungle still exists" (1985, p. 509) and in fact has become more dense and overgrown. Instead of the six approaches indicated above, the number had mushroomed to 11 approaches to the study of management science as follows: (1) the empirical or case approach, (2) the interpersonal behavior approach, (3) the group behavior approach, (4) the cooperative social system approach, (5) the socio-technical systems approach, (6) the decision theory approach, (7) the systems approach, (8) the mathematical or "management science" approach, (9) the contingency or situational approach (see above), (10) the managerial roles approach, and (11) the operational approach. Short summaries of each of these approaches are provided by Koontz (pp. 509-513). (Stayed tuned for updates on these and other development; in the meantime, we are urged to promote professional preparation program in universities that stresses an action-theory marriage resulting in basic competency attainment for the prospective manager.)

Finally, the continuing industrial revolution, and what has been called the postindustrial revolution by some because of developing cybernetics, coupled with literally fantastic advances in science and technology, has placed people in a difficult situation even in our most developed societies. These factors, along with the exploding population and the resultant development of immense urban and suburban areas, have created a situation in which a larger percentage of the personpower has been forced to concern itself increasingly with the management of the efforts of the large majority of the people in our society. The ability of a relatively few people to master this task to a reasonable degree has meant that the world as we know it may indeed continue to grow and develop. It is up to us all to do everything that we can to cut down on adverse ecological factors and human mistakes so that we may effect a steady-state society and culture.

INADEQUATE CONCERN FOR THEORY IN PHYSICAL EDUCATION AND SPORT MANAGEMENT

Little Evidence That Sport & Physical Education Managers Are Aware of Theory. It is still accurate to state that there has been relatively little evidence that managers or administrators in sport and physical education, wherever they may be functioning, are generally concerned with the theoretical aspects of management. The situation was just the opposite with the practical or technical aspects of management in the 1950s (Trethaway, 1953, p. 458 et ff.). Admittedly it appears to have been similar to the emphases indicated in educational administration research at the time where the topics investigated also shied away, or at least investigators were just beginning to understand the need for, theoretical investigation. See, for example, An analysis of doctoral research problems in school administration by H.A. Taylor, a doctoral study completed at Stanford University in 1954. The problems most investigated related to finance; business affairs; planning, maintenance, and operation of the school plant; and teacher personnel, all topics that Gross identified as specific rather than general administrative processes where motivating, communicating, etc. are involved. However, it is also important to understand that most educational administration professors' understanding of administrative theory and the meaning of terms had most definitely matured by the late 1960s (see Penny, 1968, pp. 107, 121).

Thus, there is still a paradoxical situation in physical education and athletics at the college or university when one is imprudent enough to discuss such a thing as "management theory." The paradox arises because the field seems very definitely to be divided into two groups, neither of which can see the need or importance of such a subject. These groups might be labeled as the "practitioners" and the "scientists." The practitioners don't believe such theory will help them on the job, and the scientist has yet to be convinced of the scientific quality of any such investigation.

The above notwithstanding, and despite the inadequacies in professional preparation for management in our field that have existed for decades, it must be confessed that courses in the organization and administration of physical education and athletics have been offered in our field since 1890 (Zeigler, 1951)! By 1927 they were typically included in professional curricula throughout the United States (Elliott). Since that time there has been a proliferation of similar courses relating to administration and supervision at both the undergraduate and graduate levels. In addition, literally thousands of master's theses and doctoral dissertations have been deposited on the shelves of our libraries. Most of these studies involve the descriptive method of research, or some technique thereof, and there is unquestionably a body of knowledge of sorts about practice of an administrative nature. Relatively speaking, however, there is still a paucity of research in management theory. What we have is an endless stream of articles, theses, dissertations, monographs, and texts on administration or management as a subject-matter area, but what it all adds up to is anybody's guess.

However, during the 1980s, a steady advancement was made in management science in both business and educational administration. Yet, it was still apparent that little had been done similarly to develop management competencies and skills in sport and physical education management programs. Our field was simply not ready to take a progressive step forward. We believe this to be true because the books we published promoting the case method approach to the teaching of human relations and management (1959), as well as management competency development in sport and physical education (1983), were premature. Undaunted, we now are reasonably secure in the knowledge that some progress in understanding the complexity of professional management training has been made during this intervening decade and on into the 1990s. And so, looking ahead to the remainder of the 1990s and the turn of the century, we can state again that more attention should undoubtedly be devoted to management theory and practice--not to mention the skills required to be an effective and efficient manager--if professionals in the field now understand that this is essential. We believe that a significant minority of our colleagues are now aware of this deficiency, and we trust that those involved with management training will continue to implement positive changes. We believe further that social trends and the job market is forcing professionals in the field to develop sufficiently strong attitudes (psychologically speaking) to bring about this much needed change.

STATUS OF THOUGHT, THEORY, AND PRACTICE IN PHYSICAL EDUCATION AND SPORT MANAGEMENT

What can be said at the present about the status of the development of management thought, theory, and practice in physical education and sport? If those working in the area are searching for academic respectability, and this appears to be the case, management theory in this field must somehow steadily and increasingly strive for a sound theoretical basis. The fact is that, even though organization and administration have a long history in our professional preparation programs, investigation into these topics has not achieved the recognition that has been accorded to research in, for example, sport and physical education history. Thompson (in Halpin, 1958, pp. 29-33) explained how we could improve this situation. First, the terms and concepts used must be clear, and they must be related to systematic theory. Second, the theory that we are able to develop should be "generalizable" (and therefore abstract). Third, the research endeavor should be as value-free as possible; if we want to introduce values, they should be treated as variables in the investigative methodology. Fourth, such scholarly endeavor will undoubtedly be based on the social (and primarily the behavioral) sciences. Finally, fifth, correlations are interesting and also significant, but adequate theory should, in the final analysis, clarify processes that will produce quality performance.

The Sport and Physical Activity Manager Defined. Defined traditionally, we might say that the sport and physical activity manager is one who plans, organizes, staffs, leads (or directs), and controls (i.e., monitors and evaluates) progress toward pre-determined goals within programs of developmental physical activity for people of all ages, be they in normal, accelerated, or special populations." In 1983, Zeigler & Bowie defined management more precisely as involving "the execution of managerial acts, including conceptual, technical, human, and conjoined skills, while combining varying degrees of planning, organizing, staff, directing, and controlling within the management process to assist an organization to achieve its goals."

Applied to our field, the above description of the management process would apply to any organization that somehow, somewhere in North America is offering at least some aspect of developmental physical activity in sport, exercise, dance, and play to some degree to one or more sectors of the population.

It will not be discussed here at length, but it should be understood that competitive sport in educational institutions, for example, has faced differing marketing environments in each of the past three decades (i.e., the 1960s, 1970s, and 1980s). In the 1960s there was a great need for additional revenue sources as operating costs skyrocketed. This need continued in the 1970s and was further exacerbated by changing social and economic influences (e.g., social values, slower economic growth). In the 1980s a need existed more than ever for sport programs to develop individual strategic marketing plans with concurrent evaluation schedules to serve as control mechanisms (Zeigler and Campbell, 1984).

A Slowly Growing Awareness of the Managerial Revolution. Even after efforts by a number of us over the past three or four decades to upgrade management theory and practice applied to our field--that is within educational circles in physical education and athletics at least--the new manager or administrator is typically still not truly aware of the managerial revolution that has occurred within this time period. (If he or she is aware of it, the difficult and laborious aspects of the management process is usually turned over to someone with training in business practice.) This is undoubtedly considerably less true for people who assume managerial posts in recreation and other public, semi-public and private agencies where developmental physical activity is a considerable part of the organization's program. But even those in these other groups, if they have only had one course in administration or management within one of our departments as part of their background preparation, these young men and women have only a vague understanding of the many aspects and ramifications of the position being undertaken. What's even worse is the fact that even after the individual is on the job, such a person is still not cognizant of the unbelievable complexity of the position! They learn to do what they do by trial and error! The typical approach is to work overtime to get control of the new responsibility and to meet the seemingly endless demands of higher administration, faculty, staff, and students (or the public as consumers or whatever).

Quite soon one gets the feeling that a treadmill is in operation and that the angle is getting sharper, thereby creating a situation where one must trot at a brisk pace simply not to fall off the back end! It's an uneasy feeling because the pressure is there constantly; some people end up with duodenal spasms and an ulcer. Work tends to pile up in enormous quantities when one is absent from the office for just a few short days. Then, too, all the while there is the feeling that he or she is merely doing what is practical and expedient at the moment. The pattern of operation does indeed become one of trial and error, and it seems impossible to take time out for extended future planning. Finally, because of the many, increasing, and persistent demands that are made upon his or her office, the administrator reasons that more help is needed--both administrative and secretarial. No matter whether budgetary pressures increase, and so-called management in decline becomes a perennial syndrome, there will probably continue to be an increase in positions of this type now and in the foreseeable future. It's the simple truth that "assistants need assistants of their own!" What is the answer to this dilemma? VanderZwaag (1984) offered a concise prescription for the prevailing malady: "What is needed is an integrated sport management program that proceeds from a systematic approach to management."

TIME IS RUNNING OUT ON US

We really don't have much choice at the present other than to make all possible efforts to place professional preparation for administrative leadership within our field on an increasingly academically sound basis. At present the need for vastly improved leadership comes at us from a number of different directions. We simply do not have enough fine leaders in any field--and our field is no exception to this statement. If we don't have good leadership, an organization or enterprise soon begins to falter and even to stumble. Our field needs fine people who will take charge in the behaviorally oriented work environment of today's world. We have all heard that management involves the accomplishment of an objective through the enlistment of others to work closely with management. However, as Zoffer (1985) states: "But I would add to that the need to achieve a certain excellence-- accomplishing goals efficiently, cost-effectively and imaginatively, while respecting the lives and welfare of the broader community." Interestingly, there is no doubt but that sport and physical education has achieved greater recognition within educational circles on this continent than in any other geographical area of the world. (It should be mentioned that recent developments in Japan, Europe, and Australia are encouraging for sport management.) Such achievement is an accomplished fact, but we now have to continue in the direction of upgrading professional preparation for administrative or managerial leadership so that the profession of sport and physical education will consolidate those gains made and-- like the successful basketball team--continue to "move strongly down court on balance toward the goal" (Rothermel, 1966).

Those of us who have been functioning in physical education and sport for many years often take solace in statements like, "But we are still a young field; give us time!" There may be a grain of truth here, but let's not forget that the evidence at hand points to the offering of a course in the organization and administration of physical education and athletics as far back as 1890 (Zeigler, 1951, p. 28), and by 1927 such courses were typically included in professional curricula throughout the country (Elliott, 1927, p. 46). Typically such courses were based on what might be called a "principles approach." For example, the author (EFZ) took courses at Columbia Teachers College in the 1940s that stressed the principles of physical education and sport administration according to such notable early leaders in physical education administration there as William L. Hughes, Clifford L. Brownell, Harry M. Scott, and Patricia Hagman. The authority for such principles usually emanated from the experiences of these professors themselves and, of course, their earlier teachers.

Today, courses--and entire programs--are offered at the undergraduate, master's and doctoral levels in physical education/kinesiology, and the subject matter of administration or management, broadly or narrowly defined, is included to such an extent that a disinterested observer would suspect the presence of a vast storehouse of undergirding knowledge. This is hardly true, although the situation has improved enormously since the description immediately above. This, incidentally, is the same approach that this investigator followed until about the mid-1950's when he began to question the source and validity of all of these principles he had been taught--and which principles he was presumably still using both in teaching the administration course and in practice with his associates as a chairperson. (See Zeigler, 1959.)

It is true, as stated above, that administration has been an area of limited scholarly investigation in physical education and athletics since the early days of the twentieth century. Early studies were often carried out by the administrators themselves and concerned such topics as departmental organization, staffing, and facilities. As master's programs developed in the early years of the century, and then were followed by the first doctoral programs in the 1920s, the number of topics subsumed under the administration area broadened. Soon theses and dissertations became a basic sources of research. Cureton (1949, pp. 21-59) carried out a survey of completed research for the years 1930 through 1946 and listed 420 doctoral dissertations in all sub-areas of the field in his report. Also, whenever there were such general reviews of physical education research as in, for example, the Encyclopedia of Educational Research, research about administration was typically included as a sub-topic (e.g., Esslinger, 1941, pp. 801-814; Esslinger, 1950, pp. 820-835; Rarick, 1960, pp. 973-975; and Montoye & Cunningham, 1969, 963-973). Typical headings and sub-headings were organization and administration, physical education status, administrative practices, policies and procedures, facilities, etc.

ANALYSIS OF RESEARCH REPORTS (TRETHAWAY)

Trethaway (1953) completed a doctoral study tracing early physical education research in which he examined the files of the National Research Committee, an ongoing committee project that was the predecessor of the present AAHPERD Research Council. In total, he collected the titles of 3083 research reports based on research reports of varying quality in physical education competitive athletics, and school recreation between 1895 and 1940. Then he developed a sampling of 789 abstracts from the total and summarized what he found to have been the major developments in each of the three areas.

Interestingly, there have been more studies completed in this area within physical education and athletics, as it was typically designated then, than in any other (with the possible exception of studies about the functional effects of physical activity or the physiological aspects of exercise and sport). This vast number of master's theses and doctoral dissertations may be found on the shelves of our libraries and/or electronic retrieval systems (e.g., CD/ROMs). The large majority of these investigations was carried out using descriptive method research, or a technique thereof, and there does exist undoubtedly a certain body of knowledge about the various aspects of administrative practice relating to our field.

Zeigler (1959, p. 51)), noting the overly heavy dependence on this type of research being carried out, made an effort to introduce the Harvard case method technique of research (also a descriptive research technique) to the field in the late 1950s. At that time he called for research that would contribute more significantly to administrative thought and practice. Beeman (1960), then intramural and recreational sports director at Michigan State University, completed the first doctoral dissertation of this type.

DANIELS AND MCCRISTAL EFFECT BIG TEN
BODY-OF-KNOWLEDGE PROJECT

After Arthur Daniels of Indiana University, working with King McCristal of the University of Illinois and others, effected the actual formation of the Big Ten Body-of-Knowledge Project, Zeigler & McCristal (1967) traced the history of this highly significant undertaking for the future of physical education. This "subdisciplinary approach" to the development of scientific knowledge about developmental physical activity in exercise, sport, and related expressive movement, upon the encouragement of McCristal and Zeigler included administrative theory as one of the subdisciplinary areas. At that time the availability of pure research relative to administrative theory was very poor, however. So, Zeigler encouraged Spaeth in the mid-1960's to make an assessment of its status when pressure for the field to take a "disciplinary approach" came to the fore because of Arthur Conant's criticism of administration courses in physical education. Spaeth's conclusion (1967, p. 145) was that "there is an almost total lack of theoretical orientation in the design of research and interpretation of findings in the sample of of administrative research . . . reviewed in this investigation."

> (Note: The use of the word "theoretical" means "existing only in theory, not practical; thus, a statement of a truth to be demonstrated" [*Random House Dictionary, The*, 1987, p. 1967]. "A theory is essentially a set of assumptions from which a set of empirical laws [principles] may be derived" [Griffiths, 1959, p. 28]. The matter at hand, therefore, was to assess the availability of, and possibility that, hypothetical statements may be shown to be true about the most effective means of administering programs of sport and physical activity.)

A Significant Status Assessment in the Mid-1960s (Spaeth). Spaeth (1967) recommended strongly that we must strive in future research to examine management as a process or group of processes rather than as an area of content (such as the "nuts and bolts" approach, or the "this is how you organize a round-robin tournament" explanation). The execution of studies related to the various technical concerns of managing physical education and education is, of course, highly important to the practitioner, but we must also investigate the more fundamental, broader processes of management that might be designated as decision-making, communicating, activating, planning, evaluating, etc. as they relate to our field. For the period under consideration in this monograph, it was decided that this taxonomy proposed by Gross would be followed basically.

Spaeth's analysis of the relationship of administrative theory to administrative research prior to 1967 (as paraphrased from Spaeth, 1975, Chap. 3 and her 1967 thesis) revealed an almost total lack of a theoretical orientation both in the design of the research itself and in the interpretation of the findings in the sampling that she conducted. She discovered that completed research could be classified according to task areas grouped under two major headings: program aspects (including curriculum development and evaluation and relating students to the program) and technical-managerial aspects (including personnel administration, finance and business management, facilities and equipment, and public relations).

She found further that the program aspects in order of frequency studied were: intercollegiate athletic programs for men, college physical education programs, interscholastic athletics for boys, intramural programs in colleges, elementary school physical education programs, intercollegiate athletics for women, interscholastic programs for girls, and intramural programs in public schools.

Insofar as investigation about the technical-managerial aspects of physical education and athletics in order of frequency studied were: personnel (including, in order of frequency, characteristics of men and women faculty members; job analysis of administrators, supervisors, and directors; characteristics, qualifications, and attitudes of administrators; job analysis of faculty, teachers, and coaches; department chairmen at the college and university level; administrative or leadership behavior; and selection of faculty); facilities and equipment; finance, insurance, and liability; and public relations.

It was interesting to note further that certain of the topics listed above were studied more intensively in some decades than others. Much of the research referred to fell within what might be called the traditional framework of task areas and very little to what can be called the administrative processes. Further examination of the literature within sport and physical education in the mid-1960's by Spaeth (Zeigler & Spaeth, 1975) had indicated also that the field was still almost completely unaware of the development of administrative theory and research that was taking place in other fields.

Field Is Alerted to Need for More Interdisciplinary Work (Penny). Penny (1968, reported in 1975, p. 74) found significant differences between the two groups (i.e., professors of educational administration and professors of physical education and athletics) in their understanding of the meanings of significant concepts in administrative theory. This clearly indicated that professors in physical education and sport needed more interdisciplinary work. Hunter (1971) found the same result when he investigated athletic administrators. The need for improved ordinary language and more sophisticated professional language terms was apparent then and has become even more urgent today. Fortunately, there is now a reasonable degree of consensus on the meanings of the significant concepts that appear in the developing body-of-knowledge relative to management theory and practice within public administration, business administration, and management science. This statement applies generally also to specialists in administrative theory within professional education (i.e., they attach similar meanings to specific, significant concepts associated with the subject matter).

A Plea For A Broader Approach to the Teaching of Administration Courses in Physical Education and Sport (Paton). Similarly, Paton (in Zeigler and Spaeth, 1975, p. 14) suggested a significantly broader approach to the teaching of administration courses in sport and physical education. This approach should be characterized by an emphasis in which the area of content specifically related to sport and physical education would depend increasingly on a body of knowledge developed through management research and theory in our field. Further, educational institutions provide the setting within which many sport and physical education programs are managed. Thus, current efforts to develop management theory and research about the broad administrative process mentioned above within the educational setting are still directly relevant to our field. The fact that management/administration is practiced in a specific setting has tended to obscure the fundamental similarities of the managerial process. The study of administration as administration should eventually also provide a sounder theoretical base for understanding the management process. Finally, and last but not least, underlying all management theory and research are the social sciences (and still more specifically, the behavioral sciences). Concepts and theories related to the behavior of people in organizations have much to offer to an understanding of administration or management.

Baker and Collins Continue Bibliographic Work Begun by Zeigler and Spaeth. Zeigler and Spaeth (1973) made an effort to compile the research that had been completed by offering a selected bibliography of approximately 250 studies related to the administration of physical education and athletics that had been carried out during the 45-year period from 1927 to 1972. Then, Baker and Collins (1983), after discussions with Zeigler, carried out their project involving a retrieval system extending from 1971 to 1982. They assessed the 7,855 thesis and dissertation reports that had been indexed and abstracted in Completed Research in Health, Physical Education and Recreation between 1971 and 1981 (Volumes 13-23). (Studies related specifically to the administration of intramurals and recreational sports were excluded.) General descriptors based on a modified framework of the conceptual structure employed originally by Spaeth (1967) were devised by the investigators. They added "legal considerations" as a heading in the area of "technical administrative concerns, but excluded the category of "curriculum development" (Baker and Collins, 1983, p. xiii). This change was made since King and Baker (1982) had already carried out a bibliographic compilation of curriculum studies based on completed thesis investigations. (See Fig. 1).

Interestingly, Baker and Collins reported that approximately ten per cent of completed thesis research in all of physical education could be related to administration or management. In fact, as noted earlier, completed theses in the administration or management area are exceeded only slightly by those that are "exercise physiological" in nature. For the ten-year period under consideration, the found a total of 758 studies (9.8% of all theses completed). Finally, the contents of the 758 studies were analyzed to determine a scheme of sub-groupings within each general category. As we look to the future, of course, the next step is to understand where all of these findings from these studies are, as well as what they contribute to the development of ordered generalizations or principles about management theory and practice in sport and physical education.

In an effort to establish this subprofessional aspect of the field's undergirding discipline on a sounder footing, the Stipes Publishing Co. decided to add two additional monographs to the Stipes Monograph Series on Sport and Physical Education Management. The first is the present monograph that, in addition to this historical essay, includes the earlier Zeigler/Spaeth bibliography (1973) with the addition of brief annotations to each item provided through the combined efforts of Thomas Sinclair and Zeigler, respectively. The Baker/Collins publication then extends the research retrieval from 1971 to 1982. Their listing came primarily from Completed Research for those years and indicates where a particular study may be found within these volumes (not the institution where the thesis was completed). Two interesting questions for future bibliographers to consider are (1) whether master's theses (where carried out) should be included, and (2) whether the original Zeigler/Spaeth "taxonomy," as modified by Baker/Collins, should be further adapted to the 1990s decade.

The above notwithstanding, and despite positive efforts by a steadily increasing number of scholars largely within the North American Society for Sport Management since its beginning in the mid-1980s, general awareness of the theoretic literature--or any significant contribution to it--has only increased slowly in the past thirty years since Spaeth's analysis. This seeming (evident?) lack of awareness and concern is troubling since the field has recently begun to appreciate that people should be prepared more carefully and thoroughly for the "assumption of the managerial risk." For example, since opportunities to specialize in streams or areas of concentration within physical education training programs have begun, the sport management specialization now appears to have been the most popular program of the 1980s. Further, its growth is continuing on into the 1990s. One is forced to speculate about the intellectual level of these programs when the majority of professors and instructors have typically been such reluctant, unproductive scholars.

The late University of Michigan researcher, Paul Hunsicker, suggested an aphorism to the effect that "No master's thesis or doctoral dissertation ever startled the academic world." Unfortunately, up until relatively recently (i.e., 1990) this insightful comment could well be an apt description of the status of research in management theory and practice in sport and physical education. However, one might argue that completed physical education and sport management theses have made at least some contribution to our understanding of administrative practice in the area. However, contributions to management theory still have not really made much of a dent in the bulk of the many problems and conundrums facing the professional practitioner.

THE SITUATION IN THE MID-1990s

In the mid-1990s, we really didn't have much choice other than to make all possible efforts to place professional preparation for administrative leadership within our field on a more academically sound basis. This question of leadership comes toward us from a number of different directions these days. We simply don't have enough fine leaders in any field--and our field is no exception to this statement. If we don't have good leadership, any organization or enterprise soon begins to falter and even to stumble. Our field needs fine people who will take charge in the behaviorally oriented work environment of today's world. We've all heard that management involves the accomplishment of an objective through the enlistment of others to work closely with you. However, as Zoffer (1985) stated: "But I would add to that the need to achieve a certain excellence--accomplishing goals efficiently, cost-effectively and imaginatively, while respecting the lives and welfare of the broader community."

There is no doubt but that physical education and (educational) sport has up to this time achieved greater recognition within educational circles on this continent than in any other geographical area of the Western world. Such achievement is an accomplished fact, but we now have to continue in the direction of upgrading professional preparation for administrative or managerial leadership so that the profession of sport and physical education will consolidate those gains made and--like the successful basketball team--continue to "move strongly down court toward the goal on balance" (Rothermel, 1966).

Up to this point, in addition to some introductory and background material, it has been argued essentially (a) that the world is changing and becoming increasingly complex with each passing day fostering a steadily growing development in management thought, theory, and practice, a development that has had obvious implications for the field of sport and physical education; (b) that sport and physical education needs managers who function effectively and efficiently on the basis of tenable management theory to organize and administer its far-flung programs; and (c) that we have not advanced very far in preparing our people to manage from both a theoretical and practical standpoint, an inadequacy that I believe we should correct as soon as possible by promoting sound theoretical knowledge and by implementing management competency development programs of high quality that include well-planned laboratory experiences.

Let us assume that we can agree on the need for improving the quality of sport and physical education management in the near future. This need is not peculiar to our profession, however, since we are hearing pleas from all over North America about a growing need for a higher quality in managerial performance than may have been present in the past. To meet the challenge to North American industry and business, for example, we were exhorted to consider "Theory Z" as wisdom coming from our Japanese colleagues (Ouchi, 1982)--actually a debatable assumption as it has turned out. Also, there has been a spate of books with the world "excellence" in the title. For example, in a 1980s book entitled Creating Excellence (Hickman and Silva, 1984), we are presented with a list of "new age skills" that management executives should cultivate: (a) creative insight: asking the right questions; (b) sensitivity: doing unto others; (c) vision: creating the future; (d) versatility: anticipating change; (e) focus: implementing change; and (f) patience: living in the long term (pp. 99-246). After this, you begin to "walk on water!"

THE PRESENT NEED FOR AN "ACTION-THEORY MARRIAGE"

What has been stated above provides some substantiation for the gradual emergence of management science--indeed, a need for an "action-theory marriage!" Many say that management thought is too practical, while others avow that it is usually too theoretical. This may seem to be true, but I believe it can be said more accurately that really practical administrative thought will simply have to be based on far more tenable knowledge and theory than is yet available. Scholarly investigation on this topic should be carried out to the greatest possible extent on the "observable facts of real-life administration" (Gross, 1964). A manager on the job is typically confronted with a real-life situation to resolve. To resolve the problem effectively and efficiently, something better than trial and error is needed in our increasingly complex social environment. That "something" should be the most tenable theory available. In other words, a research strategy is needed that is characterized by a "theory-research balance" based on the results of sound theoretical and applied investigation.

Even though I have been emphasizing that the manager is being faced with a relatively fast-moving social system, a condition from which managers of sport and physical education cannot (and probably should not wish to) escape, change for us has somehow not occurred as rapidly as in certain other segments of society. However, managers in our field must now recognize the fact that they too are being put on notice about the fluid nature of their environments. Managers simply must take advantage of every opportunity to prepare themselves to keep ahead (or at least abreast) of their associates intellectually. This is necessary because they must be ready to meet change head-on and make the alterations and modifications necessary so that growth (if desired and/or desirable) and survival will be ensured (the ecological approach, if you will).

Don't Forget the Carry-Over Constants and/or Generalizations. The above momentary digression is not meant to imply for an instant that there are not a great many constants and/or generalizations which carry over from yesterday to today and thence to tomorrow which help to maintain the structure and vitality of sport and physical education. This means, for example, that much of what is known about human nature today will be identical or quite similar tomorrow. It forewarns the manager that he or she shouldn't throw the baby out with the bath water just because many changes seem to be taking place. The great problem seems to be the urgent need to both strengthen and focus the body of knowledge available to the management profession so that the literally astounding development in the area of technology is reasonably approximated by the understanding and knowledge available about effective and efficient administrative behavior. While such a balance is being established, the tried-and-true constants or "principles" from the past should be used daily and only discarded or modified when there is ample evidence (scientific or normative) available to warrant any change.

Thus the manager, in addition to relying on the wisdom of the past, should make it a habit over the years to increase both his or her theoretical and practical knowledge. I believe that the field still has an opportunity to relate significantly to the developing social science of management. However, we can't dally much longer! I say this with a full understanding that so many professionals in our field are only dimly aware of the scientific development that has occurred in management science. Second, the vast enterprise that is sport and physical education for its very survival as a recognizable entity simply must relate more effectively to the urgent need for qualified sport and physical activity managers. The North American Society for Sport Management, inaugurated in the mid-1980s is making a significant contribution to this development. Additionally, such development should continue to be carried out in full cooperation with the the the National Association for Sport and Physical Education within the AAHPERD and the Canadian Association for Health, Physical Education, Recreation, and Dance.

CONCLUDING STATEMENT

At this point Peter Drucker's advice (1993, Chap. 12) about the idea of "The Educated Person" in Post-Capitalist Society seems like a good way to begin to close this essay. He states that a great transformation has been taking place in the world in regard to (a) a move from capitalism to a knowledge society, (b) a trend from nation-states to megastates, and (c) a shift from a market economy based on traditional market institutions to a market that organizes economic activity around information and knowledge (Chap. 10). In this "new world," Drucker claims that the technological revolution will gradually "engulf" our schools as we all rethink the role of the school and the way it functions. The direct challenge to our society, therefore, is the way that we use the new technology in what he calls post-capitalist society--i.e., the knowledge society (Chap. 11, 197). If we have the wisdom to shift rapidly and fully to a knowledge society that puts the person in the center of the process, we will be able to remain in the forefront of progress.

This post-capitalist society needs "a leadership group, which can focus local, particular, separate traditions onto a common and shared commitment to values, a common concept of excellence, and on mutual respect" (p. 212). However, what is required, Drucker insists, is a new and different kind of educated person than the Deconstructionists, the radical feminists, the anti-Westerners, and the Humanists want (p. 212). What is needed, he maintains, is an educated person who has the knowledge and the commitment to cope with the present situation, as well as being prepared for "life in a global world" (p. 214). Leaders in this society under transformation will use sound organizational theory as a tool enabling them to use their specialized knowledge wisely. Gross's earlier prediction about the need for an action-theory marriage will indeed come to pass (1964, pp. 844-856).

Finally, keeping the basic need for leaders ("educated persons," according to Drucker!) firmly in mind, the author should state his personal and continuing interest in a leadership spectrum (or perhaps a continuum) in which, as one moves from left to right (i.e., from anarchy to dictatorship), the manager gradually exercises greater authority and the staff members have lesser areas of freedom. (He has also employed this same continuum to the teaching act in a way similar to the approach of the late Muska Mosston; see Zeigler, 1964, pp. 258-261.) Through long experience he has developed a distinct aversion to one-person, arbitrary, authoritative decisions--especially in educational settings--although he wouldn't like to work in such a setting at any time anywhere else either.

Of course, it is appreciated that in certain lines of work, such as the military or firefighting, there typically isn't sufficient time to have discussion and then to take a vote before action is taken. Nevertheless, staff members should be involved in the decision-making process to the greatest possible extent--if they are willing to make serious efforts to be well informed on the matter at hand. Further, once a decision is made democratically by informed members of the group, the organization can and should demand loyal support from all members of the group. (The assumption here is that opportunities will be provided subsequently for people to be convinced in democratic fashion at a not-too-distant future date that a contravening decision should be made.)

In this changing (internal and external) organizational environment that we have been discussing, the interpersonal skills of the leader(s) need continuing examination and study. Certainly the leader must know himself or herself and know those with whom direct or indirect association is established. The executive needs to establish an open climate. By this is meant that (a) associates can collect information about a problem accurately, (b) bring these data back to the decision-making group, and then (c) take part in the planning and execution of future actions (Bennis & Slater, 1968).

The concept of "leadership", however, has been an elusive one down through the years. For a long time what was called "trait theory" was in vogue-- that is, there was concern about the prospective manager's personal characteristics, ones that presumably made him or her a fine leader. In the 1940s, however, trait theory declined because investigations along this line produced no clear-cut results. Thus, even though this approach had, and still has, some descriptive value, it has been supplanted to a large degree by so-called "situational theory." With this approach it is argued (a) that there are situational factors that can be delineated in a finite way and (b) that they vary according to a number of other factors (Filley, House, & Kerr, 1976). Some of these factors, for example, are (a) the leader's age and experience, (b) the size of the group led, (c) the cultural expectations of subordinates, (d) the time required and allowed for decision-making). Chelladurai (1985), in his discussion of leadership, refers to charismatic leadership and organizational leadership, the latter being "just one of the functions of a manager who is placed in charge of a group and its activities, and is, in turn, guided by superiors and organizational factors" (p. 139).

Even though it has been emphasized that the manager is now faced with a relatively fast-moving social system, a condition from which managers of sport and physical activity cannot (and probably should not wish to) escape, somehow change for us is occurring less rapidly than in certain other segments of society. However, managers must recognize the fact that they have been put on notice about the fluid nature of their particular environments as well. Managers simply must avail themselves of every opportunity to prepare themselves to keep ahead (or at least abreast) of their associates intellectually. This is the major reason why the present data base of completed research available should be continually updated and amplified. This is absolutely necessary because managerial leaders must be ready to meet change head-on. They have to understand when and how to make necessary alterations and modifications so that effective and efficient growth (if desired and/or desirable) and long-term survival will be ensured.

The Professional Task Ahead. What, then, is the professional task ahead? As a preamble to this final section on what we should do, we should be prospective enough to recognize that "our world" may be sharply different tomorrow. By that I mean that the push is on to call sport and physical education as defined by NASPE either kinesiology or exercise and sport science--the question is, I presume, "do we want to employ Greek or English?" These are seemingly the two leading appellations (of approximately 117 names now in use) being recommended for both the disciplinary core of our field and the department, division, school, or college in which it is housed (Razor, 1989).

How are the members of NASSM going to answer two burning questions confronting them at this very moment? By this, first, I am referring to the fact that a number of people are recommending that we in sport and physical activity management abandon the relatively traditional disciplinary core of physical education that has developed over the past 40 years in the field. They argue that the extra time could be well spent on further liberal arts and science training and some basic business administration courses. Our Society (NASSM) needs to appoint a commission to look into this fundamental question that will report to our executive and general assembly in the very near future. We can't afford to hang back on this question, mainly because it is so crucial to our future. Second, we should also have a group working on the development of a computerized assessment of the evolving theory and principles underlying sport and physical activity management. We need to identify the knowledge, skills, and competencies required to perform the duties of sport management effectively, efficiently, and ethically (Zeigler and Bowie, 1983).

Finally, then, as to what we should do, we should first truly understand why we have chosen this profession, and why we have specialized in sport and physical education management, as we rededicate ourselves anew to the study and dissemination of knowledge, competencies, and skills in human motor performance in sport, exercise, and related expressive movement.

Second, as either management practitioners or as professors involved in professional preparation of sport and physical education managers, we should search for young people of high quality in all the attributes needed for success in the field. We should then help them to develop lifelong commitments so that our profession can achieve its democratically agreed-upon goals. We should search especially for young people to serve in the area of sport and physical education management. Our area of specialization has been the growth curriculum in the 1980s, and there is every reason to believe that this trend will continue on into the future.

Third, we must place quality as the first priority of our professional endeavors. Our personal involvement and specialization should include a high level of competency and skill undergirded by solid knowledge about the profession. It can certainly be argued that our professional task is as important as any in society. Thus, the present is no time for indecision, half-hearted commitment, imprecise knowledge, and general unwillingness to stand up and be counted in debate with colleagues within our field and in allied professions and related disciplines, not to mention the general public.

Fourth, the obligation is ours. If we hope to reach our potential, we must sharpen our focus and improve the quality of our professional effort. Only in this way will we be able to guide the modification process that the profession is currently undergoing toward the achievement of our highest professional goals. This is the time--right now--to employ sport, exercise, dance, and play to make our reality more healthful, more pleasant, more vital, and more life-enriching. By "living fully in one's body," behavioral science men and women will be adapting and shaping that phase of reality to their own ends.

Finally, such improvement will not come easily; it can only come through the efforts of professional people making quality decisions, through the motivation of people to change their sedentary lifestyles, and through our professional assistance in guiding people as they strive to fulfill such motivation in their movement patterns. When our black brothers and sisters speak about the concept of 'soul,' they mean placing a special quality into some aspect of life (e.g., soul music). Our mission in the years ahead is to place this special quality in all of our professional endeavors.

NOTE

1. The reader should understands that this background essay is intended to be synoptic in nature. What is contained represents an updated, revised (presumably improved) version of many of the ideas, opinions, and recommendations expressed by the author about management theory and practice as applied to physical education and sport in a variety of publications over a period of approximately forty years. Prior to a recent collaborative effort with Gary Bowie (Lethbridge) designed to introduce a management competency development approach to professional preparation in physical education and educational sport, the author had collaborated earlier, also, with Marcia Spaeth (retired from SUNY, Cortland) and Garth Paton and Terry Haggerty (now both at New Brunswick, but earlier at Western Ontario). Some of this material (i.e., that related to proposed areas of administrative research and that related to the professional preparation program) has been researched by Professor Spaeth and Professor Paton, respectively and

appeared in Zeigler and Spaeth [1975]). Also, the author wishes to express sincere appreciation to Tom Sinclair who worked most closely with me in the mid-1970s, and who capably tracked down as a special project much of the information provided in many of the brief annotations related to completed research between 1927 and 1972.

REFERENCES AND BIBLIOGRAPHY

Andrews, K.R. (Ed.). (1953). *Human relations and administration.* Cambridge, MA: Harvard University Press.

Argyris, C. (1957). *Personality and organization* NY: Harper & Bros.

Baker, J.A.W. & Collins, M.S. (1983). *Research on administration of physical education and athletics 1971-1982*: A retrieval system. Reseda, CA: Mojave.

Barnard, C.I. (1938). *The functions of the executive.* Cambridge, MA: Harvard Univ. Press.

Bedeian, A.G. (1985). Management, historical development of. In L.R. Bittel, & Ramsey, J.E. (Eds.), *Handbook for professional managers* (pp. 491-496). NY: McGraw-Hill.

Bennis, W. & Slater, P.E. (1968). *The temporary society.* New York: Harper & Row.

Bittel, L.R. & Ramsey, J.E. (1985). *Handbook for professional managers.* NY: McGraw-Hill.

Brubacher, J.S. (1961). Higher education and the pursuit of excellence. *Marshall University Bulletin*, 3:3.

Chelladurai, P. (1985). *Sport management.* London, Canada: Sport Dynamics.

Cureton, T.K. (March 1949). Doctorate theses reported by graduate departments of health, physical education and recreation 1930-1946, inclusively. *Research Quarterly*, 20, 21-59.

Drucker, P.F. (1954). *The practice of management.* New York: Harper & Row.

Drucker, P.F. (1993). *Post-capitalist society.* NY: HarperBusiness.

Elliott, R. (1927). The organization of professional training in physical education in state universities. New York: Columbia Teachers College.

Encyclopedia of Educational Research, The. (1969). (4th Ed.). NY: Macmillan.

Esslinger, A.A. (1941). Physical education. In *Encyclopedia of Educational Research* (pp. 801-814). NY: Macmillan.

Esslinger, A.A. (1950) Physical education. In *Encyclopedia of Educational Research (2nd Ed.)* (820-835) NY: Macmillan..

Fayol, H.(1949). *General and industrial management.* NY: Pitman.

Filley, A.C., House, R.J. & Kerr, S. (1976). *Managerial process and organizational behavior. (2nd Ed.).* Glenview, IL: Scott, Foresman.

George, C.S., Jr. (1972). *The history of management thought. (2nd Ed.).* Englewood Cliffs, NJ: Prentice-Hall.

Goodwin, M. (1986). When the cash register is the scoreboard. *The New York Times,* June 8, 27-28.

Gordon, P.J. (Spring 1966). Transcend the current debate on administrative theory. *Hospital Administration,* 11(2), 6-23.

Gross, B.M. (1964). *The managing of organizations.* New York: The Free Press of Glencoe (Macmillan).

Halpin, A.W. (1958). The development of theory in educational administration. In A.W. Halpin (Ed.), *Administrative theory in education.* New York: Macmillan.

Hickman, C.R. & Silva, M.A. (1984). *Creating excellence.* New York: New American Library.

Hodgetts, R.M. (1979). *Management: Theory, process and practice.* (2nd Ed.). Philadelphia: Saunders.

Hower, R.M. (Sept.-Oct. 1953). Final lecture, advanced management program In Katz, R.L. (1974), Skills of an effective administrator. *Harvard Business Review,* 52, 90-112.

Hunter, J. (1971). *An analysis of meanings attached to selected concepts by administrators of the Big Ten Conference and the Central Intercollegiate Athletic Association.* Master's thesis, University of Illinois, C-U.

King, H.A. & Baker, J.A.W. (1982). Conceptualization and bibliography of research in teaching physical education based on theses and dissertations. *Journal of Teaching Physical Education,* 2(1), 63-102.

Koontz, H. (December 1961). The management theory jungle. *Journal of the Academy of Management,* 4(3), 174-188.

Koontz, H. (1985). Management theory, science, and approaches. In L.R. Bittel, & Ramsey, J.E., *Handbook for professional managers* (pp. 506-518). NY: McGraw-Hill.

Luthans, F. & Stewart, T.I. (1977). A general contingency theory of management. *Academy of Management Review,* 182, 190.

McCleary, L.E. & McIntyre, K. (March 1972). Competency development and the methodology of college teaching: A model and proposal. *The Bulletin (NASSP),* 56, 53-59.

McCleary, L.E. (1973). Competency-based educational administration and application to related fields. In *Proceedings of the Conference on Administrative Competence*. Tempe, AZ: Bureau of Educational Research, Arizona State University, 26-38.

Mintzberg, H. (1973). *The nature of managerial work*. NY: Harper & Row.

Montoye, H. & Cunningham, D. (1969). Physical education. In *Encyclopedia of Educational Research (4th Ed.)* (pp. 963-973). NY: Macmillan.

New York Times, The. (1970). Report by Commission on Tests of the College Entrance Examination Board, Nov. 2.

Odiorne, G.S. (1965). *Management by objectives*. New York: Pitman.

Ouchi, W.G. (1981). *Theory Z*. Reading, MA: Addison-Wesley.

Paris, R. (1975). A selected listing of doctoral dissertations in administrative theory and practice related to physical education and sport 1971 to 1978. In *Administrative theory and practice in physical education and athletics* (Appendix). (E.F. Zeigler & M.J. Spaeth, Eds.). Englewood Cliffs, NJ: Prentice-Hall.

Parsons, T. (1958) Some ingredients of a general theory of formal organization. In Halpin, A.W. (Ed.), *Administrative theory in education* (p. 44). New York: Macmillan.

Penny, W.J. (1968). *An analysis of meanings attached to selected concepts in administrative theory*. Doctoral dissertation, University of Illinois, C-U.

Rarick, G.L. (1960). Physical education. In *Encyclopedia of Educational Research (3rd Ed.)* (973-95). NY: Macmillan.

Razor, Jack E. (1989). What we call ourselves currently. A paper presented to the American Academy of Physical Education, Boston, MA, April 19, 1989.

Rosenberg, J.M. (1978). *Dictionary of business and management*. NY: John Wiley.

Rothermel, B.L. (1966). Conversation with the author, Oct. 3.

Snyder, R.A. & Scott, H.A. (1954). *Professional preparation in health, physical education, and recreation*. New York: McGraw-Hill.

Spaeth, M.J. (1967). *An analysis of administrative research in physical education in relation to a research paradigm*. Doctoral dissertation, University of Illinois, C-U.

Tesconi, C.A., Jr. & Morris, V.C. (1972). *The anti-man culture*. Urbana, IL: University of Illinois Press.

Thompson, J.D. (1958). Modern approaches to theory in administration. In Halpin, A.W., *Administrative theory in education*. New York: Macmillan.

Tillett, A.D., Kempner, T., & Wills, G. (1970). *Management thinkers*.

Baltimore: Penguin.

Toffler, A. (1970). *Future shock.* New York: Random House.

Toffler, A. (1980). *The third wave.* New York: William Morrow.

VanderZwaag, H.J. (1984). *Sport management in schools and colleges.*
NY: John Wiley.

Wren, D.A. (1979). *The evolution of management thought. (2nd Ed.).* NY:
Wiley.

Zeigler, E.F. (1951). *A history of professional preparation for physical
education in the United States, 1861-1948.* Eugene, OR: Microfiche
Publications, University of Oregon.

Zeigler, E.F. (1959). *Administration of physical education and athletics:
The case method approach.* Englewood Cliffs, NJ: Prentice-Hall.

Zeigler, E.F. & McCristal, K.J. (December 1967). A history of the Big Ten
Body-of-Knowledge Project. *Quest,* 9, 28-41.

Zeigler, E.F. (1972). A model for optimum professional development in a field
called "X." In *Proceedings of the First Canadian Symposium on the
Philosophy of Sport and Physical Activity.* Ottawa, Canada: Sport Canada
Directorate, pp. 16-28.

Zeigler, E.F. & Spaeth, M.J. (1973). A selected bibliography of completed
research on administrative theory and practice in physical education and
athletics. In *Proceedings of the Big Ten Symposium on Administrative
Theory and Practice,* Ann Arbor, MI, pp. 143-153.

Zeigler, E.F., Spaeth, M.J. & Paton, G.A. (1975). Theory and research in the
administration of physical education. In Zeigler, E.F. & Spaeth, M.J.,
Administrative theory and practice in physical education and athletics.
Englewood Cliffs, NJ: Prentice-Hall.

Zeigler, E.F. & Spaeth, M.J. (Eds.). (1975). *Administrative theory and
practice in physical education and athletics.* Englewood Cliffs, NJ:
Prentice-Hall.

Zeigler, E.F. (1977). Philosophical perspective on the future of physical education
and sport. In R. Welsh (Ed.), *Physical education: A view toward the future* (pp. 36-61).
Saint Louis: C.V. Mosby.

Zeigler, E.F. (1982). *Decision-making in physical education and athletics administration: A
case method approach.* Champaign, IL: Stipes.

Zeigler, E.F. & Bowie, G.W. (1983). *Management competency development in
physical education and sport.* Philadelphia: Lea & Febiger.

Zeigler, E.F. & Campbell, J. (1984). *Strategic market planning: An aid to
the evaluation of an athletic/recreation program.* Champaign, IL: Stipes.

Zeigler, E. F. (1985). The Illinois slush-fund scandal of the 1960s: A preliminary analysis. *The Physical Educator*, 42, 2 (Spring), 82-88.

Zeigler, E.F. & Bowie, G.W. (1995). *Management competency development in sport and physical education*. Champaign, IL: Stipes.

Zoffer, H.J. (1985). Training managers to take charge. In Business (Section 3, 2), *The New York Times*, Oct. 20.

CHAPTER IX

AMERICAN PHYSICAL EDUCATION
AND SPORT PHILOSOPHY:
AN HISTORICAL AND CRITICAL ANALYSIS

In this chapter the historical development of sport and physical activity philosophy in the United States will be traced. Additionally, because of the vital importance of this topic to the present development of the field of physical education and sport's present development, the present situation in connection with this topic will be analyzed critically.

Having said this, this chapter will examine:

(1) from a historical perspective how scholars in the past 100 years, variously related to the profession of physical education and (educational) sport, general philosophy, and educational theory (or philosophy of education) have sought to carry out their function as philosophic analysts of human physical activity in sport, exercise, and related expressive activities;

(2) from a "cultural criticism" perspective the use and abuse of an increasingly important social institution known as sport that functions alongside a concomitant professional movement known worldwide as physical education and sport designed to promote sound health, fitness, and lifetime sports; and

(3) from a philosophical perspective the status of so-called sport philosophy as it looks to its future in the 21st century while struggling in the Philosophic Society for the Study of Sport. In this third part of this paper several recommendations are advanced that may have the potential to raise again the status of our departmental philosophy in the eyes of the physical education/kinesiology profession and the public.

I wish to emphasize that this paper is not intended as an attack, nor is it a defense of sport and concomitant physical activity. It is initially more of an exploration of the advantages and disadvantages of sport and related physical activity for present life. I state boldly first as a given that sport has obviously become an extremely powerful social force in society. If we grant that it now has such power in our culture--a power indeed that appears to be growing steadily--we can also recognize that any such social force affecting society can be dangerous if perverted (e.g., positive nationalism to blind chauvinism, normal commercialism to excessive commercialism). Accepting the possible (apparent?) truth of these assertions, I believe that, while sport has grown as an important social force, it now also appears to have become a societal institution with an inadequately defined theory. Society, especially television producers, seems to be proceeding generally on the assumption that "sport is good, and more sport is better!"

Within this presently muddled situation in regard to sport's role in society, I feel that most people--including the writer as a sport philosopher hopefully to a significantly lesser degree--are like the proverbial blind person attempting to describe an elephant using the sense of touch only (i.e., here a trunk, there a tusk, next four leathery pillars, etc.). Even though we humans have sight we are akin to a person attempting to assemble a jigsaw puzzle without first seeing the complete picture on the cover of the box. This had led us into developing warped or truncated ideas about the big picture of sport we should be assembling in a presumably forward-looking society. Resultantly, this causes us to ignore concomitant benefits attained from participation in competitive activities.

This "head in the sand" approach is exactly what I wish to condemn. Thus, my primary concern is to state my belief that many of those who call themselves sport philosophers (or sport and physical activity philosophers, or whatever) are presently functioning like the proverbial lemmings marching off the cliff to extinction. Their philosophical approach and endeavor may be sound for what they think they should be doing, but they are suffering from the same malady besetting general philosophy and educational theory or policy (formerly called educational philosophy): they simply aren't "baking bread" in a world where competitive sport-- whether it knows it or not--is "starving for educational and ethical nourishment!" Also, at a time when physical education and (educational?) sport in North America really needs guidance, many key sport philosophers have deserted the profession. Further, we aren't even "reproducing ourselves" adequately any more because our status and space in the educational firmament is declining sharply, and positions simply "ain't out there!" How we came to be in this dilemma; why competitive sport needs educational and ethical nourishment; and what we could do about this are the topics I will discuss.

HISTORICAL REVIEW OF THE DEVELOPMENT OF OF SPORT AND PHYSICAL EDUCATION PHILOSOPHY

In this first section, I will look backward relatively briefly to refresh ourselves

255

as to how those functioning in what is now called sport and physical activity philosophy have approached their task over the past 100 years. This brief excursion away from the realms of general philosophy and departmental educational policy (i.e., philosophy of education) to what has been happening historically within the field of physical education (or whichever name you like of the more than 150 terms that are in use presently to designate the units in which most of us are employed). To do so I have roughly divided the period of a century more or less into a number of discrete (yet in several cases overlapping) periods--and will mention at least one example of "philosophizing" from each period--as follows:

(1) A commonsense/rational thought approach;
(2) a normative approach to philosophizing;
(3) a philosophy of education systems/
   implications approach;
(4) a theory-building approach;
(5) a phenomenological-existentialistic
   approach;
(6) a conceptual/language analysis approach; and
(7) an analytic approach to concepts and
   constructs.

A Common Sense/Rational Thought Approach (late 1880s through early 1920s. Early physical education philosophers, if we may call them that in today's "analytic or post-analytic environment," believed that they had the answers to most of the day's perplexing problems being faced. During the late 1800s and early 1900s, there was typically a combined "common sense and rational thought approach" to this aspect of our field. The report of the Boston Conference on Physical Training included didactic pronouncements by 33 men and women representing what is now known as "the battle of the systems" as propounded by the authorities of the time (Barrows, ed., 1899). Some of the people who philosophized about the importance of "physical training" and their work in it are still recognized today: William G. Anderson, Pierre de Coubertin, Luther Halsey Gulick, Edward Hitchcock, Heinrich Metzner, Nils Posse, and Dudley A. Sargent.

A Normative Approach to Philosophizing (mid-1920s to mid-1950s). This first period of amateur philosophizing about developmental physical activity in what might be called organized U.S. physical education was followed in the 20th century by what might be identified as a "normative philosophizing approach." Use of this second approach extended roughly from the mid-1920s to the mid-1950s at least--and for some down to the present day. This was the period when all sorts of principles texts appeared, an approach undoubtedly influenced strongly by similar scholarly endeavor emanating from both philosophy itself to a degree, but primarily from schools of education where the great philosophic traditions of Idealism, Realism, and Pragmatism were in vogue. Some influential names from professional education to be mentioned here for the period 1930-1950 might be Mortimer J. Adler, Frederick S. Breed, John S. Brubacher, John Dewey, Herman Harrell Horne, William H. Kilpatrick, and William McGucken (Henry, 1942).

Professors in what was a more unified profession of health, physical education, and recreation caught the flavor of the several philosophic traditions extant, but their analysis was not philosophical in today's scholarly, analytic way. In the late 1940s and early 1950s, here were some "great debates" by such outstanding earlier leaders such as McCloy, Nash, Oberteuffer, and Williams. Additionally, we recall the enunciation of principles during this quite long period by leaders like Clifford L. Brownell, Rosalind Cassidy, Ray Duncan, Arthur Esslinger, Clark Hetherington, William L. Hughes, Mabel Lee, R. Tait McKenzie, Elmer D. Mitchell, N.P. Neilson, Jackson Sharman, Natalie Shepard, Seward C. Staley, Arthur Steinhaus, Agnes Wayman, Thomas D. Wood, and others (names listed alphabetically).

> (**Note:** Schrag [1994], in his review of Kaminsky [1993], points out correctly that "prewar philosophers of education in the United States wrote for school teachers and administrators, among others" (p. 365). Beginning in the early 1950s, also, educational philosophers were caught in a situation where more academic respectability was desired, and they wittingly fell into a trap probably set unwittingly by a growing multitude of professors in general philosophy who barely knew such "philosophers of education" were alive. Schrag states further that "When the analysts began work in the late 1950s and 1960s they were writing primarily for each other" <p. 365>. Subsequently, in the late 1960s, I believe that a segment of those professors functioning in physical education and sport philosophy also "wittingly fell into the same sort of trap set for us quite unwittingly" by our colleagues in education--but initially, of course, by philosophers in the mother discipline. "Credit" for "laying of the bait" for physical education professors should go also to

selected, interested professors from general philosophy anxious to "show the light" to physical education professors. Examination of the proceedings of the annual meetings of the Philosophy of Education Society demonstrates with overwhelming conclusiveness that present "educational policy" professors, then known as educational philosophers, hadn't the slightest academic interest in physical education and educational sport.)

A Philosophy of Education Systems (Implications?) Approach (Mid-1950s to Mid-1960s). In the early to mid-1950s, a few physical educators sought to "key in" on what might correctly be called a "philosophy of education systems approach" and sought to employ more strictly its so-called "structural analysis or implications technique" for the analysis of different philosophies of physical education. Between 1954 and 1958, for example, Richard B. Morland carried out his monumental doctoral study at New York University in which he employed this newer approach-- to a degree at least--that sought to draw reasonable implications from metaphysical analysis to a specific philosophy of education with resultant inferences for health, physical education, and recreation. A main point of Morland's approach emphasized careful examination of a leader's writings to discover possible recurrent themes that accordingly displayed their basic beliefs as they might relate to the major systems of educational philosophy extant.

Both Davis (1961) and Zeigler (1964) used the so-called Systems/Implications Approach in their texts that exerted considerable influence on professional preparation in the 1960s. Davis's *Philosophies fashion physical education* (1963), with contributions from Burke, Oberteuffer, Holbrook, and Van Dalen, made a helpful contribution to professionals at the time. Because of criticism within educational philosophy--that it was impossible to draw conclusions without adequate evidence--Zeigler felt constrained to add a step to this technique by gathering available scientific knowledge to lend support to any implications drawn from a specific philosophical position (see note with Zeigler, 1975).

A Theory-Building Approach. A diversion from this "Systems or Implications Approach," with what may be called a "theory-building approach" was begun with some success by Lois Ellfeldt and Eleanor Metheny in the mid-1950s. This was an effort to develop a tentative general theory about the meaning of human movement-kinesthesia. Such movement was defined as "a somatic-sensory experience which can be conceptualized by the human mind" The theory was developed "within the context of the basic assumptions of the philosophy of symbolic transformation as they relate to the nature of the process which enables human being to find meaning in their sensory perceptions" (1958, p. 264). For this purpose, the investigators developed "a vocabulary to refer to these elements in their most general form" (p. 264).

A Phenomenological-Existentialistic Approach. Another interesting approach occurred when Metheny, through her own work and that of a number of her graduate students and others that began in the early 1960s, spearheaded the introduction of a movement that may be called broadly a "Phenomenological-Existentialistic Approach" (or series of techniques) to philosophical endeavor related to sport, exercise, and related human movement (see, for example, Kleinman, 1964; Thomson, 1967; Slusher, 1967; Stone, 1969;). In retrospect, because those espousing existentialism and phenomenological method in our field seem to have gone "thataway," it seems worthwhile to recall that existentialism, according to Barrett (1959, p. 126), is a philosophy that,

> confronts the human situation in its totality to ask what
> the basic conditions of human existence are and how
> man can establish his own meaning out of these
> conditions. . . . Here philosophy itself--no longer a mere
> game for technicians or an obsolete discipline superseded
> by science--becomes a fundamental dimension of human
> existence. For man is the one animal who not only can,
> but must ask himself what his life means.

Such an approach quite obviously makes this type of philosophizing potentially vital in the life of the individual because he or she is offered a way of life, of living, if you will. This is in contrast to other leading philosophic positions or approaches in which we are confronted with a depersonalized Nature, a transcendent Deity, or a State seemingly possessing both of these qualities. As Kaplan explained it, "The meaning of life lies in the values which we can find in it, and values are the product of choice" (1961, p. 105). Thus *the direction of movement within selected concepts is from existence to choice to freedom!*

A Conceptual Analysis & Philosophy of Language. However, just as the systems/implications approach to physical education and sport philosophy and an existentialistic, phenomenological approach were gathering some momentum in the mid-1960s, it became generally apparent that the field of educational philosophy had veered sharply in the direction of the analytic tradition being employed largely in general philosophy in the English-speaking world. One of the first indications of this that deserves mention was the influence of several papers and articles James Keating (1964) in regard to conceptual analysis and sport ethics in the mid-1960s. Immediately after that, other studies exploring aspects of subsequent philosophy of language/analytic approaches or techniques to doing sport philosophy may be noted as well (Paddick, 1967; Spencer-Kraus, 1969; Patrick, 1971; Pearson, 1971; Zeigler, 1974).

> (**Note**: For those who wish to review sport and physical education literature up to 1970, the monumental study employing what he called "metaphilosophic analysis" was completed by Osterhoudt [197]. This study, which won the Carl Diem Prize in 1972, provides a wealth of material based on Pearson's [1968] "Inquiry Into Inquiry" taxonomy involving construct analysis, system analysis, and concept analysis.)

A Philosophic Analysis Approach to Concepts, Constructs, and Meanings. Finally, the Yale philosopher, Paul Weiss, ushered in what became a strong trend toward "philosophic purism" in this highly interesting decade with the publication of *Sport: A Philosophic Inquiry* (1969), a work that ushered in the significant decade of the 1970s for sport philosophy. A so-called philosophic analysis approach to concepts, constructs, and meanings steadily gained momentum in the field in the 1970s and is still largely in vogue down to the present day. I believe that Sparkes (1991) has defined "analytical philosophy" well as "a wide variety of philosophical movements and tendencies" within the English-speaking world that are dissatisfied with any philosophizing that "attempts to construct large-scale theories of 'reality as a whole,'"and that stress instead "the task of critically elucidating already existing ideas and beliefs" (p. 192).

The organization of the Philosophic Society for the Study of Sport in late 1972, with Paul Weiss as the first president and Warren Fraleigh as the president-Elect, represented a significant step forward in the development of the sub-disciplinary area. Although this area was not always represented in the many "disciplinary diagrams" being formulated between 1965 and 1975, one nevertheless had the idea that prospective professionals would now increasingly receive significant help both in philosophic self-analysis and analysis of sport and physical education in society.

What did happen is not quite what I had expected--or at least what I had hoped for. I had hoped for a balance between pure and applied sport and physical education philosophy to develop within the profession. Already in 1975, in a presidential address to the PSSS, I stated that sport and physical activity philosophy was "standing at a clear and definite crossroad" (Zeigler, 1976). (Note that already I was not using the term "physical education" in my remarks to the group, because it had become out of vogue and was regarded as a bit unscholarly to do so.) I went on to decry the paucity of material in sport philosophy that related to the subject of man's nature. "Considering the many problems of a highly serious nature extant in sport today," I said, "this paucity of material almost constitutes 'dereliction of duty,' and at the very best may be classified as copying of and fearful, blind allegiance to the mother discipline's presumed correct research technique" (p. 125).

What I was saying--in a polite way--was that many scholars involved with the Philosophic Society for the Study of Sport needed to communicate more effectively with the profession and with the public by spending a *reasonable* amount of their time turning out work of an *applied* nature. Further, it had become obvious to me that the continuing, wholesale adoption of a negative attitude by the large majority of the scholars within the mother discipline of philosophy, and also within educational theory (or policy or philosophy), toward applied endeavor was a most serious mistake for which they would eventually pay in various ways. However, as Barzun (1974, p. 7) explains in referring to the contemporary artist in the mid-1970s on the basis of Daumier's slogan: "One must be of one's own time." Thus, I believe this is the explanation why sport philosophy "went that-a-way" in the early seventies in a plausible, understandable effort to do what was right--so to speak--for the subject-matter of sport philosophy.

In 1982, the Canadian Association for Sport Sciences commissioned a paper on sport and physical activity philosophy for inclusion in *The Sport Sciences* edited by J.J. Jackson and H.A. Wanger. In this paper, Zeigler (1982) sought to trace the development of the area and to assess its status at that time. Such terms as analytic philosophy, existentialism, normative philosophy, speculative philosophy, systems analysis, construct analysis, concept analysis, and metaphilosophic analysis were defined. An attempt was made to list the "leading contributors" of the time--always a "dangerous" undertaking--because in review one notable omission at least was discovered (the name of rapidly rising Scott Kretchmar). At that time I also paid tribute to the contributions of the eminent Hans Lenk (of the FRG) to sport philosophy, who has since departed from the ranks of PSSS and sport philosophy for several reasons best left unsaid. Also, I believe it is relevant at this point to mention the "balanced" philosophic endeavors of our Japanese associates, Shinobu Abe and Akio Kataoka.

Now, 30 years after I made a plea for a "balanced approach" between pure and applied philosophizing, I am asking parenthetically what all of this "pure" endeavor has indeed added to society as of today. Everything considered, I believe we need a broader, more encompassing orientation for the 1990s and thereafter. We should now return, armed with improved analytical techniques, to find at least some tentative answers to some of the very basic questions that were being asked as far back as at the end of the 19th century! Of course, whether we can expect or actually get any help from the mother discipline or the departmental discipline known as educational philosophy is moot at this point. I say this because my reading of the literature at this point tells me that there is still very little interest in these quarters, not to mention considerable controversy and, dare I say, confusion on this matter of how to practice one's craft in these sectors of North American campuses too.

THE USE AND ABUSE OF SPORT AND PHYSICAL ACTIVITY: CULTURAL & PHILOSOPHIC CRITICISM

The Need for Sport to Be Challenged. In the second section of this chapter, I reaffirm my belief that sport must be challenged on an ongoing basis by various categories of people in a variety of ways. The hope is that sport will continue to be conducted in its various settings now and in the future, both generally and specifically, in a manner that will encourage its proper educational and recreational uses. If this were to be the case, sport might possibly retain those aspects that can contribute value to individual and social living. To do this, however, we must first define our terms accurately so that we are fully aware of that which we are critiquing. Based on both everyday usage and dictionary definition, the term "sport" still exhibits radical ambiguity, and this adds to the present confusion. For the purpose of this paper, therefore, when the word "sport" is used it refers unless indicated otherwise to "an athletic activity requiring skill or physical prowess and often of a competitive nature, as racing, baseball, tennis, bowling, golf, wrestling, boxing, hunting, fishing, etc." (*The Random House Dictionary of the English Language,* 1987, p. 1944).

Two Basic Approaches to Criticizing and/or Philosophizing. In any effort to critique the use and abuse of sport, it is necessary to explain one's approach to such analysis. It can be argued that there are at least two basic ways to criticize and/or philosophize and thereby translate theory into practice: one would involve narrowing an issue down and examining it in great detail to refine possible ways to effect ends. The second would be to consider all possible ramifications of an issue in order to arrive at a synthesis and/or conclusion with the greatest possible application to life in the eyes of the majority. A triangular figure, either in its normal position or upside down with the narrow or pointed end on the bottom, can be used to explain how a philosopher could approach his or her task in one way or the other. In this paper I am obviously inclined strongly toward arriving at a synthesis and conclusion that will lend itself toward application of sport and developmental physical activity to life.

In this process of critiquing competitive sport, we should also maintain an effort to keep its drawbacks in check to the greatest possible extent. In recent decades we have witnessed the rise of sport throughout the land to the status of a fundamentalist religion. In this case sport is being called upon to serve as a redeemer of wayward youth, for example, but, in the process, is becoming a destroyer of certain fundamental values of individual and social life. Concurrently, onrushing science and technology have also become the tempters of many coaches and athletes and added another dimension to the personal and professional conduct of those people who are unduly anxious for recognition and financial gain. Beliefs such as these have created a vacuum of positive belief for others like me who would view "educational" competitive sport as a life-enhancer (e.g., intercollegiate sports that are not sustained through gate receipts--golf, tennis, gymnastics, soccer, and all of women's sport).

In this second section, therefore, I am simply stating what I believe to be the obvious: sport has become an extremely powerful social force in society. Secondly, if we grant that sport now has such power in our North American culture and around the world for that matter--a power indeed that appears to be growing--we should also recognize that any such social force affecting society can be dangerous if perverted (e.g., nationalism, commercialism). Thus, I believe that sport, albeit a powerful social force, has somehow become an active societal institution without an adequately defined underlying theory. Somehow, most of society seems to be proceeding generally on the previously stated assumption that "sport is a good thing for society to encourage, and more sport is even better!" (Also, and this adds to this confusion, the term "sport" still exhibits radical ambiguity based on both everyday usage and dictionary definition, thereby adding to the present problem and accompanying confusion. For example, in Germany what used to be called *koerperliche Erziehung* [physical education] is now incorporated into one word: *Sport*.)

Need for a Theory of Sport. I believe further that governmental agencies (especially!) sponsoring "amateur" sport competition should be able to state in their relationship to sport that, if such-and-such is done with reasonable efficiency and effectiveness within sporting activities, then such-and-such will (in all probability) result. Accordingly, we should by now be able to argue, also, that sport is a "relatively homogeneous substance" that can serve at least reasonably well as an indispensable balm or aid to human fulfillment within an individual life (Barzun, 1974, p. 12). Further, we might argue logically that--through the process of total psycho-physical involvement--sport provides "flow experiences" (Csikszentmihalyi, 1993, p. 183).

However, Wilcox (1991), for example, in his empirical analysis, challenges "the widely held notion that sport can fulfill an important role in the development of national character." He states that "the assumption that sport is conducive to the development of positive human values, or the 'building of character,' should be viewed more as a belief rather than as a fact." He concluded that his study did "provide some evidence to support a relationship between participation in sport and the ranking of human values" (pp. 3, 17, 18, respectively).

Assuming Wilcox's view has reasonable validity, those involved in any way in the institution of sport--if they all together may be considered a collectivity--should contribute a quantity of redeeming social value to our North American culture, not to mention the overall world culture (i.e., a quantity of good leading to improved societal well-being). On the basis of this argument, the following questions are postulated initially for possible subsequent response by concerned agencies and individuals (e.g., federal governments, state and

> (1) Can, does, or should a great (i.e., leading) nation produce great sport?
> (2) With the world being threatened environmentally in a variety of ways, should we now be considering an "ecology" of sport in which the beneficial and disadvantageous aspects of a particular sporting activity are studied through the endeavors of scholars in other disciplines?
> (3) If it is indeed the case that the guardian of the

"functional satisfaction" resulting from sport is (a) the sportsperson, (b) the spectator, (c) the businessperson who gains monetarily and, in some instances, (d) educational administrators and their respective governing boards, who in society should be in a position to be the most knowledgeable about the immediate objectives and long range aims of sport?

(4) Additionally, if the answer to question No.3 above is that this person should be the trained sport and physical activity professor, is it too much of a leap to also expect that this group of persons should work to achieve consensus about what sport should accomplish and then also should have some responsibility as the guardians (or at least the assessors) of whether those aims and objectives are being approximated to a greater or lesser degree?

This listing of four questions that need answers brings us to the crux of the second section of the paper. Arguably, if there could be affirmative agreement about the answers to the final two questions immediately above, sport and physical education philosophers should be about their business of determining more accurately what the aims and objectives of such human physical activity are at point as the world enters the 21st century of the common era (C.E.). Also, it can be argued reasonably that we should attain a consensus of how (and **if!**) sport, exercise, and similar physical activity, considered collectively, is currently being used to help in the fulfillment of these aims and objectives.

Following this argument a bit further, we might postulate that sport philosophers by virtue of their background and training could also be taking the lead in analyzing and promoting ethical behavior in sport. The time is past due when sport philosophers should be looking more vigorously for at least tentative answers to the questions No.1 and No.2 raised above. (How these vital questions that need answers may be approached through an improved variety of philosophic approaches, including analytic techniques, along with substantively greater production of scholarly *and* professional literature directed to the achievement of these ends, is an issue that will be discussed below in the third section of this chapter.)

Conflicting Views on Philosophy and Philosophic Thought. The pendulum swings back and forth, or the merry-go-round goes round and round. Take your pick, because we are still finding sharply conflicting views on the subject of philosophy and philosophic thought. Hartshorne (1975) arguing that philosophy concerns itself with problems more general than those functioning in the sciences:

> philosophers investigate not only facts and ideas but also
> values and ideals, and not only actualities but possibilities,
> and not only possibilities as determined by the actual
> constitution of our world (i.e., as determined by scientists),
> but also possibilities transcending the actual
> world, that is to say the possibility of natural laws other
> than those which in fact obtain. . . . (p. 8).

Hartshorne's recommendations about the proper concerns of the discipline of philosophy were part of an issue of *Philosophy in Context* in which a solid effort was made to define the nature and role of philosophy. Other insightful recommendations as to our function, approaches that could be readily adapted to departmental sport philosophy, were made by R. Fox, F.E. Sparshott, E. Shmueli, G.J. Massey, L.F. Werth, L. Armour, K. Nielsen, and H. Butler. Butler (1975), for example, to select only one other recommendation in addition to that of Hartshorne above, explained that "history demonstrates that confrontation with reality is at best difficult for man" (p. 113). He asserted further:

> For philosophers to offer any meaningful help, the
> concept of an academic philosophy must be abandoned.
> There are at least two compelling reasons for this. First,
> social practice occurs in the real world. For philosophers,
> this means that they must abandon the armchair to
> become participant observers since to do otherwise is to
> develop a theory without action. Since social practice is
> action, this is not possible. A theory of action must be
> grounded in action and becoming an actor involves risk.
> To take risks, philosophers must develop commitment.

Butler's second reason for urging "abandonment of academic philosophy" for philosophers--in some of their efforts at least--is that, to be of any assistance to the social world, a philosophy must be empirically grounded. Arguing that "concepts must emerge from action, and confirmation must occur in action," he offers as an example to prove his point the contrast between the theories of Dewey and the distortions that occurred within the progressive education movement when the practitioners subsequently attempted to do the theoretical grounding (p. 113).

Since these broadly encompassing statements were made, it has become ever more apparent that there is indeed a "need for a recovery of philosophy." This belief has come to our attention increasingly from a variety of sources over these past 30 years. One such statement was made as a presidential address before the American Philosophical Association by John E. Smith in 1981. Smith believed that three beliefs have prevented the discipline of philosophy from having the impact on society that it might have had. The first relates to the belief that it is possible to attain certainty; the second is the belief that to engage a philosophical issue our intellectual apparatus must be ordered appropriately; and the third belief is that philosophy can be made "scientific" by reducing it to irrefutable logic and certifiable scientific solutions (p. 8). In his effort to counteract these questionable beliefs, Smith spells out four conditions that, if met, would "contribute greatly to the recovery of philosophy as a significant force in American society."

Further evidence of the changing philosophical environment comes from a "minicourse" offered to senior citizens by Steven Ross (1990), a Hunter College philosophy professor, in the American Association of Retired Persons publication *Modern Maturity* [can you believe a self-respecting philosopher today analyzing philosophy here?]. Tracing developments within the discipline of philosophy, he states: "It came to seem ridiculous that philosophy could have nothing to say about ongoing moral controversies when American political life was forcing all of us to thinker harder about such things than we ever had before" (p. 57). He concludes his interesting analysis by stating:

> Philosophy will always be special in its willingness to work out abstract answers to abstract puzzles. But today philosophers interested in saying something insightful about such questions will find themselves also taking a more active, aggressive interest in those bits of everyday life that lie just behind these questions. And this great shift in orientation is no mere change in intellectual fashion: It is rather the direct result of powerful arguments made within recent philosophy itself.

Additionally, to cite another effort to analyze the situation as it applies to the departmental philosophy of education, Pratte (1992) believes that analytic philosophy has simply neglected to focus sufficiently on substantive questions. He explains that "the underlying assumptions of analytic philosophers have been challenged by a number of competing views, including postmodernism, poststructuralism, feminism, and neo-Marxism" (pp. x-xi). Thus, we are finding considerable divergence of interests along with an increasing pluralism of philosophical methods employed to confront the many normative considerations arising in contemporary society.

Finally, still further evidence of the changing philosophical environment, for example, comes from Borradori in *The American Philosopher* (1994). Here she discusses insightfully her hopes for a breaching of the "Atlantic Wall" in a period of post-analytic philosophy (pp. 3-4; see, also, Rajchman & West, 1985). While agreeing that analytic philosophy has provided "an essential means of intellectual progress," she believes that by understanding its intent a "mainly unexplored channel" has been created to narrow the philosophical gap that has developed between North America and Europe (p. 3). Also, the ultimate result of the programmatic anthology by Rajchman & West (1985) suggests consideration of the composite term "post-analytic philosophy" to describe some of the directions that American philosophy seems to be taking after the analysis era--i.e., "the emergence of a new 'public engagedness" in philosophy, a general tendency toward 'de-disciplinization' . . . ., and a renewed interest in historical perspective, completely removed from the scientific basis of the analytic genre" (p. 4). What this means, therefore, is that there has developed a move toward making American philosophy something more of a "socially engaged interdisciplinary enterprise" instead of a highly specialized occupation.

Assessment--The Aftermath of an "Elitist Approach". In my opinion we--individually as professors and collectively now as the IAPS (formerly PSSS)--have "paid dearly at the box office" for the scholarly elitism exhibited by some of us and a minute number of our erstwhile colleagues from the mother discipline starting in the early 1970s. Most of the latter were "slumming" and now have almost all parted from our midst. I said then, and I reiterate today that, because of conflicting approaches to "doing" philosophy, most of the North American members of the IASP are not communicating as well with each other as they should be, much less communicating with their colleagues in physical education/kinesiology in which many were primarily educated. The membership of a "world association" is extremely light. A NASPE (of AAHPERD) "sport and physical education presence" is barely noticeable even though, not too many years ago, 2800 members listed philosophy as their primary scholarly interest. Accordingly, despite the valiant efforts of a number in the present small membership group, I must conclude that the Association is having absolutely no impact on (a) the public generally; (b) the people active in amateur, semiprofessional, and professional sport; (c) the overwhelming majority of professors who function in the discipline of philosophy; (d) the professors teaching in educational philosophy; (e) the large majority of professors who teach in this area generally in our professional preparation programs in physical education/kinesiology in North America; and, finally, (f) the entire profession of sport and physical education within the Alliance in the USA and in CAHPERD in Canada! Obviously this is most unfortunate because of the importance of sport in world culture.

Present Improper Modeling of the Reality of Competitive Sport. To recapitulate: because there seems always to be an ever-changing pecking order among and within subject-matters in academic circles, so-called pure analytic philosophers gradually over the decades steadily assumed a more lofty position than those in their academic units struggling with other philosophic approaches, not to mention philosophy's possible application to specialized subject-matter fields (i.e., educational philosophy, physical education/kinesiology philosophy). As a result, analytic philosophers were accordingly aped by educational philosophers beginning in the mid-1950s. Then, I believe that those scholars emerging from early physical education and sport philosophy into the "true" sport philosophy of the early 1970s and thereafter have arguably become poor windows for the assessment of true reality in sport. This occurred inevitably, I believe, because those scholars attempting to function as disciplinarians alongside those laboring in the traditional academic disciplines are seemingly forced by their very specialization to avoid large, broader areas of knowledge, areas that are often much more important when the big picture is considered.

The result, I believe, is that the present overall reality of competitive sport and related physical activity in world culture is improperly modeled through the purely disciplinary approach of a relatively small group of sport philosophers. Similarly, I believe also that most scholars in the mother discipline are doing something quite similar with their own issues, as are so-called educational policy theoreticians in professional education who have merged with others in a socio-cultural area seeking to analyze the plight of the field of education as it timidly enters the 21st century. (A very close associate of ours is now functioning in a campus unit known as "cultural studies in education," and another close associate of mine is excited about the term "cultural kinesiology" to describe our field's socio-cultural aspects.)

My strong belief is that we in our field still need scholars who take a more holistic approach to doing philosophy about sport, physical activity, and expressive movement so that this aspect of professional preparation can begin to assist its *potential* publics to appreciate what the finest type of sport and physical activity can contribute to the improvement of individuals functioning in society, as well as to the actual improvement of that society as a whole.

What has happened, I believe, is that scientists and scholars functioning in the many disciplines and subdisciplines of the modern world--and this includes those presently functioning within kinesiology and human kinetics units on North American campuses--are presenting to society fragmented images of reality daily through their research reports. The attempts at transdisciplinary, crossdisciplinary, and interdisciplinary endeavor appear futile and are failing to offer people a reasonably consensual understanding of overall reality. Here is where philosophers, and interested sport philosophers if they only choose to do so diligently, are in a position to model reality for people of all ages conjecturing about the purposes of sport and physical activity in their lives. There are indeed systemic relationships that need to be clarified. We have the real life stage, the actors, the plot, the action, and the time. As Brady (1994) suggests in connection with the overall educational curriculum, we in sport philosophy with the above categories related systemically are in a position to create the picture on the lid of the jigsaw puzzle box that models sport.

At the same time those sport philosophers who follow a more specialized approach are needed to identify the inaccuracies and inconsistencies that may be apparent in the larger picture presented by the sport philosophers seeking to help people of the present and future generations to move toward understanding of the role that sport and developmental physical activity can play in their human experience.

Religion, both organized and natural, and other wisdom traditions at least provide their adherents and potential recruits with an orienting image (however dubious that may be). We of the modern age have become imbued with the tenets of science and accompanying technology, but in the process have become so specialized in our endeavors that we don't see the big picture or even any orienting image. Or, if we do postulate a "big picture," it is useful only on Sunday or special occasions and not during our workaday week.

What Is the Aim of Sport in Culture? By the way, what *is* the aim of sport and how is sport being used to help in the fulfillment of such an aim? Can we argue that sport is better than life (a truer reality)? Or do we recommend that sport be used as a means to living a better life--i.e. serve a transformational function? Or should sport involvement provide a human with a more natural life because of its spontaneity? Can we make the case in one or more of the following ways for sport participation as a sanctuary from life, as a "life-enhancer," or as a detergent that cleanses away life's many impurities? Whichever purpose is adopted, in the final analysis the guardian of the "functional satisfaction" resulting from the sport enterprise should be the sports participant and the spectator.

I ask further why we, as sport philosophers, should not understand what constitutes ethical behavior in sport? Moreover, should not the guardian of the ethics of sport be the sport philosopher? Everything considered, I believe that the time has arrived when sport philosophers should be providing at least tentative answers to these questions through a variety of approaches (including the prevailing analytic techniques).

LOOKING TO THE 21ST CENTURY

Recommended Approaches Leading to a Possible Recovery in Sport and Physical Education Philosophy. In this third section, I offer some ideas as to how we might strengthen our approaches to doing sport and physical activity philosophy in the 21st century. I point out that the "need for a recovery of philosophy" to a position of even relative eminence in society (compared to former years, that is). Such "rehabilitation" has come to our attention from a variety of sources for the past 20 years at least (e.g., see Zeigler, 1989b). If we consider the question "Who should do what to whom in this world?", it can be argued that politicians should save the cities, while do-gooders should help the disadvantaged. Accordingly, we might say that preachers should save souls, and that businessmen should make money for their stockholders. Leaping quickly to our realm, what should physical educators, coaches, and sport philosophers do? Arguably, physical educators should develop attitudes and skills that lead to healthy bodies through lifelong involvement in exercise and sport. Coaches, we might say, should help in the development of fine young people and adults through the development of skills that can be used in competitive sport. Finally, what should sport philosophers do? To answer "philosophize about sport" takes us right back to square one again.

So, after first looking backward to refresh ourselves as to where so-called sport philosophy has been over the past 100 years, we still need to actively and creatively seek some of the answers to questions that were being asked toward the end of the 19th century (and indeed as far back as the end of the Archaic Period in early Greek history).

One approach, in addition to what is presently being done and that actually was suggested by Zeigler (1975; see pages 124-160 and especially pp. 139-154) to improve the current situation, would be to examine the results of the extraordinary range of 20th-century social scientific inquiries available from history, psychology, sociology, and anthropology. Interestingly, this is exactly what Wilson (1993) has recommended for the mother discipline of philosophy and which was "seconded" by MacIntyre (1993). As Wilson states, "The truth, if it exists, is in the details." This could be supplemented in currently designated kinesiology units in universities, of course, by the ever-mounting body of evidence becoming available from the the efforts of our hard scientists (and those in related disciplines). Let us grant, however, that we shouldn't enthrone the sciences--both the social sciences and the natural sciences--by affirming that anything that can't be quantified should be regarded as useless.

A *second counterbalancing approach*, if we are indeed in "the postmodern age," would be to help humankind "create a passage beyond the failed assumptions of modernity and a radical reorientation that preserves the positive advantages of the liberal tradition and [its] technological capacities. . . ." Such a "passage" and such a "reorientation" should be "rooted in ecological sanity and meaningful human participation in the unfolding story of the Earth community and the universe" (Spretnak, 1991). Those who might be called "deconstructive postmodernists" argue basically that modernity and modern technology fled from the insights of the so-called wisdom traditions (e.g., God, Marxism, science and technology). Spretnak, who describes her position as "ecological postmodernism," critiques the deconstructive-postmodern orientation from four perspectives: ecological/cosmological, spiritual, activist-political, and feminist. Another interesting treatment titled postmodern realism is recommended by Borgmann (1992) in *Crossing the postmodern divide*. There can be little doubt but that there is a need for the development of individual and societal attitudes (psychologically speaking) toward the mounting ecological crisis (as recommended by Zeigler, 1978).

(**Note:** However, although I believe we should listen to them, I stress that I am not encouraging any significant involvement with the trendy, but obfuscating language of the deconstructionists and postmodernists. For example, I am not certain what the former mean when they call for a "critical pedagogy" based on a critique of our culture. After they "deconstruct," they need to "reconstruct!" Also, while I must agree that with the postmodernists claim that "broad social and political movements invariably suppress certain points of view," I must agree with Kneller (1994) that "Groups cannot coalesce unless some are promoted over others" (p. 184). Yet, it should be obvious to all that micropolitics should be encouraged so that specific causes seeking reform are given adequate hearings. For an insightful discussion of this topic, see McGowan (1991) whose Postmodernism and its critics explains postmodernism's precursors (e.g., Marx, Nietzsche) and the problem of freedom in postmodern theory, yet concludes with a redeeming approach to positive freedom within the political scene.)

A *third approach,* one that builds on earlier work in the 1950s by Metheny and subsequently by Kleinman, Thomson, Stone, Kretchmar and others, is that recommended by Fahlberg and Fahlberg (1994) in which investigation is based on what is termed a "realities-based framework." Titling their article "A human science for the study of movement: An integration of multiple ways of knowing," the investigators urge the use of "multiple epistemologies" in an integrated framework. They argue that, in this age of postpositivism, research questions about human movement should be viewed in relation to one integrated reality with two different levels of meaning: (1) the material world of objects moving in space that may be analyzed empirically, and (2) a human world of meaning in which the experience of the mover is determined by either psychological phenomenology and/or psychosocial hermeneutics (pp. 101-102).

A *fourth obvious approach* with the increased emphasis on applied ethics in the mother discipline is for sport/kinesiology philosophers to place greater emphasis on the topic of applied or practical philosophy and ethics. Kretchmar's (1994) *Practical philosophy of sport* represented a needed, recent contribution in this direction, as did earlier texts by McIntosh (1979), Fraleigh (1984), and Zeigler (1984). Zeigler's application of a scientific ethics to sport decisions is another effort of this type (1989a). The Center for Sport Ethics at Idaho developed by Sharon Stoll, and the Center for Applied Sport Philosophy and Ethics Research at De Montfort

University Bedford, UK where Simon Eassom labors, offer hope for the future.

A *fifth not-so-obvious approach* would be for some one sport and physical education philosopher with a historical bent, or several people if need be, to undertake an intellectual history of the subject similar to the approach of Bronowski and Mazlish (1975) that traced the Western intellectual tradition from "Leonardo to Hegel." In this case, the lives of selected scholars and leaders who spoke or wrote cogently throughout history on competitive sport and physical education could be integrated with the intellectual, political, and social developments of the period (e.g., from Plato to Weiss).

A sixth approach, similar to that adopted by the several societies within the American Philosophical Association, might be for the IASP to establish a permanent section where papers could be presented annually looking to the possible contribution that competitive sport and physical education might make toward the goal of world peace. This idea urging our profession to contribute meaningfully toward a patterned search for world peace was stressed by Zeigler (1994).

A *seventh feasible approach*, one that Zeigler (1964, 1977, 1989b) introduced to the field is called a "persistent problems approach." This could be most useful to sport and physical educational professionals today if it were employed wisely in professional preparation programs. The idea is to examine the various social forces (e.g., values, economics, ecology) and the many professional concerns (e.g., defining amateurism, semiprofessionalism, and professionalism, the role of management, coaching ethics) as they impact upon the professional practitioner (1989b, pp. 205-358).

Looking to the Future--How 'Resuscitation' Could Be Applied to Sport and Physical Education Philosophy. In defense of the scholarly output of the IASP, I am prepared to argue that in the long run we will discover that its scholarly output through its journal is helpful in ways other than procuring publications, some travel money, and possible tenure of employment for the relatively few involved. *However, the public, people active in all levels of sport, and the members of the profession of sport and physical education need so much more assistance with their understanding of the aims and objectives of competitive sport and developmental physical activity.*

What happened during the turmoil of the 1960s and early 1970s is that many of us professing in this area "threw out the baby with the bath water." In so many instances the *principles* of physical education course was eliminated except in those universities where the faculty members concerned with philosophy were out of touch with the academic world of philosophy. What was substituted for the old "principles" course was typically buffetted about in the curricular struggle of the time because staff members in other subdisciplines, having themselves as students taken "useful" courses could not understand the possible value of the newer analytic approach. Soon sport philosophy was typically relegated to elective status, and in my opinion it has never filled the bill for professional physical education/kinesiology students. Of course, I am not advocating a return to *exactly* the same sort of unsophisticated principles course today that was taught formerly. I am recommending, however, an approach that includes a required course in this area in every curriculum that introduces people to *applied* sport and physical education philosophy, an approach that urges students to take their first philosophy course in the philosophy department, and that then goes on in our unit to give them a working understanding of applied ethics as related to our own field.

This curricular idea can--and should--be carried out most effectively by physical educators with solid interests in philosophy and by those associated with the Philosophy Academy of NASPE within the Alliance. (I would hope that the Executive Committee of the IASP might lend support to this recommendation, and that this be the decision of *all* of the members of the Society--not just the Executive.) No group other than NASPE's Philosophy Academy, with the possible exception of the National Association for Kinesiology and Physical Education in Higher Education (NAKPEHE), seems ready and willing and is reasonably capable of using its influence to restore a required, applied sport and physical education philosophy course for the benefit of the profession.

And so, in conclusion, I urge you--in fact, as a dedicated professional I implore you--to give this recommendation top priority right now. I believe the basic and applied knowledge and possible subsequent "ethical competency" that would accrue to our professional students--and eventually to all with whom they come in contact--are vital for our profession in the years immediately ahead. Our struggle as a field for true professional status is far from won yet. A sound understanding of our philosophic base--the meaning and significance of what the profession stands for--must undergird our development at all times.

Finally, all of this leads to the thought that, if we as sport and physical education philosophers are truly to make a contribution to humankind, we should be examining the ways in which sport as a social institution can contribute positively and increasingly to our culture's development. Also, we should be experimenting with new approaches to philosophizing that can truly serve humankind. In this sense we would be affirming the thesis that "sport was made for man, and not man for sport" (Steinhaus, 1952), as well as the idea that such men and women in their various sport undertakings should in no way defile the earth as a result of human thoughtlessness.

NOTE

1. I want to express my gratitude and appreciation to Dick Morland, Professor Emeritus, Stetson University, DeLand, Florida for his comments after carefully reading this paper. Of course, he should not be held responsible for anything said in the final version.

REFERENCES

Barrett, W. (1959). *Irrational man: A study in existential philosophy*. Garden City, NY: Doubleday.

Barrows, I.C., ed. (1899) *Proceedings of the Conference on Physical Training.* Boston: Press of G. H. Ellis.

Barzun, J. (1974). *The use and abuse of art.* Princeton: Princeton Univ. Press.

Borgmann, A. (1993). *Crossing the postmodern divide.* Chicago: University of Chicago Press.

Borradori, G. (1994). *The American philosopher.* Chicago: Univ. of Chicago Press.

Brady, M. (March/April 1994). Correspondence. *Utne Reader*, 62: 6-7.

Bronowski, J. & Mazlish, B. (1975) *The Western intellectual tradition.* NY: Harper & Row.

Butler, H. (1975). Lifting the veil of ignorance with a philosophy of commitment. *Philosophy in Context*, 4: 111-117.

Csikszentmihalyi, M. (1993). *The evolving self: A psychology for the third millennium.* NY: HarperCollins.

Davis, E.C. (1961). *The philosophical process in physical education.* Philadelphia: Lea & Febiger. (Includes several excellent analyses by Roger Burke.)

Davis, E.C. (1963). *Philosophies fashion physical education. Dubuque*, IA: Wm.C.Brown.

Ellfeldt, L.E., & Metheny, E. (1958). Movement and meaning: Development of a general theory." *Research Quarterly*, 29, 264-273.

Fahlberg, L.L., & Fahlberg L.A. (1994). A human science for the study of movement: An integration of multiple ways of knowing. *Research Quarterly for Exercise and Sport.* 65, 100-109.

Fraleigh, W.P. (1984). *Right actions in sport.* Champaign, IL: Human Kinetics.

Hartshorne, C. (1975). The nature of philosophy. *Philosophy in Context*, 4: 7-16.

Henry, N.B., ed. (1942). *The Forty-First Yearbook of the National Society for the Study of Education.* (Part I). Chicago: University of Chicago Press.

Kaminsky, J. (1993). *A new history of educational philosophy.*

Westport, CT: Greenwood Press.

Kaplan, A. (1961). *The new world of philosophy*. NY: Random House.

Keating, J.W. (1964). Sportsmanship as a moral category. *Ethics,* LXXV, 1:25-35.

Kleinman, S. (1964). The significance of human movement--a phenomenological approach. A paper presented to the National Association of Physical Education for College Women Conference, June 17.

Kretchmar, R.S. (1994). *Practical philosophy of sport*. Champaign, IL: Human Kinetics.

Macintyre, A. (August 29, 1993). The truth is in the details. *The New York Times Book Review*.

McGowan, J. (1991). *Postmodernism and its critics*. Ithaca: Cornell University Press.

McIntosh, P. (1979). *Fair play*. London: Heinemann.

Morland, R.B. (1958). *A philosophical interpretation of the educational views held by leaders in American physical education*. Ph.D. dissertation, New York University.

Nietzsche, F. *The use and abuse of history*.

Osterhoudt, R.G. (1971). *A descriptive analysis of research concerning the philosophy of physical education and sport*. Ph.D. dissertation, University of Illinois, C-U.

Paddick, R.J. (1967). *The nature and place of a field of knowledge in physical education*. M.A. thesis, University of Alberta.

Patrick, G.D. (1971). *Verifiability (meaningfulness) of selected physical education objectives*. Ph.D. dissertation, University of Illinois, C-U.

Pearson, K. (1968). "Inquiry into inquiry." An unpublished paper presented to the graduate seminar at the Univ. of Illinois, C-U.

Pearson, K. (1971). *A structural and functional analysis of the multi-concept of integration-segregation (male and/or female) in physical education classes*. Ph.D. dissertation, University of Illinois, C-U.

Pratte, R. (1992). *Philosophy of education--two traditions*. Springfield, IL: Charles C. Thomas.

Rajchman J. & West, C. (Eds.). (1985). *Post-analytic philosophy*. NY: Columbia Univ. Press.

Random House Dictionary of the English Language, The. 1987. (2nd

Ed., Unabridged). NY: Random House.

Rorty, R. (1982). *Consequences of Pragmatism* Minneapolis: Univ. of Minnesota Press.

Ross, S. (1990). Rethinking thinking, *Modern Maturity*, 33, 1:52-61.

Schrag, F. (1994). A view of our enterprise. *Educational Theory*, 44, 3:361-369.

Slusher, H.S. (1967). *Man, sport and existence*. Philadelphia: Lea & Febiger.

Smith, J.E. (September 1982). The need for a recovery of philosophy. In *Proceedings and Addresses of the American Philosophical Association*, 56, 1: 5-18.

Sparkes, A.W. (1991). *Talking philosophy: A wordbook.* London and NY: Routledge.

Spencer-Kraus, P. (1969). *The application of "linguistic phenomenology" to the philosophy of physical education and sport.* M.A. thesis, University of Illinois, Urbana.

Spretnak, C. (1991). *States of grace: The recovery of meaning in the postmodern age.* NY: Harper/SanFrancisco.

Stevenson, L. (1987). *Seven theories of human nature.* (2nd Ed.). NY: Oxford Univ. Press.

Steinhaus, A.H. (1952). Principal principles of physical education. In *Proceedings of the College Physical Education Association.* Washington, DC: AAHPER, pp. 5-11.

Stone, R. (1969). *Meanings found in the acts of surfing and skiing.* Ph.D. dissertation, University of Southern California.

Thomson, P.L. (1967). *Ontological truth in sports: A phenomenological analysis.* Ph.D. dissertation, University of Southern California.

Weiss, P. (1969). *Sport: A philosophic inquiry.* Carbondale, IL: Southern Illinois Press.

Wilcox, R.C. (1991). Sport and national character: An empirical analysis. *Journal of Comparative Physical Education and Sport,* XIII, 1: 3-27.

Wilson, J.Q. (1993). *The moral sense.* NY: The Free Press.

Zeigler, E.F. (1964). *Philosophical foundations for physical, health, and recreation education.* Englewood Cliffs, NJ: Prentice-Hall.

Zeigler, E.F. (1972). The black athlete's non-athletic problems. *Educational Theory*, 22, 4, 420-426.

Zeigler, E.F. (1974). A brief analysis of the ordinary language employed in the professional preparation of sport coaches and teachers. A paper presented to the Philosophy of Sport and Physical Activity Section, Canadian Association for Health, Physical Education and Recreation, Ottawa, May 27.

Zeigler, E.F. (1975). An analysis of the implications of reconstructionism for physical, health, and recreation education. In E.F. Zeigler, *Personalizing sport and physical education philosophy*. Champaign, IL: Stipes. (Originally presented to the AAHPERD Convention, Cincinnati, OH, May 1, 1964).

Zeigler, E.F. (1976). In sport, as in all of life, man should be comprehensible to man. *Journal of the Philosophy of Sport*, III, 121-126.

Zeigler, E.F. (1977). *Physical education and sport philosophy*. Englewood Cliffs, NJ: Prentice-Hall.

Zeigler, E.F. (1982). Philosophy of sport and developmental physical activity, in *The Sport Sciences* (Eds. J.J. Jackson and H.A. Wenger). Victoria, BC: Physical Education Series (Number 4).

Zeigler, E.F. & Rosenberg, D. (1983). Methodology and techniques employed in philosophic inquiry in sport and physical education. An unpublished paper.

Zeigler, E.F. (1984). *Ethics and morality in sport and physical education: An experiential approach*. Champaign, IL: Stipes.

Zeigler, E.F. (Late Winter 1988). How the profession "lost its principles." *The Physical Educator*, 45, 1, 14-18.

Zeigler, E.F. (1989a). Application of a scientific ethics approach to sport decisions, in P.J. Galasso, (Ed.), *Philosophy of sport and physical activity* (pp. 83-89). Toronto: Canadian Scholars' Press.

Zeigler, E.F. (1989b). *Sport and physical education philosophy: An Introduction*. Dubuque, IA: WCBrown/Benchmark.

Zeigler, E.F. (1994). *Physical education and kinesiology in North America: Professional & scholarly foundations*. Champaign, IL: Stipes.

CHAPTER X

THE SOCIAL FORCE OF ECOLOGY CONFRONTS THE PROFESSION

The subject of ecology has developed relatively rapidly as a vital social force confronting the profession of physical education, kinesiology, and educational sport. The influence of ecology, a term that may be defined as the study of the interrelationship between and among living organisms and their physical environment, began to be felt by North American society during the 1970s.

As a matter of fact, this problem has been with us increasingly over the centuries. However, because the earth's population was relatively small, the dangers that people faced in this regard seemed slight. However, no longer--as it has almost always been possible in the past--can people simply move elsewhere to locate another abundant supply of game to hunt, water to drink, or mineral resources to exploit when natural resources are depleted. Now the fundamental problem of implementing sound ecological principles throughout our culture is here to stay.

More than 30 years ago, Grahame Smith (1971), in an article titled "The Ecologist at Bay," explained: "The decline in quality of this planet and the precarious aspect of continued existence of life on Earth are largely the results of this comfortable shell of consumer technology with which each American is surrounded" (p. 69). Thus, ecologists find themselves in a situation in which they comprehend fully the dangerous position in which some people of Earth are right now, and in which most of the earth's population may well find themselves in a few short years. However, for ecologists to cry out in alarm to the general populace in the favored countries more vigorously, and to have them truly understand the reality of the precarious approach being followed, often risks being ridiculed and branded as pessimists and doom-sayers.

Exactly such a cavalier attitude shown toward this most important worldwide problem was being shown at the century's end by certain journalists like Gregg Easterbrook (1995) who clearly feels that misguided environmentalists are "making much to do about nothing." In fact, the impression is created clearly that these people are recommending a return to a hunter-gatherer existence instead of appreciating the fact that man is actually helping nature in many instances! One wonders where Mr. Easterbrook has been the past 20 or 30 years as the world's population was increasing exponentially.

So, since the large majority of people still conduct their lives in an "Easterbrook-oriented manner," it is quite clear that these unsuspecting (or deliberately destructive?) people still do not appreciate the gravity of the situation. We can therefore only conclude that somehow the urgency of the matter has not been brought home in a stark, strongly impressionistic manner. (Witness the attitude of the United States in regard to the Kyoto Accord.) Also, either there is evidently a lack of deep understanding and appreciation of the problem by the leaders of the world's 206 (or so) political entities, or else they are faced with so many other problems that their attention and efforts are vitiated by the multiplying demands of the times.

However, the growing impact of ecology as a vital social force is definitely here, and it cannot be escaped by closing our eyes. As Pogo, the cartoon possum, has stated--and it is a remark we must accept ruefully--"We have met the enemy, and he is us!" Actually, this influence became truly recognizable and significant during the 1980s. And, it was in 1984, for example, that the Worldwatch Institute sparked by the leadership of Lester R. Brown and associates published the first issue of the highly regarded State of the world report that explains annually what progress (or retrogression!) has been made toward the establishment of an ongoing sustaining world society. The 1995 edition of this truly significant effort was translated into 27 languages and is now used widely in colleges and universities both as a text and reference work.

Of course, in the 1990s as today, we were being flooded daily through the media with all sorts of dire warnings about what lies ahead for humankind if poor earth husbandry practices are continued. However, even though we humans are being warned from a variety of directions, the large majority of the population continues to go about its business as usual. Somehow a general lack of serious concern still prevails; so, it is not unusual that very little attention has been paid to the environmental crisis by those in the field of kinesiology, physical education, and educational sport. However, our profession can now be criticized if it does not very soon join forces strongly with selected other professions in regard to this failing.

BRIEF HISTORICAL BACKGROUND

The number of people on Earth is more than six billion. At the beginning of the Christian era, that figure was only 250 million. By the time North America was settled by Europeans, the figure had been doubled to about 500 million, in a period of only 1,600 years. By 1830 the figure had increased twofold again to 1 billion in somewhat less than 200 years. In the next 100 years, the amount doubled again to 2 billion, and now, in about only 60 years, the total number of men, women, and children on Earth has surpassed 4 billion! As Huxley (1963, p. 2) warned 40 years ago, "By the year 2,000. unless something appalling bad or miraculously good should happen in the interval, six thousand millions of us will be sitting down to breakfast every morning." (He was correct, of course.) To make matters worse, it is in the underdeveloped countries that the rate of increase is so much higher than the average. It will presumably not be possible for such nations to move ahead to full industrialization because of the inevitable drain on their resources caused by such rapid growth.

In another realm--that of poor husbandry insofar as land and animal use are concerned--our careless and ignorant abuse of the planet probably goes as far back as 8000 years ago when we first began to farm the land. There are today innumerable archeological sites that were once thriving civilizations. For a variety of reasons, including poor use of land, most of these locations are now dusty and desolate ruins. An example of such an area is North Africa, which was once exploited extensively by the Romans. Here, valuable topsoil was eroded by poor farming techniques, incorrect grazing of livestock, and flagrant abuse of timberland. One can also go back to ancient Greece to find another example of once fertile land with an abundant supply of water and forested hills. Now much of the area is blighted, with rocky hills and barren lowlands denuded of topsoil. Wildlife is almost extinct as well.

Much the same story can be related about what came to be known as Turkey. Early port cities, such as Ephesus and Tarsus, offer no evidence today of their history as trading ports. The Fertile Crescent of biblical times has long since gone, and the "land between the rivers" (the Tigris and the Euphrates) shows almost no evidence of its former luxuriant vegetation. Thus, turn where one will--to areas desolated by 15th-century sheep raisers in Spain, to the pre-Columbia North American civilization on Monte Alban in Mexico--one is apt to find examples of poor management and land and forest degradation. Obviously, some peoples have managed their resources wisely--The Netherlands, Japan, and modern Israel, for example--but they are rare exceptions in an otherwise bleak picture. The discussion that follows will describe concisely why the coming century will need to be characterized by a concern never shown before.

ECOLOGY DEFINED

Hawley (1966) defined ecology early on as the field of study that treats the relationships and interactions of human beings and other living organisms with each other and with the natural, or physical environment in which they reside (p. 1). Until the 1970s very few scientists were known as ecologists; they were identified either as biologists or zoologists, or perhaps as conservationists. Now many of these scientists have been asked to consider our plight in relation to the environment in a much broader perspective than that in which an experimental scientist typically functions. The experimental outlook for these people must be macroscopic as well as microscopic.

Resultantly, many scientists find it difficult to make this transition in their lives with some unusual in-service experience or outside prodding. In his insightful theoretical essay, for example, Hawley explained how he developed his thought about human ecology within the broader subject. Recognizing that "adaptation is a system phenomenon," he inquired about the individual's position within developing ecological theory. In summary, Hawley postulated (1986) that:

(1) "every human being requires access to environment";
(2) "interdependence with other human beings is imperative";
(3) the individual "is a finite creature in a finite world";
(4) the human "possesses an inherent tendency to preserve and expand life to the maximum attainable under prevailing conditions"; and, finally,
(5) "the intrinsic limitation on the human being's behavioral variability is indeterminate" (pp. 4-6).

Keeping the above in mind, then, what has happened is that, for a variety of reasons, we can no longer proceed on the assumption that our responsibility is to "multiply and replenish the earth" in the sense that these words were originally intended. In the past we have been exhorted to both increase the population and develop an economy to cope with the various demands. Now there are more than six billion people on Earth, and approximately five or six babies are being born somewhere in the world every second!

In an effort to do something about this growth, French (1995) reported more than 160 countries approved what has been called a World Population Plan of Action at the Cairo Conference, a program that it is hoped will result in keeping the world population below 9.8 billion in 2050 (p. 176). It has become starkly obvious to many reflective people that strong attitudes favoring population control must be developed, because we continue to see some version of the Malthusian law operative--and its operation may become more massive as time passes.

Although there are those who disagree with such a statement based on early Malthusian law today, the reader will recall that Malthus theorized in 1798 that the population tends to increase more rapidly than the food supply--a question of geometric progression as opposed to arithmetical progression. Sadly, this idea still seems valid today, with the only possible checks being war, disease, natural catastrophes, famine, and birth control.

Moving directly into the realm of economics, it has been pointed out that the United States has some extremely difficult choices to make in the next few decades. In fact. a number of these choices may be made because of the severe crises the nation will encounter. Those who look ahead optimistically, Murray (1972) had explained seem willing to allow a continuous-growth economic system, whereas those who will probably be classified as pessimists argue for a no-growth system (p. 38). It is imperative for us all to understand that the forecasting models developed by economists and ecologists quite typically differ sharply. The consequences of their recommendations, respectively, are completely different. Certainly all are aware of contradictory economic theories that appear in the daily press, but it is also obvious that very few people, relatively speaking, are aware of the collision course seemingly being taken if the ecologic models have any validity at all.

A major problem facing the world's economy is that a ever-increasing "culture of consumption" has developed in the world's leading countries economically, and that this demand for for so-called physical goods has brought with it a concomitant demand for all types of materials from which such goods can be created. Thus, as Young and Sachs (1995) report that the world is faced with an urgent need to crate a "sustainable materials economy" as soon as possible. The "traditional materials economy" has become hopelessly inefficient in the face of such gargantuan demands by consumers (pp. 76-78).

For example, there is a need for a systems approach that will provide a comprehensive system for the collection of waste, recycling it, and transforming it into all sorts of new products. Approaching this problem from another angle, if more durable products are made for people's consumption the amount of reprocessing will be cut down proportionately. Also, if the specifications for reworking materials systematically include the right sort of information about how such processing might affect the environment, this in turn would be one more step in the right direction (pp. 83-86).

All of the above steps will be to limited avail, however, unless these reprocessed goods are marketed effectively and efficiently along with government requirements stipulating that, all else being at least approximately equal, goods made from second materials must be purchased. Further, there can be additional pay-offs from such economic planning. For example, a great variety of reprocessing employment opportunities will be created, and the beauty of this arrangement is that such positions could be continued indefinitely. This would be so because employment of this nature does not depend on presently finite mineral and timber supplies, for example, Finally, such development is especially important in heavily industrialized nations where increased attention to materials efficiency could revitalize (pp. 91-94).

In an effort to consider the problem more carefully, and in the process to place it in some perspective for members of the physical education and sport profession as well as those in our allied professions, we will (1) offer a few definitions, (2) analyze the extent of it in our society, (3) put the environmental crisis in some philosophical perspective for our profession, and (4) offer a concluding statement.

SOME FURTHER DEFINITION OF TERMS

As a result of the development of ecology, and what has by some been called "environmental science," many new words and phrases have been added to our vocabulary: Huxley (1963) had described ecology as "the science of the mutual relations of organism with their environment and with one another" (p. 6). Or, to be somewhat more precise, Murray (1972) then stated that "ecologists study competition between individuals and between populations for resources, the growth of populations, and the movement of materials (e.g., water and minerals) in ecological systems (ecosystems)" (p. 36).

It is not possible or pertinent to define even the most common terms usually employed in this area of study here, but it should be understood that we have polluted the Earth--and are doing so now and may continue to do so in the future--in both the biosphere (the zone of life) and in the remainder of the atmosphere. This includes the area from 35,000 feet up to perhaps 600 miles above the Earth. Kunz (1971) explained that the biosphere is "that envelope made up of the Earth's waters, land crust, and atmosphere where all organisms, including man, live" (p. 67).

An ecosystem is "an integrated unit or 'system' in nature, sufficient unto itself to be studied as a separate entity--e.g., a rotting log in the forest, a coral atoll, a continent, or the earth with all its biota." Fortunately, many of these common terms are recognizable, and their continued use in the various communications media is making them part of everyday vocabulary. A few of these terms are: allowable release level, biodegradable, biota, carcinogen, coliform bacteria, compost, decibel, demography, effluent, energy cycle, green revolution, greenhouse effect, herbicide, atmospheric inversion, nonrenewable resource, recycling, smog, sonic boom, symbiosis, thermal pollution (p. 67).

THE EXTENT OF THE PROBLEM IN MODERN SOCIETY

What then is the extent of the environmental crisis in modern society? Very simply, then, in regard to the ecological situation, we humans have achieved a certain mastery over the physical world in which we have found ourselves because of our scientific achievements and accompanying technology. (Aha! Now we have still another persistent historical problem--science and technology--to add to the growing list; see Zeigler [1994, pp. 381-391] for a brief explanation of social influences.) We are at the top of the food chain because of our mastery of much of Earth's flora and fauna. Because of the exponential, geometric, explosion of the human population, Mergen (1970) explained that increasingly greater pressures "will be placed on our lands to provide shelter, food, recreation, and waste disposal areas. This will cause a greater pollution of the atmosphere, the rivers, the lakes, the land, and the oceans" (p. 36).

All of this was explained graphically also 35 years ago by the National Geographic Society (1970) in a chart titled "How Man Pollutes His World." Here the earth is "divided" into air, land, and sea. It is vital to understand that this satellite is self-sustaining; is possessed of only a finite quantity of oxygen, water, and land; and it has no means of reconstituting itself with further natural resources once the present supply is exhausted. This means that we must given immediate attention to the effect of supersonic aircraft on the atmosphere at various levels; to what increasing urbanization will mean insofar as the strain on the physical environment is concerned; to how significant the stripping of vegetation is to the Earth's soil supply and to its ability to produce oxygen; to how dangerous the effects of mercury waste, harmful pesticides, chemical fertilizers, and trash and sewage disposal are to the natural environment; and to what the oil spills and dumping at sea will mean to the Earth's great bodies of water and their ability to sustain fish, bird, and bottom life. We need to ask ourselves questions about the extent to which nature's self-renewing cycles are being disturbed. To repeat a point made earlier, what sort of world will the more than 6 billion inherit in the 21st century?

In North America alone, many rivers, lakes, and streams are being used as sewers; the air in some cities is so polluted that one might as well be smoking a pack of cigarettes daily; New York City alone is estimated to have as many rats as it has people (more than 9 million); overall about 5 billions tons of garbage are produced each year; more than four-fifths of the original forests have been converted for other purposes, as have about 300 million acres of crop and range land; and at least 3,500 acres a day are covered with concrete and other substances. And, of course, many other nations in the world are following the same path.

If all this sounds a bit melodramatic, keep in mind that there is a global network of international agricultural research centers that is facing ever-increasing demands from all parts of the Earth for assistance in increasing food production because countries' populations are outstripping their capacity to put sufficient nutritional food on the table for all of their citizens. And still further, is the situation better today than in 1975? The New York Times reported then, for example, that air pollution plagued several large and populous areas along the Eastern seaboard today, causing serious potential hazards for people with respiratory or other health problems and at least some discomfort for countless others" (1975, p. 37).

For the answer to this question, one only has to turn to State of the world in, for example, 1995. Writing about "Nature's limits," Brown makes it crystal clear that "nature's limits are beginning to impose themselves on the human agenda, initially at the local level, but also at the global level" (p. 5). As can be appreciated, the earth's natural limits insofar as food production is concerned have been slowed already in regard to oceanic fish yields, availability of fresh water, and the quantity of fertilizer that present crop varieties can use effectively. This means that that seafood prices, for example, will probably keep rising indefinitely as long as the world's population continues its exponential growth. And, as we recognize, when demand exceeds supply in relation to any desired product, the progression is from stability to instability followed by collapse in that respect with possible resultant intensification of pressures in other areas.

This diatribe could be continued, but the point must have been made several paragraphs ago! Certainly the gravity of prevailing patterns of living is recognized by many, but such recognition must become knowledge about which positive attitudes are formed by a great many more people who are in a position to act even more aggressively in the immediate future (i.e., the U.S. president and Congress). Interestingly enough, many laws have been passed, but enforcement is difficult, and the fines for lawbreaking in this regard are evidently not sufficiently high. Other seemingly more pressing demands tend to take precedence over environmental concerns (e.g., the destruction of lakes and ponds by various industries through air pollution that falls as rain depending on prevailing wind patterns). It has now been almost 35 years since Smith (1971) decried the "fragmented approach that we tend to take in seeking solutions" (p. 69), and appointed presidential councils are perennially accused of dodging the evident crises. Fortunately, ministerial groups are placing some emphasis on what has been called a "theology of survival."

MEANING AND SIGNIFICANCE VIEWED PHILOSOPHICALLY

How does one approach a question such as the influence of ecology or the environmental crisis philosophically? Presumably no one philosophical position or stance would actually include any tenets designed to bring about an end to life on Earth as it has been known. Of course, some particularistic approaches might be overly optimistic about our future on Earth, and others might contain dicta which, if carried out assiduously, might hasten the time when the Earth's resources could no longer sustain its population. Other approaches might be so despairing and pessimistic about the future that the inevitability of our consciously (or even unconsciously) destroying ourselves is a distinct possibility.

This subject brings us close to the subject of ethics, that phase of societal values and norms treating what is good and bad and what actions are right or wrong. In an interesting article, Holmes Rolston (1975) asked what to many might seem like a contradictory question--"Is there an ecological ethic?" He inquired whether an environmental ethic--the values that we hold about our environment--is based simply on a specific ethical approach (e.g., with a philosophical position) or whether there is actually a built-in naturalistic ethic in the universe.

Commencing from the position that the dividing line between science and ethics is definite if one but accepts the philosophical categories of descriptive law and prescriptive law as being separate and distinct. Descriptive law, presented in the indicative mood, is employed in science and history. Prescriptive law, on the other hand, is used in ethics, and the imperative mood is involved implicitly or explicitly. Thus, in moral philosophy the quickest way to be accused of committing a naturalistic fallacy is to blithely assume an "ought" from an "is"--at least in the eyes of an analytic philosopher with a scientific orientation. Transposed to the discussion of ecological ethics, environmental science should tell us what we think we know through observing, hypothesizing, experimenting, and generalizing about the environment. Environmental ethics, on the other hand, means presumably that we have applied one or another approach to moral philosophy to our understanding of and relationship to the environment.

Rolston (1975) stated that those who argue for a built-in ecological morality have differences in opinion that divide them into two groups: (1) those who equate homeostasis with morality, and (2) those who appear to go even further by arguing that there is "a moral ought inherent in recognition of the holistic character of the ecosystem" that results in an ecological ethic (p. 94). In assessing the first group, Rolston seeks a "moral translation" from the paramount law in ecological theory-- that of homeostasis (a closed planetary ecosystem, recycling transformation, energy balance).

A bit earlier Sears (1969) argued that:

> "probably men will always differ as to what constitutes the good life. The need not differ as to what is necessary for the long survival of men on earth. . . . As living beings we must come to terms with the environment about us, learning to get along with the liberal budget at our disposal . . .we must seem to attain what I have called a steady state." (p. 401)

Here the argument appears to be as follows: If you wish to preserve human life--and you ought to want to do so--the ecological law (that the life-supporting ecosystem must recycle or all will perish) indicates that technically you ought not to disturb the ecosystem's capability to recycle itself. According to moral law (which equates with natural law), you ought to assist such recycling wherever possible. With this approach, values are not strictly inherent in the makeup of the world. They are actually ascribed to it by us attempting to employ careful husbandry with what we have assumed to be our possession (the Earth!). Rolston (1975) argued that we can call the balance of nature (and the ends that we seek, which are presumably compatible with an ecosystemic balance) "ultimate values if we wish, but the ultimacy is instrumental, not intrinsic" (p. 98).

The other major claim referred to above allows one to use the term ecological ethic without quotation marks, because the assumption is that "morality is a derivative of the holistic character of the ecosystem" (p. 98). Rolston appreciated then that this was a radical idea that would not receive ready acceptance. It endows nature and its integral ecosystem with value. This is obviously a proposal for the broadening of the concept of value-- nature in and of itself would have value whether anyone was here to appreciate it and function on that basis. The leap is made from "is" to "ought" because "the values seem to be there as the facts are fully in" (p. 101).

Because of past philosophical and religious speculation, not to mention what is called philosophy of science, it is extremely difficult to find a logical place for a primary ecological ethic in which the long-standing classical ought "has been transformed, stretched, coextensively with an ecosystemic ought" (p. 104). Are human beings ready to agree that "egoism should be transformed into ecoism" (p. 104)? If the answer is "yes," then the self would be identified with nature with Nature as one of its components, as part of the ecosystem. It would not be human beings and nature; it would be human beings in nature with such a transformation of outlook. In this way we would have a much stronger obligation to preserve nature's balance, because we are truly a part of the world--and the world is a part of our bodies.

With such an outlook, we would create what might be called the ecological person. It was exactly such a person postulated by Rolston (1975) who might be able today to postulate an authentic naturalistic ethic:

> Man, an insider, is not spared environmental pressures, yet in the full ecosystemic context, his integrity is supported by and rises from transaction with his world and therefore requires a corresponding dignity in his world partner. Of late, the world has ceased to threaten, save as we violate it. How starkly this gainsays the alienation that characterizes

modern literature, seeing nature as basically rudderless, antipathetical, in need of monitoring and repair. More typically modern man, for all his technological prowess, has found himself distanced from nature, increasingly competent and decreasingly confident, at once distinguished and aggrandized, yet afloat on and adrift in an indifferent, if not a hostile, universe. His world is at best a huge filling station, at worst a prison or "nothingness." Not so for ecological man; confronting his world with deference to a community of value in which he shares, he is at home again. (pp. 107-108)

IMPLICATIONS FOR THE EDUCATION PROFESSION

Above we have explained the difficulty of moving from an ecological "is" to an ecological "ought" in the realm of science and ethics. Nevertheless, the concept of the ecological man and woman has a definite appeal. Regardless of your position on this interesting question, there are quite obviously many scientific findings classified as environmental science that should be made available to people of all ages whether they are enrolled in educational institutions or are part of the everyday world. Simply making all the facts available will, of course, not be any guarantee that strong and positive attitudes will develop on the subject.

It is a well-established fact, however, that the passing of legislation in difficult and sensitive areas must continue to take place through responsible political leadership. Also, attitude changes often follow behind--albeit at what may seem to be a snail's pace. The field of education must play a vital role in the development of what might be termed an "ecological awareness." This is much broader than what was called the conservation movement within forestry and closely related fields that was bent on the preservation of this or that feature of nature. Now ecology (or environmental science) places all these individual entities in a total context in which the interrelationship of all parts must be thoroughly understood.

Sound educational planning should take place at all levels, from early childhood education through the free tuition courses now being offered to many older citizens by certain universities. As Mergen stated 35 years ago, "The knowledge that has been accumulated is vast, and ecological principles should be made part of the educational menus for economists, city planners, architects, engineers, the medical profession, the legal profession, religious groups, and all people concerned with the public and private management of natural resources, as well as politicians and governmental employees" (1970, p. 37).

Obviously, those concerned professionally with sport and physical education, health and safety education, and recreation and parks administration from the standpoint of professional preparation have an equally important stake in this total educational process. As a matter of fact, these three allied professions are more concerned than most with humans and their relationship to the total environment, whether natural or artificial.

Presumably the usual struggle will take place among those who want to introduce a new subject into the curriculum, those who will demand that environmental science be taught incidentally as part of existing subjects within the educational program, and those who will see no need for the study of environmental relationships to be in the basic curriculum. Further, some will want the subject matter taught as facts and knowledge in a subject-centered curriculum based on a logical progression from the simple to the complex, whereas others will stress that interest on the part of the learner should dictate if and how the subject should be introduced, because this is the way people learn best. Regardless, the urgency of the ecological crisis warrants an approach that veers neither to the right nor left of center. The point is simply that a potentially devastating problem is upon us, and that we should move ahead rapidly to see that some of the basics of environmental science are made available to all. These issues have been with us for so many centuries, of course, that they will not be solved tomorrow. What is critical right now is that we start to move as strongly as possible to foster understanding and the development of attitudes leading to corrective action.

It is difficult to state that certain information and attitudes should be taught to the population of pluralistic societies--and then to look forward confidently to the effective execution of such a pronouncement throughout North America. This is simply not the way things happen in countries like the United States, for example, where educational autonomy prevails in the individual states. All that can be hoped is that knowledge about the several positions regarding economic growth will be made available in a fair manner to the people as a controversial issue. What should be made known is that certain ecologic and economic theories and recommendations are diametrically opposed. Which one should be followed and how far is something that the people in a democratic type of government must soon decide ("like yesterday"!).

Somehow we don't hear much about it today, but the ecologist, B.G. Murray (1972), made it crystal clear in the early 1970s that citizens of the United States were definitely being placed in a position where a decision would have to be made between a continuous-growth economy policy or a no-growth one (p. 38). Somehow it has happened that the very large majority of citizens are not even aware that some scholars are recommending such a thing as a no-growth policy. Is this continent not one where capitalism and democracy prevails, where a steadily increasing gross national product is a strong indicator of economic prosperity? Is it a case where the eternal optimists seem to be saying, "Full speed ahead, if we ever hope to remain 'Number 1' and reduce poverty." "The United States can do no wrong!"

To this the pessimists respond with an incantation that "population and economic growth must strive for a steady state during the 21st century (if that is not already too late)." Whoever heard of such nonsense as a steady-state situation when the United States is encouraging immigration from around the globe? This is the almost impossible task educators face as they attempt to explain and then carry forward to fruition and implementation the required forecasting models developed by researchers in both the natural and social sciences.

In a comparison of conflicting ecological and economic models, Murray (1972) examined the concepts of growth, movement of materials, and competition. In regard to growth, he explained that all types of biological growth follow a characteristic pattern that in time reaches a steady state or equilibrium in which as many organisms are dying as are being born into the system. (Think of this in relation to the massive problem being faced by China where a birth-control policy has been operational for some time.) In United States business, however, the high standard of material living has been reached by continuously increasing GNP to meet the needs and demands of a continuously increasing population. Question: How long can this growth curve be maintained--and at what cost, including the rest of the world? It is explained further that continuous growth curves are not unknown in biological and physical systems (p. 38). However, the result is usually disaster-- death of the host organism as when uncontrolled cell growth takes place in cancer, or even when the chain reaction of fissioning uranium-235 nuclei results in the inefficient use of energy in nuclear explosions (p. 39). The axiom of the ecologist here is that a system will eventually collapse unless it stops growing at some point and recycles.

The second concept discussed is the movement of materials, and here reference is being made to the bio-geochemical cycles operative within nature--"the movement within ecosystems of minerals, water, oxygen, carbon dioxide, and other nutrients essential for life" (p. 39). One example of this process, of course, is that which carbon dioxide follows in its cyclic path between Earth's atmosphere and the many organisms that inhabit this planet. Interestingly enough, the recycling that takes place is not completely efficient, with the result that the process known as "succession" results in a somewhat different makeup based on the ecosystem's chemical composition. The serious difficulty created by human beings is that both food requirements and the demands of technological advancement are simply not recycled in such a way as to sustain even a steady-state situation indefinitely. In other words, the movement of materials is all in one direction--for the temporary service of an expanding population that is increasing in number exponentially.

Third, and last, the other fundamental rule of ecology is discussed. Sooner or later competition excludes some of the competing species. Practically this means that, if two organisms are competing for an exhaustible resource (and which one isn't in a closed system?), one of the competitors will be dispensed with by its rival "either by being forced out of the ecosystem or by being forced to use some other resource" (p. 64). Thus, there exists a basic contradiction between the economic theory that competition is supposed to maintain diversity and stability of systems, and the contrasting theory based on the ecological model described above.

By now it should be readily apparent that this issue of conflicting models and resultant (presumably correct) operative theories should have an overriding priority for inclusion somewhere, somehow, and immediately in our culture and its educational systems. We simply have to know what all this means for such cherished concepts as increasing growth, competition, capitalism, and advancing technological revolution. The merging of tenable principles of environmental science with altered societal values and norms into acceptable and high desirable social policy and accompanying educational theory and practice is an urgent challenge for all politicians and educators in North America.

IMPLICATIONS FOR PHYSICAL EDUCATION, KINESIOLOGY AND EDUCATIONAL SPORT

If our culture and its educators have a definite responsibility and strong obligation to present the various issues revolving about what has become a crucial social force (persistent historical problem) in North America, this duty obviously includes the professionals at all levels of education and in society at large. After having the matter called to my attention originally in the summer of 1970, I soon decided that it, too, should be considered a persistent problem demanding the field's attention in the same way as the other five social forces of values, politics, nationalism, economics, and religion (Zeigler, 1977). Having written about this problem since then (e.g., 1989, 2003), my primary concern in this context now is, of course, that the kinesiology, physical education, and educational sport professional, along with his colleagues in the allied professions, take tangible steps to incorporate in their curricula the means by which an awareness is kept ever-present in the minds of young people.

It will be appreciated immediately, of course, that these fields, along with dance, are now designated as the allied professions in the United States, whereas physical and health education and recreation and parks administration are separate professions in Canada. We need to keep in mind further that many physical educators/coaches get involved with certain duties that are often carried out by the professional practitioners to a greater or lesser extent in the allied field. The same can be said, of course, for personnel functioning in the other professions.

A BROAD GENERAL EDUCATION RESPONSIBILITY

Physical education and educational sport teacher/coaches functioning in public education settings, like those practicing in the other allied professional fields within the educational system, quite naturally have a broad general education responsibility to all participants in classes or community recreation programs. Thus, they are directly concerned with our relationship with ourselves, our fellow human beings, other living organisms, and the physical environment. Responsible citizens and educators will have an understanding of worldwide population growth and what problems such growth will present. Granted that there are conflicting views on this matter, students should at least be able to expect that instructors will have a reasoned position about this issue that is so important, yet seemingly so highly controversial.

The physical educator/coach should also understand how continuous-growth economic theories contradict basic ecological theory. There can be no argument about the fact that both population growth and advancing technology--the latter with the capability to improve the material living standard of all to the extent possible--seem to be leading Earth's population to a position at which some fundamental changes in attitudes and practices will probably necessarily result (or ought to change, at any rate). Although attitudes toward improved international relations have waxed and waned over the decades, the responsible sport and physical education professional will realize that the quality of life cannot be steadily improved in some countries on earth without due consideration being given to improving the conditions of all people everywhere.

Finally, the informed citizen/professional we are discussing will be aware of the urgent need to take care of the manifold ecosystems on this "closed" planet and will do all in his or her power to assist with the necessary recycling so that a "reconstituted" Earth will be transmitted to future generations.

SPECIFIC IMPLICATIONS FOR THE PRACTICING PROFESSIONAL

Now we must consider whether there are any specific implications for physical educator/coaches as they face their own professional task. As matters stand now, they are confronted daily with the fact that for a variety of reasons modern, urbanized, technologically advanced life in North America has created a population with a very low level of physical fitness, with a resultant decrease in overall total fitness.

What makes this matter so extremely difficult is that the large majority of the population has been lulled into a false sense of complacency by what Herbert Spencer (1949) in the 1860's called a "seared physical conscience" that is unable to "monitor" the body properly and accurately (p. 197). As a result of this presumed sense of complacency, there is an unwillingness to lead a life that may be characterized as "physically vigorous." What we have created, therefore, is a ridiculous situation in which people on this continent are to a large extent overfed, overweight, and poorly exercised, whereas a multitude of people on other continents are often underfed, underweight, and often strenuously exercised. All of this adds up to a world situation that may well bring disaster to us all before we are far into the 21st century.

The facts about this incipient tragedy are now being brought home to us daily at dinnertime on our television screens! Although many professions are already focusing in on this dilemma, as the author (Zeigler, 1964) stated--now so long ago--it is the sport and physical education profession that is uniquely responsible for the exercise programs that will enable men and women "to be rugged animals fit to withstand the excessive wear and tear that life's informal and formal activities may demand" (p. 55). Additionally, it is this same physical educator--perhaps more so now in Canada than in the the United States--who gets involved with health and safety education courses in which nutritional practices and habits are discussed.

As Spencer (1949) indicated, "generally, we think, the history of the world shows that the well-fed races have been the energetic and dominant races" (p. 55). He explained further that animals can work harder when they are fed more nutritiously. The point he wished to make is that a sound diet is necessary for both energy and growth (p. 191). What this adds up to is that the sport and physical education professional is also in a situation in which he or she teaches about nutrition at least indirectly in daily practice--and quite often directly in classroom situations. Thus, he or she can to some extent advise students about the correct food to eat for a physically vigorous life, as well as which amounts of what food will ensure adequate nutrition to maintain normal health--not to mention advice about how to keep from being overweight or underweight.

A vigorous exercise program and correct nutritional instruction relate quite directly to two aspects of the ecological crisis discussed earlier--that is, the pollution of Earth and its atmosphere, and adequate nutrition for the children born on this earth. Without getting involved in the moral question of birth control--an issue that will have to be resolved from an ecological standpoint sooner or later--sport and physical education professionals should do all in their power to control pollution because it will in a short time, and in a variety of ways, make it increasingly difficult for us in the urban centers at least to exercise vigorously and to maintain physical fitness. When the air we breath and the water we drink become increasingly impure, how, then, will we maintain the fitness of all?

Second, there is the matter of adequate nutrition for the rapidly increasing population in the countries least able to feed their offspring. Although some may believe that the Malthusian principle should be allowed to take effect and that the favored nations should take care of their own needs, it would seem more humane to keep the world's hungry people as adequately supplied with staples as possible. But at the same time we in the profession should redouble our efforts to make certain that young people learn correct eating habits to guarantee relatively lean and fat-free bodies that are capable of vigorous exercise to ensure physical fitness. There is so much food wasted on this continent that our moral sense should be affronted. For example, how many people could be kept alive with our garbage? Or to view the question in a different way, is it quite so necessary that millions upon millions of dogs and cats can be sustained when human beings here and abroad are dying of malnutrition?

In addition, people at all stages of life show evidence of a variety of remediable physical defects, but there is typically an unwillingness on the part of the public to make exercise therapy programs readily available through public and private agencies. Many physiotherapy programs are available briefly after operations or accidents and may be covered by health insurance programs. (Such coverage is more readily available in Canada, but must be carried out by registered physiotherapists upon medical prescription.) Such assistance is typically helpful and fills an important need. However, our concern here is with the unavailability of exercise therapy programs in the schools and certain private agencies under the supervision of qualified exercise specialists in our profession after the initial need for physiotherapy modalities and assistance is past.

Keeping in mind the ecological principle that "competition kills competitors," it would appear to be the direct responsibility of sport and physical education professionals to involve all young people in a vigorous program of developmental physical activity--human motor performance in sport, exercise, and related expressive activities--that can be characterized as interesting, joyful, and exuberant. If this were done early, regularly, and in an interesting manner, it is quite possible that such interest would be maintained throughout life. Our society could then be characterized as a nation of fit people explained by Spencer (1949) as able to meet the necessary first condition for the maintenance of independence and prosperity-- physical fitness within a concept of total fitness (p. 177). In the process we should, to the best of our ability, guide young people away from such "sporting" activity as the use of snowmobiles and speedboats and auto racing, which pollute the environment, tend to destroy the ecosystemic balance, and provide merely a mechanical means for propelling the body from one point to another.

Developmental physical activity in sport, physical education, and related expressive activities can play an important role in the social and psychological development of both sexes and all ages, whether from accelerated, normal, or special populations. As important as the element of competition may have been in the past--and should continue to be in the future--it is now time to place at least equal emphasis on the benefits to be derived from cooperation in the various aspects of sport competition. Most certainly the future of life on this planet will present all sorts of opportunities for cooperative effort both at home and abroad. A wholesome balance between competition and cooperation in a child's and young person's education can serve to develop highly desirable personality traits, while at the same time offering numerous occasions for the release of the overly aggressive tendencies present in so many individuals for a variety of explainable reasons.

As indicated earlier, those teaching sport and physical education skills often get involved directly or indirectly with health and safety education and or (at least) physical recreation education. These instructors have some contact with practically every student in the school. Thus, they have great potential for conveying knowledge and assisting in the formation of correct attitudes about all four allied field through effective teaching. Additionally, the physical educator/coach can set an example personally for all young people to follow. For example, the area of health and safety education provides innumerable ways to demonstrate safety practices, personal hygiene, and attitudes (and practice) toward the use of alcohol, tobacco, marijuana, and (what are presumably) the more harmful drugs. Wholesome attitudes and practice in the area of sex and sex education are also extremely important--the whole area of family life education, for that matter, should be taught well by both precept and practice.

Similarly, the area of recreation education within the allied profession of recreation offers many opportunities for education in ways that will promote improved ecological understanding. In the first place, a challenge in leisure values-- at least as they have now been established by many--should take place. Through recreation education it should be possible to promote an understanding of and respect for the world's flora and fauna, not to mention the whole concept of ecosystemic balance. Even though our so-called post-industrial society is not reducing working hours at the rate predicted earlier and many in leadership roles are putting in even longer hours, there is still an urgent need to promote the concept of creative leisure. We need a return to what used to be considered the simple recreational pleasures, perhaps with certain variations to appeal to the young. The sport and physical education professional should promote the concept of physical recreation for all, of course, but by precept and example the idea of a young person getting involved with aesthetic and creative activities and hobbies should be fostered, as well as involving what have been called "learning" recreational interests.

CONCLUDING STATEMENT

The influence of ecology is now such that it must be included as a persistent historical problem and a strong social force along with the other social forces of values, politics, nationalism, economics, religion, and science & technology (Zeigler, 1989, p. 259). Although there is a dividing line between science and morality, perhaps the time has come for morality to be viewed as being derived from the fundamental, all-encompassing nature of the ecosystem.

This plea for the broadening of the concept of value--a truly naturalistic ethic--has direct implications for the future of the world. Accordingly, it has both direct and indirect implications for our culture and educational systems. Presumably it is possible to view this topic philosophically using the same approach that was employed with all other vital social forces.

Speaking personally, I have refrained from doing this to avoid conflict if at all possible. In this instance, we must not follow the previous path in which traditional philosophic divisions have almost automatically occasioned divided approaches to controversial issues. I believe that, because of the vital urgency of this stark problem, all mature people in our society must be led to develop an "ecological awareness" as soon as possible. French (1995) believed that this situation has now reached the point where a full-fledged environment agency should be created within the United Nations system as soon as possible (p. 183).

The physical education, kinesiology, and educational sport professional, as well as those functioning in the allied professions, should take up this worldwide challenge as well. We are presumed to be informed citizens in society. However, we additionally have a unique role to play in helping people of all ages and conditions develop and maintain physical fitness within a concept of total fitness to the extent possible for the individual. Such fitness should further be based on a goal of international understanding and concern for all humanity.

REFERENCES

Brown, L.R. *et al.* (1995). Nature's limits. In L.R. Brown (Ed. & Au.), *State of the world* (pp. 3-20). NY: W.W. Norton.

Easterbrook, G. (1995). *A moment on the earth*. NY: Viking.

French, H. (1995). Forging a new global partnership. In L.R. Brown (Ed. & au.), *State of the world (1995)* (pp. 170-190). NY: W.W. Norton.

Hawley, A.H. (1986). *Human ecology: A theoretical essay*. Chicago: The University of Chicago Press.

Huxley, J. (1963). *The politics of ecology*. Santa Barbara, CA: Center for the Study of Democratic Institutions.

Kunz, R.F. (Jan. 2, 1971). An environmental glossary. *Saturday*

Review, 67.

Mergen, F. (May 1970). Man and his environment. *Yale Magazine,* XXXIII(8): 36-37.

Murray, B.G., Jr. (Dec. 10, 1972). What the ecologists can teach the economists. *The New York Times Magazine:* 38-39, 64-65, 70, 72.

National Geographic Society, The. (1970). How man pollutes his world. Washington, DC: The Society. (This is an explanatory chart).

New York Times, The (May 1, 1970). Foul air poses health threat to east.

Rolston, H. (Jan. 1975). Is there an ecological ethic? *Ethics,* 85(2): 93-109.

Smith, G.L.C. (Jan. 1, 1971). The ecologist at bay. *Saturday Review,* 68-69.

Spencer, H. (1949). *Education: Intellectual, moral, and physical.* London: Watts.

Young, J.E., Sachs, A. (1995). Creating a sustainable materials economy. In L.F. Brown (Ed. & Au.), *State of the world (1995)* (pp. 76-94). NY: W.W. Norton.

Zeigler, E.F. (1964). *Philosophical foundations for physical, health, and recreation education. Englewood Cliffs, NJ:* Prentice-Hall.

Zeigler, E.F. (1989). *An introduction to sport and physical education philosophy.* Carmel, IN: Benchmark.

Zeigler, E.F. (Ed. & Au.). (1994). *Physical education and kinesiology in North America: Professional & scholarly foundations.* Champaign, IL: Stipes.

Zeigler, E.F. (2003). *Socio-Cultural Foundations of Physical Education and Educational Sport.* Aachen, Germany: Meyer and Meyer Sports.

CHAPTER XI

THE EMERGING POSTMODERN AGE:
GLOBAL TRENDS IN PHYSICAL EDUCATION

North Americans do not fully comprehend that their unique position in the history of the world's development will in all probability change radically in the 21st century. For that matter. the years ahead are really going to be difficult ones for all of the world's citizens. The United States, as the one major nuclear power, has assumed the ongoing, massive problem of maintaining large-scale peace. Of course, a variety of countries, both large and small, may or may not have nuclear arms capability as well. That is what is so worrisome.

Additionally, all of the world will be having increasingly severe ecological problems, not to mention the ebbs and flows of an energy crisis. Generally, also, there is a worldwide nutritional problem and a devastating health problems known colloquially as AIDS. Additionally, there is an ongoing situation where the rising expectations of the underdeveloped nations, including their staggering debt (and ours!), will somehow have to be met. These are just a few of the major concerns looming on the horizon.

Initially, as a first objective in this chapter, I believe we need to review briefly the prevailing situation internationally to set the stage for what follows. Then the second objective of this chapter will be an exploratory effort to discover something of what professionals in our field are experiencing firsthand "out there" in certain countries on the various continents of the world.[1] Over the years I have been doing my best to keep informed about global trends. Yet, even with the generally improved quality and availability of information from the various media, I still felt inadequate to speak with reasonable assurance of accuracy on the topic of "global trends." Despite the continuing efforts of such fine international organizations as ISCPES, ICHPER-SD, and ICSSPE, there still exists a significant, ongoing need for improved communication worldwide insofar as the development of physical education and educational sport are concerned.

Indeed, although it is seemingly more true of the United States than Canada, history is going against the U.S.A. in several ways. This means that their previous optimism must be tempered to shake them loose from delusions they have acquired, some of which they still have. For example, despite the presence of the

United Nations, the United States has persisted in envisioning itself--as the world superpower--as almost being endowed by "the Creator" to make all crucial political decisions. Such decisions, often to act unilaterally with the hoped-for, but belated sanction of the United Nations, have resulted in United States-led incursions in the Middle East in the two wars and into Somalia for very different reasons. And there are other similar situations that are now history (e.g., Cuba Afghanistan, the former Yugoslavia, Rwanda, Sudan, Haiti, etc., respectively, not to mention other suspected incursions).

Nevertheless, there is reason to expect selected U.S. retrenchment brought on by its excessive world involvement and enormous debt. Of course, any such retrenchment would inevitably lead to a decline in the economic and military influence of the United States. But who can argue logically that the present uneasy balance of power is a healthy situation looking to the future? Norman Cousins appeared to have sounded just the right note more than a generation ago when he stated that "the most important factor in the complex equation of the future is the way the human mind responds to crisis" (1974, 6-7). The world culture as we know it must respond adequately to the many challenges with which it is being confronted. The societies and nations must individually and collectively respond positively, intelligently, and strongly if humanity as we have known it is to survive.

SIGNIFICANT DEVELOPMENTS HAVE "TRANSFORMED" OUR LIVES

In this discussion of national and international developments, with an eye to achieving some historical perspective on the subject, we should also keep in mind the specific developments in the last quarter of the 20th century. For example, Naisbitt (1982) outlined the "ten new directions that are transforming our lives," as well as the "megatrends" insofar as women's evolving role in societal structure (Aburdene & Naisbitt, 1992). Here I am referring to:

(1) the concepts of the information society and
    the Internet,
(2) "high tech/high touch,"
(3) the shift to world economy,
(4) the need to shift to long-term thinking in
    regard to ecology,
(5) the move toward organizational decentralization,
(6) the trend toward self-help,

(7) the ongoing discussion of the wisdom of
participatory democracy as opposed to
representative democracy,

(8) a shift toward networking,

(9) a reconsideration of the "north-south" orientation, and

(10) the viewing of decisions as "multiple option"
instead of "either/or."

Add to this the ever-increasing, lifelong involvement of women in the workplace, politics, sports, organized religion, and social activism, Now we begin to understand that a new world order has descended upon us as we begin the 21st century.

Moving ahead in time slightly beyond Naisbitt's first set of Megatrends, a second list of 10 issues facing political leaders was highlighted as "Ten events that shook the world between 1984 and 1994" (Utne Reader, 1994, pp. 58-74). Consider the following:

(1) the fall of communism and the continuing rise
of nationalism,

(2) the environmental crisis and the Green movement,

(3) the AIDS epidemic and the "gay response,"

(4) continuing wars and the peace movement,

(5) the gender war,

(6) religion and racial tension,

(7) the concept of "West meets East" and resultant
implications,

(8) the "Baby Boomers" came of age and "Generation
X" has started to worry and complain because of
declining expectation levels,

(9) the whole idea of globalism and international markets, and

(10) the computer revolution and the specter of Internet.

THE WORLD HAS THREE MAJOR TRADING BLOCKS

Concurrent with the above developments, to help cope with such change the world's "economic manageability" may have been helped by its division into three major trading blocs: (1) the Pacific Rim dominated by Japan, (2) the European Community very heavily influenced by Germany, and (3) North America dominated by the United States of America. While this appears to be true to some observers, interestingly perhaps something even more fundamental has occurred. Succinctly put, world politics seems to be "entering a new phase in which the fundamental source of conflict will be neither ideological nor economic." In the place these, Samuel P. Huntington, of Harvard's Institute for Strategic Studies, believes that now the major conflicts in the world will actually be clashes between different groups of civilizations espousing fundamentally different cultures (The New York Times, June 6, 1993, E19).

These clashes, Huntington states, represent a distinct shift away from viewing the world as being composed of first, second, and third worlds as was the case during the cold war. Thus, Huntington is arguing that in the 21st century the world will return to a pattern of development evident several hundred years ago in which civilizations will actually rise and fall. (Interestingly, this is exactly what was postulated by the late Arnold Toynbee in his earlier famous theory of history development.)

Thus, internationally, with the dissolution of the Union of Soviet Socialist Republics (USSR), Russia and the remaining communist regimes are being severely challenged as they seek to convert to more of a capitalistic economic system. Additionally, a number of other multinational countries have either broken up, or are showing signs of potential break-ups (e.g., Yugoslavia, China, Canada). Further, the evidence points to the strong possibility that the developing nations are becoming ever poorer and more destitute with burgeoning populations and widespread starvation setting in.

Further, Western Europe is facing a demographic time bomb even more than the United States because of the influx of refugees from African and Islamic countries, not to mention refugees from countries of the former Soviet Union. It appears further that the European Community will be inclined to appease Islam's demands. However, the multinational nature of the European Community will tend to bring on economic protectionism to insulate its economy against the rising costs of prevailing socialist legislation.

Still further, there is some evidence that Radical Islam, along with Communist China, may well become increasingly aggressive toward the Western culture of Europe and North America. At present, Islam gives evidence of replacing Marxism as the world's main ideology of confrontation. For example, Islam is dedicated to regaining control of Jerusalem and to force Israel to give up control of land occupied earlier to provide a buffer zone against Arab aggressors. (Also, China has been arming certain Arab nations. But how can we be too critical in this regard when we recall that the U.S.A. has also armed selected countries in the past [and present?] when such support was deemed in its interest?)

As Hong Kong is absorbed into Communist China, further political problems seem inevitable in the Far East as well. Although North Korea is facing agricultural problems, there is the possibility (probability?) of the building of nuclear bombs there. (Further, there is the ever-present fear worldwide that small nations and terrorists will somehow get nuclear weapons too.) A growing Japanese assertiveness in Asian and world affairs also seems inevitable because of its typically very strong financial position. Yet the flow of foreign capital from Japan into North America has slowed down somewhat because Japan is being confronted with its own financial crisis caused by inflated real estate and market values. There would obviously be a strong reaction to any fall in living standards in this tightly knit society. Interestingly, still further, the famed Japanese work ethic has become somewhat tarnished by the growing attraction of leisure opportunities.

The situation in Africa has become increasingly grim because the countries south of the Sahara Desert (that is, the dividing line between black Africa and the Arab world) experienced extremely bad economic performance in the past two decades. This social influence has brought to a halt much of the continental effort leading to political liberalization while at the same time exacerbating traditional ethnic rivalries. This economic problem has accordingly forced governmental cutbacks in many of the countries because of the pressures brought to bear by the financial institutions of the Western world that have been underwriting much of the development. The poor are therefore getting poorer, and health and education standards have in many instances deteriorated even lower than they were previously.

THE IMPACT OF NEGATIVE SOCIAL FORCES HAS INCREASED

Now, shifting the focus of this discussion from the problems of an unsettled "Global Village" back to the problem of "living the good life" in the 21st century in North America, we are finding that the human recreational experience will have to be earned typically within a society whose very structure has been modified. For example, (1) the concept of the traditional family structure has been strongly challenged by a variety of social forces (e.g., economics, divorce rate); (2) many single people are finding that they must work longer hours; and (3) many families need more than one breadwinner just to make ends meet. Also, the idea of a steady surplus economy may have vanished, temporarily it is hoped, in the presence of a substantive drive to reduce a budgetary deficit by introducing major cutbacks in so-called non-essentials.

THE PROBLEMS OF MEGALOPOLIS LIVING
HAVE NOT YET BEEN SOLVED

Additionally, many of the same problems of megalopolis living described as early as the 1960s still prevail and are even increasing (e.g., declining infrastructure, rising crime rates, transportation gridlocks, overcrowded schools). Interestingly, in that same year of 1967, Prime Minister Lester Pearson asked Canadians to improve "the quality of Canadian life" as Canada celebrated her 100th anniversary as a confederation. And still today, despite all of Canada's current identity problems, she can take some pride in the fact that Canada has on occasion been proclaimed as the best place on earth to live (with the United States not very far behind). Nevertheless, we can't escape the fact that the work week is not getting shorter and shorter. Also, Michael's' prediction about four different types of leisure class still seems a distant dream for the large majority of people.

Further, the situation has developed in such a way that the presently maturing generation, so-called Generation X, is finding that fewer good-paying jobs are available and the average annual income is declining (especially if we keep a steadily rising cost of living in mind). What caused this to happen? This is not a simple question to answer. For one thing, despite the rosy picture envisioned a generation ago, one in which we were supposedly entering a new stage for humankind, we are unable today to cope adequately with the multitude of problems that have developed. This situation is true whether inner city, suburbia, exurbia, or small-town living are concerned. Transportation jams and gridlock, for example, are occurring daily as public transportation struggles to meet rising demand for economical transport within the framework of developing megalopolises.

Certainly, megalopolis living trends have not abated and will probably not do so in the predictable future. More and more families, where that unit is still present, need two breadwinners just to survive. Interest rates, although minor cuts are made when economic slow-downs occur, remain quite high. This discourages many people from home ownership. Pollution of air and water continues despite efforts of many to change the present course of development. High-wage industries seem to be "heading south" in search of places where lower wages can be paid. Also, all sorts of crime are still present in our society, a goodly portion of it seemingly brought about by unemployment and rising debt at all levels from the individual to the federal government. The rise in youth crime is especially disturbing. In this respect, it is fortunate in North America that municipal, private-agency, and public recreation has received continuing financial support from the increasingly burdened taxpayer. Even here, however, there has been a definite trend toward user fees for many services.

WHAT CHARACTER DO WE SEEK FOR PEOPLE?

Still further, functioning in a world that is steadily becoming a "Global Village," we need to think more seriously than ever before about the character and traits for which we should seek to develop in people. The so-called developed nations can only continue to lead or strive for the proverbial good life if children and young people develop the right attitudes (psychologically speaking) toward (1) education, (2) work, (3) (use of leisure), (4) participation in government, (5) various types of consumption, and (6) concern for world stability and peace. Make no mistake about it. If we truly desire "the good life," education for the creative and constructive use of leisure--as a significant part of ongoing general education-- should have a unique role to play from here on into the indeterminate future.

What are called the Old World countries all seem to have a "character." It is almost something that they take for granted. However, it is questionable whether there is anything that can be called a character in North America (i.e., in the United States, in Canada). Americans were thought earlier to be heterogeneous and individualistic as a people, as opposed to Canadians. But the Canadian culture--whatever that may be today!--has changed quite a bit in recent decades toward multiculturalism--not to mention French-speaking Quebec, of course--as people arrived from many different lands. (Of course, Canada was founded by two distinct cultures, the English and the French.)

Shortly after the middle of the twentieth century, Commager (1966), the noted historian, enumerated what he believed were some common denominators in American (i.e., U.S.) character. These, he said, were (1) carelessness; (2) openhandedness, generosity, and hospitality; (3) self-indulgence; (4) sentimentality, and even romanticism; (5) gregariousness; (6) materialism; (7) confidence and self-confidence; (8) complacency, bordering occasionally on arrogance; (9) cultivation of the competitive spirit; (10) indifference to, and exasperation with laws, rules, and regulations; (11) equalitarianism; and (12) resourcefulness (pp. 246-254).

What about Canadian character as opposed to what Commager stated above? To help us in this regard, A generation ago, Lipset (1973) made a perceptive comparison between the two countries. After stating that they probably resemble each other more than any other two countries in the world, he asserted that there seemed to be a rather "consistent pattern of differences between them" (p. 4). He found that certain "special differences" did exist and may be singled out as follows:

> Varying origins in their political systems and national identities, varying religious traditions, and varying frontier experiences. In general terms, the value orientations of Canada stem from a counterrevolutionary past, a need to differentiate itself from the United States, the influence of Monarchical institutions, a dominant Anglican religious tradition, and a less individualistic and more governmentally controlled expansion of the Canadian than of the American frontier (p. 5).

WHAT HAPPENED TO THE ORIGINAL ENLIGHTENMENT IDEAL?

The achievement of "the good life" for a majority of citizens in the developed nations, a good life that involves a creative and constructive use of leisure as a key part of general education, necessarily implies that a certain type of progress has been made in society. However, we should understand that the chief criterion of progress has undergone a subtle but decisive change since the founding of the United States republic, for example. This development has had a definite influence on Canada and Mexico as well. Such change has been at once a cause and a reflection of the current disenchantment of some with technology. Recall that the late 18th century was a time of political revolution when monarchies, aristocracies, and the ecclesiastical structure were being challenged on a number of fronts in the Western world. Also, the factory system was undergoing significant change at that time. Such industrial development with its greatly improved machinery "coincided with the formulation and diffusion of the modern Enlightenment idea of history as a record of progress. . . ." (Marx, 1990, p. 5).

Thus, this "new scientific knowledge and accompanying technological power was expected to make possible a comprehensive improvement in all of the conditions of life--social, political, moral, and intellectual as well as material." This idea did indeed slowly take hold and eventually "became the fulcrum of the dominant American world view" (Marx, p. 5). By 1850, however, with the rapid growth of the United States especially, the idea of progress was already being dissociated from the Enlightenment vision of political and social liberation.

TECHNOLOGY AND LIFE IMPROVEMENT

By the turn of the twentieth century, "the technocratic idea of progress [had become] a belief in the sufficiency of scientific and technological innovation as the basis for general progress" (Marx, p. 9). This came to mean that if scientific-based technologies were permitted to develop in an unconstrained manner, there would be an automatic improvement in all other aspects of life! What happened--because this theory became coupled with onrushing, unbridled capitalism--was that the ideal envisioned by Thomas Jefferson in the United States had been turned upside down. Instead of social progress being guided by such values as justice, freedom, and self-fulfillment for all people, rich or poor, these goals of vital interest in a democracy were subjugated to a burgeoning society dominated by supposedly more important instrumental values (i.e., useful or practical ones for advancing a capitalistic system).

So the fundamental question still today is, "which type of values will win out in the long run?" In North America, for example, it seems that a gradually prevailing concept of cultural relativism was increasingly discredited as the 1990s witnessed a sharp clash between (1) those who uphold so-called Western cultural values and (2) those who by their presence are dividing the West along a multitude of ethnic and racial lines. This is occasioning strong efforts to promote fundamentalistic religions and sects--either those present historically or those recently imported--characterized typically by decisive right/wrong morality.

POSTMODERNISM AS AN INFLUENCE

The orientation and review of selected world, European, North American, regional, and local developments occurring in the final quarter of the 20th century might seem a bit out of place to some who read this book. It could be asked whether this has a relationship to the value system in place in America. My response to this question is a resounding "Yes." The affirmative answer is correct, also. if we listen to the voices of those in the minority within philosophy who are seeking to practice their profession, or promote their discipline. as if it had some connection to the world as it exists. I am referring here, for example to a philosopher like Richard Rorty (1997). He, as a so-called Neo-pragmatist, exhorts the presently "doomed Left" in North America to join the fray again. Their presumed shame should not be bolstered by a mistaken belief that only those who agree with the Marxist position that capitalism must be eradicated are "true Lefts." Rorty seems truly concerned that philosophy once again become characterized as a "search for wisdom," a search that seeks conscientiously and capably to answer the myriad of questions looming before humankind all over the world.

While most philosophers have been "elsewhere engaged," what has been called postmodernism has become a substantive factor in intellectual circles. I must confess up front that I've been grumbling about--and seeking to grapple with--the term "postmodern" for years. Somehow it has now become as bad (i.e., misunderstood or garbled) as existentialism, pragmatism, idealism, etc.). I confess, also, that I have now acquired a small library on the topic. At any rate, I recently read Crossing the Postmodern Divide by Albert Borgman (Chicago, 1992). I was so pleased to find something like this assessment of the situation. I say this because, time and again, I have encountered what I would characterize as gobbledygook describing what has been called "civilization's plight." By that I mean that what I encountered time and again was technical jargon, almost seemingly deliberate obfuscation by people seemingly trying to "fool the public" on this topic. As I see it, if it's worth saying, it must be said carefully and understandably. Otherwise one can't help but think that the writer is a somewhat confused person.

At any rate, in my opinion this effort by Borgman is solid, down-to-earth, and comprehensible up to the final two pages. At the point he veers to Roman Catholicism as the answer to the plight of moderns. It is his right, of course, to state his personal opinion after describing the current situation so accurately. However, if he could have brought himself to it, or if he had thought it might be possible, I would have preferred it if he had spelled out several alternative, yet still other desirable directions for humankind to go in the 21st century.

Is this modern epoch or era coming to an end? An epoch approaches closure when many of the fundamental convictions of its advocates are challenged by a substantive minority of the populace. It can be argued that indeed the world is moving into a new epoch as the proponents of postmodernism have been affirming over recent decades. Within such a milieu there are strong indications that all professions are going to have great difficulty crossing this so-called, postmodern gap (chasm, divide, whatever!). Scholars argue that many in democracies, undergirded by the various rights being propounded (e.g., individual freedom, privacy), have come to believe that they require a supportive "liberal consensus" within their respective societies.

Post-modernists now form a substantive minority that supports a more humanistic, pragmatic, liberal consensus in society. Within such a milieu there are strong indications that present-day society is going to have difficulty crossing the "designated," postmodern divide. Traditionalists in democratically oriented political systems may not like everything they see in front of them today, but as they look elsewhere they flinch even more. After reviewing where society has been, and where it is now, two more questions need to be answered. Where is society heading? And. most importantly, where should it be heading?

Some argue that Nietzsche's philosophy of being, knowledge, and morality supports the basic dichotomy espoused by the philosophy of being in the post-modernistic position. I can understand at once, therefore, why it meets with opposition by those whose thought has been supported by traditional theocentrism (i.e., in the final analysis, it is God "who calls the shots."). It can be argued, also, that many in democracies undergirded by the various rights being propounded (e.g., individual freedom, privacy) have come to believe--as stated above--that they require a supportive "liberal consensus." However, conservative, essentialist elements functioning in such political systems feel that the deeper foundation justifying this claim of a requisite, liberal consensus has been never been fully rationalized--keeping their more authoritative orientations in mind, of course. The foundation supporting the more humanistic, pragmatic, liberal consensus, as I understand it, is what may be called postmodernism by some.

Post-modernists subscribe largely to a humanistic, anthropocentric belief as opposed to the traditional theocentric position. They would subscribe, therefore, I think, to what Berelson and Steiner in the mid-1960's postulated as a behavioral science image of man and woman. This view characterized the human as a creature continuously adapting reality to his or her own ends.

Thus, the authority of theological positions, dogmas, ideologies, and some "scientific infallibilism" is severely challenged. A moderate post-modernist--holding a position I feel able to subscribe to once I am able to bring it all into focus--would at least listen to what the "authority" had written or said before criticizing or rejecting it. A strong post-modernist goes his or her own way by early, almost automatic, rejection of tradition. Then this person presumably relies on a personal interpretation and subsequent diagnosis to muster the authority to challenge any or all icons or "lesser gods" extant in society.

If the above is reasonably accurate, it would seem that a post-modernist might well feel more comfortable by seeking to achieve personal goals through a modified or semi-post-modernistic position as opposed to the traditional stifling position of essentialistic theological realists or idealists. A more pragmatic "value-is-that-which-is proven-through-experience" orientation leaves the future open-ended. Whatever your personal orientation may be, you will be faced with decisions of varying complexity that must be made every day of your life. One can theorize tentatively that current social forces (e.g., the many ongoing wars throughout the world in, the economic downturn (and "upturns") with their inevitable influence on education at all levels, and the "return to essentials" in much of the educational thought we are hearing) are effecting often debatable curricular changes in programs worldwide. But, in truth, how accurate is such conjecture? To get some feel for what was happening "out there," a decade ago I decided to contact individuals in the 33 countries represented in the membership list of the International Society for Comparative Physical Education and Sport. Each person was sent a pre-tested questionnaire designed to elicit answers to selected questions that would afford insight to the main problem of this investigation. By the very nature of this sample, no claim can be made in regard to the accuracy of the sum of the findings. However, the author reasoned that the responses obtained would "fortify" to a degree his personal theory on the question of global trends in physical education and educational sport. Before such a survey could be carried out, I undertook to examine the available periodical literature about the world situation and develop my own preliminary assessment of the prevailing situation internationally.

STATEMENT OF THE SURVEY'S MAIN PURPOSES

In essence, this investigation has two broad, main purposes: (1) to carry out a preliminary analysis of global trends in physical education and (educational) sport and (2) to make some recommendations regarding what the field should do in the immediate future. To accomplish this, it was decided to follow a sequence of sub-problems as follows: (1) to set the stage with a brief, general assessment of the international situation; (2) to obtain some specific reactions about what was happening in regard to physical education and educational sport in each of the 33 countries represented in the 1993 membership list of the ISCPES; (3) to consider the topic of futurology by offering one futuristic approach that has been recommended to cope with the "Great Transition" that the world has been undergoing; (4) keeping the possible, probable, and preferable futures, to offer my personal observations and understanding about how the greatly strengthened undergirding knowledge available to the profession of physical education and educational sport around the world might help in addressing the field's future; (5) to make some recommendations to cope with the "modifications" that the field has been undergoing during the past 30 years to effect improved professional development as the field looks somewhat hesitatingly looks to an indeterminate future; and (6) to delineate the basic considerations and strategy required to cope with the professional task ahead.

RESEARCH METHODS EMPLOYED

The investigation employed both historical method and broad descriptive methodology, as well as what may be called "philosophical assessment" as to field's current direction and immediate future. The broad-based historical analysis of the emerging international situation, based on secondhand literature, was followed by the employment of a descriptive questionnaire technique to gather the required data about the status of physical education and sport internationally. (A pre-tested questionnaire was specially designed for, and distributed to, one member selected from each of the 33 countries represented in the ISCPES membership.) Next, the greatly enlarged, undergirding body of knowledge available to the profession was reviewed to assess the field's "current strength" through a statement of "principal principles" that support the field's professional endeavor. Then one futuristic approach to the "world situation" was used a guide available to the profession for consideration as it faces an uncertain future. Next, a type of historical analysis was then carried out in regard to the numerous "modifications" that the profession has undergone in the past 30 years. Finally, by employing a type of "philosophical analysis," the necessary steps required to accomplish the professional task immediately were delineated and offered as recommendations for strategic professional action in the first quarter of the 21st century.

The difficulty of developing scientific hypotheses for an analysis of this type was recognized. Strictly speaking, hypotheses are statements about the relationship between variables. They also embody an understanding as to how such a relationship may be established (i.e., substantive hypotheses are transposed to [null] hypotheses for statistical testing, for example). For example, it was simply not possible in my present circumstance as a retired person with no university financial support to contact even every member of the ISCPES. Also, this relatively small membership group does not qualify as a "world sampling," so to speak. Further, I had to be satisfied with a 60% response (20 out of 33 questionnaires sent were returned). Advice was sought in this regard from Prof. E. Ebanks (an authority on research design and statistics in the Dept. of Sociology, The University of Western Ontario), who recommended that "what I had" was quite simply the opinion about the status of physical education and educational sport from one professionally minded person in 20 of the 33 countries surveyed. Fortunately, the people who responded were representative of countries widely dispersed in all parts of the world, and they made a sincere effort to respond to the questions raised.

With the exploratory survey phase of this study, it was decided that these "status" subproblems could simply be phrased as questions. Then, using simple descriptive statistics with the results expressed in categories relating to percentage values determined, the data gathered were numerically tabulated, and the responses were summarized by percentage values based on the predetermined questions. The results from each question asked were followed immediately by related discussion to each question asked. With several questions it was possible to double up with the responses (e.g., No. 13 and No. 14 that were closely related). With certain questions, because of the type and information sought, agreement was arbitrarily indicated as follows: *SUBSTANTIAL MAJORITY* (75%-100%), *MAJORITY* (50%-75%), *SUBSTANTIAL MINORITY* (25%-50%), and *INSUBSTANTIAL MINORITY* (0%-25%).

FINDINGS FROM SUBPROBLEMS INCLUDED: PRESENTED SEQUENTIALLY (INCLUDING DISCUSSION WHERE APPROPRIATE)

The Present International Situation. Before reporting the limited findings about the status of physical education and educational sport in selected world countries, the present international scene was summarized in the first section of this chapter. Humankind's rapid progress in science and technology in the 20th century, and people's retrogression, or dubious progress at best, in the realm of social affairs, have forced intelligent men and women everywhere to take stock. It may well be impossible to gain objectivity or true historical perspective on the rapid change that is taking place. Today, a seemingly unprecedented burden has been imposed on people's understanding of themselves and their world. Many leaders must certainly be wondering whether "the whole affair can be managed."

You will recall that, at the beginning of this discussion about social affairs, I told how I understood that our profession was fighting an uphill struggle when I entered the field 65 years ago. Well, as we understand from the work of scholars in several disciplines, progress is never a straight-line affair. The pendulum does indeed swing to the right and the left and never seems to stop in the middle. So now, as I am of necessity winding down my years in the field, physical education-- and art and music too--are still facing a severe, uphill struggle. Where physical education, for example, once was a required subject in North America (e.g., for three and one-half years when I went to college), it is now often fighting to remain as an elective offering at many schools, colleges, and universities in various states and provinces in North America. Additionally, where physical education may be scheduled, the important aspects of health education (e.g., AIDS, drugs, and smoking) are encroaching on the already limited time given over to physical activity within the class period. Fortunately, the presence of a physical education requirement is at least present in 16 of the countries included in the present survey.

To single out the United States specifically, the NASPE News of AAHPERD's National Association for Sport and Physical Education released its "Latest Shape of the Nation Report" in which it is explained that "three years after our federal government established daily physical education for all students in kindergarten through grade 12 as a physical activity and fitness goal of Healthy People 2000, Illinois remains the only state requiring daily physical education for all students, K-12" (Winter 1994, 1, 14). In this same issue of the newsletter, another article titled "Experts Release New Recommendations to Fight America's Epidemic of Physical Inactivity" highlights a new updated recommendation from the American College of Sports Medicine (p. 7). It is interesting that the publication of this information was necessary just at the time that we now have the evidence that, in addition to enabling a person to live life more fully, steady involvement in the right kind of developmental physical activity throughout life will also help a person to live longer.

FINDINGS FROM QUESTIONS ASKED (I.E., SUBPROBLEMS)

1. Everything considered, do you feel that the physical education program in your country, generally speaking, has improved during the 1980s?

Results: A *MAJORITY* believed that the physical education program, generally speaking, had improved in the 1980s (13 or 65% = 50%-75% grouping).

Discussion: In a way this was a surprising but encouraging finding to the investigator whose thinking was undoubtedly influenced by the North American scene. Of course, in some instances the status may have been quite low, and the status simply improved.

2. To the best of your knowledge, has the actual physical fitness of students in schools improved or declined or "stayed the same" in the past decade?

Results: A *SUBSTANTIAL MINORITY* believed the level of physical fitness had declined in the 1980s (8 or 40% = 25%-50% grouping).

Discussion: Note that 5 or 25% believed that the level of physical fitness had improved, whereas 5 or 25% felt that it had stayed about the same. Two respondents were not able to form a judgment.

3. What name (or names?) is currently assigned to our field (the subject-matter) in your country's schools, colleges, and universities?

Results: A *SUBSTANTIAL MAJORITY* use the name physical education at the school level (20 or 100% = 75%-100% grouping). A *MAJORITY* have not made a name change at the university (13 or 65% = 60%-75% grouping).

Discussion: Name changes have been made at the university level during the past 10 years in those institutions where the units are striving for academic status in a competitive environment. In the U.S.A., at last count, more than 150 different names have been introduced at the college & university level.

4. Is physical education a requirement in your country's schools?

Results: Physical education is required in a *SUBSTANTIAL MAJORITY* of countries (17 or 85% = 75%-100% grouping. The requirement ranges from a low of three (3) years to a high of 14 yrs.

Discussion: Only four (of the 20) countries that responded have no national requirement in physical education: Canada, India, Malawi, and the United States of America.

5. In your schools is competitive sport included under physical education, or is it separate?

Results: Competitive sport of varying "intensity" is considered to be part of the overall physical education program in a *MAJORITY* of the schools (11 or 55% = 50%-75% grouping). It is considered extra-curricular in a *SUBSTANTIAL MINORITY* of countries (9 or 45% = 25%-50% grouping).

Discussion: It is not clear in this instance to what extent competitive sport is regarded as a "educational experience" in the same way as what is typically called physical education. At any rate, this matter has not been resolved yet for a variety of reasons. It is certain that in all countries competitive sport is available outside of of the school authority through one of a number of private, semi-public, and public agencies.

6. Where are physical education and organized sport located administratively in your country (e.g., to a national ministry)?

Results: Physical education comes under the jurisdiction of a national ministry in a *MAJORITY* of the countries surveyed (14 or 70% = 50%-75% grouping). Organized sport is considered sufficiently important in a *MAJORITY* of the countries to report to a national ministry (12 or 60% = 50%-75% grouping). In six countries physical education is considered an aspect of education, education being the responsibility of a state or province within a country.

Discussion: The location of organized sport within governmental frameworks does not appear to follow any definite pattern. Physical education, on the other hand, is always located within the governmental bureau concerned with education of the populace (i.e. an office or bureau of education in the capital of the country concerned.

7. Does physical education count for credit as a course experience toward a diploma or degree in schools, colleges, or university (excluding a diploma or degree in physical education)?

Results: Physical education does count for credit in a *MAJORITY* of the countries surveyed (14 or 70% = 50%-75% grouping).

Discussion The results here are blurred, because there is a great range in the academic credit granted--that is, from no credit in 7 countries to full acceptance as a tertiary entrance subject in a number of Australian states. Underlying this whole issue, of course, is the question of whether the physical education course experience and subsequent grade awarded--especially in those instances when there is no theoretical component included in the grade allotted--should be averaged in with other course grades to determine a GPA (overall grade-point average).

8. What are the basic areas or activities generally included (e.g. fitness activities, sport skills, rhythmic activities) in this subject matter at the *ELEMENTARY, MIDDLE, HIGH SCHOOL,* and *UNIVERSITY* levels (excepting those included in the physical education degree or diploma program, of course)?

Results: It is not possible to classify the responses given to this question by each of the 20 respondents. However, a few generalizations are possible:

(a) Generally speaking, The curriculum and instructional methodology are fairly standardized from country to country. Note: It is not possible without first-hand study to make any comparative assessment between or among countries.
(b) Fundamental movement skills and games of low organization are standard at the elementary-school level
(c) Sports skills instruction and fitness activities are introduced gradually at the middle-school level and continued on through the high school level on either a required or elective basis
(d) A theoretical component in instructional programs is almost completely lacking (except in a few countries in specific states or provinces)
(e) Lifetime sport and physical recreation instruction is often offered in the upper high-school years
(f) Extramural competitive sport within education is offered only in Canada, Japan, Nigeria, and the U.S.A.
(g) University programs, where offered, are largely elective and typically include voluntary sport and physical recreation and fitness-oriented activities. (A few countries (Israel, Philippines, Slovakia, and in a rela-few universities in the U.S.A.) have a one- or two-year requirement)

9. Is there any highly unusual or unique aspect in your country's physical

education curriculum or instructional methodology?

Results: The respondents were almost unanimous in affirming that there was nothing "highly unusual or unique" in their countries' physical education curriculum or instructional methodology.

Discussion: This is a disturbing finding. For recognition it seems evident that the introduction of more theoretical material is necessary to provide undergirding for the skills instructional program. Australia and Canada report that in certain states or provinces highly sophisticated theory courses using texts have been introduced in the upper-level, high-school courses, the results of which are fully credited for university entrance. Also, Japan has been making extensive use of video cameras to provide sport-skill feedback to students at the high-school level.

10. What is your assessment of the present, overall status of the subject of physical education in relation to other curricular subjects within the field of education in your country (i.e., higher, lower, about the same level)? Please describe, also, any present strengths, weaknesses, and your estimate of what physical education's status will be 10 years from now?

Results:

(a) The present status of physical education was rated lower than other subjects in the curriculum by a *SUBSTANTIAL MAJORITY* (i.e., almost unanimously--18 or 90% = 75%=100% grouping). In two countries (Nigeria, Taiwan), the respondents believed that physical education's status was equal.

(b) As to the future (i.e., 10 yrs. from now) status of physical education, a *MAJORITY* (12 or 60% = 50%-75% grouping) believe that the status will be better. Four respondents (20%) believe that PE's status will be about the same, and four respondents (20%) feel that the status will be worse.

Note: The four countries where the respondents felt that PE's status would be worse are Canada, England, Israel, and the U.S.A.

(c) Special open-ended comments from certain respondents were as follows:

- In six countries, the respondents believed that physical activity's contribution to health status would help the field to gain more recognition for its contribution

- In three countries, the respondent felt that improved teacher preparation was needed

- In two countries (Canada and the U.S.A.), legislation had served to improve the level of adapted physical education provided significantly.

- In one country (Australia) a recent national conference report about the prevailing situation has brought improvement to the field.

CONCLUDING STATEMENT

In this chapter an effort was made initially to present an overview of the developing world situation in what has been called the postmodern age. After having achieved some perspective in relation to the global situation, the North American development was considered more specifically. This was followed by a presentation of the findings from a limited worldwide survey of the prevailing situation in physical education and educational sport.

NOTE

1. The results of this (delimited) world survey were presented as an invited paper to the 10th Commonwealth & International Scientific Congress, Univ. of Victoria, Brit. Col., Canada, August 13, 1994. A few words and tenses have been changed here and there.

CHAPTER XII

LOOKING TO THE FUTURE

ORIENTATION TO THE FUTURE
OF THE PROFESSION

In this final chapter you will be offered information and ideas from a more general social perspective, and also possibly in a more normatively philosophical manner, than what you might expect to read in a history text. There is no doubt that what we call "sport and physical education" within the National Association for Sport and Physical Education within the American Alliance for Health, Physical Education, Recreation, and Dance has been undergoing modification--if we want to use such a neutral term. For example, there are now four allied professions within the AAHPERD, not to mention several other associations and academies, as well as a number of extremely loosely related "outside" societies of a disciplinary nature. (A close colleague--an outstanding physical educator and scientist!--told me recently that he felt that we had become "so splintered" that he felt we were simply spinning off centripetally in the direction of eventual "nothingness." I fervently hope that such a prediction doesn't turn out to be true!) The modification of the past 60 years or so occurred to a certain extent, of course, because of the impact of the various social forces that we have discussed, but also because of our many sins of omission and commission.

The situation in physical education and educational sport in educational institutions globally may well continue to deteriorate in the years immediately ahead. Education is literally reeling at present because of increases in certain negative social forces caused by a changing social environment. However, because of what is now known about the potential beneficial effects that properly conceived developmental physical activity in exercise, sport, and related expressive movement can have on people of all ages and conditions, we should not--we dare not--as a profession become pessimistic about the wisdom of striving to create a social situation in which the salutary effects of appropriate developmental physical activity will be introduced into people's lives. However, humankind's needs will be met if-- and only if--(1) public support for our efforts is earned and (2) highly trained leadership is made available to earn such public support and then to bring about these desirable educational and developmental outcomes.

As professionals, we already have a good understanding of the effects of physical activity as demonstrated by the steadily improving quantitative and qualitative, natural-science type of investigation that has been carried out over the past 50 years. However, I firmly believe, also, that a full understanding of our endeavor as developmental physical activity professionals can only become possible through an ever-greater and stronger understanding of how the social sciences and the humanities can also influence our work as well. Obviously, the bio-science aspects of developmental physical activity are highly important, but people need to understand also that in the final analysis a more balanced, across-the-board approach to scholarly investigation is required to help us achieve the field's true potential in the service of humankind.

Also, the concept of "growth and development" has been well understood and applied for decades in the field of physical education and sport. This perception is accordingly transferable to the process of growth and development that usually occurs throughout the life of a person working in the field as well. My generation of physical educators and coaches was typically optimistic about the future despite the strong social forces and accompanying persistent professional problems that have influenced physical education and educational sport from decade to decade down through the 20th century. As I see it, my generation and the "baby boomer's generation" too have an obligation to pass on as much of that optimism as possible to "Generation X" (and whatever comes next) as this age group strives with considerable difficulty to become a legitimate partner in our profession for the first quarter of the 21st century at least. I will try to explain how and why this can be done in this chapter.

After this introductory section, the following topics phrased as questions will be considered: (1) to what extent is it possible to forecast the future? (2) what should we avoid on the way to the 21st century? (3) what do we believe we know (i.e., the underlying knowledge needed to practice as professionals)?, (4) what should we do (literally!) as we look to the future? and, finally, (5), what do all of these interpretations and assertions mean for the professional task that lies ahead of us?

FORECASTING THE FUTURE

As we begin, I must state initially that I believe that our optimism in regard to automatic progress has blinded us so we have not been able to truly comprehend how such unrealistic expectations came about. Within this vortex of social forces and professional concerns, I have been searching for some guidance to the profession as we look to the future. Thinking back a bit, we can recall the words of Heilbroner when he postulated that, "The problem then. . .is to respond to the technological, political, and economic forces which are bringing about a closing of our historic future" (1960, p. 178). He was arguing that we could only cope with this most difficult, present period by changing our "structure of power" and also the very "common denominator of values"--two developments for which he did not hold out much hope in the immediate future. He was correct in his assessment. We had all realized that the 1970s were going to be difficult years; that there were great ecological problems to be overcome; that there was a worldwide nutritional problem; that the present energy situation had lulled us in relation to a crisis of enormous proportions that will develop in the future; and that the tide of rising expectations of the underdeveloped nations would somehow need to be met. However, and this is the crucial point, we had still not fully awakened to the fact that history is actually going against us in North America and will continue to do so for some time. Naturally, it would not make sense to expect our presidents in America to be pessimists, but on the other hand "optimism as a philosophy of historic expectations can no longer be considered a national virtue. It has become a dangerous national delusion" (Heilbroner, 1960, p. 178). We simply have to learn that the unique quality of the American experience can't be adapted to all historic experience--now and in the future.

If the tide has seemed to turn against us in regard to world opinion, for example, we must ask ourselves a disturbing question: "What happened?" Then, as responsible professionals, we must search for the missing attributes that have somehow been lacking in recent decades. Heilbroner's analysis offers three missing attributes for consideration. The first is history's inertia, a fact that is typically overlooked as a determining "force" in history because it is so dull and unobtrusive. Humans have a very long history of being almost unbelievably resistant to change-- whether it be for good or bad. Second, we find that the philosophy of optimism has another missing attribute that has caused difficulty down through the ages. This we may characterize as the human's seeming inherent unwillingness to assess present status in a truly realistic manner--and then to make a positive effort to improve the situation! And, if our society is not willing to act now to rectify life's innumerable injustices at home and abroad, it can only be hoped that others less privileged here and elsewhere will be willing to bide their time as the "haves" move ever so slowly to help the "have-nots." But to hope that slow steps toward improvement will be taken without violence and great suffering is not realistic. We can only feel some sense of sorrow for life's tragic victims who are seemingly selected at random.

Finally, the third aspect of history that seemingly works to confound a philosophy of optimism is the "ambiguity of events" (1960, pp. 201-204). Heilbroner stresses here the sociological dictum that "progress is never a straight-line affair upward." Somehow progress in any aspect of life has never been a simple matter of heaping one success upon another until utopia is indubitably within our grasp. (Recall that a definition of utopia is "that desired place or state of affairs, the next step toward which we cannot presently envision".) This dialectic of history, as it was designated by Marx and Hegel, will not cease when an ideal state of communism is achieved (as Marx believed quite naively).

The "grand dynamic of history" as it is occurring today makes it almost presumptuous to speak about the dignity of the individual (1960, p. 205), but we simply can't give up hope that such a state may be realizable in the future after the difficult period ahead. We in America can't retreat to a state of defiant isolation in regard to the rest of the world and thereby lose our capacity to serve as resource persons and helpers. In the process we must recognize further that we won't be calling the shots as some of our leaders still think we are entitled to do. The question is whether we will have the patience and the good will to live within history, to be fully aware of it, to bear somewhat more than our fair share of the burden ("Ay, there's the rub"), and to maintain our integrity as we strive for the ideal, long-range goals of human freedom and dignity that we cherish.

What I have been writing about relates actually to getting in league with the future, so to speak. This can initially be carried out best, I presume, by making a sincere, solid effort to understand what futuristics or futurology is all about. From there one could take the next step and apply these findings to one aspect of our lives--in this case, the possible future of the profession of sport and physical education. Here, then, I will turn first for some guidance to *Visions of the Future*, a publication of the well-known Hudson Institute. Initially, we are urged to tailor our thinking to three ways of looking at the future: (a) the possible future, (b) the probable future, and (c) the preferable future (Melnick, 1984, p. 4).

As you might imagine, the possible future includes everything that could happen, and thus perceptions of the future must be formed by us individually and collectively. The probable future refers to occurrences that are likely to happen, and here the range of alternatives must be considered. Finally, the preferable future relates to an approach whereby people make choices, thereby indicating how they would like things to happen. Underlying all of this are certain basic assumptions or premises such as (1) that the future hasn't been predetermined by some force or power; (2) that the future cannot be accurately predicted because we don't understand the process of change that fully; and (3) that the future will undoubtedly be influenced by choices that people make, but won't necessarily turn out the way they want it to be (Amara, 1981).

As we all appreciate, people have been predicting the future for thousands of years, undoubtedly with a limited degree of success. Considerable headway has been made, of course, since the time when animal entrails were examined to provide insight about the future (one of the techniques of divination). Nowadays, for example, methods of prediction include forecasting by the use of trends and statistics. One of the most recent approaches along these lines has been of great interest to me. I have been using a variation of this technique for more than 30 years with a persistent problems approach (originated by John S. Brubacher) leading to the analysis of our field (Zeigler, 1964, 1968, 1977, 1979, 2003, and now in this text). Here I am referring to the work of John Naisbitt and The Naisbitt Group as described in *Megatrends*. These people believe that "the most reliable way to anticipate the future is by understanding the present" (1982, p. 2). Hence they monitor occurrences all over the world through a technique of descriptive method known as content analysis. They actually monitor the amount of space given to various topics in newspapers--an approach they feel is valid because "the news-reporting process is forced choice in a closed system" (p. 4).

Melnick and associates, in *Visions of the Future* (1984), discuss a further aspect of futuristics--the question of "levels of certainty." They explain that the late Herman Kahn, an expert in this area, often used the term "Scotch Verdict" when he was concerned about the level of certainty available before making a decision. This idea was borrowed from the Scottish system of justice in which a person charged with the commission of a crime can be found "guilty," "not guilty," or "not been proven guilty." This "not been proven guilty" (or "Scotch") verdict implies there is enough evidence to demonstrate that the person charged is guilty, but that insufficient evidence has been presented to end all reasonable doubt about the matter. Hence a continuum has been developed at one end of which we can state we are 100 percent sure that such-and-such is not true. Accordingly, at the other end of the continuum we can state we are 100 percent sure that such-and-such is the case (pp. 6-7). Obviously, in between these two extremes are gradations of the level of certainty. From here this idea has been carried over to the realm of future forecasting.

Next we are exhorted to consider the "Great Transition" that humankind has been experiencing, how there has been a pre-industrial stage, an industrial stage and, finally, a post-industrial stage that appears to be arriving in North America first. Each of the stages has its characteristics that must be recognized. For example, in pre-industrial society there was slow population growth, people lived simply with very little money, and the forces of nature made life very difficult. When the industrial stage or so-called modernization entered the picture, population growth was rapid, wealth increased enormously, and people became increasingly less vulnerable to the destructive forces of nature. The assumption here is that comprehension of the transition that is occurring can give us some insight as to what the future might hold--not that we can be "100 percent sure," but at least we might be able to achieve a "Scotch Verdict" (p. 47). If North America is that part of the world that is the most economically and technologically advanced, and as a result will complete the Great Transition by becoming a post-industrial culture, than we must be aware of what this will mean to our society. Melnick explains that we have probably already entered a "super-industrial period" of the Industrial Stage in which "projects will be very large scale, services will be readily available, efficient and sophisticated, people will have vastly increased leisure time, and many new technologies will be created" (pp. 35-37).

It is important that we understand what is happening as we move further forward into what presumably is the final or third stage of the Great Transition. First, it should be made clear that the level of certainty here in regard to predictions is at Kahn's "Scotch Verdict" point on the continuum. The world has never faced this situation before, so we don't know exactly how to date the beginning of such a stage. Nevertheless, it seems to be taking place right now (the super-industrial period having started after World War II). As predicted, those developments mentioned above (e.g., services readily available) appear to be continuing. It is postulated that population growth is slower than it was 20 years ago, yet it is true that people are living longer. Next it is estimated that a greater interdependence among nations and the steady development of new technologies will contribute to a steadily improving economic climate for underdeveloped nations. Finally, it is forecast that advances in science and accompanying technology will bring almost innumerable technologies to the fore that will affect lifestyles immeasurably all over the world.

This discussion could continue almost indefinitely, but the important points to be made here are emerging rapidly. First, we need a different way of looking at the subject of so-called natural resources. In this interdependent world, this "global village" if you will, natural resources are more than just the sum of raw materials.

They include also the application of technology, the organizational bureaucracy to cope with the materials, and the resultant usefulness of the resource that creates supply and demand (p. 74). The point seems to be that the total resource picture (as explained here) is reasonably optimistic if correct decisions are made about raw materials, energy, food production, and use of the environment. These are admittedly rather large "ifs" (Melnick, pp. 73-97).

Finally in any attempt to forecast the future, the need to understand global problems of two types is stressed. One group is called "mostly understandable problems," and they are solvable. Here reference is made to (a) population growth, (b) natural resource issues, (c) acceptable environmental health, (d) shift in society's economic base to service occupations, and (e) effect of advanced technology. However, there is a second group classified as "mostly uncertain problems," and these are the problems that could bring on disaster. First, the Great Transition is affecting the entire world, and the eventual outcome of this new type of cultural change is uncertain. Thus we must be ready for these developments attitudinally. Second, in this period of changing values and attitudes, people in the various countries and cultures have much to learn and they will have to make great adjustments as well. Third, there is the danger that society will--possibly unwittingly--stumble into some irreversible environmental catastrophe (e.g., upper-atmosphere ozone depletion). Fourth, the whole problem of weapons, wars, and terrorism, and whether the world will be able to stave off all-out nuclear warfare. Fifth, and finally, whether bad luck and bad management will somehow block the entire world from undergoing the Great Transition successfully--obviously a great argument for the development of management art and science (pp. 124-129).

WHAT SHOULD WE AVOID?

We have considered the question of "future forecasting" briefly. Keeping the the present worldwide and North American situation in physical education and educational sport in mind, it would be logical at this point to recommend what we should do in the years immediately ahead. However, just before we do that, we should undoubtedly give brief consideration to the question of what to avoid along this path (adapted from Zeigler in Welsh, 1977, pp. 58-59). First, there is evidence to suggest that we must maintain a certain flexibility in philosophical approach. This will be difficult for some who have worked out definite, explicit philosophic stances for themselves--especially those people who have positions that are extreme either to the right or left. For those who are struggling along with only an implicit sense of life (as defined by Rand, 1960), having philosophic flexibility may be even more difficult--they don't fully understand where they are "coming from!" All of us know people for whom Toffler's concepts of "future shock" (1970) and "third wave world" (1980) have become a reality. Life has indeed become stressful for these individuals.

Second, I believe that we as individuals must avoid what might be called "naive optimism" or "despairing pessimism" in the years ahead. What we should assume, I believe, is a philosophical stance that may be called "positive meliorism'-- a position that assumes that we should strive consciously to bring about a steady improvement in the quality of our lives. This second "what to avoid" item is closely related to the recommendation above concerning flexibility in philosophical approach, of course. We can't forget, however, how easy it is to fall into the seemingly attractive traps of either blind pessimism or optimism.

Third, I believe the professional in physical education and (educational) sport should continue to strive for "just the right amount" of freedom in his or her life generally and in professional affairs as well. Freedom for the individual is a fundamental characteristic of a democratic state, but it must never be forgotten that such freedom as may prevail in all countries today had to be won "inch by inch." It is evidently in the nature of the human animal that there are always those in our midst who "know what is best for us," and who seem anxious to take hard-won freedoms away. This seems to be true whether crises exist or not. Of course, the concept of "individual freedom" cannot be stretched to include anarchy; however, the freedom to teach responsibly what we will in physical education and sport, or conversely the freedom to learn what one will in such a process, must be guarded almost fanatically.

A fourth pitfall in this matter of avoidance along the way is the possibility of the development of undue influence of certain negative aspects inherent in the various social forces capable of influencing our culture and everything within it (including, of course, physical education and sport itself). Consider the phenomenon of nationalism and how an overemphasis in this direction can soon destroy a desirable world posture or even bring about unconscionable isolationism. Another example of a "negative" social force that is not understood generally is the seeming clash between capitalistic economic theory and the environmental crisis that has developed. The world must not proceed indefinitely with the idea that "bigger" is necessarily "better."

Fifth, moving back to the realm of education, we should be careful that our field doesn't contribute to what has consistently been identified as a fundamental anti-intellectualism (e.g., a coach mouthing ungrammatical platitudes). On the other hand, "intelligence or intellectualism for its own sake" is far being being the answer to our problems. As long ago as 1961, Brubacher asked for the "golden mean" between the cultivation of the intellect and the cultivation of a high degree of intelligence because it is need as "an instrument of survival" in the Deweyan sense (pp. 7-9).

Sixth, and finally, despite the continuing cry for a "return to essentials"--and I am not for a moment suggesting that Johnny or Mary shouldn't know how to read or calculate mathematically--we should avoid imposing a narrow academic approach on students in a misguided effort to promote the pursuit of excellence. I am continually both amazed and discouraged by decisions concerning admission to undergraduate physical education programs made solely on the basis of numerical grades, in essence a narrowly defined academic proficiency. Don't throw out academic proficiency testing, of course, but by all means broaden the evaluation made of candidates by assessing other dimensions of excellence they may have! Here, in addition to ability in human motor performance, I include such aspects as "sensitivity and commitment to social responsibility, ability to adapt to new situations, characteristics of temperament and work habit under varying conditions of demand," and other such characteristics and traits as recommended so long ago by the Commission on Tests of the College Entrance Examination Board (*The New York Times*, Nov. 2, 1970)

WHAT DO WE KNOW?
(AN ASSESSMENT OF THE PROFESSION'S PRESENT BODY OF KNOWLEDGE)

A third objective of this chapter is a brief summary of the status of our field's ever-increasing body of knowledge as it effects developmental physical activity in the lives of people of all ages and conditions. Professionals in the field are gradually, but steadily, being overwhelmed by periodical literature, monographs, books, texts, and conference proceedings. Much of this is interesting and valuable, but it is often not geared to our individual professional and disciplinary interests. This knowledge explosion is also occurring in allied professions and related disciplines with knowledge often overlapping some of our findings. Further, and of serious concern, much material available is either unintelligible or unavailable to the general public on whose behalf we are presumably carrying out our work.

To make matters worse, we as individual professionals and scholars are often missing out on important findings published originally in languages other than our own that happens to be English (e.g., German, Russian, Japanese, Finnish--just to mention a few in which scholarly work is being reported regularly). The result is that we simply do not know where we stand in regard to the steadily developing body of knowledge in the many sub-disciplinary and sub-professional aspects of developmental physical activity in exercise, sport, and related expressive movement. Nowhere do we have an inventory of scientific findings arranged as ordered generalizations to help us in our work as professional practitioners, be it as teacher, coach, scholar, researcher, administrator. This deficiency must be rectified on a local, regional, national, hemispheric, and worldwide basis! To give an indication of what we are missing typically, in this third section of this paper, I will offer 13 "principal principles" that research evidence of recent decades has made available for practicing professionals. This concise summary of our field's "principal principles" at this time may surprise the reader.

Keeping in mind what was reported in Chapter 11 as to the worldwide status of physical education and sport, and before discussing the changes or modifications that have occurred in the past 30 years in the field, permit me to offer a succinct assessment of the significant increase that has taken place in the body of knowledge undergirding our professional task. First, permit me to refer to a now historical statement made on December 28, 1951. Speaking at the general session of the former College Physical Education Association in Chicago, Illinois, the late, eminent Arthur H. Steinhaus, M.D. of George Williams College, Chicago, with "many misgivings," offered what he called the four "principal principles" of physical education to the profession (1952). As he explained, the term "principal principles can and does mean the most important or chief fundamental theories, ideas, or generalizations" (p. 5).

This effort preceded the approach taken in "The Contributions of Physical Activity to Human Well-Being," a supplement to the *Research Quarterly* in May, 1960. There, as explained by Dr. Raymond Weiss, a highly regarded professor at New York University, a joint effort was made by scholars in the allied professions to present evidence that physical activity can indeed contribute to human well-being (Foreword). These scholarly professionals were stating to the best of their ability what we really knew and what we were close to knowing at that time.

As we in physical education and sport have passed the now almost mythical year 2000, we can affirm with considerable assurance that our steadily growing body of knowledge has provided our profession with a more substantive knowledge base than existed at the middle of the 20th century. In addition to the "principal principles" listed by Professor Steinhaus, with reasonable assurance resulting from consistent data analysis over the years, I am now suggesting that physical education's principal principles have increased in number from four to thirteen! Building on the work of Steinhaus and others since that time, these recommended principles will be listed below.

It is perhaps pointless to attempt to determine precisely to what extent this increase can be attributed more to the efforts of the profession's natural science scholars than to those of the more recently added social science and humanities scholars. Also, we must not forget the contributions emanating steadily from our allied professions and related disciplines. That there is some overlap in "what we believe we now know" seems obvious, but this increase in the number of principal principles points to the wisdom of searching for evidence wherever it is to be found from whatever discipline.

In concluding his now historical proclamation in 1951, Steinhaus summarized as follows:

1. The principle of overload charters physical education as a unique force in the growth and development of man;
2. The principle of reversibility discloses the fleeting effect and dictates its practice at every age;
3. The principle of integration and integrity raises physical education to the human level and governs its contribution to mental strength and morality; and
4. The principle of the priority of man makes of physical education a socially useful servant, possessed of capacity to produce a better generation (p. 10).

> **Note**: In the 13 principal principles formulated below, Steinhaus' principles are included; note, however, that his "principle of integration and integrity" has been divided in two thereby creating two separate principles. (In passing, I believe we should all express sincere appreciation to the many scientists and scholars--within our field, the allied professions, and the related disciplines--whose efforts have made the following statement of these 13 principal

principles possible at this time.)

Principle 1: The "Reversibility Principle". The first principle affirms that circulo-respiratory (often called cardio-vascular) conditioning is inherently reversible in the human body; a male, for example, typically reaches his peak at age 19 and goes downhill gradually thereafter until eventual death. This means that you must achieve and maintain at least an "irreducible level" of such conditioning to live normally.

Principle 2: The "Overload Principle". The principle here is that a muscle or muscle group must be taxed beyond that to which it is accustomed, or it won't develop; in fact, it will probably retrogress. Thus, a human must maintain reasonable muscular strength in his/her body to carry out life's normal duties and responsibilities and to protect the body from deterioration.

Principle 3: The "Flexibility Principle". This principle states that a human must put the body's various joints through the range of motion for which they are intended. Inactive joints become increasingly inflexible until immobility sets in. If inflexibility is a sign of old age, the evidence shows that most people are becoming old about age 27! Maintenance of flexibility in body's joint must not be neglected.

Principle 4: The "Bone Density Principle". This principles asserts that developmental physical activity throughout life preserves the density of a human's bones. The density of human bones after maturity is not fixed or permanent, and the decline after age 35 could be more rapid than is the case with fat and muscle. After prolonged inactivity, adequate calcium in your diet and weight-bearing physical activity is absolutely essential for the preservation of your bones. Remember that prevention of bone loss is much more effective than later efforts to repair any bone damage that might have been incurred.

Principle 5: The "Gravity Principle". This principle explains that maintaining muscle-group strength throughout life, while standing or sitting, helps the human fight against the force of gravity that is working continually to break down the body's structure. Maintaining muscle group strength and tonus and the best possible structural alignment of one's bones through the development of a proper "body consciousness" will help a person to fight off gravity's potentially devastating effects as long as possible.

Principle 6: The "Relaxation Principle". Principle 6 states that the skill of relaxation is one that people must acquire in today's increasingly complex world. Oddly enough, people often need to be taught how to relax in today's typically stressful environment. Part of any "total fitness" package should, therefore, be the development of an understanding as to how an individual can avoid chronic or abnormal fatigue in a social and physical environment that is often overly taxing.

Principle 7: The "Aesthetic Principle". This principle explains that a person has either an innate or culturally determined need to "look good" to himself/herself and to others. Socrates is purported to have decried "growing old without appreciating the beauty of which the body is capable." This is evidently a "need" to make a good appearance to one's family, friends, and those who one meets daily at work or during leisure. Billions of dollars are spent annually by people striving to "make themselves look like something they are not" naturally. Why do people do this? Quite probably, they go through these "body rituals" to please themselves and because of various social pressures. Thus, if one is physically active, while following the above six principles, one's appearance can be improved normally, naturally, and inexpensively.

Principle 8: The "Integration Principle". Principle 8 asserts that developmental physical activity provides an opportunity for the individual to get "fully involved" as a living organism. So many of life's activities only challenge a person fractionally in that only part of the individual's sensory equipment and even less of the motor mechanism are involved. By their very nature, physical activities in exercise, sport, play, and expressive movement demand full attention from the organism--often in the face of opposition--and therefore involve complete psycho-physical integration.

Principle 9: The "Integrity Principle". The "integrity principle" goes hand in hand with desirable integration of the human's various aspects [so-called unity of body and mind in the organism explained in Principle 8 immediately above]. The idea of integrity implies that a completely integrated psycho-physical activity should correspond *ETHICALLY* with the avowed ideals and standards of society. Fair play, honesty, and concern for others should be uppermost in one's individual pattern of developmental physical activity.

Principle 10: The "Priority of the Person Principle". Principle 10 affirms that any physical activity in sport, play, and exercise sponsored through public or private agencies should be conducted in such a way that the welfare of the individual comes first. Situations arise daily in all aspects of social living where this principle--stressing the sanctity of the individual--is often forgotten. In a democratic society, a man or woman, or boy or girl, should never be forced or encouraged to take part in some type of developmental physical activity where this principle is negated because of the desire of others to win. The wholeness of one's personal life is more important than any sport in which an individual may take part. Sport must serve as a "social servant."

Principle 11: The "Live Life to Its Fullest Principle". This principle explains that, viewed in one sense, human movement is what distinguishes the individual from the rock on the ground. Unless the body is moved with reasonable vigor according to principles 1-6 above, it will not serve a person best throughout life by helping a person to meet the normal daily tasks and the unexpected sudden demands that may be required to take advantage of life's many opportunities or to protect a person from harm.

Principle 12: The "Fun and Pleasure Principle". Principle 12 states that the human is normally a "seeker of fun and pleasure," and that a great deal of the opportunity for such enjoyment can be derived from full, active bodily movement. The physical education profession stresses that the opportunity for such fun and pleasure will be missing from life if a person does not maintain at least an "irreducible minimum" level of physical fitness.

Principle 13: The "Longevity Principle". This final principle affirms that regular developmental physical activity throughout life can help a person live longer. The statistical evidence is mounting that demonstrates the wisdom of maintaining an active lifestyle throughout one's years. Succinctly put, all things being equal, if a human is physically active, he or she will live longer (Zeigler, 1994c)

GETTING "IN LEAGUE THE FUTURE"

So "What is the problem?" you might ask. "If we indeed have made so much headway in the development of our body of knowledge, admittedly with significant help also from the efforts of those in our allied professions and related disciplines, why can't we just 'get on with it'?" This is a good question, but it also reflects our collective naiveté. As a profession we simply have not been able to "get in league with the future." We haven't even as a profession begun to officially recognize what the scholarly and scientific advances as explained above in the past three decades, much less what must be done to rescue us from the present doldrums in which we are reclining because of changing social conditions.

First, I believe that we must make a concerted effort to understand what futuristics or futurology is all about. The next step should be to apply these findings to one aspect of our professional lives--in this case, the possible future of the profession of physical education and educational sport. In *Visions of the Future*, a 1984 publication of the Hudson Institute, three ways of looking at the future. They are described as (1) the possible future, (2) the probable future, and (3) the preferable future (p. 4).

As one might imagine, the possible future includes everything that could happen, and thus perceptions of the future must be formed by us individually and collectively. The probable future refers to occurrences that are likely to happen, and so here the range of alternatives must be considered. Finally, the preferable future relates to an approach whereby people make choices, thereby indicating how they would like things to happen. Underlying all of this are certain basic assumptions or premises such as (1) that the future hasn't been predetermined by some force or power; (2) that the future cannot be accurately predicted because we don't understand the process of change that fully; and (3) that the future will undoubtedly be influenced by choices that people make, but won't necessarily turn out the way they want it to be (Amara, 1981).

A variety of people have been predicting the future for thousands of years, undoubtedly with a limited degree of success. Considerable headway has been made, of course, since the time when animal entrails were examined to provide insight about the future (one of the techniques of so-called divination). Nowadays, for example, methods of prediction include forecasting by the use of trends and statistics. One of the most recent approaches along these these lines has been of great interest to me because I have been using a variation of this technique for more than 30 years with a persistent problems approach (originated by John S. Brubacher, 1947) leading to the analysis of our field (Zeigler, 1964, 1968, 1977a, 1977b, 1979, 1989, 2003). I am referring to the work of John Naisbitt and The Naisbitt Group as described in *Megatrends* (1982) and *Megatrends 2000* (1990). These people believe that "the most reliable way to anticipate the future is by understanding the present" (p. 2). Hence they monitor occurrences all over the world through a technique of descriptive method known as content analysis. They actually keep track of the amount of space given to various topics in newspapers-- an approach they feel is valid because "the news-reporting process is forced choice in a closed system" (p. 4). One of the "millennial megatrends" delineated by the work of the Naisbitt Group that appears to have significant implications for physical education and sport has been designated as the "Age of Biology" (1990, pp. 241-269). Explaining that biotechnology is rapidly becoming a powerful influence in our lives, Naisbitt and Aburdene stress that people should not be "somewhat put off by technology, and the confusing ethical component of biotechnology" because "the issues of biotechnology will not got away" (p. 242). The possibility of ultimately being able to manipulate inherited characteristics will have tremendous implications for the future as humans get involved in developmental physical activity in exercise and sport.

The work of Melnick and associates in *Visions of the Future* (1984), was discussed earlier in this chapter. They consider, also, a further aspect of futuristics (i.e., the question of "levels of certainty)." They explain that the late Herman Kahn, an expert in this area, often used the term "Scotch Verdict" when he was concerned about the level of certainty available prior to making a decision. This idea was borrowed from the Scottish system of justice in which a person charged with the commission of a crime can be found "guilty," "not guilty," or "not been proven guilty." This "not been proven guilty" (or "Scotch") verdict implies there is enough evidence to demonstrate that the person charged is guilty, but that insufficient evidence has been presented to end all reasonable doubt about the matter. Hence a continuum has been developed at one end of which we can state we are 100% sure that such-and-such is not true. Accordingly, at the other end of the continuum we can state we are 100% sure that such-and-such is the case (pp. 6-7). Obviously, in-between these two extremes are gradations of the level of certainty. From here this idea has been carried over to the realm of future forecasting.

Next we are exhorted to consider the "Great Transition" that humankind has been experiencing, how there has been a pre-industrial stage, an industrial stage and, finally, a post-industrial stage that appears to be arriving in North America first. Each of the stages has its characteristics that must be recognized. For example, in pre-industrial society there was slow population growth, people lived simply with very little money, and the forces of nature made life very difficult. When the industrial stage or so-called modernization entered the picture, population growth was rapid, wealth increased enormously, and people became increasingly less vulnerable to the destructive forces of nature. The assumption here is that comprehension of the transition that is occurring can give us some insight as to what the future might hold--not that we can be "100% sure," but at least we might be able to achieve a "Scotch Verdict" (p. 47). If North America is that part of the world that is the most economically and technologically advanced, and as a result will complete the Great Transition by becoming a post-industrial culture, than we must be aware of what this will mean to our society. Melnick explains that we have probably already entered a "super-industrial period" of the Industrial Stage in which "projects will be very large scale, services will be readily available, efficient and sophisticated, people will have vastly increased leisure time, and many new technologies will be created" (pp. 35-37).

It is important that we understand what is happening as we move further forward into what presumably is the final or third stage of the Great Transition. First, it should be made clear that the level of certainty here in regard to predictions is at Kahn's "Scotch Verdict" point on the continuum. The world has never faced this situation before, so we don't know exactly how to date the beginning of such a stage. Nevertheless, it seems to be taking place right now (the super-industrial period having started after World War II). As predicted, those developments mentioned above (e.g., services readily available) appear to be continuing. It is postulated that population growth is slower than it was 20 years ago; yet, it is true that people are living longer. Next it is estimated that a greater interdependence among nations and the steady development of new technologies will contribute to a steadily improving economic climate for underdeveloped nations. Finally, it is forecast that advances in science and accompanying technology will bring almost innumerable technologies to the fore that will affect life styles immeasurably all over the world.

The important points to be made here are emerging rapidly. First, we need a different way of looking at the subject of so-called natural resources. In this interdependent world, this "global village" if you will, natural resources are more than just the sum of raw materials. They include also the application of technology, the organizational bureaucracy to cope with the materials, and the resultant usefulness of the resource that creates supply and demand (p. 74). The point seems to be that the total resource picture (as explained here) is reasonably optimistic if correct decisions are made about raw materials, energy, food production, and use of the environment. These are admittedly rather large "ifs" (pp. 73-97). Kennedy (1993) also pointed out the difficulty "of international reform" in this connection as he writes of the "apparent inevitability of overall demographic and environmental trends" that the world is facing (p. 335).

Finally in this "forecasting the future" section, the need to understand global problems of two types is stressed. One group is called "mostly understandable problems," and they are solvable. Here reference is made to (1) population growth, (2) natural resource issues, (3) acceptable environmental health, (4) shift in society's economic base to service occupations, and (5) effect of advanced technology. However, it is the second group classified as "mostly uncertain problems," and these are the problems that could bring on disaster. First, the Great Transition is affecting the entire world, and the eventual outcome of this new type of cultural change is uncertain. Thus we must be ready for these developments attitudinally. Second, in this period of changing values and attitudes, people in the various countries and cultures have much to learn, and they will have to make great adjustments as well. Third, there is the danger that society will--possibly unwittingly--stumble into some irreversible environmental catastrophe (e.g., upper-atmosphere ozone depletion). Fourth, the whole problem of weapons, wars, and terrorism, and whether the world will be able to stave off all-out nuclear warfare. Fifth, and finally, whether bad luck and bad management will somehow block the entire world from undergoing the Great Transition successfully (pp. 124-129)--obviously a great argument for the development of management art and science .

WHAT WE SHOULD DO IN THE NEAR FUTURE?

What should we do--perhaps what must we do--to ensure that the profession will move more decisively and rapidly in the direction of what might be called true professional status? Granting that the various social forces will impact upon us willy-nilly, what can we do collectively in the years immediately ahead? These positive steps should be actions that will effect a workable consolidation of purposeful accomplishments on the part of those men and women who have a concern for the future of developmental physical activity as a valuable component of human life from birth to death. The following represent a number of categories joined with action principles that relate directly to the "modifications" that have occurred in recent decades in North America at least. We have now reached the point where we should seek a world consensus on the steps spelled out below. If such could be achieved, we could then, as dedicated professionals, take as rapid and strong action as we can be mustered through national and international professional associations, not forgetting any assistance we can obtain from our allied professions and related disciplines. These recommended steps are as follows:

1. A Sharper Image. Because in the past the field of physical education and educational sport has tried to be "all things to all people," and now doesn't know exactly what it does stand for, we should now sharpen our image and

improve the quality of our efforts by focusing primarily on developmental physical activity--specifically, human motor performance in sport, exercise, and related expressive movement. As we sharpen our image, we should make a strong effort to include those who are working in the private agency and commercial sectors. This implies further that we will extend our efforts to promote the finest type of developmental physical activity for people of all ages whether they be members of what are considered to be "normal, accelerated, or special" populations.

2. Our Profession's Name. Because all sorts of name changes have been implemented (a) to explain either what people think we are doing or should be doing, or (b) to camouflage the presumed "unsavory" connotation of the term "physical education" that evidently conjures up the notion of a "dumb jock" moving the lesser part of a tri-partite human body, we should continue to focus primarily on developmental physical activity as defined immediately above while moving toward an acceptable working term for our profession. In so doing, we should keep in mind any profession's bifurcated nature in that it has both theoretical and practical (or disciplinary and professional) aspects. At the moment we are called physical education and sport quite uniformly around the world.

(Note: A desirable name might be developmental physical activity, and we could delineate this by the addition of such "in sport, exercise, and expressive movement." Then we could be "physical activity educators"! The terms "kinesiology" and "human kinetics" are looming up in both the United States and Canada as new names for the undergraduate degree program in our field. However, it is most difficult to see this word catching on in the close to 190 countries now registered in the United Nations.)

3. A Tenable Body of Knowledge. Inasmuch as various social forces and professional concerns have placed us in a position where we don't know where or what our body of knowledge is, we will strongly support the idea of disciplinary definition and the continuing development of a body of knowledge based on such a consensual definition. From this must come a merging of tenable scientific theory in keeping with societal values and computer technology so that we will gradually, steadily, and increasingly provide our members with the knowledge that they need to perform as top-flight professionals. As professionals we simply must possess the requisite knowledge, competencies, and skills necessary to provide developmental physical activity services of a high quality to the public.

4. Our Own Professional Associations. Inasmuch as there is insufficient

support of our own professional associations for a variety of reasons, we need to develop voluntary and mandatory mechanisms that relate membership in professional organizations both directly and indirectly to stature within the field. We simply must now commit ourselves to work tirelessly and continually to promote the welfare of professional practitioners who are serving the public in areas that we represent. Incidentally, it may be necessary to exert any available pressures to encourage people to give first priority to our own groups (as opposed to those of disciplinary-oriented societies, related disciplines, and/or allied professions). The logic behind this dictum is that our own survival has to come first for us!

5. Professional Licensing. Although most teachers/coaches in the schools, colleges, and universities are seemingly protected indefinitely by the shelter of the all-embracing teaching profession, we should now move rapidly and strongly to seek official recognition of our endeavors in public, semi-public, and private agency work and in commercial organizations relating to developmental physical activity through professional licensing at the state or provincial level. Further, we should encourage individuals to apply for voluntary registration as qualified practitioners at the federal level in their countries.

6. Harmony Within The Profession. Because an unacceptable series of gaps and misunderstandings has developed among those in our field concerned primarily with the bio-scientific aspects of human motor performance, those concerned with the social-science and humanities aspects, those concerned with the general education of all students, and those concerned with the professional preparation of physical educators/coaches, managers, and scholars and scientists-- all at the college or university level--we will strive to work for a greater balance and improved understanding among these essential entities within the profession.

7. Harmony Among The Allied Professions. Keeping in mind that the field of physical education has spawned a number of allied professions down through the years of the 20th century, we should strive to comprehend what they claim that they do professionally, and where there may be a possible overlap with what we claim that we do. Where disagreements prevail, they should be ironed out to the greatest extent possible at the national level in all countries.

8. The Relationship With Competitive Sport. Because for several reasons an ever-larger wedge is being driven between units of physical education and competitive sport in those relatively few countries where within educational institutions gate receipts are a basic factor in the continuance of sporting

competition, such a rift serves no good purpose and has become contrary to the best interests of both groups. In these countries, the organized profession should work for greater understanding and harmony with those people who are primarily interested in the promotion of highly organized, often commercialized sport. At the same time it is imperative that we do all in our power to maintain competitive sport in a sound educational perspective within our schools, colleges, and universities where it is presently offered.

9. The Relationship with Intramurals and Recreational Sports. Intramurals and recreational sports is in a transitional state at present in that it has proved that it is "here to stay" at the college and university level. Nevertheless, intramurals hasn't really taken hold yet, generally speaking, at the high school level, despite the fact that it has a great deal to offer the large majority of students in what may truly be called recreational (educational?) lifetime sport. Also, there are a minority of administrators functioning at the college level who would like to adopt the term "campus recreation" as their official designation, but there is not consensus on whether this is appropriate or whether an effort should be made to encompass all recreational activities on campus within the sphere of what is now typically intramurals and recreational sports only.

(Everything considered, I believe (a) that--both philosophically and practically--intramurals and recreational sports ought to remain within the sphere of the physical education and sport profession; (b) that it is impractical and inadvisable to attempt to subsume all non-curricular activities on campus under one department or division; and (c) that departments and divisions of physical education and sport ought to work for consensus on the idea that intramurals and recreational sports are co-curricular in nature and deserve regular funding as laboratory experience in the same manner that general education course experiences in sport and physical education receive their funding for instructional purposes.)

10. Guaranteeing Equal Opportunity. Because "life, liberty, and the pursuit of happiness" are guaranteed to all in North American society, as a profession we should move positively and strongly to bring about equal opportunity to the greatest possible extent to women, to minority groups, and to special populations (e.g., the handicapped) as they seek to improve the quality of their lives through the finest type of experience in the many activities of our field.

11. The Physical Education and (Educational) Sport Identity. In addition

to the development of the allied professions (e.g., school health education) in the second quarter of the twentieth century, we witnessed the advent of a disciplinary thrust in the 1960s that was followed by a splintering of many of the various "knowledge components" and subsequent formation of many different societies nationally and worldwide. These developments have undoubtedly weakened the field of physical education and educational sport. Thus, it is now more important than ever that we hold high the physical education and sport identity as we continue to support those who are developing our profession's undergirding body of knowledge. Additionally we should re-affirm, but also delineate even more carefully, our relationship with our allied professions.

12. Applying the Competency Approach. Whereas the failures and inconsistencies of the established educational process have become increasingly apparent, we will as a profession explore the educational possibilities of the competency approach as it might apply to general education, to professional preparation, and to all aspects of our professional endeavor in public, semi-public, private, and commercial agency endeavors

13. Managing the Enterprise. All professionals in the unique field of physical education and sport are managers--but to varying degrees. The "one course in administration" approach of earlier times that included no laboratory or internship experience is simply not sufficient for the future. There is an urgent need to apply a competency approach in the preparation (as well as in the continuing education) of those who will serve as managers either within educational circles or elsewhere promoting exercise and sport in the society at large.

14. Ethics and Morality in Physical Education and Sport. In the course of the development of the best professions, the various, embryonic professional groups have gradually become conscious of the need for a set of professional ethics--that is, a set of professional obligations that are established as norms for practitioners in good standing to follow. Our profession needs both a universal creed and a reasonably detailed code of ethics right now as we move ahead in our development. Such a move is important because, generally speaking, ethical confusion prevails throughout the world. Development of a sound code of ethics, combined with steady improvement in the three essentials of a fine profession (i.e., an extensive period of training, a significant intellectual component that must be mastered before the profession is practiced, and a recognition by society that the trained person can provide a basic, important service to its citizens) would relatively soon place us in a much firmer position to claim that we are indeed members of a fine

profession. (Zeigler, 1984).

15. Reunifying the Profession's Integral Elements. Because there now appears to be reasonable agreement that what is now called the field of physical education and educational sport is concerned primarily with developmental physical activity as manifested in human motor performance in sport, exercise, and related expressive movement, we will now work for the reunification of those elements of our profession that should be uniquely ours within our disciplinary definition.

16. Cross-Cultural Comparison and International Understanding. We have done reasonably well in the area of international relations across the world due to the solid efforts of many dedicated people over a considerable period of time, but now we need to redouble our efforts to make cross-cultural comparisons of sport and physical education while reaching out for international understanding and cooperation in all sections of the world. Much greater understanding on the part of all of the concepts of "communication," "diversity," and "cooperation" is required for the creation of a better life for all in a hopefully peaceful world. Our profession can contribute significantly toward this long-range objective.

17. Permanency and Change. Inasmuch as the "principal principles" initially espoused for physical education and sport by the late Arthur Steinhaus of George Williams College can now be expanded significantly and applied logically to our professional endeavors, we will emphasize that which is timeless in our work, while at the same time accepting the inevitability of certain societal change.

18. Improving the Quality and Length of Life. Since our field is truly unique within education and in society, and since fine living and professional success involve so much more than the important verbal and mathematical skills, we will emphasize strongly that education is a lifelong enterprise. Further, we will stress that now both the quality and length of life can be improved significantly through the achievement of a higher degree of kinetic awareness and through heightened experiences in sport, exercise, and related expressive movement.

19. Reasserting Our "Will to Win". Although the developments of the past 40 years have undoubtedly created an uneasiness within the profession, and have raised doubts on the part of some as to our possession of a "will to win" through the achievement of the highest type of professional status, we pledge ourselves to make still greater efforts to become vibrant and stirring through absolute dedication and commitment in our professional endeavors. Ours is a high

calling since we seek to improve the quality of life for all people on earth through the finest type of human motor performance in sport, exercise, and related expressive movement (adapted from Zeigler, 1990, Chap. 11).

CONCLUSIONS AND RECOMMENDATIONS: THE PROFESSIONAL TASK AHEAD

What, then, is the professional task ahead? First, we should truly understand why we have chosen this profession as we rededicate ourselves anew to the study and dissemination of knowledge, competencies, and skills in human motor performance in sport, exercise, and related expressive movement. Concurrently, of course, we need to determine more exactly what it is that we are professing.

Second, as either practitioners or instructors involved in professional preparation and scholarly endeavor, we should search for young people of high quality in all the attributes needed for success in the field, and then help them to develop lifelong commitments so that our profession can achieve its democratically agreed-upon goals. We should also prepare young people to serve in the many alternative careers in sport, exercise, dance, and recreative play that are becoming increasingly available in society.

Third, we must place quality as the first priority of our professional endeavors. Our personal involvement and specialization should include a high level of competency and skill undergirded by solid knowledge about the profession. It can certainly be argued that our professional task is as important as any in society. Thus, the present is no time for indecision, half-hearted commitment, imprecise knowledge, and general unwillingness to stand up and be counted in debate with colleagues within our field and in allied professions and related disciplines, not to mention the general public.

Fourth, the obligation is ours. If we hope to reach our potential, we must sharpen our focus and improve the quality of our professional effort. Only in this way will we be able to guide the modification process that the profession is currently undergoing toward the achievement of our highest professional goals. This is the time--right now--to employ exercises, sport, and related expressive movement to make our reality more healthful, more pleasant, more vital, and more life-enriching. By "living fully in one's body," behavioral science men and women will be adapting and shaping that phase of reality to their own ends.

Despite the above admonitions about the professional task ahead, you may be saying to yourself: "Fine, but how can we begin right now to implement these "what to do" items to help our developing profession achieve its lofty goals? We are currently mired into a state of semi-rigidity!" Well, every great idea is conceived in the mind of one individual. Further, some wise person is purported once to have said, "If you want to accomplish something big in this life, do not expect people to roll stones out of your path; in fact, do not be surprised if they heap boulders in your way." (If you don't believe this, ask Bill and Hillary Clinton about the size of the boulders in their path!)

Frankly, at this point I am not anticipating the presence of stones of any size to be heaped on our path in the years immediately ahead. However, based on past experience, I just know that they are going to be there. The political powers that be are simply not going to say "Eureka, you've got a vital answer to the world's plight! Here's a billion dollars to organize, develop, and begin the administration of a worldwide plan to make field of physical education and educational sport a full-fledged, respected profession. I don't propose to repeat here and now what might be their arguments as rebuttals to any proposal we might make. Further, I would not be the least surprised if we as professionals were to prove to be our own worst enemies as we traverse this rocky path.

Nevertheless, without attempting to enumerate specifically where any stumbling blocks might loom in our path, I would like to propose four major processes (March and Simon, 1958, pp. 129-131) that could be employed chronologically, as we seek to realize the desired immediate objectives and long-range goal:

1. Problem-solving: Basically, what is being proposed here is a problem for our profession to solve or resolve. We must move as soon as possible to convince others of the worthwhileness of this proposal. Part of our approach includes assurance that the objectives are indeed operational (i.e., that their presence or absence can be tested empirically as we progress). In this way, even if sufficient funding were not available--and it well might not be--the various parties who are vital or necessary to the success of the venture would at least have agreed-upon objectives. However, with a professional task of this magnitude, it is quite possible, even probable that such consensus will not be achieved initially. But it can be instituted--one step at a time!

2. Persuasion: For the sake of argument, then, let us assume that our

objectives on the way toward the achievement of long-range aims are not shared by the others whom we need to convince, people who are either directly or indirectly related to our own profession or are in allied professions or related disciplines. On the assumption that the stance of the others is not absolutely fixed or intractable, then this second step of persuasion can (should) be employed on the assumption that at some level our objectives will be shared, and that disagreement over sub-goals can be mediated by reference to larger common goals. (Here we should keep in mind that influencing specific leaders in each of the various "other" associations and societies with which we are seeking to cooperate can be a most effective technique for bringing about attitude change within the larger membership of our profession everywhere.)

> **Note**: If persuasion works, then the parties concerned
> can obviously return to the problem-solving level (#1).

3. Bargaining: We will now move along to the third stage of a theoretical plan on the assumption that the second step (persuasion) didn't fully work. This means obviously that there is still disagreement over the operational goals proposed at the problem-solving level (the first stage). Now the profession has a difficult decision to make: do we attempt to strike a bargain, or do we decide that we simply must "go it alone?"

The problem with the first alternative is that bargaining implies compromise, and compromise means that each group involved will have to surrender a portion of its claim, request, or argument. The second alternative may seem more desirable, but following it may also mean eventual failure in achieving the final, most important objective.

> **Note**: We can appreciate, of course, that the necessity
> of proceeding to this stage, and then selecting either of
> the two alternatives, is obviously much less desirable than
> settling the matter at either the first or second stages.

4. Politicking: The implementation of the fourth stage (or plan of attack) is based on the fact that the proposed action of the first three stages has failed. The participants in the discussion cannot agree in any way about the main issue. It is at this point that the recognized profession has to somehow expand the number of parties or groups involved in consideration of the proposed project. The goal, of course, is to attempt to include potential allies so as to improve the chance of

achieving the desired final objective. Employing so-called "power politics" is usually tricky, however, and it may indeed backfire upon the group bringing such a maneuver into play. However, this is the way the world (or society) works, and the goal may be well worth the risk or danger involved.

> **Note:** Obviously, we hope that it will not be necessary to operate at this fourth stage continually in connection with the development of our profession. It would be most divisive in many instances and time consuming as well. Therefore, we would be faced with the decision as to whether this type of operation would do more harm than good (in the immediate future at least).

Finally, the recommendations for worldwide improvement of the status of the professional of physical education and sport will not come easily. It can only come through the efforts of professional people making quality decisions, through the motivation of people to change their sedentary lifestyles, and through our professional assistance in guiding people as they strive to fulfill such motivation in their movement patterns. Our mission in the years ahead is to place a special quality--a quality bespeaking excellence and dedication--in all of our professional endeavors.

REFERENCES AND BIBLIOGRAPHY

Aburdene, P. & Naisbitt, J. (1992). *Megatrends for women*. NY: Villard Books. 388 p.

Amara, R. (1981 February). The futures field. *The Futurist*.

Brubacher, J.S. (1947). *A history of the problems of education*. New York: McGraw-Hill.

Brubacher, J.S. (1961). Higher education and the pursuit of excellence. *Marshall University Bulletin*, 3:3.

Contributions of physical activity to human well-being. (May 1960) *Research Quarterly*, 31, 2 (Part II):261-375.

Huntington, H.P. (June 6, 1993). World politics entering a new phase, The New York Times, E19.

Kennedy, P. (1993). *Preparing for the twenty-first century*. New York: Random House.

March, J.G. & H.A. Simon. (1958). *Organizations*. New York: Wiley.

Melnick, R. (1984). *Visions of the future*. Croton-on-Hudson, NY:

Hudson Institute.

Naisbitt, J. (1982). *Megatrends*. New York: Warner.

Naisbitt, J. & Aburdene, P. (1990). *Megatrends 2000*. New York: Wm. Morrow.

New York Times, The. (1970). *Report by Commission on Tests of the College Entrance Examination Board*, Nov. 2.

Rand, A. (1960). *The romantic manifesto*. New York: World Publishing.

Steinhaus, A.H. (1952). Principal principles of physical education. In *Proceedings of the College Physical Education Association*. Washington, DC: AAHPER, pp. 5-11.

Ten events that shook the world between 1984 and 1994. (Special Report). (March/April 1994). *Utne Reader*, 62, 58-74.

Toffler, A. (1970). *Future shock*. New York: Random House.

Toffler, A. (1980). *The third wave*. New York: Bantam Books.

Zeigler, E.F. (1964). *Philosophical foundations for physical, health, and recreation education*. Englewood Cliffs, NJ: Prentice-Hall.

Zeigler, E.F. (1968). *Problems in the history and philosophy of physical education and sport*. Englewood Cliffs, NJ: Prentice-Hall.

Zeigler, E.F. (1977a). Philosophical perspective on the future of physical education and sport. In R. Welsh (Ed.), *Physical education: A view toward the future* (pp. 36-61). St. Louis: C.V. Mosby.

Zeigler, E.F. (1977b). *Physical education and sport philosophy*. Englewood Cliffs, NJ: Prentice-Hall.

Zeigler, E.F. (1979). *Issues in North American physical education and sport*. Washington, DC: AAHPERD (Leaders Speak Series).

Zeigler, E.F. (1986). *Assessing sport and physical education: diagnosis and projection*. Champaign, IL": Stipes Publishing Co.

Zeigler, E.F. (Ed. & au.). (1988). *A history of physical education and sport* (Revised edition). Champaign, IL: Stipes.

Zeigler, E.F. (1989). *Sport and physical education philosophy*. Dubuque, IA: Benchmark/W.C. Brown.

Zeigler, E.F. (1990) *Sport and physical education: past, present, future*. Champaign, IL: Stipes Publishing Co.

Zeigler, E.F. (Ed. & Au.). (1994a). *Physical education and kinesiology in North America: Professional and scholarly foundations*. Champaign, IL: Stipes.

Zeigler, E.F. (1994b). *Critical thinking for the professions of*

health, sport and physical education, recreation, and dance.
Champaign, IL: Stipes Publishing Co.

Zeigler, E.F. (1994c September). Physical Education's 13 Principal Principles. *JOPERD*, 64, 4-5.

Zeigler, E.F. (2003). *Socio-cultural foundations of physical education and educational sport.* Aachen, Germany: Meyer and Meyer Sports.

APPENDIX A

CHRONOLOGY OF EVENTS OF INTEREST IN THE HISTORY OF AMERICAN PHYSICAL EDUCATION AND EDUCATIONAL SPORT (1492-1950)

(Note: This chronological listing is not intended to be all-inclusive. Occasional dates unrelated to physical education are included to put it all in perspective.)

Date	Event
1492	Columbus discovers a land mass that was eventually called America.
1609	The beginning of what Norma Schwendener termed the "Colonial Period" of American physical education that extended to 1781.
1636	Harvard College founded.
1647	In New England the (so-called) General Court outlaws certain forms of gaming.
1665	The first commercially organized horse race took place in New York City.
1776	War of Independence of the United States from Great Britain began.
1776	United States of America founded.
1781	The beginning what Schwendener called the "Provincial Period" of American physical education that extended to 1885.
1790	Noah Webster proclaimed the value of exercise, particularly for youth.
1812	The War of 1812.
1812	First public high established in Massachusetts.
1819	Articles on sport written by John Stuart Skinner appear in the *American Farmer*.
1820	Capt. Alden Partridge, a former West Point director, was concerned about youth fitness in America. He worked to encourage schools and universities to include

	strenuous physical activities in their programs.
1824	Karl Beck and Karl Follen emigrated from Germany to the United States. This was the start of the German gymnastics movement, an important development.
1825	The struggle for the development of the American state system of schools was underway (i.e., the beginning of the "Architectural Period" of American education).
1829 (Sept.)	First issue of the *Journal of Health* praised by Edward Hitchcock, the first professor of physical education (Amherst College). It only survived four years as there was significant hostility toward physicians.
1830	Between 1830 and 1878 Catharine Beecher worked tirelessly to improve the health and fitness of American women. Her *A Course of Calisthenic for Young Ladies in Schools and Families*, published in 1831, was read widely.
1833	Oberlin College founded as the first coeducational college.
1834	*Thoughts on Physical Education* by Charles Caldwell advocated physical activity in a balanced life.
1835	The first homeopathic medical school , the Allentown Academy, was established by Dr. William Wesselhoeft in Bath, Pennsylvania
1835	*The House I Live In* by William Alcott stressed exercise, cleanliness, and diet along with a simple anatomical guide.
1839	The first state normal school for training teachers began in Concord, Vermont in 1939.
1846	John C. Warren's *Physical Education and the Preservation of Health* urged young women to get more involved in physical education even if this meant that mental culture suffered somewhat.
1848	The first Turnverein in the United States was the Cincinnati *Turngemeinde* opened in November of this year. Some 22 of these groups were organized by 1851. All promoted German gymnastic programs.
1850s	Activities known as gymnastics and calisthenics at this time were primarily indoor exercises, not sports and games. Such activities had not yet attracted much attention despite earlier efforts by such leaders as

Edward Hitchcock and William Alcott to promote them. Also, such activity had been promoted at selected school for young ladies because German gymnastics were felt to be too strenuous by many. In the late 1850s there was considerable emphasis on the idea that the body was more than a "container for the soul" and that perfection of the body had a connection with Christian morality.

1852	First intercollegiate athletic sporting competition held: a rowing race between Harvard and Yale.
1853	Lectures on Life and Health: or The Laws and Means of Physical Culture, written by William Alcott, was published. This prolific writer was a leader in the lay health movement.
1853	Russell Trall, a physician, authored the *New Hydropathic Cook-Book*. In it he stated "Nutrition is the replenishment of tissue, not the accumulation of fat. . The latter is a disease, and a fattened animal, be it a hog or an alderman, is a diseased animal."
1856	*Physiology and Calisthenics for Schools and Families* by Catharine Beecher. NY: Harper Bros.
1857	*The Illustrated Family Gymnasium* was published by Trall with the accompanying thought that "physical" activity might also improve "mental" faculties.
1859	Collegiate baseball got its start with early competition among "Ivy League" universities.
1859	Charles Darwin published his theory about evolution in *Origin of the Species*.
1860s	This decade saw a shift in emphasis in helping Americans either to become healthy or regain health. There was a movement to improve building ventilation and sanitary conditions. Postwar fitness emphases were linked to the concept of "Muscular Christianity." George Windship "burst upon the scene" as the "Roxbury Hercules" who held a medical degree and lectured eloquently. Windship maintained a relationship with Dr. Dudley A. Sargent of Bowdoin College and then of Harvard University.
1860	By 1860 Harvard, Yale, and Amherst had gymnasia constructed on their campuses.
1860	Dioclesian Lewis gave an invited lecture on "light

gymnastics to the American Institute of Instruction on August 21, 1960. For health reasons it was evidently felt there was a need for physical activity in the schools.

1861	Abraham Lincoln elected president of the United States.
1861	Dioclesian Lewis started the first "teacher-education" program in physical education at his Normal Institute for Physical Education in Boston on July 8, 1961.
1862	Dioclesian Lewis published *New Gymnastics*. It was widely read and decried the bodily health and "mental condition" of many Americans.
1862	Passing of the Morrill Land Act brought about military-drill activity was often substituted for physical education at the college level. Educators criticized this practice.
1866	The first ["abortive"] state legislation for physical education was passed in 1866.
1866	The Normal College of the American Gymnastic Union began in New York City. It was a "traveling school," so to speak, as it moved from city to city at first.
1866	*The Indian Club Exercise* published by S.D. Kehoe was extremely well received.
1866	Peck and Snyder of New York made available a "complete" home gymnasium.
1867	Edward Payson Weston was featured as the foremost "Pedestrian" in *Harper's Weekly* on Nov. 16 (p.724).
1868	The New York Athletic Club was established.
1869	Princeton and Rutgers played the first football game in the United States.
1870	Interest in cycling grew sharply in the 1870s.
1873	America's first collegiate track and field meet was held.
1876	Yale and Harvard began to race against each other in rowing annually near New London, CT.
1879	Interest in pedestrian racing was so high that *The Boston Globe* published 1,415 articles on the topic in 1879.
1879	After this year, departments of pedagogy for the training of teachers began to spring up in colleges and universities.
1879	William Blaikie's *How to Get Strong and How to Stay So* helped to promulgate the efforts of Dr. D. A. Sargent at his Boston Normal School of Gymnastics and also in connection with his Harvard appointment in Boston, MA.

1880	The influence of the North American *Turnerbund* was very strong in the "Mississippi Valley Corridor" from Milwaukee to New Orleans. The Turners were responsible for the introduction of German gymnastics in many school systems and helped to bring about state legislation for physical education.
1885	The Association for the Advancement of Physical Education was founded. The word "American" was added in 1886.
1885	This year was the beginning of what Schwendener defined as "The Period of the Waning of European Influence" that carried through to 1918.
1885	Edward M. Hartwell began his publishing efforts as America's first specialist in comparative physical education. He wrote extensively on the history of physical education based on keen analyses after travel.
1885	The Barnett (Improved) Rowing Machine for home use became available about this time.
1888	The Amateur Athletic Union was founded.
1889	The Boston Conference of 1889 brought together leaders of the various systems of physical activity in vogue in a search for the best type of program for American physical education.
1890	This was "the time of" Eugene Sandow whom Dr. Sargent lauded as "the most wonderful specimen of man I have ever seen."
1891	The game of basketball was invented by James Naismith, a Canadian who was teaching at Springfield College.
1891	The first women's athletic association was founded at Bryn Mawr with many other eastern institutions following this lead. Athletic programs were integral parts of the existing physical education programs.
1892	Biddle University played Livingstone College in the first football game between Black colleges.
1892	Corbett defeated Sullivan for heavyweight boxing championship in New Orleans
1895	The game of volleyball was invented by William Morgan.
1897	An important development was the establishment of the Harvard Summer School of Physical Education.

1899	John Dewey published *School and Society*.
1902	The first Rose Bowl football game was held.
1902	The township high school at Joliet, Illinois became the first public junior college in the United States through the encouragement of William Rainey Harper, the president of the University of Chicago.
1903	New York City began the Public School Athletic League as an experiment in high school athletics
1905	Football "brutality" became a national issue after 18 deaths were recorded. President "Teddy" Roosevelt was involved as a mediator and later a national meeting of university representatives was convened. Rule changes were recommended and a blueprint for supervision called for the establishment of the Intercollegiate Athletic Association of the United States. (This association later evolved as the National Collegiate Athletic Association.)
1906	The Playground Association of America was founded.
1910	National Collegiate Athletic Association was founded.
1910	The beginning of public junior colleges started in this year in California
1912	Jim Thorpe, an outstanding all-round athlete at the Carlisle Indian School if Pennsylvania, won the decathlon event in track and field at the 1912 Olympic Games in Stockholm. Later, because he received money for playing "summer baseball," his medals were taken from him. They were returned much later to the man called by many "America's athlete of the mid-century."
1913	Both the University of Michigan and Ohio State University appointed the first intramural athletics directors in America. Elmer D. Mitchell of Michigan was an early leader in the movement.
1913	Clark Hetherington's Child Demonstration Play School was established at the University of California, Berkeley with the philosophy that "play is the child's chief business in life."
1914	A joint committee meeting of the YMCA, A.A.U., and the N.C.A.A. brought uniformity to rules for basketball in the United States.
1914	The Smith-Lever Act stimulated agricultural extension

	service in education.
1915	The "sports and games approach" as the way to carry out a program of physical education, was still far from holding sway against the various gymnastic systems extant.
1916	Some 140 colleges and universities reported having some type of intramural sports programs.
1916	John Dewey's *Democracy in Education* published.
1917	The United States enters World War I as combatant.
1917	The Athletic Conference of American College Women (ACACW) was organized under the leadership of Blanche Trilling of Wisconsin.
1918	By 1918 compulsory attendance laws had been passed in all states.
1918.	In this year the Education Commission Report of 1918 announced the "Seven Cardinal Principles of Education."
1918	The date at which Schwendener believes "The Period of American Physical Education" started.
1920	The 19th Amendment to the Constitution is ratified thereby giving women the right to vote.
1923	The White House Conference on Women's Athletics was held.
1924	All American Indians were made citizens of America.
1925	By this year state high school athletic associations existed in every state.
1925	The Scopes Trial in Tennessee was about the teaching of evolution in the schools.
1926	The American Association for Adult Education was established.
1929	The Stock Market Crash of 1929 took place.
1929	The George-Reed Act of 1929 allowed secondary vocational education to be increased.
1930	Some 39 states have a type of physical education legislation. (By the mid-1970s that all had a law.)
1930	Physical education suffered sharp setbacks with the budgetary cutbacks of the Great Depression.
1931	Mabel Lee became first woman president of the American Physical Education Association.
1936	Jesse Owens won three gold medals in track and field at

	the Olympic Games in Berlin, Germany.
1941	Beginning of World War II.
1950	Founding of the National Intramural Association.

REFERENCES

Brubacher, J.S. (1966). *A history of the problems of education* (2nd ed.). New York: McGraw-Hill.

Butts, R.F. (1947). *A cultural history of education.* NY: McGraw-Hill.

Frazier, B. F. (1933). Bulletin No. 10. In *National survey of the education of teachers.* Washington, DC: U.S. Govt. Printing Office. (In Volume Five of this survey, part one dealt with the "History of the professional education of teachers in the United State.")

Green, H. (1986) *Fit for America: Health, fitness, sport, and American society.* Baltimore, MD: The Johns Hopkins University Press.

Mechikoff, R. & Estes, S. (1991). *A history and philosophy of sport and physical education.* Dubuque, IA: WCB: Brown & Benchmark.

Schwendener, N. *A history of physical education in the United States.* NY: A.S. Barnes.

Spears, B. & Swanson, R.A. (1988). *History of sport and physical education in the United States.* Dubuque, IA: Wm. C. Brown.

Weston, A. (1968). *The making of American physical education* (NY: Appleton-Century-Crofts.

Zeigler, E.F. (1975) (Ed. & Au.). *A history of physical education & sport in the United States & Canada: Selected topics.* Champaign, IL: Stipes.

Zeigler, E.F. (1988). *History of physical education and sport* (Rev. ed.). Champaign, IL: Stipes. (Selected chapters were written by M.L. Howell, R. Howell, R. G. Glassford, G. Redmond, R.K. Barney, and G.A. Paton.)

Zeigler, E.F. (1990). *Sport and physical education: Past, present, future.* Champaign, IL: Stipes.

Zeigler, E.F. (2003). *Socio-cultural foundations of physical education and educational sport.* Aachen, Germany: Meyer and Meyer Sports.

APPENDIX B

Illustrations (Satirical Cartoons)
Relating to the
History of American Physical Education

(Note: These "satirical cartoons" were created by Dr. M. Chris (Kent) Rogers. They were used in her unique historical investigation titled *A Satirical Interpretation of the History of Selected Persons, Organizations, and Events in American Physical Education.* This was a doctoral study completed at The University of North Carolina at Greensboro in 1981

Explanatory Note: The famous 1889 Conference brought together proponents of many foreign system of gymnastics and physical education.

Courtesy of Dr. M. Chris (Kent) Rogers. Taken from *A Satirical Interpretation of the History of Selected Persons, Organizations, and Events in American Physical Education* (a doctoral study completed at The University of North Carolina at Greensboro in 1981).

Explanatory Note: Luther Halsey Gulick, late 19th century leader in physical education and recreation, was identified largely with Springfield College. James Naismith, a Canadian, is credited with the invention of basketball while working there.

Courtesy of Dr. M. Chris (Kent) Rogers. Taken from *A Satirical Interpretation of the History of Selected Persons, Organizations, and Events in merican Physical Education* (a doctoral study completed at The University of North Carolina at Greensboro in 1981).

Explanatory Note: Dr. Dudley Allen Sargent became director of the Hemenway Gymnasium at Harvard where he also directed the famous Harvard Summer School of Physcal Education. The numerous pulley devices he invented for strength training became known worldwide.

Courtesy of Dr. M. Chris (Kent) Rogers. Taken from *A Satirical Interpretation of the History of Selected Persons, Organizations, and Events in merican Physical Education* (a doctoral study completed at The University of North Carolina at Greensboro in 1981).

Explanatory Note: This is a gentle parody of Miss Amy Morris Homans, Director of Physical Education at Wellesley College. The "image" created was evidently most important in her judgment. Miss Homans, on behalf of her benefactors Mrs. Mary Hemenway, used these funds for many worthwhile physical education programs.

Courtesy of Dr. M. Chris (Kent) Rogers. Taken from *A Satirical Interpretation of the History of Selected Persons, Organizations, and Events in merican Physical Education* (a doctoral study completed at The University of North Carolina at Greensboro in 1981).

Explanatory Note: Each person elected to fellowship in the American Academy of Physical Education receives a number.

Courtesy of Dr. M. Chris (Kent) Rogers. Taken from *A Satirical Interpretation of the History of Selected Persons, Organizations, and Events in merican Physical Education* (a doctoral study completed at The University of North Carolina at Greensboro in 1981).

Explanatory Note: Columbia Teachers College and New York University were leaders and arch rivals in early graduate study in physical education.

Courtesy of Dr. M. Chris (Kent) Rogers. Taken from *A Satirical Interpretation of the History of Selected Persons, Organizations, and Events in merican Physical Education* (a doctoral study completed at The University of North Carolina at Greensboro in 1981).

Explanatory Note: Dr. McCloy (Iowa) and Dr. Williams (Columbia Teachers College) were leading exponents, respectively, of essentialism (education of the physical) and progressivism (education **through** the physical) in the mid-20th century.

Courtesy of Dr. M. Chris (Kent) Rogers. Taken from *A Satirical Interpretation of the History of Selected Persons, Organizations, and Events in merican Physical Education* (a doctoral study completed at The University of North Carolina at Greensboro in 1981).

Explanatory Note: Women in physical education in higher education in mid-20th century were divided on the question of unification in one association with men.

Courtesy of Dr. M. Chris (Kent) Rogers. Taken from *A Satirical Interpretation of the History of Selected Persons, Organizations, and Events in merican Physical Education* (a doctoral study completed at The University of North Carolina at Greensboro in 1981).

ISBN 1-41205897-X